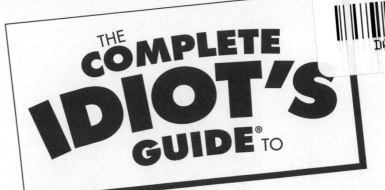

THE **COMPLETE IDIOT'S GUIDE**® TO

European History

by Nathan Barber

ALPHA

A member of Penguin Group (USA) Inc.

For Christy, Noah, and Emma

ALPHA BOOKS

Published by the Penguin Group

Penguin Group (USA) Inc., 375 Hudson Street, New York, New York 10014, U.S.A.

Penguin Group (Canada), 10 Alcorn Avenue, Toronto, Ontario, Canada M4V 3B2 (a division of Pearson Penguin Canada Inc.)

Penguin Books Ltd, 80 Strand, London WC2R 0RL, England

Penguin Ireland, 25 St Stephen's Green, Dublin 2, Ireland (a division of Penguin Books Ltd)

Penguin Group (Australia), 250 Camberwell Road, Camberwell, Victoria 3124, Australia (a division of Pearson Australia Group Pty Ltd)

Penguin Books India Pvt Ltd, 11 Community Centre, Panchsheel Park, New Delhi—110 017, India

Penguin Group (NZ), cnr Airborne and Rosedale Roads, Albany, Auckland 1310, New Zealand (a division of Pearson New Zealand Ltd)

Penguin Books (South Africa) (Pty) Ltd, 24 Sturdee Avenue, Rosebank, Johannesburg 2196, South Africa

Penguin Books Ltd, Registered Offices: 80 Strand, London WC2R 0RL, England

Copyright © 2006 by Nathan Barber

International Standard Book Number: 1-59257-489-0
Library of Congress Catalog Card Number: 2005937207

08   07   8 7 6 5 4

Interpretation of the printing code: The rightmost number of the first series of numbers is the year of the book's printing; the rightmost number of the second series of numbers is the number of the book's printing. For example, a printing code of 06-1 shows that the first printing occurred in 2006.

Printed in the United States of America

Note: This publication contains the opinions and ideas of its author. It is intended to provide helpful and informative material on the subject matter covered. It is sold with the understanding that the author and publisher are not engaged in rendering professional services in the book. If the reader requires personal assistance or advice, a competent professional should be consulted.

The author and publisher specifically disclaim any responsibility for any liability, loss, or risk, personal or otherwise, which is incurred as a consequence, directly or indirectly, of the use and application of any of the contents of this book.

Most Alpha books are available at special quantity discounts for bulk purchases for sales promotions, premiums, fund-raising, or educational use. Special books, or book excerpts, can also be created to fit specific needs.

For details, write: Special Markets, Alpha Books, 375 Hudson Street, New York, NY 10014.

Publisher: *Marie Butler-Knight*
Editorial Director: *Mike Sanders*
Senior Managing Editor: *Jennifer Bowles*
Senior Acquisitions Editor: *Randy Ladenheim-Gil*
Senior Development Editor: *Phil Kitchel*
Production Editor: *Megan Douglass*
Copy Editor: *Ross Patty*
Cartoonist: *Richard King*
Book Designer: *Trina Wurst*
Cover Designer: *Bill Thomas*
Indexer: *Angie Bess*
Layout: *Ayanna Lacey*
Proofreading: *John Etchison*

Contents at a Glance

Part 1:   Climbing Out of the Middle Ages (c.1300–1600)   1

   1   The End of the World as We Know It   3
If you think only modern humans have ever considered the end of the world then think again. In this chapter you'll learn how Europe faced some major disasters and felt as though the world was on the verge of destruction. Needless to say, the world didn't end then.

   2   Civilization Reborn   21
In this chapter you'll see how society was transformed by the rebirth of ideas from ancient Greece and Rome. The progress and achievement in this chapter are among the greatest in European history.

   3   Time for a Change in the Church   39
The emphasis on learning in the Renaissance and the invention of the printing press encouraged Europeans to think for themselves. Here you'll learn how the emphasis on learning, reading, and thinking changed religion and in fact the history of the world.

   4   Time for an Alternative to the Church   57
Here you'll discover that there were many alternative religious ideas that grew out of cries for reform. Though really different in some ways, these new religious views all shared anti-Catholic perspectives.

   5   The Catholic and Counter Reformations   75
In this chapter you'll see how the Catholic Church reacted to calls for reform and to the mass exodus from Catholicism.

Part 2:   Might Makes Right, Right? (c.1450–1750)   89

   6   God, Gold, and Glory   91
Everyone knows the rhyme about Christopher Columbus and the ocean blue. Here you'll find the rest of the story about him and the other explorers who risked their lives on expeditions including why they went and what they hoped to find.

   7   Our Religion Is Better Than Your Religion   107
In this chapter you'll see firsthand how some Europeans reacted to the rise of new religious ideas. You may be surprised what people did to other people in the name of religion.

8   The Rise and Fall of the Holy Roman Empire   123
    *The Holy Roman Empire was once one of the greatest
    political powers in all of Europe. So what happened? In
    this chapter you'll learn how a few guys getting tossed from
    a window eventually led to the fall of the Holy Roman
    Empire.*

9   Am I in Charge? Absolutely!   139
    *Louis XIV ruled France longer than any other monarch in
    European history. In this chapter you'll see what measures
    he took to keep order and what other rulers like him did to
    justify their absolute reigns.*

10 The Eastern Absolutists   157
    *Louis XIV wasn't the only absolute ruler. Eastern European
    monarchs tried their hand at absolute rule. In this chapter
    you'll find out how they stacked up against the Sun King.*

Part 3: Revolutions Galore (c.1500–1800)   173

11 Revolt of the Scientists   175
    *Here you'll discover that much of our current scientific
    knowledge about the universe actually isn't that old. This
    chapter tells the story of a few individuals who questioned
    traditional knowledge and practices and, in the process,
    made some amazing earth-shattering discoveries.*

12 Enlightening the Public, Not the People   189
    *Have you ever heard of the philosophes? Not philosophers,
    philosophes. What's the difference? You'll find out here.*

13 The Agricultural Revolution and an Expanding
    Europe   205
    *What impact on European society could be made by a seed
    drill and some turnips? You'll find the answer to that
    question in this chapter.*

14 The French Revolution   219
    *In this chapter you'll see what happens when hungry,
    oppressed people get mad. You'll also see what happens when
    absolute power falls into the hands of the wrong people.
    Fasten your seatbelts for this one.*

Part 4:   **You Say You Want More Revolution? (c.1776–1900)**   235

15 A "Little" Guy Named Napoleon, a Big Wig Named
Metternich   237
*Napoleon really wasn't all that short. He was that important,
though. So was a snobby aristocrat named Metternich. Here
you'll see how these two dominated Europe for half a century.*

16 The Industrial Revolution   257
*Just like today, humans used machines to make their lives
better two hundred years ago. In this chapter you'll see what
inventions led to a fully-industrialized society and you'll get
a look at the underbelly of industrialization.*

17 Intriguing New Ideologies   275
*Intellectuals and workers alike saw industrialization as
potentially harmful for the working class people of Europe.
They developed some theories about the working class and
property that would have an effect even on modern European
governments.*

18 Nineteenth-Century Growing Pains   291
*Europe hit a growth spurt in the 1800s and it wasn't always
pretty. In this chapter you'll see what problems grew out of
the desire for less oppressive governments. You'll also experience the miracle of birth as two important nations are born.*

19 What a Tangled Web   307
*Some people say you can never have too many friends. In this
chapter, you'll find evidence to the contrary. You'll also see
how Europeans competed to grab as much of the world's land
as possible out of a sense of competition with one another.*

Part 5:   **Big Wars and Big Bangs (Twentieth Century)**   323

20 Turning the World Upside Down   325
*The world did get turned upside down during the first 30
years of the twentieth century. In this chapter you'll see how
a world war, a major revolution, and a depression left Europe
reeling.*

21 World War: Second Verse, Worse Than the First   345
*This chapter will explain how the First World War never
really ended but just got put on hold while a few ruthless
dictators rose to power. If you thought the First World War
was rough, just wait till you read this.*

22 The Cold War Era   365
    *Two unlikely sides cooperated to defeat the enemy in World
    War II but the two sides weren't friends. Here you'll see how
    the drama unfolds as the two sides give each other the cold
    shoulder for a generation.*

23 Changing Millennia   383
    *Whoever said "All good things must come to an end" should
    have said "All Communist things must come to an end."
    That's exactly what happens in this chapter as democracy
    triumphs over communism and then creates a whole new set
    of challenges for our children and grandchildren to sort out.*

Appendixes

A   Major Events in European History   401
    *Everything that ever happened in European history is in this
    timeline. Actually, that's not true but many of the landmark
    events are here in order so you can see how the whole story
    fits together.*

B   Online Resources for Further Research   407
    *Here you'll find a collection of just a few of the best websites
    available for the subjects covered in each chapter.*

    Index   417

Contents

Part 1: Climbing Out of the Middle Ages (c.1300–1600) 1

1 The End of the World as We Know It 3

Introducing the Middle Ages 4
The Bubonic Plague 5
   Fleas and Rats 5
   Sicily First, Then All of Europe 5
   The Black Death 6
   After the Plague 6
The 116 Years' War 7
   The Original Hatfields and McCoys 7
   Chivalry Is Dead 8
   England's Fleeting Victory 9
   Joan of Arc 10
From Two Kingdoms to Two Nations 11
The Church's Black Eye 12
   The Crusades 13
   Babylonians in Europe? 14
   The Great Schism and the Conciliar Movement 15
   Why Didn't God Stop the Madness? 16
When Peasants Are Hungry and Taxed 17
   The Jacquerie 17
   The Peasants' Revolt of 1381 18

2 Civilization Reborn 21

Introducing the Renaissance 21
Why Italy? 23
   The Commercial Revival 24
   The Power of Banking Families 24
   Communes, Republics, and City-States 26
   Balance of Power Politics 27
The Isms 27
   Humanism 27
   Secularism 29
   Individualism 30

How Great the Art 30
   Changes in Artistic Techniques *30*
   The Changing Status of the Artist *31*
   The Hall of Fame *32*
The Printing Press 33
   Gutenberg's Invention *33*
   The Effects of the Printing Press on Europe *34*
Better Late Than Never: Northern Renaissance 34
   Renaissance with a Twist *35*
   The Christian Humanists *35*
   Art in the North *36*

3   Time for a Change in the Church   39
The Reformation 40
Mumblings and Grumblings About the Church 40
   John Wycliffe and the Mumblers *41*
   Jan Hus *43*
   A Plethora of Problems *44*
The Monk with a Mission 46
   Luther's Early Days *46*
   Luther Struggles with Salvation *47*
   Tetzel Ticks Him Off *48*
Luther vs. the Church 49
   Just the Beginning *50*
   The Worms Diet and Its Undesired Results *51*
   Protestant Thought vs. Catholic Dogma *52*
The Far-Reaching Effects of Luther's Ideas 53
   Peasants Pick Luther *54*
   Princes Pick Luther *55*
   Luther and the Status of Women *55*

4   Time for an Alternative to the Church   57
The Reformation Goes International 58
Instituting a New Form of Protestantism 59
   Welcome to Geneva *59*
   Another Would-Be Lawyer Chooses Religion *60*
   Calvin's Theocracy *60*
   TULIP *61*
From Scotland to Geneva and Back Again 62
   Knox and Presbyterianism *62*
   Becoming the Scottish National Church *63*

The Fringe Groups of the Reformation 64
   The Anabaptists *65*
   The Amish and the Quakers *66*
The English Reformation Soap Opera 67
   The Torch is Passed in England *68*
   I'm Henry VIII I Am *68*
   The Reformation Parliament *70*
   The Church of England *71*
   Protestant, Catholic, and Protestant Again *72*

5 **The Catholic and Counter Reformations**   **75**

Renewal and Reform 76
   Let's Get Fired Up *77*
   Time for a Tune-Up? *78*
Who's Trent? 79
   Reconcile? Inconceivable *79*
   Reformed or Reaffirmed? *80*
Order, Order 82
   The Society of Jesus—No Girls Allowed *83*
   The Ursuline Order—No Boys Allowed *84*
   Visions of Avila *84*
Expect the Inquisition and the Index 85
   Hunting for Heretics *85*
   Bad, Bad Books *86*

Part 2:   **Might Makes Right, Right? (c.1450–1750)**   **89**

  6 **God, Gold, and Glory**   **91**

Europe Looks Beyond the Horizon 91
Europeans Begin Overseas Exploration 92
   Cutting-Edge Technology *93*
   Going East by Sailing West *95*
What's Your Motive? 95
   God *96*
   Gold *96*
   Glory *96*
Guys Who Sailed the Ocean Blue 97
   Columbus—Hero or Hack? *98*
   The Conquistadors *100*
   More Who Explored *102*
   Going Dutch *103*

The Making of the Armada 104
The Booming Economy *104*
The Finest Fleet *105*

7   Our Religion Is Better Than Your Religion   107

The Habsburgs and the Valois 108
The Many Wars of Religion 110
War of the Three Henrys *111*
Paris Is Worth a Mass *112*
The Naughty Netherlands 113
The Rule of Philip II *113*
The Revolt of the Netherlands *114*
Protestants vs. Catholics in England 115
Bloody Mary *115*
The Virgin Queen *116*
Down with the Armada *117*
How to Find Witches 118
The Changing Status of Women *119*
The Great Witch Hunt *120*

8   The Rise and Fall of the Holy Roman Empire   123

The Holy Roman Empire 124
Neither Holy nor Roman nor an Empire *125*
Church and State *126*
Europe's Most Powerful Family *127*
The Thirty Years' War 129
Out the Window *129*
The Bohemian Phase (1618–1625) *130*
The Danish Phase (1625–1630) *131*
The Swedish Phase (1630–1635) *132*
The French Phase (1635–1648) *132*
Aftermath and Fallout 133
The End of an Empire *134*
Agricultural, Economic, and Population Disaster *135*

9   Am I in Charge? Absolutely!   139

Planting the Seeds of Absolutism 140
Henry IV *140*
Sully and Richelieu *141*
Mazarin *143*

The Sun King 144
  Becoming an Absolutist *144*
  Using Versailles *145*
  One French Religion *146*
  Colbert and Mercantilism *146*
  Louis on the Battlefield *147*
  "L'etat, c'est moi" *148*
Absolutism in England 148
  King James *149*
  Charles I and the English Civil War *150*
  Cromwell and the Protectorate *151*
  The Restoration *153*
The Death of English Absolutism 153
  The Glorious Revolution *154*
  Limits on the Crown *155*

10 The Eastern Absolutists   **157**

The Plight of the Peasants 157
Austria After the War 158
  More Serfs and Fewer Protestants *159*
  Habsburgs After the War *159*
  The War on Louis *160*
  The Pragmatic Sanction *161*
Prussia (with a P!) 161
  The Hohenzollerns *161*
  Fredericks, Fredericks Everywhere *162*
Russia on the Rise 164
  No More Mongol Yoke *164*
  Hail Czar *165*
  Was Ivan Really Terrible? *165*
To Modernize or to Westernize? That Is the Question 166
  Peter the Great *166*
  Reforming Russia *167*
  The City in the Swamp *168*
If It Ain't Baroque ... .169
  Baroque Art *169*
  Using the Baroque to Bolster Absolutism *170*

Part 3:   Revolutions Galore (c.1500–1800)   173

11   Revolt of the Scientists   175

A New Worldview 176
   The "Old" Worldview *176*
   The Copernican Hypothesis *177*
   Brahe, Kepler, and Galileo *178*
On the Shoulders of Giants 180
   Sir Isaac Newton *180*
   Principia *181*
The Reaction of Religion 181
   Luther and Calvin Sound Off *182*
   The Church Chimes In *182*
Cooking with Bacon and Descartes 184
   Sir Francis Bacon and Inductive Reasoning *184*
   René Descartes and Deductive Reasoning *185*
Consequences of the Scientific Revolution 186
   Foundations of the Modern Scientific Method *186*
   A Community of Science *187*
   Science Saving Lives *187*

12   Enlightening the Public, Not the People   189

Linking the Revolution and the Enlightenment 190
   Science Chic *190*
   Applying What We've Learned *190*
   Why So Skeptical? *191*
   The tabula rasa *193*
The Philosophes 193
   Intellectual Freedom in France *194*
The Encyclopedia 196
Tolerance: A Reasonable Expectation 196
   a.k.a. Voltaire *197*
The Later Enlightenment 198
   Baron d'Holbach, Atheist *199*
   David Hume, Also an Atheist *199*
   Rousseau's Different Take on Society *199*
The Oxymoron of Enlightened Absolutists 201
   Frederick the Great *201*
   Catherine the Great *202*
   Maria Theresa and Joseph II *203*

13   The Agricultural Revolution and an Expanding Europe   205

Seeds of Revolution 205

Open and Closed 206

The Open-Field System 207

Enclosure 208

Revolutionary Agricultural Technology 208

Nitrogen Replenishing Crops 209

New Agricultural Techniques 210

People, People Everywhere! 211

The Chain Reaction 211

Limiting Population Growth 212

The Cottage Industry 212

Rural Industry or the Putting-Out System 213

Proto-Industrialization and Textiles 213

The Atlantic Economy 214

Colonies as a Function of Mercantilism 215

Adam Smith 216

Slavery 217

The Triangle Trade 217

14   The French Revolution   219

Trouble for the Brits 220

The Colonies Get Mad 220

The Colonies Declare Independence 221

The Colonies Get Help from France 222

The French Get an Idea 222

Louis XVI's Dilemma 223

Thanks, Sun King 223

Trouble over Taxes 223

The National Assembly and Revolution 224

The Three Estates 224

Becoming the National Assembly 225

Bastille and the Great Fear 226

The National Assembly Takes Over 227

Declaration of the Rights of Man 228

What About the Women? 228

National Assembly Makes Some Changes 229

Europe's Response to Revolution 229

Off with His Head: The Reign of Terror 230
The Girondists and the Mountain 230
Robespierre and the Reign of Terror 231
The Thermidorian Reaction 233
The Establishment of the Directory 234

Part 4: You Say You Want More Revolution? (c.1776–1900) 235

15 A "Little" Guy Named Napoleon, a Big Wig Named Metternich 237

The Little Man with Big Plans 238
The Kid from Corsica 238
Napoleon's Military Career 239
First Consul, Then Emperor 240
Napoleonic France 240
Changes in Government 241
Civil Code of 1804 241
Napoleon Can't Get Enough of Europe 242
The Coalitions 242
The Grand Empire 243
The Original Waterloo 243
Life After Napoleon and Balance of Power Politics 245
Maintaining a Delicate Balance 245
The Bourbon Dynasty Restored 246
The Congress of Vienna 247
More Isms 249
Nationalism 249
Liberalism 250
Conservatism 251
Prince Klemens von Metternich 252
The Epitome of Conservatism 253
The Holy Alliance 253
Long Live the Status Quo 254

16 The Industrial Revolution 257

Shop Britain First 258
Why Britain? 258
The First Factories 259
The Luddites 260
State-of-the-Art Technology 261
New Sources of Energy 262
The Railroads 263

Labor and Reform 264
  Better Wages but Worse Conditions 264
  Exploitation of Children 265
  Blame It on the Factory Owners 265
  The Reform Movement 266
  Early Labor Movements 266
The Sewer of City Life 267
  The Growing Cities 267
  Overpopulation 268
  Sanitation? What's That? 268
  Cleaning Up Their Act 269
How Romantic 270
  Romantic Ideals 270
  Romantic Literature 271
  Romantic Art and Music 272

17 Intriguing New Ideologies   **275**

Socialism 276
  French Utopian Socialism 276
  Early Attempts at Utopia 278
Marx and the Manifesto 278
  Not One of the Marx Brothers 279
  Workers of the World, Unite 281
The Socialist Movement 282
  Early Socialists 282
  Socialism and Labor 283
New Ideas About Family 284
  An Emerging Middle Class 284
  Women's Changing Roles 286
  New Attitudes Toward Children 287

18 Nineteenth-Century Growing Pains   **291**

Before the Watershed 291
1848: Year of Revolts 292
  Revolution in France 293
  Revolution in Austria 294
  Prussians Make Demands 295
Another Napoleon 296
  How to Get Elected Using a Famous Name 296
  First a Republic, Then an Empire 297
  Cleaning Up the Mess 298

Nation Building: Italy and Germany 298
  Unification of Italy *299*
  Unification of Germany *300*
Reforming Russia 303
  The So-Called Great Reforms *304*
  Catching Up with the Rest of Europe *305*

19 What a Tangled Web   307

A Global Market 308
  The Growing Gap *309*
  Foreign Investment and Markets *309*
  Opening the East *310*
  Europeans Scatter Throughout the World *310*
The White Man's Burden 312
  New vs. Old Imperialism *312*
  Justification for Imperialism *313*
  The Land Grab in Africa *314*
Entangling Alliances 315
  Ground Rules for the Land Grab *316*
  Too Many Treaties, Allies, and Enemies *316*
Too Much Tension 318
  Keeping Up with the Joneses *318*
  The Balkan Powder Keg *319*
  Nationalism in the British Isles *320*
  A Sordid Affair *321*

Part 5: Big Wars and Big Bangs (Twentieth Century)   323

20 Turning the World Upside Down   325

The War That Was Supposed to End All Wars 326
  How Did This Happen? *326*
  War on the Western Front *327*
  Life in the Trenches *328*
  War Spreads Across Europe *329*
  The Total War Effort *330*
The Russian Revolution 331
  The End of the Czars *331*
  The Provisional Government *333*
  The Bolshevik Revolution *334*
  The Bolsheviks Win *335*

Let's Call the Whole Thing Off 336
  The Treaty of Versailles 337
  Failings of the Treaty 338
  An Exhausted Europe 339
The Age of Anxiety 339
  Unsettling Philosophy 340
  New Physics 341
  Art and Literature Break All the Rules 342
  The Great Depression 343

21 World War: Second Verse, Worse Than the First   345

Continental Drift 345
Dictators Seize Power 346
  The Rise of Stalin 347
  The Rise of Mussolini 349
  The Rise of Hitler 350
Appeasement—Seemed Like a Good Idea at the Time 352
  The Rough Interwar Years 353
  Hitler Breaks Some Rules 354
  The Price of Appeasement 355
Total War 355
  Britain and France Finally React 356
  Russia and the United States Get Involved 357
  No Quiet on the Eastern Front 358
  Unconditional Surrender 359
The Holocaust 360
  He Said It in Mein Kampf 361
  The Jewish Problem 362
  Concentration Camps 362
  The Nuremburg Trials 363

22 The Cold War Era   365

Nations United or United Nations? 366
  Pre–Cold War Tensions 367
  East vs. West 368
  NATO and the Warsaw Pact 369
Rising from the Ashes 370
  The Devastation of the War 370
  Western Europe Prospers 371
  The EEC 372

A Nicer USSR? 373

    No More Stalin 373

    De-Stalinization 374

    The Brezhnev Doctrine 376

    Détente? 377

Letting Go Is Hard to Do 377

    From British Empire to British Commonwealth 378

    French Decolonization 379

The Economy Worsens 379

    The Fall of the Dollar 380

    The OPEC Embargo 380

    Keeping an Eye on the USSR 381

23 Changing Millennia   **383**

The Decline and Fall of Communism 384

    One Last Soviet Stand 384

    Poland Makes Waves 385

    Reagan and the Pope Take on Communism 386

    1989 387

    Germany Reunites 388

    The Collapse of the USSR 389

Bad Days in the Balkans 391

    The Breakup of Yugoslavia 392

    The Yugoslav Wars 392

    Ethnic Cleansing 393

The European Union 394

    The Single European Act and the Maastricht Treaty 394

    Here Comes the Euro 396

The More Things Change 396

    Responding to Terror 397

    Challenges for the Future 399

Appendixes

  A Major Events in European History   **401**

  B Online Resources for Further Research   **407**

  Index   **417**

Introduction

History is much more than names and dates. History is a story of people, real people who really lived. Some of the people in the story are wonderful and others are downright despicable; some make bad decisions and some are brilliant; some change history accidentally and others set out with a great sense of purpose. The story is an interesting mix of cause and effect, of chain reactions and random events. Some events change the world all at once, while other events create a ripple effect. Some events create a frenzy only for the event to be forgotten, while other events seem to linger in people's minds for all of history.

History in general, and the history of Europe especially, contains themes that turn up over and over again—not only in Europe but in American history and the rest of the world, too. Especially important to the history of Europe are the themes of struggle and resolution, cause and effect, the desire for improvement, and most importantly the desire to control one's destiny and make one's own decisions, especially in light of the repeated attempts of absolutists to keep that control out of the people's hands.

These themes shouldn't sound foreign to you or to me, because the characters in the story of history were just like you and me. They may have lived in a different era, on a different continent, in a different socio-economic category, or under a different style of government, but in the end people are the same today as they were 600 years ago. Just like you and me, Europeans wanted food to eat, a place to call home, something to believe in, freedom to make their own choices, and security.

In my experience as a teacher and as a writer, I've found that people generally aren't interested in mountains of facts and lists and dates and statistics. People want to know the stories. Therefore, what you won't find in this book are pages of names and dates and lists to be committed to memory. All the facts in the world won't help you understand history. What you will find in this book is a big story composed of many smaller, interconnected stories. The history of modern Europe is really just the story of modern Europe.

What You'll Learn in This Book

Part 1: "Climbing Out of the Middle Ages (c.1300–1600)"

If you want to study modern European history and really understand it, you have to begin in medieval Europe. The major events of the Middle Ages in Europe were not so pleasant and life was tough for nearly all medieval Europeans. They constantly dealt with war, disease, and the uncertainty of religious conflict. In many ways, at the low point of the Middle Ages Europeans probably felt like the end of the world was just around the corner.

After the terrible wars and diseases of the Middle Ages, things looked brighter. Europe reconnected with its historical roots, scholarship and art flourished, and humanity achieved glorious new heights in painting, sculpture, and architecture. The printed word became available everywhere, to everyone. The spread of both new and rediscovered ancient ideas encouraged people to think and express themselves. People began questioning traditions, especially those dealing with religion. Before long, independent thinkers broke away from established religion and approached it from new perspectives, much to the dismay of the established Church. Just like today, people throughout European history had a hard time accepting new ideas. Needless to say, religion will be a major issue for the rest of the story.

Part 2: "Might Makes Right, Right? (c.1450–1750)"

The emphasis on learning made Europeans curious about the world around them. This curiosity led certain Europeans to bravely explore uncharted oceans and mysterious lands in search of fame and fortune—and, of course, to impose their "superior" European ideas on whomever they found. Overseas they found beautiful lands full of untold riches. However, they also found new peoples with different ideas than their own. The courageous and daring explorers who traveled the world for the first time made amazing and remarkable discoveries that forever changed the world, but the clash of cultures in the New World wasn't pretty.

Back in Europe, ideas about religion grew more and more diverse. Religious and political leaders grew uncomfortable with that diversity and used whatever means necessary to either bring the strays back into the fold or to get rid of them altogether. This lack of tolerance and understanding produced a great deal of violence. Many politicians believed that the way to keep the violence and disagreements in check was to establish total control. The monarchs who successfully did this defined their cultures and single-handedly directed the course of their nations' history, but the people who lived under them burned for the chance to live without oppression and make their own decisions about government, religion, and more. This, too, will be a major theme in the story.

Part 3: "Revolutions Galore (c.1500–1800)"

Revolutions have come in a wide variety of forms. Some have been military and political revolutions. Some have been intellectual and philosophical revolutions. Some have been religious revolutions and still others have been technological revolutions. Somehow, though, all successful revolutions share two common characteristics. First, revolutions are a reaction and, second, revolutions cause change.

Humans have always had a desire to improve themselves, the conditions in which they live, and the world around them. Europeans got tired of being told that the current way to do something is the best and only way, and the current body of knowledge is the absolute, unchangeable truth. Industrious Europeans set out to question the answers they had been given and to find new and better ways of doing things. The results were intellectual revolutions and a technological revolution of sorts. The intellectuals reached heights that equaled or surpassed everyone who had ever come before them. While the intellectual revolutions didn't have many immediate effects on the average European, the technological revolution in agriculture sure did. As a result of the ingenuity of a few Europeans, millions enjoyed a higher quality of life.

Politically, Europeans looked for better ways of doing things but found themselves held up against the wall by rulers who wouldn't give them an opportunity to test their new political ideas. In those cases, the Europeans armed themselves and took the opportunity by force. Over and over in the story, people will take what governments are not willing to give if they believe the governments are being unfair and unreasonable.

Part 4: "You Say You Want More Revolution? (c.1776–1900)"

It's human nature for a person to want what another person has. Europeans were the same way. When they saw the revolutionary successes of one country, they wanted the same freedoms and opportunities. Much to the chagrin of the classes who traditionally held power in Europe, the revolutionary spirit spread through Europe. A driving force behind that revolutionary spirit was a sense of community and belonging called nationalism, which was very similar to patriotism.

Nationalism and the desire for a group of like-minded people with much in common to rule themselves turned into powerful forces. Nationalism toppled regimes, united people scattered over large areas, and inspired progress, unity, and pride. Unfortunately, some Europeans forgot what oppression felt like. A fierce competition developed between the powerful nations to see who could conquer the most land and build up the biggest armies. The tensions created by that competition will come back to bite Europe more than once.

In a truly remarkable chapter of European history, Europeans once again reached incredible new heights by using their minds to overcome problems and challenges. Another incredible technological revolution changed the world forever, again. The products of the technological revolution improved people's lives, made transportation easier and faster, and provided much needed work. With the new technological revolution, though, came growing pains and unforeseen challenges to overcome. Europeans created wonderful, helpful inventions but they also devised new ways to threaten and harm one another. For the remainder of the story, Europeans will struggle to keep that technology in check and out of the hands of those who will use the technology against other humans.

Part 5: "Big Wars and Big Bangs (Twentieth Century)"

The final chapter of the story features the age-old struggle between good and evil. The good news is that the good guys win over and over, but at a high price each time. After Europeans have had centuries to develop their own ideas, their own national identities, their own religious beliefs, and their own political preferences, disagreements were bound to arise. In the final chapter all the themes, all the major issues, and all the trends play out. The result is a tumultuous struggle for the truth, for freedom, for self-determination, for tolerance, and for a better way of life.

For all the struggle and hardship in the story of modern Europe there is even more beauty and creation and achievement. In spite of the conflict, Europe produced much of the world's finest literature, art, music, architecture, philosophical ideas, ideas about government, and ideas about religion. Over and over the human spirit triumphs over those who try to suppress it. If you want to study modern European history and really understand it, start in the Middle Ages, and read the history like a story.

Appendix A: "Timeline of Major Events in European History"

If you're like me, a visual learner, then a timeline is a great way to organize a list of events. A timeline is great not necessarily because the dates and events are listed side by side, though that is helpful. A timeline is great for historical events because a timeline makes it easy to follow chains of events and easy to see the cause-and-effect relationship between events.

Appendix B: "Online Resources for Further Research"

Today's students, readers, history buffs, and scholars have a wonderful resource in the World Wide Web. The Internet is a fantastic place to find resources that you can't find in a brick-and-mortar library, in addition to the resources at the library or when you can't get to the library. This compilation of websites will give you some great places to further your knowledge of some of the subjects covered in each chapter.

Sidebars

Sidebars provide additional information and insight, and they often expand upon, or clarify, the main text. To make it easier to locate (or identify) different kinds of information, there are three categories of sidebars:

 **As a Matter of Fact**
Longer sidebars that give you further background on historical events or people.

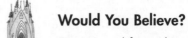 **Would You Believe?**
Figures and factoids to enhance your understanding of events.

 **Continental Quotes**
The wit and wisdom of historical figures, in their own words.

 Define Your Terms
Definitions of difficult words and elusive concepts.

Acknowledgments

This project would not have been possible without the significant contributions of some very important people. Thanks first and foremost to my family for allowing me the time to work. Thanks to Jackie Sach for helping me land the project. Thanks to Randy Ladenheim-Gil for getting this project off on the right foot. Many, many thanks to Phil Kitchel, without whom this book would look nothing like it does now, for his tireless work and invaluable input on the manuscript.

Special Thanks to the Technical Reviewer

The Complete Idiot's Guide to European History was reviewed by an expert who double-checked the accuracy of what you'll learn here, to help us ensure that this book gives you everything you need to know. Special thanks are extended to Dave White.

Part 1

Climbing Out of the Middle Ages (c.1300–1600)

This is the place to start for modern European history, as Europe emerged from the Middle Ages, changed by major events such as the Crusades, the Black Death, the Hundred Years' War, and scandal in the Church. These events laid the foundations for future events like the Renaissance and the Reformation. This part also shows how European curiosity led to the discovery of ancient texts and far-off lands never before seen by Europeans. Part 1 also demonstrates the importance of religion to Europe as the Church and the faithful struggled, sometimes against one another, to find the truth about God.

The End of the World as We Know It

In This Chapter

- ◆ Why the Middle Ages are called the Middle Ages
- ◆ The worst disease ever
- ◆ The Hundred Years' War
- ◆ Big problems in the Church
- ◆ Peasant revolts

The term Middle Ages comes from the Latin *medium aevum*, from which we derive the word medieval. The terms Middle Ages and medieval are virtually synonymous, historically speaking. Europeans who lived in the fifteenth century and after looked back at the years between the fall of the Roman Empire and the dawn of the Renaissance as the middle, hence the name Middle Ages.

For medieval Europeans, the times probably seemed more like the *end* of time than anything else. Between 476 C.E. when Rome fell to the barbarians and the 1400s when signs of the Renaissance began to appear in Italy, Europe experienced difficult times. For roughly 400 years after the fall of Rome, with no Romans and no stable governments to maintain order, barbarian tribes had their way with Europe. Conditions weren't exactly ideal for human advancement in areas like technology, science, education—or anything else for that matter. In fact, things were so dismal that many modern historians have labeled those first centuries after the fall of Rome as the Dark Ages.

Introducing the Middle Ages

So when did Europe emerge from the dark? Some credit must go to Charlemagne, who forged a stable central government for the Franks and made them the greatest of the barbarian kingdoms. Charlemagne wasn't finished, though. In 800 C.E., he became Holy Roman Emperor and solidified a relationship between church and state that would last for a very long time. The position of Holy Roman Emperor went hand in hand with that of the pope. The pope was the final authority on all spiritual matters in the Catholic world, and the Holy Roman Emperor had supreme political authority in the Catholic world.

Some credit must also be given to William, Duke of Normandy, better known as William the Conqueror. In 1066 C.E., William successfully invaded England, taking control after a decisive victory at the Battle of Hastings. Once in control of England, William established the system of *feudalism*. He divided his kingdom among a number of nobles. These were his vassals, and the pieces of land he gave each of them were called fiefs. Each noble was then responsible for supplying soldiers for the royal army. To do this, the nobles divided their land among vassals of their own in exchange for military service and loyalty. This process continued until all tracts of land in the kingdom were of a manageable size and until the royal army was of a sufficient size. The feudal system would dominate most of Europe for centuries—as long as 900 years in some regions.

> **Define Your Terms**
>
> **Feudalism** was a political, economic, and social system in which landowners (lords) granted land (fief) to another person of lower status (vassal) in exchange for loyalty, military service, and rents.

For those uncomfortable with the judgment implied in the term "Dark Ages," the Middle Ages can be divided into the Lower Middle Ages, the centuries after the fall of Rome, and the High Middle Ages, the centuries just prior to the Renaissance. While life in the Lower Middle Ages held plenty of uncertainty for most of Europe, life during the High Middle Ages couldn't have been much better, despite the presence of some stable governments. The High Middle Ages were never as they appear in romantic tales or Hollywood movies, with happy peasants, beautiful castles, brave knights, and lovely ladies—in fact, they were fraught with political and religious turmoil, disease, and war.

The Bubonic Plague

The fourteenth century proved to be one of the worst centuries ever for the people of Europe. The population was the largest it had ever been—or would be again for hundreds of years. The density placed a strain on the land and created bitter competition for work. Furthermore, poor agricultural techniques, poor climatic conditions, and poor harvests early in the century combined to disastrous effect. Because the common person's immune system was weakened by a poor diet, many, many people fell victim to sickness, fatigue, malnutrition, or starvation. The timing hardly could have been worse. In October 1347, traders from Genoa arrived in Italy with an unexpected stowaway: the *bubonic* plague.

Define Your Terms

Bubonic is taken from the word *bubo*, the name for the large, swollen lymph nodes that caused great pain and discomfort for victims of the plague.

Fleas and Rats

The plague originated with rodents, specifically black rats. In fourteenth-century Europe, sanitation was, in a word, nonexistent. City streets flowed with sewage. Garbage and waste were not disposed of properly. Where there was garbage there were rats. Where there were rats there were fleas.

Rats couldn't transmit the disease to humans, but fleas could. In a Europe where people rarely bathed, rarely wore clean clothes, and often shared beds with several other people, fleas were part of everyday life. If a flea bit an infected black rat and then bit a human, the human would almost certainly contract the disease. An infected human could then spread the disease by coughing and sneezing or by touch.

Sicily First, Then All of Europe

In the 1330s, China suffered from an outbreak of the plague. Unfortunately for Europe, one of the most lucrative trade routes for Italian merchants went through the

Black Sea region to China. The traders from Genoa who unwittingly brought the plague to Italy more than likely contracted the disease in the Black Sea from traders who carried it there from China. When the ships arrived in Sicily, the plague already had a death grip on many of the travelers. It didn't take long for the disease to spread throughout Sicily. The Sicilians ran the traders out of town, but the damage had been done. Within days the disease spread into the countryside.

By August of 1348, the plague had moved across Europe and reached into England. The disease spread so quickly that by the time a town realized it had fallen victim to the disease, it was too late. People frequently traveled through one town, contracted the disease, then unknowingly carried the disease to the next town. Eventually towns grew wary of any travelers, but even cautious towns and cities couldn't prevent the plague from preying on their inhabitants.

The Black Death

Never before had Europe experienced anything like the plague—the Black Death, as it came to be known. Approximately two thirds of all who contracted the disease died. Victims suffered excruciating deaths, with awful black sores on their skin and swollen glands in the neck, armpit, and groin. The only good news was that victims usually suffered only briefly. The author Boccaccio commented that victims of the Black Death "ate lunch with their friends and dinner with their ancestors in paradise."

People lived in constant fear of the dreaded disease. Medicine had no answer for it. Doctors of the day had relatively no understanding of infectious diseases, so they could do little to combat the spread of the plague and even less to treat the victims. Europe felt helpless.

The Black Death left millions of dead in its wake. Within five years, an estimated one third of Europe's population disappeared. Population estimates vary, but commonly accepted numbers range from 25 million to 33 million dead. Death tolls were generally lower in the countryside, but many cities lost as much as 50 percent of their population. The epidemic subsided after several years, but the threat of the plague lingered for centuries as outbreaks continued to strike Europe.

After the Plague

Few would argue that the loss of so many lives was a tragedy of epic proportions, but there was actually a silver lining. Before the Black Death struck Europe, the continent was overpopulated, underfed, and underpaid. After the plague ran its course and the population leveled off, there actually was a shortage of labor. This meant that workers enjoyed an increase in wages, and the once-underfed population now had plenty of food. Ironically, the health and the economic status of Europeans improved.

There were, however, negative consequences. As the disease raged out of control, people needed an explanation for the tragedy. Many claimed that the disease was the wrath of God being visited upon a wicked continent. The Church instructed people to pray hard for relief, but the relief never came. Many lost faith in God and in the power of the Church. Some who didn't subscribe to the "wrath of God" theory pointed their fingers at the Jews. Conspiracy theorists proposed that the Jews poisoned the wells in an attempt to destroy Christendom. This led to much violence against Jews all over Europe. Many Europeans were left bitter and jaded regardless of why they thought the disease struck.

The 116 Years' War

Between 1337 and 1453, England and France engaged in a series of raids, guerilla actions, and all-out battles in what has become known as the Hundred Years' War. The struggle actually lasted 116 years, to be exact, but it should be noted that the fighting was not continuous over the entire time span. There were cease-fires and periods of little or no fighting, but these times of peace rarely lasted more than a few years.

The Original Hatfields and McCoys

There must have been a major disagreement for two kingdoms to slug it out for over a hundred years. In the case of the Hundred Years' War, there were actually two major disagreements, combined with the fact that the English and French really didn't like each other.

The first disagreement was over land, specifically English holdings in southwestern France that were rich in trade goods. In a disastrous minor war earlier in the fourteenth century, England lost most of its holdings and wanted desperately to recover the land.

The second disagreement arose over the inheritance of the French throne. In 1328, the French king, Charles IV, also called Charles the Fair, died without a son to inherit the throne. This was a crisis for France; for centuries there had been no succession problems within the Capetian dynasty, or the rule of the Capet family. Now, however, things got complicated.

The closest male relative of the dead king was his nephew, Edward III, the teenage king of England; Edward's mother was the dead French king's sister, Isabella. According to Edward III, the decision about who should be king of France was a no-brainer: He, clearly, was next in line.

If Edward had been French there would have been no problem. However, the French nobility couldn't stomach the thought of a foreigner, an *Englishman*, on the French throne. French legal scholars did their homework and found a very old law that prevented property and other inheritances from passing through a female line. That was good enough for France. They refused Edward's claim to the throne and opted for a distant relative of the dead king.

Over the next several years, tension mounted between France and England. Edward III reluctantly recognized Philip VI as the new king, and France reluctantly allowed England to maintain some of its last holdings in France. Events came to a head, though, when France allied with Scotland as the Scots tried to win independence from England. During Scotland's fight for freedom, Philip VI seized the English land in France. Edward III saw this as the perfect opportunity to make his move. He reasserted his claims to the French throne and to the lost lands in France. Fighting broke out and the Hundred Years' War was underway.

Define Your Terms

Chivalry comes from the French word *chevalier* which means "horseman." Knights were bound by the Code of Chivalry, which governed their conduct in life, loyalty, and war.

Initially, there was significant popular support for the war in both England and France. The nobility supported the war because *chivalry* and feudalism held war to be glorious and virtuous. The lesser nobles saw the war as their opportunity for social mobility, or the possibility of moving up socially. The nobles could not have realized, however, that chivalry would meet its demise in what is remembered as the last great medieval war.

Chivalry Is Dead

At the outbreak of the war, the two feudal kingdoms were poised to fight in two different styles. The English couldn't match the French army in sheer numbers; they knew they would have to avoid engaging the massive armies on the open battlefield. Instead, English forces planned to use sneak attacks and guerilla raids—which weren't chivalrous—to fight their neighbors across the English Channel.

The French, on the other hand, depended on traditional feudal battle strategies. They had many knights in heavy armor mounted on horses, a mainstay of feudal warfare, in addition to archers and foot soldiers. The English had knights on horseback, but not as many as the French, so they intended to rely primarily on scores of archers gathered from every corner of England. For generations, the knights were the dominant fighting force in medieval warfare. Little did France know that was all about to change.

On August 26, 1346, on a battlefield at Crécy in northern France, approximately 36,000 French squared off against about 12,000 Englishmen, nearly 7,000 of them archers using longbows. The battle began in late afternoon with the English dug in atop a hill and the powerful, mounted French knights charging up the slippery slope. After some eight bloody hours, the French quit, having lost nearly 10,000 men. English losses numbered only in the hundreds. The longbowmen reigned triumphant; mounted knights were suddenly obsolete. English archers prevailed again at Poitiers in 1356 and at Agincourt in 1415. The English proved that knights could be defeated with unorthodox tactics—and unchivalrous methods.

> **Would You Believe?**
>
> After the Hundred Years' War, many knights found themselves no longer in demand. Warfare, for the most part, had passed them by. As a result, tournaments featuring jousting and other knightly activities sprung up around Europe to give knights an arena in which to showcase their talents.

England's Fleeting Victory

From the beginning of the conflict in 1337, the Hundred Years' War was defined not by sustained warfare but by many smaller raids and skirmishes and a few major battles such as Crécy, Poitiers, and Agincourt. After the Battle of Agincourt in 1415, it seemed as though the conflict would finally draw to a close. Led by King Henry V, who later was immortalized by Shakespeare, English archers once again dominated the French.

Victory at Agincourt gave Henry V the upper hand as he gained control of Normandy, Paris, and more. Henry forced the Treaty of Troyes in 1420 and, as a result, married Catherine, the daughter of France's arguably insane King Charles VI. The treaty declared Charles's son illegitimate and the future offspring of Henry and Catherine the true and lawful king of England and France. The plan would have worked brilliantly had not both kings died by 1422, leaving Henry's infant son the rightful heir. This unfortunate event ushered in the final stage of the war, the French reconquest of their homeland, and the expulsion of the English.

Continental Quotes

"We few, we happy few, we band of brothers;
For he to-day that sheds his blood with me
Shall be my brother; be he ne'er so vile,
This day shall gentle his condition:
And gentlemen in England now a-bed
Shall think themselves accursed they were not here,
And hold their manhoods cheap whiles any speaks
That fought with us upon Saint Crispin's day."

—Henry V's speech to his troops before the Battle of Agincourt from Shakespeare's play *Henry V.*

Joan of Arc

As late as 1429, the English still had the French on their heels. Amidst this turmoil, now nearly a hundred years in duration, a peasant girl from Domrémy, France, emerged as the most unlikely of heroines. Joan regularly reported hearing voices and seeing visions of saints. Reportedly, one of the voices told Joan to go to the French king and assist him with the resistance effort.

Eventually Joan was granted an audience with King Charles VII. She convinced Charles that God had sent her to him to help drive the English out of France. The king gave Joan command of an army at Orléans, an army which, under her leadership, broke the English siege of the city. After rallying the French troops, she went on to a number of other successful victories and eventually led Charles to Reims for his official coronation.

Would You Believe?

Pope Calixtus III declared Joan innocent in 1456. Almost 500 years later, in 1920, the Catholic Church canonized Joan. Joan had gone from peasant girl to military heroine to heretic to the patron saint of France.

The following year, Joan returned to the battlefield. After an unsuccessful attack, Joan fell into the hands of the English, who, along with their supporters, put Joan on trial for heresy. Joan was tried, condemned for heresy, and burned at the stake in 1431.

Despite the execution of Joan of Arc, the tide turned in favor of France and the English slowly lost their grip. By 1450, Calais remained the last English stronghold in France. Three years later, the French won the final battle of the war, the Battle of Castillon. There was no treaty; the two exhausted pugilists simply quit fighting.

As a Matter of Fact

During World War II, the Vichy Regime of Nazi-occupied France (see Chapter 21) used Joan of Arc as a propaganda tool. The Vichy Regime hoped to inspire in the French a new sense of national pride and confidence in the new government. The Vichy Regime also hoped the use of Joan of Arc would inspire anti-English sentiments. The French Resistance, on the other hand, used Joan of Arc to fight the Vichy Regime. The Resistance played up Joan's efforts to liberate France from invaders and emphasized that Joan was a native of the region of Lorraine, occupied by the Nazis during the war.

From Two Kingdoms to Two Nations

Technically, France won the war, but only because they effectively rid themselves of the English. Practically speaking, both sides suffered tremendous losses, and both were economically devastated by the war effort. A hundred years of war was unimaginably exhaustive for both national economies. France suffered even greater economic hardship because the majority of the fighting took place on French soil— not on large battlefields but on farms and estates and in towns and villages. The English raid-and-pillage tactics wrought total destruction, and soldiers often carried off whatever they didn't destroy.

Both England and France suffered socially as a result of the war, too. It goes without saying that more than a hundred years of warfare resulted in tremendous loss of life and depopulation for both sides. There probably didn't exist a family in England or France that remained unaffected by the war either from losing loved ones or from seeing loved ones return home as changed men. Soldiers returning home had a difficult time peacefully assimilating back into society. Veterans often acted out violently or became aimless thieves and vagabonds. Many veterans chose not to return to a normal life and traveled to other parts of Europe seeking work as mercenaries.

Politically, England and France took different paths after the war. England's nobles, tired of endless taxation to pay for the war effort, began to explore a parliamentary form of government in which much political power lay in the hands of a national assembly. In France, though, neither the king nor the nation's provincial assemblies wanted to give up such power to a national assembly. These trends would continue for centuries in each nation.

Perhaps the most significant and long-lasting effect of the Hundred Years' War for England and France was the rise of nationalism or the development of the nation-state. In 1337, when England and France entered into the conflict, the feud lay not between the *people* of England and France but between the *kings* of England and France. At that time, England and France were feudal kingdoms. Each king required his vassals to raise an army; those vassals called upon their vassals, and so on, until an army was raised. Each man who fought did so out of a sense of duty and loyalty to his feudal lord.

Seeds of dislike between England and France had been planted even before the war began. However, this dislike intensified, and, as the war dragged on, an "us versus them" mentality developed on each side of the English Channel. Each government used propaganda to help develop and perpetuate this mentality. By the end of the war, the fighting was no longer between the king of England and the king of France—it was between the English and the French. Thus began a long history of deep-rooted animosity between the two peoples that remained for centuries. The spirit of *nationalism*, a collective sense of loyalty to one's nation instead of one's king, became a permanent fixture not only in England and in France but eventually in other lands throughout Europe.

> **Define Your Terms**
>
> **Nationalism** is a sense among a population of being a nation, a unified state; it is similar to patriotism. Nationalism is fostered and enhanced by such things as a common history, common geography, a common language, common culture, and a common enemy.

The Church's Black Eye

As Europe moved into the High Middle Ages, the Catholic Church's power and influence reached far and wide across Europe. A Christian tradition began in the fifth and sixth centuries, when Clovis introduced Christianity to the Franks. Over the centuries, the Church in Rome sent missionaries to the farthest reaches of Europe to establish monasteries and spread its message. Charlemagne aided in this effort by lending his support to the construction of monasteries and monastic schools throughout his empire. Kings built beautiful cathedrals and other religious architecture, much of which still stands in Europe today. Pilgrims made religious journeys to holy places to show religious devotion, religious orders grew by leaps and bounds, and local churches played a major role in the everyday lives of common Europeans.

By the twelfth century, the Church had become such an integral part of European life that historians have nicknamed the Middle Ages the Age of Faith. Over a period of several hundred years, however, poor decisions, poor leadership, power struggles, and unfortunate events caused a serious decline not only in the prestige of the Church and the papacy but also in their power and influence.

The Crusades

Prior to the twelfth century, even though Muslims controlled the Holy Land, Christian pilgrims often visited sacred sites such as Jerusalem. As time wore on, relations between the Muslims and the Christians who traveled there grew unfriendly.

In the late twelfth century, the Muslims threatened the security of Constantinople and the Byzantine Empire, the home of the Eastern Orthodox Church. The Byzantine emperor sent a plea for help to Pope Urban II. Pope Urban responded in 1089 by calling for a Crusade, or an organized Christian military expedition, to protect the Byzantine Empire. The pope then went a step further. He also called for the Christian crusaders to travel to the Holy Land to take back the holy places from the hands of the Muslims, or infidels, as they were called. Urban made numerous emotional appeals to European Christians. To further entice people to "take up the Cross," as crusading was known, he said crusaders could keep whatever they captured. As icing on the cake, Urban promised that any who died while crusading would receive remission of their sins; in other words, their sins would be forgiven and their souls would go directly to heaven.

Urban received an overwhelming response to his call. Kings, nobles, peasants, and townspeople from across Europe sold their possessions or simply walked away from their lives to rid the Holy Land of infidels. For 200 years, Europeans crusaded very frequently; after that, crusading continued but not with the same frequency.

Much to the chagrin of Christendom, the Crusades never really worked out the way everyone imagined. Crusaders often bickered, argued, and fought amongst one another all the way to Jerusalem. Kings offended other kings and armies refused to cooperate. Expeditions ran out of food and supplies and resorted to stealing from towns along the way. Emotionally charged fighters routinely killed Jews they encountered; some crusaders even attacked the Byzantines when they passed through Constantinople. Only a few of the Crusades resulted in Christian control of Jerusalem and the surrounding areas. Worst of all, even the success of the "successful" Crusades was short-lived. Without exception, each time the crusaders scored a victory, the Muslims regained control of the Holy Land within a few years.

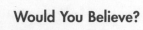

Would You Believe?

Overall, the Crusades were disastrous for Europe. However, Europeans did gain valuable knowledge in such areas as mapmaking, shipbuilding, and castle construction. Europeans also experienced new luxury goods like spices and silks as a result of the Crusades.

Rather than leaving the Catholic world triumphant, the Crusades caused many to lose heart. God had not delivered the holy places into Christian hands as the pope said He would. Kings—Richard of England and Philip of France, for example—resented one another after failing to get along on the Crusades. The relationship between the Eastern Orthodox Church and the western Catholic Church grew bitter and tense. Perhaps worst of all, though, tens of thousands of Crusaders and Muslims alike died in the historic clashes. The Crusades remain a relatively dark spot on the record of the Church.

Babylonians in Europe?

As the 1300s rolled around, the Church found itself in quite a quandary. Pope Boniface VIII pushed papal power to the limits and tried to increase his political power, angering France's King Philip the Fair, among others. After a bitter feud, Boniface *excommunicated* Philip. Philip's men then attacked and kidnapped the pope, who died shortly after being released. A Frenchman became Pope Clement V, who decided to break with tradition and choose a city other than Rome as his home. He settled in Avignon, France, at least partially to try to help end the feud between England and France. Clement also hoped to prevent Philip the Fair from trying the now-dead Pope Boniface for heresy.

Define Your Terms

Excommunication means being officially kicked out of or cut off from the Catholic Church. This is significant because, according to Catholic theology, one must go through the Church in order to receive

Regardless of why Clement decided to move the papacy to Avignon, traditional Catholics, particularly those in Rome, were shocked. This had never been done before. Furthermore, Rome suffered terribly from the move. The papacy is big business. Many, many pilgrims and travelers from all over Europe visit the pope every year. Heads of state from across the continent have official ambassadors permanently assigned to the papacy. Writers and artists flock to the pope to employ their skills. The administrators and the entourage of the pope often numbered in the hundreds. All of these people generate revenue for the local economy. If all these sources of revenue were summarily removed from a city, that city's economy faced serious hardships. Such was the case with Rome. Avignon, on the other hand, stood to gain tremendously from the move, especially considering that Clement's administration and entourage was nearly triple the size of popes who had gone before him.

The Italian writer Francisco Petrarch articulated the frustrations of many people when he called the situation the "Babylonian Captivity of the papacy." He compared the situation to the time when the Hebrews were exiled from their homeland and taken to Babylon as prisoners. Furthermore, the papacy appeared to most observers to be growing more and more eccentric, ostentatious, and concerned with wealth and extravagance. Many concerned Catholics, including pious women such as Catherine of Siena, urged the papacy to return to Rome. Despite the complaints and pleas, the papacy remained in Avignon for decades.

Finally, in 1377, Pope Gregory XI decided to take the papacy back to Rome, only to discover a city in shambles. The blow to Rome's economy had far-reaching effects. The beautiful places in Rome had become run-down and crime had increased. It didn't take long for Gregory to change his mind and head back to Avignon. Within a few months, though, Gregory was dead and the Church was left to choose a new pope.

The Great Schism and the Conciliar Movement

The cardinals charged with electing the next pope faced a monumental challenge. The Church needed a strong leader. However, the people of Rome were adamant that the cardinals choose an Italian pope so the papacy would return to its proper home. When a mob of Romans stormed the Vatican and threatened to do some real damage, the conclave of cardinals elected Urban VI, an Italian. Immediately Urban took a "holier than thou" attitude and called out many Church officials; in other words, he attacked many individuals for what he considered unholy behavior when his behavior hardly qualified as holy or righteous. Completely lacking in social skills, Urban alienated pretty much everyone who wasn't a close friend of his. His ranting, raving, and finger-pointing cost him the support of most of those who initially favored him.

The French cardinals, put off by Urban, claimed they elected him under duress. They denounced Urban and elected a new pope, Clement VII, who returned to Avignon. The Church and the people of Europe faced an unimaginable dilemma: there were two popes. The magnitude of this problem hardly can be overstated. The pope is the official head of the Catholic Church, the mouthpiece of God on earth, the final authority on matters of spiritual significance and theology. Furthermore, the pope appoints clergy and weighs in on legal and political issues. The people of Europe were forced to make a decision: which pope was the true pope? Most people had no idea how to decide. What might be the consequences should people follow a false pope?

Would You Believe?

The Italian pope and his supporters referred to Clement as the anti-pope in an attempt to dissuade people from supporting Clement.

Finally, the nations and kingdoms of Europe picked sides, based more on politics than on religious conviction. The French and their allies supported Clement. The English, Germans, Poles, and most of the governments in Italy supported Urban. The division in Europe over who was the real pope did nothing to ease political tensions that already existed between many governments. This division of Europe is known as the Great Schism.

The crisis in the Church caused many to question its authority in worldly affairs and, more specifically, the nature of the authority of the pope. Those interested in reforming the Church hierarchy joined together in councils; thus began the Conciliar Movement. These councils applied great pressure on the papacy, in both Italy and France, to resolve the dispute. When no headway was made, a council of cardinals met, deposed both popes, and appointed a new pope, John XXIII. Rather than fixing the problem, the presence of yet a third pope complicated matters even more. The Conciliarists were beginning to realize that they couldn't fix the problems in the Church. Holy Roman Emperor Sigismund called for a meeting of the general council of the Church, which came to be known as the Council of Constance. Constance, located in Germany, was an important city in the Catholic world because it had been given imperial status. Constance was subject only to the power and authority of the Holy Roman Emperor.

The Council of Constance initially dealt with issues like heresy but later focused on the problem of the papacy. Finally, between 1415 and 1417, nearly 40 years after the Schism began, the Council deposed two popes, accepted the resignation of a third, and then appointed a new pope, Martin V. More importantly, the Council of Constance issued a decree in which it claimed that its power was derived directly from Christ and that all men, including the pope, were subject to its authority. A century earlier such a decree would have been unthinkable. Popes would now be forced to accept limits on their power and influence, limits like the Pragmatic Sanction of 1438 that severely limited papal authority in France. The conciliar threat to papal power was compounded by other European states that sought to decrease papal authority within their borders the way France had.

Why Didn't God Stop the Madness?

For the political powerbrokers of Europe, issues like the failure of the Crusades, the turmoil of the Babylonian Captivity, and the subsequent Schism affected them politically more than anything else. Furthermore, the heads of state viewed disasters like the plague and the Hundred Years' War from a much different perspective than the common man.

For the common people of Europe, these crises represented perhaps a flaw or a weakness in the Church's message and the Church's power to save people. Life was plenty difficult already for medieval Europeans without the problems of disease, famine, warfare, and turmoil at the highest levels of the Church. The Church's prestige wasn't what it had once been, thanks in no small part to its inability to fix the problems that struck Europe during the High Middle Ages. Until this point, the Church had been able to explain away disasters and turmoil as the wrath of God, God testing His people, or simply the presence of evil in the world. These explanations no longer sufficed for Europeans and, in fact, spawned a new sense of curiosity that led many Europeans to look elsewhere for answers to questions that had been raised in light of recent events.

When Peasants Are Hungry and Taxed

Throughout history, peasants have consistently demonstrated one thing, regardless of when and where they were: when they get hungry and when they believe they are being overtaxed, there are going to be problems.

Nowhere was this more true than in Europe during the Middle Ages. Peasants, the poor who lived and worked in the countryside, always numbered more than any other demographic group during the Middle Ages. However, under feudalism, the greatest financial burden fell on the peasants. Peasants knew this, but they were trapped. The one thing that kept them hanging on was the promise that the afterlife would be better than the earthly life. As a result, the European peasants behaved themselves most of the time.

When food supplies ran low, though, peasants tended to get cranky. When they felt overtaxed, in addition to being hungry, peasants often created problems for governments. Fortunately for those governments, peasant revolts rarely threatened national stability. Peasants had no way of organizing on a large scale, nor of acquiring weapons and supplies.

The Jacquerie

In 1358, France was embroiled in the Hundred Years' War and peasants were forced to deal with food shortages and farmland ravaged by war. To make matters worse, mercenaries constantly pillaged the already-plundered land.

According to the unwritten rules of the feudal system, peasants paid rents and taxes to their lords in exchange not only for use of the land but also for protection. In France, the lords still demanded the rents and taxes, but they offered little or no protection. The peasants finally grew tired of the food shortages, the attacks, and the continued heavy taxation and did what most peasants do when they get hungry and mad: they revolted.

Define Your Terms

The name of the revolt, **Jacquerie,** probably comes from the French term for a peasant, Jacques Bonhomme.

The revolt broke out north of Paris and spread quickly. Peasants destroyed property and committed acts of violence until their leader was finally beheaded. Nobles and government officials took the opportunity to react violently toward the unruly peasants and squelch the rebellion. The revolt never threatened the national government or national security, but it was a headache.

The Peasants' Revolt of 1381

As in France, English peasants felt the strain of the Hundred Years' War and had little patience for anyone intent on taking advantage of them.

In Essex, a group of peasants, out of frustration, reacted violently to a tax collector who attempted to enforce a poll tax; the poll tax was intended to finance England's military campaigns abroad. The defiant attitude spread from village to village as other peasants joined in the reaction against taxes and tax collectors. Soon the defiance turned to violence and spread across southeast England. While peasants continued to destroy property in the countryside, some took their grievances to London. Some even managed to get an audience with King Richard II.

Would You Believe?

Though known as the Peasants' Revolt of 1381, many of those who revolted were townspeople and not rural residents.

The peasants demanded changes in the feudal system and even abolition of feudal obligations in some cases. The leader of the uprisings in London eventually died as a result of being stabbed while in Richard's presence. When the peasants saw their leader dead in a field, they calmed down. Elsewhere, the revolts were crushed by nobles who had no mercy on the peasants. To the peasants' credit, however, no medieval English government attempted a poll tax again.

The Least You Need to Know

◆ In the mid-fourteenth century, traders from abroad landed in Italy infected with the bubonic plague. Over the course of just a few years, the Black Death would claim one of every three people in Europe.

◆ Called the last great medieval war, the Hundred Years' War pitted England against France over land and a dispute over the French throne in a series of raids and battles that lasted 116 years. France finally ran English forces out of France after Joan of Arc helped turn the tide for the French.

◆ The Church faced crisis after crisis during the High Middle Ages, including failed crusading attempts, a period with two popes, and failure to stop the death and destruction of medieval wars and disease.

◆ While peasants never toppled any medieval governments, they did rebel against those in power when they ran low on food and when they believed they were being taxed unfairly.

Chapter 2

Civilization Reborn

In This Chapter

- Why the Renaissance is called the Renaissance
- Italy in the fifteenth century
- The art of the Renaissance
- Effects of the printing press
- The Northern Renaissance

The word *Renaissance* literally means "rebirth." Many people know this but, unfortunately, many people also believe that somebody during the Renaissance declared, "This must be the rebirth of blah blah blah." In truth, the historical era known as the Renaissance wasn't referred to as such until centuries later.

Introducing the Renaissance

Historians have the distinct advantage of hindsight when examining an historical era such as the Renaissance. Looking back on a particular era or on particular events, historians can look for patterns and trends that weren't quite so apparent when they were occurring. The Renaissance is a perfect example. To be fair, though, there is an inherent danger in trying

Define Your Terms

The Swiss historian Jacob Burckhardt, who published *The Civilization of the Renaissance in Italy* in 1860, generally gets both the credit and the criticism for the modern use of the term **Renaissance** as it applies to the era of European history.

to compartmentalize a period of history. Many critics of the term Renaissance argue that some if not much of the rebirth attributed to fifteenth century scholarship actually began during the Middle Ages.

In terms of chronology, the Renaissance occurred after the Middle Ages and, more specifically, after landmark events such as the Black Death and the Hundred Years' War. However, to say that all things were different in the Renaissance than in the Middle Ages would be a grave mistake. In fact, the Renaissance is most distinguishable from the Middle Ages only in intellectual and cultural terms, particularly in terms of art and architecture. No vertical line intersects a horizontal timeline and separates one historical era from another. Historical eras often bleed into one another. Such is certainly the case with the Renaissance.

So why do historians refer to the period following the Middle Ages as a time of rebirth? There are two primary reasons. First, following the death and destruction that plagued Europe in the thirteenth and fourteenth centuries, the next few centuries seem in retrospect as a time in which civilization was reborn, was given a second chance at life. That is not to say the Renaissance was a time of peace and stability across Europe. Italy, for example, struggled with widespread political instability and intrigue before and during the Renaissance. Relatively speaking, though, life after plague and war seemed pretty okay.

Secondly, historians remember the Renaissance as a time when classical texts and classical ideas were resurrected. As scholars throughout Europe, not just in Italy, began to realize their common heritage, an ancestry traced back to ancient Greece and Rome, the desire to collect and study classical Greek and Roman texts grew. These texts served a number of purposes. In education, these texts became the focal points of instructional curriculum. Many students and religious scholars learned both Greek and Latin by studying the original classical texts. This was a departure from medieval scholarship, which often studied commentaries on the classical texts and not the texts themselves.

Studying the original texts, Renaissance scholars brought back classical Greek and Roman ideals. Some of the greatest Renaissance artists traveled to Rome to measure and sketch great Roman ruins, statues, and other relics of antiquity. As a result, much classical art, in a sense, was reborn as well. To be fair, though, interest in the classics dates back to the twelfth and thirteenth centuries, considered the Middle Ages.

Why Italy?

As the saying goes, you gotta start somewhere. Italy was that place for the Renaissance, though neither by accident nor coincidence.

During the Middle Ages, Italy was in a unique situation. To begin with, both before and during the Renaissance, there was no country or nation named Italy. Instead, there was a geographic area that stretched from the vicinity of Venice and Milan in the north along "the boot" to Naples and the island of Sicily in the south. Italians were Italians based roughly on a common geography and language. Cities known as *city-states* dominated the political, cultural, and economic scene in Italy, and that alone went a long way toward keeping Italy fragmented.

Define Your Terms

A **city-state** is a political unit, or state, the size of a city. A city-state often controls the land immediately surrounding the city. Ancient Sparta and Athens are great examples of city-states.

It also could be argued that, throughout the Middle Ages, Italy never quite fit the definition of "European." Italy sat south and east of Europe, west of the Ottoman Empire and north of Africa. This great location gave Italy access that Europe did not have to the rest of the world. In terms of politics and economics, Italy never found itself dominated by feudalism like the rest of Europe. Furthermore, while trade stagnated and even dried up in some parts of Europe during the Middle Ages, Italy always had at least some trade. Granted, the Crusades opened up Europe to some trade, but for Italy the Crusades bolstered trade that was already bustling. In fact, Italy's prominence after the Middle Ages can be attributed almost entirely in one way or another to trade and commerce. Dating back to the days of the Roman Empire when "all roads led to Rome," much of the Mediterranean world's trade flowed through Italy. The perception of Rome and Italy as the world's trade center never completely disappeared even after the fall of Rome.

The monetary benefits of trade need little explanation. If a city-state exported more than it imported, it profited. This made several city-states and many individuals very wealthy. However, trade did much more for Italy than just fill up bank accounts. Trade centers like the Italian city-states, even dating back to classical Athens, have always had the unique qualities of sophistication and cosmopolitanism. If a city wanted to be successful in the world of trade, it had to be willing to open its doors to outsiders. Merchants from other parts of the world flooded trade centers with not only new goods from other parts of the world but also with new languages and new ideas. Cities such as Venice, Milan, Rome, and especially Florence became the cultural centers of Italy and Europe because they first were the financial centers.

The Commercial Revival

Trade and commerce served as the catalyst for the Renaissance in Italy and later in the rest of Europe. Were it not for cities, though, trade and commerce would have had no place to call home. The cities of Italy grew and became bustling urban areas rich with both money and culture. But where did the cities get the cash to finance the rebirth of civilization?

A large portion of the revenue of the Italian city-states flowed into the cities from trade. Italy exported wool from Flanders and from Italy to foreign traders who then took the goods and resold them elsewhere. The Italian merchants then used the money to purchase imported goods such as spices, silks, and other luxury items to resell throughout Italy and Northern Europe.

With the growth of cities across Europe came the regional fairs. These fairs, which were both carnivals and open-air markets, attracted vendors of all descriptions from across Europe. These fairs gave locals a chance to purchase luxury items they otherwise would never have been able to purchase, and Italian merchants were more than willing to sell them. Unsavory though it may seem today, Italy benefited from the slave trade as well. Slavery was indeed a vital element of Italy's economic success. Echoing the Roman days, Italian cities brought people from around the Mediterranean area to be bought and sold all across Europe and on into Asia.

By the end of the Middle Ages, Italy had established quite a network of buyers and sellers all over Europe and the Mediterranean region. This made many men extremely wealthy. However, trade wasn't the only way to make a buck in Italy. While merchants made their fortunes by peddling goods, financiers made their fortunes by peddling, well, their fortunes.

The Power of Banking Families

Perhaps the one constant across Europe throughout the Middle Ages was war. Kings, princes, and even the pope engaged in war on a regular basis. Sometimes war served offensive and expansionist purposes; other times war was the only way to defend against invasion. One fact remained constant: War was very, very expensive. Many times monarchs emptied their coffers to pay for war efforts only to find themselves at war again long before the coffers were refilled by the outrageously high taxes they levied. Furthermore, the administration of newly conquered lands also cost dearly. What was a king to do?

Similarly, the Church always sought to expand its sphere of influence by building churches, monasteries, and schools along the frontiers of the continent. Just as it cost kings to manage their holdings, so, too, did it cost the Church to build and maintain its holdings. What was the Church to do?

Italy found itself in a win-win situation with the financial crises of the princes and pontiffs. Because of the success of trade, plenty of individuals had money to loan to whoever needed it; whether the borrowers were secular or religious made no difference to the moneylenders.

After generations of money lending by a number of families throughout Italy, one family emerged as the most powerful and influential of all. The Medici family of Florence reigned supreme. Their fortune was uncountable and their power was unrivaled. By the time the Medici family reached the pinnacle of their power, the Renaissance truly was in full effect in Italy.

Would You Believe?

The famous financial district of London, Lombard Street, was so named because of the Italian financiers who established themselves there during the Middle Ages.

The Medici family made its mark on Renaissance Italy not because of the size of its accounts and estates but because of the breadth of the family's influence on politics and culture. Cosimo de' Medici (1389–1464) epitomized the mighty Medici family. Cosimo controlled virtually all the politics in his hometown of Florence, yet he never held office. He controlled the elections and persuaded elected officials to do as he wished. Cosimo's son Lorenzo de' Medici (1449–1492) proved to be a shrewd banker and negotiator like his father. Often known as Lorenzo the Magnificent, he expanded the Medici influence beyond Florence. Lorenzo managed to single-handedly cause Naples and the pope to declare war on Florence and then talked his way out of the mess. Lorenzo's son, Giovanni (1475–1521), did more than just engage the pope in negotiations. Giovanni actually *became* pope. Known as Pope Leo X, Giovanni de' Medici did as his father did and his father's father did: he dominated the political landscape of Florence, then Italy, as well as the cultural landscape.

Would You Believe?

Niccolo Machiavelli's classic handbook for rulers, *The Prince*, was written for Lorenzo de' Medici. Machiavelli had fallen out of favor with the government so he decided that writing a book for Lorenzo the Magnificent was the ideal way to kiss up and win back the job he had lost.

The influence of the Medici family on Florentine and Italian politics and culture cannot be overstated. Beginning with Cosimo and continuing with both Lorenzo and Giovanni, or Pope Leo X, the Medici family took great pride in its benevolence. Perhaps it was a result of vanity and pride more than generosity, but the Medicis spent obscene amounts of money sponsoring the greatest painters, sculptors, and architects of their day. By allowing Italy's finest artists to do what they did best, the Medici family arguably helped define the legacy of the Italian Renaissance.

Continental Quotes

"He who wishes to be obeyed must know how to command."

—*The Prince,* by Niccolo Machiavelli

Communes, Republics, and City-States

Dating back to the Middle Ages, the Northern Italian cities were communes composed of free men who did not wish to live under the rule of local lords as other Europeans did under feudalism. Many nobles settled in these cities because of the lucrative business opportunities. There they married into prominent merchant families and essentially created a wealthy merchant class similar to nobility that ultimately would rule these cities.

The wealthy had the political power; the working classes had none. The *popolo*, as the common workers were known, often demanded political power. The *popolo* formed militia-like groups and competed for power with the urban nobles. When the *popolo* were successful, they established republican governments within the cities, but these governments eventually failed.

Define Your Terms

An **oligarchy** is a government in which power lies in the hands of only a few people. In Venice, for example, the "few" were wealthy noble businessmen.

In the event of a failed government, city-states would often turn over power to the *signori*, or tyrant-like rulers. The *signori* controlled all major political issues and appointed who they wished to office. In other cases, *oligarchies* ruled city-states when republics failed. Venice was a classic example of a highly successful oligarchic government.

Florence was a mighty city-state that succeeded in making the republican form of government work. To do that, though, Florence had to make a few adjustments that eventually would prohibit newcomers from ever having a say in politics. In Florence, disputes over citizenship and the right to participate in the political system eventually resulted in an uprising known as the Ciompi Revolt. The Ciompi were unskilled laborers who revolted against the authorities. After several weeks, though, the revolt was crushed and the leaders were imprisoned or exiled. Power stayed in the hands of the wealthy upper class for a while, then passed into the hands of Cosimo de' Medici.

Balance of Power Politics

Unlike in the rest of Europe, the city-states dominated Italy. There was no nation of Italy or even a kingdom of Italy. Rather, the land called Italy provided a home for dominant city-states like Florence, Venice, Milan, the Papal States, and Naples. The city-states never united because of the intense competition amongst them. To further complicate matters, city-states allied with each other to gain an edge in commerce and in political power, but these political alliances shifted like the wind.

Occasionally a city-state or an alliance would rise up and appear to hold too much power. Eventually the city-states realized the potential dangers and established permanent ambassadors to each city-state. They established a policy known as balance of power politics. If one city-state grew so powerful that it threatened the balance of power in Italy, the rest of the city-states would ally against the insurgent to keep it in check. This proved effective until the late fifteenth century, when forces from Europe turned their eyes toward Italy and began to ravage the region.

The Isms

Many eras throughout history are studied in light of the values, ideals, and schools of thought that symbolize them. The Renaissance can be studied in light of what some historians lightheartedly refer to as the "isms": humanism, secularism, and individualism. The influence of the three may not have been as apparent during the Renaissance as they are to historians looking back, but the three isms together help capture and illustrate the spirit found in the art, literature, and culture of the Renaissance.

Humanism

The greatest intellectual movement of the Renaissance was the *studia humanitatis*, or *humanism*. Humanism figures greatly into why historians equate the Renaissance with the rebirth of classical ideas. Perhaps more often than most people realize, medieval scholars did

Define Your Terms

Humanism is a school of thought emphasizing the importance of man, man's greatness, and man's potential, *or* the cultural movement of the Renaissance that emphasized rediscovery of ancient Greek and Roman ideas, ideals, and values.

use classical texts in their studies, but not until the Renaissance did scholars devote their entire careers to the rediscovery of Greek and Roman texts and the study of Greek and Latin. By reviving the classical texts and studying the languages using the classical texts as primary sources, Renaissance scholars indeed revived many of the ideals and values that the classical civilizations held in high esteem.

Initially, humanism hardly included more than the study of rhetoric and literature as part of the educational model for elite Italians. That would change as humanists moved education away from the futile philosophy and semantics of scholasticism, a centuries-old approach to education that involved the critical reading, analysis, and then discussion between teacher and students about classical texts. Despite living amongst the ruins of ancient Rome, most Italians never thought twice about the great civilization that lay beneath them. Italians later took notice, though, when the father of humanism sought to better his world by embracing the cultural and moral values of Rome and the blueprint for government laid out by the ancient Romans.

Francisco Petrarch (1304–1374) hoped to change the world by bringing back the glory of Rome. He could arguably be classified as an intellectual snob for the way he looked down his nose at all things medieval. After all, according to Petrarch, very little of intellectual value came out of the several centuries of European history before his lifetime. Petrarch hoped that a renewed interest in classical Rome would bring about a change for the better. For Petrarch, Italy ideally would rediscover and then adopt the long-forgotten culture of Rome. In fact, Petrarch devoted much of his life to learning Latin and translating classical texts. He even wrote and distributed letters in Latin in hopes of inspiring others to fall in love with the language and culture as he had. Petrarch believed that if those around him consumed the ancient culture the way he did, they literally would begin to recreate the culture and live the way the Romans did. He believed that the teachings of the moral philosophers of Rome, those who didn't just teach virtue but taught people to be virtuous, were just what Italy needed in the fourteenth century. To some extent, his dream was realized.

> **Define Your Terms**
>
> Francisco Petrarch coined the phrase **Dark Ages** to describe the barbaric, uncivilized world that existed between the fall of Rome and his day and age in Italy. Historians have long fought over whether that age really was "dark."

Petrarch probably shouldn't receive all the credit for the revival of classical ideals such as honor and virtue in Italy during the Renaissance, but he deserves a great deal. Those who came after Petrarch embraced the classical spirit, and humanism manifested itself in many places. The educated elite, especially in Florence, made the classical languages and texts part of their educational curriculum. Painters turned from the medieval techniques and themes and painted heroes of old. Sculptors created marvelous figures of marble and bronze. Even architects used arches and columns so often found in antiquity.

On another level, for many scholars and historians, humanism is synonymous with the glorification of humanity and its potential. Also part of humanism was the fascination with the beautiful creation or work of art called the human body. It should be no surprise to anyone that this ideal was plucked right out of classical Greece and Rome. Classical artists and sculptors created magnificent works of art that depicted nude, muscular, heroic men, and classical writers told tales of great men who went on great adventures.

This elevated view of humanity resurfaced during the Renaissance. Pico della Mirandola (1463–1494), in his *Oration on the Dignity of Man*, passionately maintained that man's potential had no limits and that man was the pinnacle of God's creation. The writers and artists and politicians of the Renaissance, including Mirandola, were more than gifted and they knew it. Many believed their work rivaled the greatest that Rome had to offer. Perhaps they were right. Or perhaps they simply were celebrating the Renaissance man, his achievements, and his potential for greatness.

Secularism

The prestige of the Church took a major hit during the Middle Ages after its involvement in such scandalous affairs as the Babylonian Captivity. Also, the Church's inability to launch a successful crusade and to stop the devastation of the Black Death did little to enhance the image of the Church and religion. As a result, the Church lost importance in the lives of many Renaissance Europeans. People began to focus more on the secular, the things of this world, than on religion and things related to the afterlife. Obviously all of Italy did not turn its back on religion. However, a marked difference in attitude did surface.

> **Define Your Terms**
>
> **Secularism** placed less emphasis on the religious and supernatural and more emphasis on things of the earthly world.

After the Hundred Years' War and the Black Death, many Europeans adopted an "eat, drink, and be merry" attitude. They started to realize that their days were numbered and that there were no guarantees in their already-tough lives. Generally speaking, Renaissance man cared far more about such worldly things as wealth, fashion, and art than did medieval man, which accounts at least partially for the resurgence of interest in art and architecture.

A few writers such as Lorenzo Valla went even further and argued that pleasing the senses and feeding man's appetites should be perfectly acceptable. Unquestionably, the Renaissance spirit embraced this secular attitude. Even the Church bought into this to some extent. Many cardinals and popes were great patrons of art and architecture, not to mention fans of an extravagant lifestyle.

Individualism

With the focus shifting away from religion and more toward man during the Renaissance, it should be no wonder that *individualism* appeared during this time. Humanism focused on the greatness of all humanity, but individualism shined the spotlight on the individual. In other words, the writer was as important as the manuscript, the artist was as important as the artwork. The Renaissance celebrated the genius of man so it was only natural that great individuals basked in the limelight.

Define Your Terms

Individualism is a school of thought emphasizing the importance of the individual.

Individualism helps explain the dramatic increase in the number of portraits commissioned during the Renaissance. Rich people loved nothing better than to look at large, beautiful paintings of themselves—and famous artists loved nothing more than to receive huge kudos for their work.

How Great the Art

When they want to sound really smart and rather cultured, historians refer to the *quattrocento* and *cinquecento*, Italian for "1400s" and "1500s." For many, art defined the Renaissance and it is easy to understand why. Much of the artwork epitomized the isms. Many classical themes, thinkers, and characters appeared in Renaissance art. Many features of Renaissance architecture mirrored that of the mighty Roman structures that once stood on the same land.

Changes in Artistic Techniques

Italian Renaissance artists, perhaps more than any other group, scoffed at the primitive, inferior Middle Ages. For Renaissance artists, art regressed after classical Greece and Rome went by the wayside. Classical Greek and Roman sculptures accentuated the beautiful bodies and glorified the achievements of heroes both mortal and immortal. The classic artists worked hard to create realistic works of art.

In contrast, medieval art placed basically no emphasis on realism and detail. Medieval artists painted flat, two-dimensional figures that frequently seemed out of proportion with everything else in the piece. Furthermore, subjects of medieval art included primarily religious icons, scenes from peasant life, or scenes from wars. Finally, the art often served a greater purpose: glorifying God or the Church but not the artist.

Beginning in the 1400s, the *quattrocento*, artists experimented with new techniques that would redefine art for the next half-millennium. First, artists experimented with new mediums. No longer were all paintings done on wood or as frescos, or paintings done on wet plaster. Innovative artists began using a new medium: canvas. Artists also experimented with a vast array of colors. For the most part, medieval artists used drab colors. Renaissance artists, however, made their work bold and bright. The Renaissance artists created a new "international style" that emphasized these bold new looks.

Two of the most significant techniques employed by Renaissance artists were the use of light and shadow and the use of perspective. Artists used perspective to give paintings depth. Rather than everything in a painting depicted as the same size, objects meant to be close were larger; smaller objects were farther away. Artists did this by creating a vanishing point in their paintings. In other words, everything in a given painting receded to a far-off single point.

The other watershed technique of Renaissance artists, called *chiaroscuro* or "light and dark" in Italian, gave an added third dimension to objects. By shading part of an object and lighting other parts, a Renaissance artist of great skill could make a painting come alive.

A wise man once said that art imitates life. Perhaps that wise man meant that Renaissance art imitated life. After all, the art of the Renaissance reflected the Renaissance isms. Humanist art depicted classical heroes and stories of classical lore, not to mention beautiful human bodies. Secularism showed in the works of artists who strayed from religious themes and the works of artists who used nudes in religious paintings. Individualism became more deeply rooted in Renaissance art every time an artist signed his name to a painting or won a huge commission as a result of some patron's bidding war.

The Changing Status of the Artist

Most people have heard the term "starving artist." While many modern artistic ideas actually can be traced back to the Renaissance, this term cannot. In fact, Renaissance artists, at least the great ones, achieved rock-star status. Wealthy individuals, princes, and even the Church became patrons or financial supporters of artists. The patrons commissioned portraits, paintings, sculptures, and buildings, and they paid handsomely. Usually the patrons used the art to flaunt their wealth and to one-up the neighbors. Popes did the same thing. They often felt they had to outdo the pope who came before by commissioning bigger projects by the greatest artists.

Regardless of the motives of the patrons, the creative genius and brilliant talents of history's finest artists were not only recognized but richly rewarded. Many of the finest artists of the day trained under a master and spent years working for little or no recognition. For those who found independence, the reward very often was worth the wait.

The Hall of Fame

Though there were many wonderful and exciting artists of the Renaissance era, a few stood head and shoulders above the rest. Often considered the founder of the Renaissance style of painting, Masaccio (1401–1428) painted humans with a sense of realism. In his paintings, he used light from one source to create consistent shadows throughout. Masaccio also used perspective brilliantly.

A pioneer in mathematics and perspective, Brunelleschi (1377–1446) achieved legendary status when he engineered and constructed the dome of Florence Cathedral. He combined a feat of engineering with classical Roman form and Renaissance style.

Define Your Terms

The term **Renaissance man** over time has come to mean one who is talented in a variety of areas or skills. As in Castiglione's *The Courtier*, the ideal man should be skilled in such things including but not limited to art, rhetoric, riding, dancing, and more. Leonardo comes as close as any to being the true "Renaissance man."

As Masaccio pioneered painting, Donatello (1386–1466) pioneered Renaissance sculpting. His masterpiece in bronze, *David*, epitomized his style. Donatello created figures who stood with their weight on one leg while the rest of their body was relaxed. This style was known as *contrapposto*.

One of the most famous of all Renaissance artists, both then and now, was Leonardo da Vinci (1452–1519). Even though fewer than two dozen of Leonardo's paintings exist today, Leonardo holds a high place in the Hall of Fame. Leonardo did more than paintings, though. He sketched thousands of pages of figures ranging in topic from anatomy to

botany to wild inventions. Perhaps the
crowning achievements of his career
were the *Mona Lisa* and the *fresco The Last
Supper*.

Define Your Terms

A **fresco** is a painting
done on wet plaster.

Painter of the great *School of Athens*, Raphael
(1483–1520) became a master at the tender age
of 17. He did many works for the Vatican and grew incredibly popular not only with
the patrons but with the ladies, too. Raphael's works, especially *School of Athens*, embody
the ideals of the Renaissance as well if not better than the works of any other
Renaissance artist.

Considered by many to be the greatest artist of all time was Michelangelo (1475–
1564). Lorenzo the Magnificent took Michelangelo under his wing and sponsored
the young master. Michelangelo painted, sculpted, wrote, and more. As a painter,
Michelangelo reached the status of "divine," as he was sometimes called, when he
completed the masterpiece of all master-
pieces, the Sistine Chapel, for Pope Julius II.
As a sculptor, Michelangelo's *David* and *Pietà*,
both of which are highly detailed works in
marble, did what no one else could—create
emotional, lifelike beings from stone. Oddly,
Michelangelo, for all his skill and wealth,
lived alone and lonely, unlike other popular
Renaissance artists.

Would You Believe?

Michelangelo com-
pleted the ceiling of the Sistine
Chapel in 1512—four years
after beginning work.

The Printing Press

European texts prior to the Renaissance were almost exclusively manuscripts, or
books written by hand. This was a tedious and time-consuming process that produced
few and very expensive books. An alternative to handwritten texts existed in China
for centuries prior to the Renaissance: the printing press. However, the Chinese
press printed one page or one image at a time, so its versatility was severely limited.
Europeans used this block-printing technique until the middle of the fifteenth century, when a German made an adjustment that was to change the world.

Gutenberg's Invention

In the 1450s, a German goldsmith named Johann Gutenberg (1399–1468) employed
his knowledge and skill in metalworking to fashion single letters and words out of

metal, which could be combined in trays to form words and sentences. In other words, the printing press no longer had to be limited to a single page printed by a wooden block. Rather, the press could print countless combinations of words simply by rearranging the *movable type*.

Gutenberg's invention allowed books to be mass-produced in a fraction of the time and at a fraction of the cost of books copied by hand or printed by the block-printing technique. Almost overnight, books and other printed materials were mass-produced and disseminated throughout Europe.

The Effects of the Printing Press on Europe

The printing press made it possible for printed material to be distributed across Europe quickly and inexpensively. This had profound effects on all of Europe.

Having words, stories, and names printed the same way over and over again contributed greatly to the standardization of language in many countries. No longer was language at the mercy of someone writing everything by hand and possibly misspelling words or misusing grammar. This aided in making vernacular literature, or literature written in one's native language rather than a language such as Latin, very popular. Because books were available to people in their own language, people read more than ever, and the literacy rate increased across Europe as a result.

Ideas that were printed spread quickly across Europe, ideas such as those upheld by Christianity. Many of the first documents printed on the movable type press were Christian texts, either Bibles or pamphlets dealing with Christian theology. Europeans consumed the printed word at an astonishing rate and ideas spread like wildfire.

Better Late Than Never: Northern Renaissance

As the calendar approached the sixteenth century, the Renaissance spirit moved northward from Italy to the rest of Europe. People began to see the relevance of the ideals of past civilizations to their own lives and to contemporary events and issues. However, as the Renaissance sprawled across Europe it did not manifest itself in the same way it did in Italy.

Renaissance with a Twist

The Northern Renaissance, as the movement was known, moved across the rest of Europe in the late fifteenth century and lasted perhaps until the turn of the seventeenth century. While Europe did experience a rebirth of sorts, as had Italy, the Renaissance took a different form and was colored by Christianity rather than by the secular spirit of Italy.

This Christian spin on the Renaissance has come to be called Christian humanism. While the idea of humanism colored by Christianity may seem oxymoronic, it makes a great deal of sense. In Italy, intellectuals used humanism to improve education and politics. The intellectuals sought classical models to copy so as to improve politics and the educational curriculum. Christian humanism also was characterized by an interest in the classics. However, Christian humanism sought to use the primary source texts to come to a better understanding of the early Church and of man's understanding of God. Christian humanism tried to use the model of Christianity taken from the classical texts to improve not only the modern Church and modern Christianity but also modern society. To go a step further, Christian humanism advocated the study of classical languages in order to better understand what the classical authors truly intended the scriptures to say.

The Christian Humanists

The best examples of Christian humanism are found in the lives of Sir Thomas More (1478–1535) and Desiderius Erasmus (1466–1536) of England and Rotterdam, respectively. Sir Thomas More most often is remembered for his work *Utopia*, a book about an ideal society. More's book was an indirect slam on the current state of politics and society in both England and the rest of Europe. He worked closely with King Henry VIII of England and actually never really had the chance to put into practice the ideas he set forth in *Utopia*. More wanted to create a better world by combining elements of humanism and Christianity. He was also an idealist. When Henry VIII broke away from the papacy and the Church, More refused to recognize the king as the head of the new Anglican Church. For his stubbornness, Henry rewarded More with a prison sentence and beheading.

Define Your Terms

While the term **utopia** has come to be synonymous with a perfect place or a paradise, the original translation of the word from Greek means "no place." More's *Utopia* described an ideal society. Could it be that by saying the ideal society was in Utopia, More was actually saying that the ideal society did not exist?

While More worked in public service, one of the virtues that dated back to the days of antiquity, Erasmus avoided politics and public service. Once confined to a monastery, he devoted his life to using classical texts to promote his platform: the education of Christians. Erasmus believed that the way to improve society was to educate society. What better texts for use in education existed than the classical texts of Christianity? Erasmus taught what he called the "philosophy of Christ." He hoped to instill in people the true nature of Christianity, and that, he believed, was found not in some deep theology but in the example and actions of Christ. By combining these Christian principles with the classical virtues, Erasmus formed a message that he hoped would keep society on the straight and narrow.

Art in the North

There was a Renaissance in art in northern Europe, but it was of a different sort than what took place in Italy. Italian artists had the luxury of Roman art and ruins all around them to study. Much of the Italians' attention to lifelike detail came as a result of their study of classical examples. Since other Europeans did not have the same luxury, they painted objects and people as they appeared. Using the innovative oil-on-canvas techniques that Italians used, artists of the Northern Renaissance created bold, vivid, nearly three-dimensional paintings that awed the viewer. In fact, some portraits were so realistic that princes occasionally chose brides based on their appearance in portraits. Northern artists also perfected the technique of giving far-off objects a hazy, blurred appearance.

One interesting way that Northern Renaissance art differed from its Italian counter-part was the artists' attention to detail. While Italian artists used detail to conform to mythic standards of beauty for their subjects, Northern Renaissance artists were much more, well, honest. For example, an unattractive person would have been painted as-is by northern artists; they would not have been made to look like a hero, god, or goddess. Also, many artists of the Northern Renaissance, such as Jan van Eyck (1390–1441) painted many domestic scenes; Italian artists used very formal settings instead.

The Least You Need to Know

♦ The Renaissance, or rebirth, began in Italy because Italy was the major trade and banking center, and eventually the cultural center, of Europe.

♦ Renaissance ideals of humanism, secularism, and individualism were evident in the art, philosophy, and general culture of the Renaissance era.

◆ Renaissance art differed from the art of the Middle Ages because Renaissance artists used new techniques like perspective and light and shadow and new mediums like canvas.

◆ The printing press made books more affordable and more available for Europeans. Literacy rates rose and ideas spread faster than ever before.

◆ The Northern Renaissance differed from the Italian Renaissance in that it centered on Christian humanism, an ideological movement that sought to better society through a combination of humanist interest in the classics and principles of Christianity.

Chapter **3**

Time for a Change in the Church

In This Chapter

- ◆ Problems in the Church and reformers who pointed them out
- ◆ The monk named Martin Luther
- ◆ Martin Luther's beef with the Church
- ◆ The religious fallout from Luther's theology
- ◆ The social and political ramifications of Luther's theology

During the Middle Ages and the Renaissance, some believed the Catholic Church developed a number of serious problems. Those who complained, pointed fingers, and generally caused headaches for the Church are now referred to as reformers. At the time, however, the Church probably thought of the "reformers" as, at best, pains in the neck.

Historians refer to the period in which these reformers worked to bring about changes in the Church as the Reformation. To reform is to change, improve, or restructure. Therefore, the reformation of an institution should bring a change for the better, an improvement. Those who played a role in the Reformation sought initially to do just that. Things just didn't work out exactly as these reformers hoped.

Introducing the Reformation

The Reformation often is synonymous with the name Martin Luther because of the major role he played in the eventual splintering of the Catholic Church into a number of denominations. However, it would be erroneous to say that the Reformation began with Luther. It probably would be more accurate to say that the Reformation climaxed with him. Luther and his teachings were perhaps the straw that broke that camel's back.

Luther was not the first to talk about problems in the Church or to talk about fixing these problems. Like a number of figures who worried about some of the same issues before him, he never intended to break up the Church. Luther and the others simply wanted to address the problems and clean things up a little.

The Church's prestige took major hits during the Middle Ages (see Chapter 1) and during the Renaissance (see Chapter 2). As a result of crises like the bubonic plague, the famine, and the warfare of the High Middle Ages, many Europeans became jaded and turned away from the Church. Renaissance Europeans became more concerned with temporal and material things than with matters of religion, the supernatural, and the afterlife. To complicate the situation, crises within the Church such as the Babylonian Captivity and the Great Schism further alienated people.

The Church was losing souls at a record pace. Those still devoted to the Church believed the Church needed to respond with compassion and concern. They believed the Church needed to be the beacon of piety that Europe needed to see. What many found, upon examination of the Church, was corruption—greed for wealth, property, and political power. Those who spoke and wrote against the shortcomings of the Church and the clergy found that, for the most part, the hierarchy of the Church had little or no interest in hearing what the reformers had to say.

Mumblings and Grumblings About the Church

In addition to glaring problems like the failure to stop the Black Death and the presence of two and even three popes at a time, several issues just as serious concerned some of the devout religious leaders of the fourteenth and fifteenth centuries. Ironically, the most pressing issues were not doctrinal or theological but were related to the hierarchy and governance of the Church and the actions of clergy at all levels.

Except in a few cases, reformers rarely disagreed with the teachings of the Church. Instead they argued that the leaders of the Church had, in many cases, lost their focus or lost their way and the Church was no longer doing its job correctly. The Church did not take too kindly to the accusations that its leaders were corrupt and launched counterattacks. In the eyes of the Church, these "reformers" were something more along the lines of *heretics*.

Define Your Terms

A **heretic** is one who is guilty of going against the official teachings of the Church, or committing heresy. The punishments for heretics ranged from excommunication to imprisonment to death.

John Wycliffe and the Mumblers

Whereas many of the later reformers disagreed mostly with Church *practice*, one of the earliest reformers, John Wycliffe (c.1320–1384), disagreed with plenty of Church *doctrines*. The Englishman studied at Oxford and went on to teach both philosophy and theology there. Wycliffe lived through the Babylonian Captivity and the Great Schism, so he had reason for his beef with the Church. Additionally, Wycliffe had witnessed much corruption within the Church in England. These problems prompted Wycliffe to take a stand and speak out against the Church.

A foundation of Wycliffe's belief system was that the Church had grown too interested in wealth and property. The Church in England had vast estates and numerous properties. Furthermore, many of the clergy, not only in England but throughout Europe, had lavish lifestyles. The Church even went so far as to claim a tax-exempt status on all its lands in England. Wycliffe maintained that the Church had forsaken the teachings of the Bible, which called for poverty on the part of the Church. The Church's extravagance didn't sit well with Wycliffe and his followers in light of the poor and starving peasantry in England.

Wycliffe took exception to another practice of the Catholic Church when members of the clergy began selling *indulgences*, or pardons, to finance political and military exploits. Luther would later disagree with the Church over indulgences, too.

Wycliffe differed from the Church on the issue of spiritual and temporal authority, an especially sensitive topic for the Church. The Church had always taught that the Pope held

Define Your Terms

An **indulgence** is a pardon that could be purchased from the Church, often in lieu of doing penance. Indulgences eventually became "get out of jail free" passes that were purchased ahead of time for sins yet to be committed.

supreme authority and that what the pope said was equal to the Bible in importance. Wycliffe believed that the Bible was the ultimate and final authority on everything and should be interpreted literally. Contrary to the teachings of the Church, he even taught that men should be able to interpret the Bible for themselves, not have to rely on the Church to interpret the Bible for them. Because the Bible didn't establish the pope as the head of the Church, Wycliffe maintained that the papacy was created by man and not by God.

Wycliffe further knocked the papacy when he challenged the idea that members of the clergy could or should hold positions of earthly political authority. Wycliffe reminded the Church that Christ and the apostles submitted to earthly authority. He proposed that in matters of the kingdom, the king should be supreme, not the pope. Needless to say, questioning the authority of the pope made the Church hierarchy very angry.

Would You Believe? ___

Wycliffe believed so strongly that men should be able to read the Bible for themselves that he had the Bible translated into English. Exactly how much translating Wycliffe did himself is up for debate.

Define Your Terms ___

The name for the followers of Wycliffe, **Lollards,** most likely was a derogatory term. The word "Lollards" means "those who mutter or mumble."

Wycliffe didn't stop with the pope when it came to debating dogma. He refuted one of the fundamental parts of the sacrament of the Eucharist, or the Lord's Supper. A sacrament is a religious act or ceremony through which a person receives grace from God. Under the Catholic doctrine of transubstantiation, the bread and wine of the Eucharist, symbolizing the body and blood of Christ, actually undergoes a physical transformation into the real body and real blood of Christ.

Not so, said Wycliffe. He argued that there was no physical transformation but rather Christ's *spirit* was present in the bread and wine. Traditional, hard-line Catholics found Wycliffe's argument hard to swallow. Wycliffe eventually was branded a heretic.

Wycliffe's teachings did not fall completely on deaf ears. His followers, or *Lollards*, carried on his works and defended his ideas even after his death. They completed and distributed the English translation of the Bible and spread the word of God as they interpreted it through the teachings of the "poor priests." In 1395, the Lollards presented *Conclusions*, their statement of beliefs, to the English parliament. In it they bashed transubstantiation, purgatory, confession, and clerical celibacy, all foundations of Catholic dogma. The teachings of Wycliffe and the Lollards affected people in England and as far away as Bohemia.

As a Matter of Fact

Lollardy, or following the teachings of reformers such as Wycliffe, enraged the Church because of the Lollards' belief in lay priesthood and a vernacular Bible—not to mention their disapproval of clerical celibacy, confession to priests, and the Church's monopoly on interpreting scripture. However, the traditionally nonviolent Lollards found themselves out of favor with secular authorities in England, too. Despite the fact that Wycliffe and other Lollards strongly opposed the Revolt, one of the leaders of the Peasant Revolt of 1381 was a Lollard named John Ball, "the mad priest of Kent." The Lollard preacher actually advocated the killing of English nobles. For his insurrection, Ball was hanged, then drawn and quartered, and Lollards fell out of favor with the English government.

Jan Hus

The teaching and preaching of Wycliffe and his "poor priests" made a significant impact on a Bohemian named Jan Hus (1371–1415). Hus attended Charles University in Prague, where he earned degrees in theology. Hus, like Wycliffe, witnessed first-hand the crisis in the Church. Not only a professor of theology but also a priest, he spoke out against the Church in his sermons. Among other things, he denounced the practice of allowing only certain Christians to partake of the Eucharist. As he grew bolder, Hus berated clergy who held secular political positions. Like Wycliffe, Hus argued that the Church had no business governing political affairs. The clergy were meant to rule in spiritual matters only. Many clergy, including his own archbishop, were fuming at the message Hus was spreading.

Hus remained undeterred. He went on to write a powerful work, *The Church*, in which he spoke of the Church as a body of believers with Christ as the head. This, of course, meant that the pope should not be the head of the Church. Hus went on to condemn the sale of indulgences. Finally, the Catholic Church had had enough, and his archbishop excommunicated him in 1412 for insubordination. Perhaps the true cause for his excommunication was Hus's choice of pope during the Schism. Regardless, Hus had been taught a lesson ... or had he?

The Council of Constance (see Chapter 1) summoned Hus to appear in 1414. The Council ordered him to recant for teaching a number of doctrines that flew in the face of Catholic dogma. Hus responded that he never taught the doctrines in question and refused to admit he had. The Council, however, had already decided about Hus. Having just resolved the Schism, it was not about to allow him to get away with

Would You Believe?

The followers of Hus became known first as the Czech Brethren and later as the Moravians, a church that thrives today around the world. When the Moravians came to the United States in the 1700s, they established two main Moravian centers, one in Bethlehem, Pennsylvania, and one in Winston-Salem, North Carolina.

questioning the nature and authority of the pope. The Council of Constance condemned Jan Hus for heresy and burned him at the stake in 1415.

Rarely does the execution of a leader of a movement have the desired effect. Such was the case with the Council of Constance and Jan Hus. The execution of Hus did not squelch his reformist movement. Rather, his followers grew stronger and even defeated armies sent to crush them. The Bethlehem Chapel in Prague where Hus preached became a major center of the Czech reformation efforts. His followers eventually would be influential in the Lutheran movement that was just over the horizon.

A Plethora of Problems

Wycliffe, Hus, and others compiled quite a list of grievances against the Church: overstepping political boundaries, corruption, greed, false doctrines. The efforts of these reformers focused attention on the Church but not the kind of attention the Church wanted. In the centuries leading up to Martin Luther, the more the reformers examined the Church, the more problems they found.

The papacy had a huge target on its back throughout the Middle Ages and the Renaissance. Not taking the Babylonian Captivity and Schism into consideration, the papacy had plenty of other issues causing public relations nightmares for the

Would You Believe?

Some of the more notorious popes lived lifestyles complete with debauchery and intrigue. Alexander VI, for example, had illegitimate children running around all over Europe, and Julius II bribed the cardinals to elect him pope!

Church. Several popes fell into the trap of ostentation, or the flaunting of enormous wealth. While Christ and the apostles lived in poverty, the papacy often ignored that example. Popes lived in a lavish palace with obscenely expensive art and furnishings. They wore the finest clothes and the most stunning jewels. They dined on extravagant feasts. Perhaps if just the pope participated in such a lifestyle few would have noticed. However, the entire papal entourage often enjoyed the same luxuries as the pope. For a continent ravaged by disease, war, and famine, the ostentation of the papacy made no sense.

The clergy beneath the pope also had targets on their backs. Many reformers, Hus included, took exception to an old practice known as *simony*, or the selling of positions in the Church. Many nobles in many kingdoms purchased positions over the years. Nobles sought bishoprics because of the great income potential. After all, the bishop's income came off the top of the collected *tithes*, or traditionally ten percent of one's income required by God to be paid to the Church, so if all the souls in an area paid up, a great deal of money passed through the bishop on the way to Rome. And the Church loved to sell these positions because nobles paid huge sums of money to be Bishop of This or Archbishop of That.

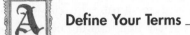

Define Your Terms

Simony is the act of selling an influential position within the Church, a position such as bishop or archbishop.

Similar to the practice of simony was the practice known as *lay investiture*. In the practice of lay investiture, kings and powerful nobles often appointed their friends and family members to high positions in the Church. For example, the King of England might appoint his cousin Bishop of York. Reformers argued that such practice was fraught with conflicts of interest; appointees often struggled over loyalties to family as opposed to loyalties to the Church.

Two practices that gave reformers fits were pluralism and absenteeism, which had become common and accepted in the Church. Pluralism was the practice of holding more than one clerical position at once. Reformers wondered how one person could minister to two districts at once. Absenteeism was the practice of holding a clerical position from afar, such as someone who was a bishop of a diocese that he never visited.

Though reformers pointed their fingers at the hierarchy of the Church, they found fault with the common parish priests as well. Many parish priests ignored the Church's rule about celibacy. Many priests had fallen into lifestyles that involved drinking and gambling. Perhaps worst of all, illiteracy ran rampant among the common clergy. How could priests shepherd their flocks and teach them the Word of God if they couldn't read?

For generations the Church managed to avoid addressing many of the grumblings and criticisms of the reformers. Unfortunately for the Church, that was about to change. While there had been a few individuals in recent centuries willing to question the Church, the rise in intellectual curiosity brought by the Renaissance certainly contributed to the growing numbers of Christians who wanted the Church to answer some tough questions.

The Monk with a Mission

Perhaps the greatest figure of the Reformation was the would-be-lawyer-turned-monk-turned-renegade-reformer, Martin Luther. Like the early reformers, Luther never set out to break away from the Church or to start a new religion. He wanted to reform the Church. As it turned out, though, Luther set in motion events that would help change not just the religious history but the social and political history of Europe, and, indeed, the world.

Luther's Early Days

Martin Luther (1483–1546) was born to a relatively well-to-do mining family in Mansfeld, Germany. Luther was very bright as a young boy, but he faced undue pressure to succeed from his father, who decided early on that Martin would become a lawyer. Many biographers go so far as to say that Luther's father, Hans Luther, probably abused him both physically and emotionally. To say the least, it was a tough childhood for Luther. He worked hard in school, studying the traditional subjects like Latin, music, and religion.

As a Matter of Fact

While at the university at Erfurt, Martin Luther honed his musical skills. Among other things, the musically inclined Luther played the lute. Some historians note that Luther may have helped pay his way through school by singing and playing music in the streets. His love of music led him to compile a number of hymnals including hymns that he wrote.

After excelling as a youngster, Luther moved on to university at Erfurt. There he studied logic, rhetoric, and more Latin, the usual subjects for a lawyer-to-be. A staunchly devout Catholic, Luther practiced his religion faithfully through daily prayer and mass, growing more and more interested in his faith. He did well at the university and received his degree in 1502, then taught at the university for a few years while he worked on a more advanced degree, which he received in 1505. Despite being unhappy about attending law school, Luther honored his father's wishes. He worked hard, but his heart was never in it—and, as it turned out, he didn't stay very long.

As the story goes, Luther was headed home to Mansfeld from Erfurt one stormy night in May of 1505. Thunder and lightning raged as he walked along the road. The intense weather had Luther on edge. Suddenly lightning struck dangerously close, or so he later claimed. In sheer panic and terror, he cried out to St. Anna and begged for his life. Luther feared for his life, but he also feared damnation upon death. Luther's strict upbringing included a heavy dose of vengeful, wrath-of-God religion. According to the Catholicism Luther had been taught, the Maker whom he feared he was about to meet could be unforgiving. Luther vowed that if his life were spared, he would join a monastery.

While most people conveniently forget promises made under such extreme circumstances, Luther believed he was bound by his word. He kept his vow and, to the dismay of his friends and family, entered the Augustinian monastery at Erfurt.

Luther Struggles with Salvation

If ever there was a model monk, it was Luther. He prayed hard, went to confession, memorized much of the Bible, and studied Greek and Hebrew. After a few years of diligent work at the monastery, Luther became a priest. Once again, his father expressed his discontent with Martin's decision.

Ironically, Hans Luther wasn't the only one with doubts. Martin should have felt great about becoming a priest, yet he felt a deep sadness and despair. For years he'd had questions about his own salvation, and these doubts only intensified after he joined the monastery. Dating back to his early education, Luther had been taught the traditional Catholic idea that salvation came through a combination of God's grace and good works through the Church. Luther knew there was nothing more he could do for himself. He did as the Church suggested and, as one of the most devout Catholics, became a monk. He worked as hard if not harder than anyone else at being a monk. He even practiced flagellation, or physically hitting himself to punish his flesh for sinning. Luther was convinced he had done everything he could—but he wasn't convinced that God saw it that way. In his heart, he believed that man couldn't do enough to save himself.

Luther continued to study and visit with other members of the clergy in a search for the answer. He visited Rome hoping that he might find answers, but returned to Germany more disillusioned than when he left.

Finally, after years of studying the Bible, Luther's doubts began to fade while he spent time at the monastery in Wittenberg. The more he studied the scriptures, the more he believed that the Bible was a divine text more

Would You Believe?

Instead of finding a sacred, holy city in Rome, Luther discovered that the headquarters of the Catholic Church had become taken with materialism and corruption. His image of the city, and to some extent the holiness of the Church, was shattered.

important than any other source. While in the tower at the monastery, Luther re-discovered a passage that spoke to him:

> *I am not ashamed of the gospel, because it is the power of God for the salvation of every-one who believes: first for the Jew, then for the Gentile. For in the gospel a righteous-ness from God is revealed, a righteousness that is by faith from first to last, just as it is written: "The righteous will live by faith."* Romans 1:16–17

The passage focused on faith in the sacrifice of Jesus on the cross as the key to salva-tion. In this passage, Luther found perhaps the key theological tenet of the entire Reformation. No amount of good works could equal Christ's sacrifice; therefore, God required faith in the sufficiency of the sacrifice rather than works for salvation. In other words, Luther determined that there was no amount of good works and good deeds that man could do to earn salvation. For Luther, salvation came only from a believer's faith in God's grace. This was welcome news for Luther theologically; however, it tormented him concerning his relation-ship with the Church. He had taken an oath to interpret the Bible in light of Church tradition. In his mind, though, Church tradition and his inter-pretation of this passage didn't mesh. No longer was the Church necessary for man to be saved.

> **Continental Quotes**
>
> "All who call on God in true faith, earnestly from the heart, will certainly be heard, and will receive what they have asked and desired."
>
> —Martin Luther

Tetzel Ticks Him Off

After his epiphany, Luther didn't exactly run out and challenge the pope, open his own church, or start an insurrection. Rather he kept to himself and went about his duties. It came to his attention, though, that some of the parishioners from Witten-berg had traveled to nearby towns to purchase indulgences.

Luther never really had any problems with indulgences because they were part of Church tradition, dating back many centuries. However, indulgences had traditionally served as restitution, or satisfaction, as part of penance for sins. In 1517, though, the pope used indulgences as a fundraiser. Pope Leo X, a Medici by birth, needed money to complete the construction of St. Peter's Church in Rome. Because of his family's long history of managing money, Leo was no stranger to fundraising. To raise the cash, the pope signed scores of indulgences to be sold throughout Europe. One par-ticularly good salesman, a preacher named Johann Tetzel, made his way through Germany, raking in the cash. The indulgences he peddled were hot commodities, because the pope claimed that they were good not only for the remission of past sins but also for future sins not yet committed. Furthermore, the indulgences could be purchased for friends, family, or anyone else—living or dead. What a deal!

Luther knew that the pope, Tetzel, and the other salesmen were abusing indulgences. Although he was upset, he didn't want to raise a big stink. He did, however, wish to debate the issue at the local university. According to legend, although there is no historical evidence that he actually did it, Luther nailed his *95 Theses* to the church door at Wittenberg, the customary way to post a topic for debate.

Would You Believe?

Indulgences could be purchased for those who were already dead to release their souls from purgatory. According to Catholicism, God required payment or restitution for sins, so even the dead whose sins were forgiven still owed payment. Those dead went to purgatory, where their sins would be purged, before they entered heaven.

The document itself, of course, is in no historical doubt. Officially titled *The 95 Theses Against the Sale of Indulgences*, Luther's landmark document laid out his arguments for why the Church's recent sale of indulgences was an abuse of the practice with no basis in scripture and no place in Catholicism.

A good clue that Luther never meant to mix things up with the Church is the fact that the document was written in Latin. The document clearly was intended for academics, scholars, and theologians; common people could barely read or write their own language and certainly couldn't read Latin. Luther did put some thought into the way he wrote the document, but he probably should have known that the episode would not be pretty. Several significant scholars before him questioned the Church on that very issue and most of them ended up dead as heretics.

Luther vs. the Church

The Church also never imagined that a simple document like Luther's *95 Theses* would spark a revolution, but Luther and the Church quickly found themselves in opposite corners—and once the dispute began, the fight was no longer between Luther and the Church but between the Church and half the continent.

Those who fell in line behind Luther did so for a variety of reasons. The issue of indulgences was just the beginning. At the heart of the disagreement were topics like the nature of the pope, the way salvation is achieved, the true number of sacraments, and the value of laypeople to the Church. After a while, the opposition was no longer just those who believed as Luther did but all sorts of Christians. On certain issues, many couldn't have disagreed more with Luther, but they followed his lead and voiced their disapproval of and disagreements with the Church. For all the diversity and varied motivations of the "reformers" who followed Luther, the *95 Theses* served as the catalyst for their actions.

Just the Beginning

Not long after Luther put forth his document, an archbishop reported him to Rome. The pope initially didn't think much of it and basically ignored Luther. However, someone also reprinted the document in German and distributed it widely. The Germans who read it threw their support behind Luther. He had articulated their growing suspicions about and frustrations with the Church.

As the document circulated, scholars blasted Luther and one of the pope's closest advisors called him a heretic. Horrified, Luther asked to answer the charges of heresy, and explained his point of view in a document titled *Resolutions Concerning the Virtue of Indulgences* in 1518. It didn't make much of a stir—except for the part of the document in which he said that all humans were imperfect, thus even a pope could make a mistake. Oops!

Luther later wrote a letter to the pope to try to make peace and explain his side of the story. The pope summoned Luther to Rome, but Luther knew he might be tried and executed if he returned to the city he loathed so much. Some politicians pulled some strings and arranged for Luther to be heard in Augsburg, Germany, instead.

Would You Believe?

Luther could have written 24 hours a day, but without Gutenberg's printing press Luther's ideas could not and would not have spread so far and so quickly upon completion. Many of Luther's writings were printed and disseminated even without Luther's knowledge.

The hearing didn't go so well, and Luther reached an impasse with the cardinal overseeing the proceedings. The deadlocked hearing led to another debate, this time between scholars in the city of Leipzig. The debate took place in July of 1519 and covered a range of topics including purgatory, penance, free will, and, of course, indulgences. Luther offered his opinions and things heated up. By the end of the debate, the cardinal had likened Luther to the heretic Jan Hus, and Luther didn't entirely object. The battle lines had been drawn and Luther was ready to roll up his sleeves and write.

The Worms Diet and Its Undesired Results

After arguing intensely with his former friend and colleague, John Eck, at the hearing in Augsburg, Luther decided to put his ideas in writing. His partner in crime was Phillip Melanchthon, a theologian and former professor who maintained that Luther criticized only practices and not Christianity itself. Over the next few months, Luther and Melanchthon worked on Luther's ideas and tried to get them down on paper. Luther wrote pamphlets dealing with the Eucharist, or Lord's Supper, the papacy, and the issue of good works. Even at this point, Luther advocated reform and change within the Church, not a new religion. However, the three watershed pamphlets Luther wrote became the foundation for what would become Lutheranism. Realistically, what Luther proposed could never have happened; it would have required the Church to turn its back on centuries of tradition.

Meanwhile, Pope Leo had had enough. He issued a papal bull, or an official decree, demanding that Luther recant or be excommunicated. Luther had 60 days to respond. Luther did respond: he took the bull and burned it, along with some pro-papacy books, in public in Wittenberg. When news of the bull spread across Germany, support for Luther grew. When news of Luther's little bonfire spread across Germany, support for Luther swelled tremendously. Still at a loss for how to deal with the renegade monk, the Church summoned Luther to appear before the Holy Roman Emperor Charles V at Worms, Germany, in a proceeding known as the *Diet of Worms*.

Although Luther had been promised safe passage to Worms, he didn't trust the Church. Scores of people accompanied him on his journey to Worms and he arrived safely; even more supporters met him in Worms and cheered him wildly. Once there, the officials accused Luther of heresy once again and demanded that he recant. Luther refused. He said he would if and only if someone could, using the scriptures, justify the disputed teachings of the Church and disprove his beliefs. The emperor realized that nothing was being accomplished and he allowed Luther to leave.

Define Your Terms

A **diet** was a gathering of important political and religious leaders at which important issues were discussed.

It is fair to say that the Diet of Worms marked the official end of Luther's relationship with the Church. He went into hiding in Wartburg Castle after leaving Worms, spending his time translating the New Testament into German. In the infamous Edict of Worms, the emperor declared Luther an outlaw.

The Diet of Worms also marked the beginning of a new religious movement outside the confines of the Church, a new religious movement with plenty of new ideas.

Would You Believe? _____

Once again, a person intended to be the sacrificial lamb turned out to be a martyr of sorts and a hero of the people. The fact that Luther was made to be a criminal and a rebel appealed to the people, though authorities had hoped for exactly the opposite effect. The papal bull and the Diet of Worms actually fueled the Reformation fire that was about to consume Germany.

Protestant Thought vs. Catholic Dogma

So what was all the arguing about, anyway? Was there really enough difference between Luther and his supporters' theology and that of the Church that people had no other option than to break away from the Catholic Church?

In a word, yes. The differences weren't just theological. Some differences had to do with salvation and the nature of God, while others had to do with the pope and the clergy. Arguably, salvation was the most important issue dividing the two sides. The Catholic Church taught that salvation could be achieved only through a combination of God's grace and good works. In other words, after works had been done to pay for sin, God's grace allowed man to be saved. Luther disagreed and said that no amount of works could save man's sinful soul. Only faith in God's grace and Christ's sacrifice on the cross was sufficient for salvation.

Define Your Terms _____

Those who protested the Catholic Church and broke away from the Church eventually became known as **Protestants**.

The beliefs about the relationship between God and man differed in the two camps. Catholicism held that man needed a mediator, or middle-man, to reach God. Luther argued that Christ alone was the bridge between man and God. The Church required man to go to a priest for confession and for intercession. According to Luther, every believer was his own priest. In other words, every believer could enter the presence of God, could pray directly to and have a relationship with God. This doctrine came to be called "the doctrine of the priesthood of the believer."

Along the same line, Luther believed that believers didn't need the Church to interpret the Bible for them. Christians were free to read and interpret the Bible for themselves. This flew in the face of the Church's insistence that only the Church had the right and the authority to interpret scriptures.

Luther also disagreed with the Church about how man received grace. Church tradition determined that there were seven sacraments: baptism, confirmation, marriage, the Eucharist or Lord's Supper, ordination, and last rites. Luther argued that the only sacraments were baptism and the Lord's Supper. The other five, he said, were created by man.

Luther also disagreed on the nature of the Lord's Supper. The Church taught the doctrine of transubstantiation, or that the bread and wine of the Lord's Supper actually changed into the flesh and blood of Christ. Luther claimed that there was no physical change but that Christ was present in the bread and wine, a belief known as *consubstantiation*.

Define Your Terms

Luther explained **consubstantiation** using an illustration. He said that Christ was in the bread and wine in the same way that fire was in a piece of iron that turned red after being in a fire.

One of the most contentious arguments between Luther and the Church occurred over the importance of the Bible relative to Church tradition. The Church taught that Church tradition and the Bible, as well as decisions made by the pope, were of equal weight and importance. Luther vehemently disagreed and claimed that the Bible alone should be the source of authority for Christians. Taken a step further, if man-made institutions like the Church and the papacy weren't in the Bible, Christians had no use for them.

The Far-Reaching Effects of Luther's Ideas

Luther's ideas were obviously dangerous to the Church on a number of levels. If taken to the logical extreme, Luther's beliefs made the Church obsolete. The Church faced the possibility of a mass exodus of souls. If the Church was no longer necessary for man's salvation, why should anyone continue to submit to the Church's authoritarian rule? Why should anyone continue to send money to Rome to support the lavish lifestyle of the pope? If, instead of the clergy holding the highest place, all believers were equally important in the eyes of God, who would respect the current clergy—and who would join the clergy in the future? What if entire kingdoms turned their backs on the Church?

No one, least of all Luther, could have had any idea how his new religious ideas would change the landscape of Europe and then the rest of the world. Clearly there would be religious changes all over Europe—but other changes were also taking place.

Peasants Pick Luther

Preachers all over Germany used Luther's writings when they delivered sermons. Germans tired of being oppressed by the Church devoured Luther's ideas about spiritual freedom. A frenzy seized the general population of Germany, and fired-up Germans heralded Luther as their champion. Luther, they believed, recognized the plight of the common people of Germany—the peasants—writing that Germany would be "drenched in blood" and that the people will "no longer submit to oppression by force."

Would You Believe?

The effect of the printing press on the spread of the Reformation spirit cannot be overstated. Were it not for the invention of the printing press only 70 years earlier, Luther's ideas never would have spread so quickly and to so many people.

In true Lutheran fashion, the peasants put their frustrations in written form in a document known as the *Twelve Articles*. Most of the articles demanded of their lords relief from tithes, feudal obligations, and the like. The Twelfth Article, again in true Lutheran fashion, said the peasants would withdraw their grievances if someone showed that their grievances were against the teachings of the Bible. Soon a full-blown peasant revolt erupted, and, much to the shock of Luther, the leaders seemed to point to Luther as their inspiration.

Luther faced a dilemma. He criticized the nobility for possibly causing the revolt. However, he also criticized the peasants for mistaking spiritual liberty with liberty from earthly rulers. In his notorious *Against the Murdering, Thieving Hordes*, Luther encouraged the nobility to use force to put down the "insurgents" that threatened social and political stability in Germany. The German princes jumped at the chance to crush the peasants, and they did just that. Perhaps 100,000 or more peasants were dead by the time the nobility restored order. The princes were grateful to Luther for his endorsement, even though he wouldn't have condoned their brutality, while the peasants felt betrayed.

Historians have debated the extent to which Luther was responsible, but the peasants' revolt left the princes in total control and the peasants totally irrelevant. Additionally, after Luther sold them out, from their perspective, the Lutheran movement didn't have the same appeal it once did among the common people and peasants.

Princes Pick Luther

In 1526, a number of Lutheran representatives met with representatives of the Holy Roman Emperor at the famous Diet of Speyer. The Holy Roman Empire knew that it would eventually have to deal with the presence of two religious factions, the Catholics and the Protestants, but the Empire granted concessions to the Protestants and decided to deal with the problem later.

At the time, Germany was not a nation or even a kingdom. It was a geographic area that included around 300 independent principalities or states ruled by princes. The major concession of the diet allowed the ruler of each principality to decide for himself if his kingdom would be Catholic or Lutheran. Many princes chose to stay true to Catholicism. However, many saw the opportunity to get out from under the influence of Rome—and avoid sending money to Rome every year. As a result, many princes chose Lutheranism.

Only three years later, the emperor revoked the edict from the Diet of Speyer in an attempt to stop the spread of Lutheranism. It was too late, though. Lutheranism had taken hold. After years of failed diplomacy and widespread violence, the two sides agreed on the Peace of Augsburg in 1555, which basically upheld the original edict of the Diet of Speyer in 1526. Princes were allowed to choose their religion, the emperor was to stay out of religious affairs, and people were allowed safe passage to other cities of their religion.

Luther and the Status of Women

As a monk, Martin Luther took a vow of celibacy. In other words, he was to remain chaste his entire life. The Catholic Church prohibited its clergy from marrying or from having sexual relations of any kind. As Luther developed his ideas about religion, he questioned this practice just as he questioned others. Because the clergy were, in his opinion, not necessary for man's salvation, Luther saw no reason for them to be celibate. Eventually, Luther married a nun named Catherine von Bora and went on to have a happy marriage complete with six children.

As a result of Luther's happy marriage to his soul mate, Luther developed an interesting new attitude toward women. The Catholic Church never considered women to be equal to men in any respect, not even in a spiritual sense. Luther questioned this and said that women were equal in the eyes of God. He encouraged women to have a greater role in the home and the spiritual community. Luther believed women should be in charge of the Christian education of children in the home and in Christian educational settings. He did not, however, believe that women were to be equal in social status or in the public eye.

The Least You Need to Know

- ◆ Early reformers like Wycliffe and Hus questioned the authority of the pope, argued for the supremacy of the Bible and called for reform in the Church.

- ◆ Problems in the Church pointed out by reformers included corruption, ostentation, simony, lay investiture, and illiteracy among priests.

- ◆ The issue of the abuse of the sale of indulgences served as the final straw for Luther, who wrote his *95 Theses* in response to Tetzel's sales campaign.

- ◆ Luther didn't intend to start a new religion, but his beliefs eventually blossomed into a new religious movement that began in Germany.

Time for an Alternative to the Church

In This Chapter

- John Calvin's highly structured theology
- Calvin's influence on the formation of the Presbyterian Church
- Protestants form more and more denominations
- Henry VIII creates the Anglican Church
- England flip-flops between Catholicism and Protestantism

Prior to the spread of the Reformation spirit in Europe, reformers frustrated with the state of the Church had no recourse other than to push for change from within. The earliest reformers never conceived of breaking with the Church or forming new religious institutions or communities. The fact that Luther dared to be different and stand up for his religious convictions inspired others throughout Europe to search for a more meaningful religious experience.

The Reformation Goes International

People's priests, or priests hired by municipalities to care for their people, carried many of Luther's ideas and ideas related to the Reformation movement across Europe. The spread of these ideas among the common people of Europe has been referred to as what else but the "Reformation of the Common Man."

One such people's priest lived in Zurich, a man named Ulrich Zwingli (1484-1531). About the same time Luther made his stand in Germany, Zwingli was relying more and more on the Bible in his sermons and less and less on Church tradition. Ultimately, Zwingli convinced the city council of Zurich to side with him and other reformers in a public debate over religious issues and effectively ended the control of the Church over Zurich. Zwingli's ideas, presented in his *Sixty-Seven Conclusions*, included the rejection of monastic life, the rejection of the idea of purgatory, the rejection of clerical celibacy, and the belief that only God can forgive sins.

Things changed dramatically in Zurich over the following years. Services no longer included the mass, and religious images, or *icons*, disappeared from churches. Christianity in Zurich looked less and less like Catholicism every year. That phenomenon spread from town to town as Europe moved deeper into the Reformation.

> **Define Your Terms**
>
> **Icons** were religious symbols such as statues and stained glass windows depicting saints, among other things. Many reformers disapproved of the veneration of saints, which was part of Church tradition, so they removed the "idols" from churches. These destroyers of icons were known as iconoclasts.

> **As a Matter of Fact**
>
> While many contemporaries of Luther sought alternatives to the Church, not all of them agreed with Luther on theology. For many, Luther remained too Catholic for their tastes. Zwingli was a prime example. While Luther believed in consubstantiation, Zwingli argued that the bread and wine of the Lord's Supper merely symbolized the body and blood of Christ. For the most part, though, Protestants were on the same page.

The first public forum for Protestants was held at the Colloquy of Marburg in 1529. Protestants including Luther and Zwingli agreed on 14 different Protestant ideas, but failed to find consensus regarding the Lord's Supper. Interestingly, in the name of unity and cooperation, Zwingli agreed to disagree with Luther on that point, but

Luther would have nothing to do with it. Luther and Zwingli eventually published work after work bashing one another for their beliefs about the Lord's Supper. Thankfully for the Protestant movement, the debate didn't deter many Europeans from turning away from Catholicism the way Luther and Zwingli had.

In 1531 civil war erupted in Switzerland between Catholics and the followers of Zwingli. Zwingli was wounded in a battle and discovered by Catholic forces who then killed him, quartered him, and burned his body. The war ended with a treaty stating Zurich would remain Protestant and the other Swiss states, or Cantons, would remain Catholic.

Instituting a New Form of Protestantism

Luther's ideas spread quickly from Germany and caught the attention of many believers throughout Europe. One such person, who eventually would leave his own indelible mark on the Reformation movement, was John Calvin. Calvin respected Luther and Luther's ideas but he had in mind yet another form of Christianity different from the Church and from Lutheranism. Calvin envisioned a form of Christianity somewhat different than the Catholic Church and even different than the reformed Church Luther initially wanted. Calvin would get the chance to help develop his branch of Christianity in the city of Geneva.

Welcome to Geneva

Until the 1530s, Geneva, Switzerland, remained a predominantly Catholic city loyal to Rome and to the Church. Geneva, however, was far from a holy or even righteous city. The materialism that gripped other cities, including Rome, also influenced Geneva.

In an attempt to reform the Church in Geneva—and the city itself—a reformer named Guillaume Farel (1489–1565) worked with the few people in Geneva who were interested in Protestantism. At first behind closed doors and then later in public, Farel called for change. After being called before a council in 1532, he was reprimanded and run out of town—in fact, Farel barely escaped. He didn't stay gone long, though, and he returned to Geneva in 1533.

Somehow, after two years of hard work, Farel managed to turn the city toward Protestantism. In 1535, the Council of Two Hundred, the dominant city council in Geneva, officially adopted Protestantism for the city. As in other towns touched by Protestantism, Geneva did away with mass and the icons. Geneva went a step further, though. The Council passed new laws that enforced strict guidelines on the behavior of its citizens—laws that banned gambling, dancing, and other unruly behavior. In reality, the laws did little to change the city.

Another Would-Be Lawyer Chooses Religion

In the midst of the struggle to get Geneva on track, Farel encountered a young man traveling through Geneva on his way to Strasbourg—a man named John Calvin (1509–1564).

Born not far from Paris, John Calvin received a terrific education as a young man. He began theology studies at the age of 14 and continued them until his father decided John should be a lawyer. John studied law and the humanities for a few years until his father died, then resumed studies that included Greek and Hebrew.

Not long after he renewed his religious studies, John had a change of heart about religion and the Church. Unfortunately, his interest in Protestantism came at a time when Protestants were being persecuted in and around Paris, so he left Paris and knocked around for a few years. On his way to Strasbourg, he ran into Farel and his life changed forever.

Farel was so impressed by Calvin that he extended him an invitation to stay in Geneva and help spread Protestantism. Calvin refused over and over, until Farel basically threatened to place a curse on him if he didn't stay and help. How could Calvin say no to that?

Calvin's Theocracy

Calvin faced an uphill battle in a city that seemed apathetic toward religion and downright immoral. Calvin's challenge was to change not only what people believed but also how they acted. Calvin and Farel drew up a list of articles that the city councils adopted in 1537. Included in these articles were rules that created an early curfew and banned gambling, card playing, dancing, and lewd songs. Citizens faced severe punishment for breaking these rules. The citizens of Geneva didn't take kindly to Calvin's theocracy, nor to a government with laws based on a system of religious beliefs and values.

A group known as the Libertines challenged Calvin's ideas, eventually taking control of the councils and ordering Calvin to lay off the people of Geneva. Finally, after a dispute arose over the Lord's Supper on Easter Sunday, the Council of Two Hundred banished Calvin and Farel.

Farel went one way and Calvin the other, to Strasbourg where he further refined his theology. While Calvin was busy working, writing, and getting married in Strasbourg, Geneva fell into disarray. When the Council of Two Hundred felt it had no alternative, it asked Calvin to return and get the city headed in the right direction again. Hesitantly, he returned.

Calvin immediately had the council pass a new constitution for the Church in Geneva. He established a rigorous routine: he taught and he preached, he wrote and he debated. He was determined to have an effect on the city this time around. To benefit the citizens of Geneva, he helped build new hospitals, schools, and industries, but these improvements came at a price.

Calvin was no less the authoritarian and disciplinarian that he had been during his first stay in Geneva. He established a panel of 12 men called the *consistory*, who oversaw the discipline of lawbreakers, specifically those who opposed Calvinism. What must have seemed like a good idea at the time resulted in a very strict system of rules. To enforce the rules and to punish violators, the consistory often tortured and banished people. Occasionally the consistory excommunicated and even executed the serious criminals. While this punishment seems extremely harsh, execution for heresy took place on a regular basis all over Europe in the days of Calvin and Luther. Strangely enough, such treatment of nonbelievers fell in line with the theology of Calvin and his followers—a theology that was organized in a rather systematic manner, unlike the theology of Luther.

As a Matter of Fact

One of the best examples of the harshness of Calvin's theocracy in Geneva was the case of Michael Servetus (1511–1553), a Spaniard who happened to escape the Spanish Inquisition (see Chapter 5). After Servetus arrived in Geneva, it was discovered that Servetus was a Unitarian; he denied the existence of the trinity, or God the father, son, and holy spirit. That didn't sit well with Calvin. Servetus refused to recant and Calvin allowed him to be burned at the stake.

TULIP

In 1536, Calvin published the first edition of his landmark work, *Institutes of the Christian Religion*, one of the most definitive volumes concerning Protestant beliefs. He later revised the work several times and expanded his system each time. To understand Calvin's theology, it is important to remember his background in law and in logic. Calvin didn't use it, but you can use the acronym TULIP to remember his system of theology.

Calvin, as evidenced in his theocracy in Geneva, believed that the civic or state government should be subject to the laws of God. This is in stark contrast to Luther, who believed the two should be separate and that the church should be subordinate to the laws of a just, earthly government. The church, according to Calvin, existed to help the elect live just lives, lives that would make the elect worthy of being called Christians. Arguably, Calvin's role in the Reformation was second only to Luther's with regard to the impact and influence of his actions and theology.

Would You Believe?

Luther, like Calvin, also believed in predestination, though it never became the focal point of his theology.

From Scotland to Geneva and Back Again

Many of the first reform-minded men appeared in Scotland when England began persecution of the Lollards. Many Lollards feared for their lives and escaped to Scotland. Early reformers in Scotland had little luck with their messages there. All too often, Lollards, Hussites, and Lutherans alike met the same fate: burning at the stake at the hands of Catholic officials.

Nevertheless, Reformation ideas crept into Scotland and took hold. Despite the best efforts of clergy there to keep the Bible and Reformation literature out of the hands of the Scots, the Scottish people read anyway. Frustrations with the unusually corrupt Scottish Church mounted, and, after reading the scriptures for themselves, the people of Scotland were primed for a Reformation of their own.

Knox and Presbyterianism

The Scot John Knox (c.1505–1572), on his own amazing journey from being merely an uneducated priest, led the Reformation movement in Scotland. Theologically, John Calvin had perhaps the greatest influence on Knox. In life, though, a man named George Wishart (1513–1546) caught Knox's attention.

Wishart, a reformer in Scotland, served as Knox's mentor until Wishart was burned at the stake in 1546. Wishart's followers asked Knox to take over the Scottish reform movement later that year. Knox knew his safety could be in jeopardy but he agreed anyway. Catholic officials arrested Knox and others and he was sent to be a galley slave aboard a French ship for a year and a half.

Upon his release, Knox traveled to England and joined the Anglican Church. From there he could safely preach against the corruption of the Catholic Church. He did just that until the Catholic Mary Tudor took the throne in England. Knox did the smart thing and fled to Geneva. (More on this later.) Knox studied Calvin and the things he was doing in Geneva. After a time, Knox returned briefly to Scotland— only to turn right around and return to Geneva. Finally, in 1559, Knox returned to Scotland for good.

Becoming the Scottish National Church

As soon as Knox arrived in Scotland, he took over as Scotland's most important reformer and preached passionately against the Church. Soon violence broke out across Scotland as Protestants smashed windows and statues and stormed monasteries. Knox didn't incite the violence, but he didn't stop it, either.

Protestantism spread like wildfire. In 1560, the Scottish parliament ratified the *Scots' Confession of Faith*, legislation that officially wiped Catholicism out of Scotland. Although he had some help, Knox did most of the work on the *Confession*. The document addressed theological issues like the sacraments and the Lord's Supper, two of the major points of difference between Catholicism and Protestantism. The Protestants in Scotland were so different from the traditional Catholic Church that they actually asked citizens to report errors in the *Confession*, as long as the Bible supported the refutations.

Knox and his advisors got to work organizing a new church for Scotland. They wrote *The First Book of Discipline*, which helped outline the organization and basic beliefs of the new church. Three years later, Knox added *The Book of Common Order*. They designed the church so that it was led by elders, much the way the New Testament Church had been. Because elders were such a vital part of the leadership of the church, it became known as the Presbyterian Church—the word *presbyterian* means "elder" in Greek.

This was yet another example of how Scottish Protestantism differed greatly from Catholicism; both clergy and nonclergy, or laymen, could become elders and hold leadership positions. In the Catholic Church, laymen were not considered equal with clergy. Individual Presbyterian congregations were governed by a *presbytery* in much the same way Catholic congregations belonged to a diocese. Collectively, all the

Presbyterian congregations belonged to a *synod*. Knox and the others purposely designed the structure of the Presbyterian Church so that the people, not a pope, made the decisions that affected the members.

Knox had managed to turn a Catholic country into a Protestant country, but his hard work almost went up in smoke. In 1561, Mary Queen of Scots (1542–1587) returned to the throne of Scotland, having been in France most of her life. Mary tried hard to return the country to Catholicism. She started by attending her own private mass, something that was forbidden by the Scottish parliament. Mary brought Knox before her and tried to intellectualize a return to Catholicism. Knox didn't budge, so she resorted to lying, bribing, and threatening anyone she could in an attempt to bring back her religion. Before long, virtually no one supported Mary. Although she was arrested, Mary escaped and fled to England where she eventually was beheaded for leading several assassination plots against her cousin Queen Elizabeth I, a Protestant.

Knox died in 1572, so he never saw the official adoption of Presbyterianism as the national religion of Scotland in 1590. Nonetheless, what he and his followers accomplished in Scotland was nothing short of remarkable. The Reformation in Scotland likely never would have taken place without John Knox.

The Fringe Groups of the Reformation

The Lutherans, Calvinists, and Presbyterians boasted some of the greatest numbers of followers during the Reformation. However, several smaller groups or movements emerged at various times, especially near the beginning of the movement. These smaller groups of believers tended to have more radical religious beliefs and agendas than Luther, Calvin, and the others—which endeared these groups to … well, practically no one during this time.

The Church looked at them with the same disdain it had for all the reformers. Other Protestant reformers looked at them as a little bizarre and, frankly, thought of them as hindrances to the spread of their own ideas. Governments who had to deal with these groups looked at them as troublemakers and rebels.

Despite being the odd men out, the smaller reform movements that began around the 1520s persevered, and somehow many of their beliefs survived persecution from all sides. Many of their ideas remain today in denominations around the world.

What was it about these groups that put them on the same side of the Reformation as the Lutherans and Calvinists, for example? And what set them apart from other Protestant groups?

The Anabaptists

The two major theological differences between the smaller, radical groups and the Catholic Church were the issues of the Lord's Supper and infant baptism, on which they didn't see eye to eye with the leaders of the Reformation, either.

The common denominator for the smaller groups was baptism. Luther and other Protestant groups, along with the Catholic Church, practiced infant baptism. According to Catholic tradition and some interpretations of the Bible, all babies since the fall of man in the Garden of Eden have been born in sin, thought to be part of man's makeup. Baptizing infants, it was believed, protected them from so-called original sin. The smaller, radical Reformation groups believed that infant baptism had no biblical basis and was, therefore, wrong. They believed in adult baptism. These radical groups believed that only adults who confessed their sins to God and committed to a life of Christianity should be baptized, not infants.

Because of their belief, their contemporaries referred to them as the "Anabaptists," or "re-baptizers." To be sure, their contemporaries never meant for the term to be a compliment. Many religious groups fell under the Anabaptist umbrella, finding success in Germany, Switzerland, Moravia, and as far away as the Netherlands.

The Anabaptists also differed with the Church and other Protestant groups about the Lord's Supper. They believed neither in transubstantiation nor consubstantiation; they believed Christ intended the Lord's Supper to be completely symbolic. Furthermore, they didn't practice the Lord's Supper in churches but in believer's homes as a literal supper. This drew sharp criticism from pretty much everyone who wasn't an Anabaptist.

The Anabaptists were neither a denomination nor an organized church. The name was applied to any number of groups who had common ideas about infant baptism and the Lord's Supper. But the similarities among Anabaptist groups went beyond just those ideas. Anabaptist groups held similar beliefs about the Bible, arguing like other Protestants that the Bible reigned supreme on all religious matters, but taking the Bible much more literally.

In fact, the Anabaptists often took ideas in the Bible to extremes. For example, the belief that Christians should not be part of the temporal world led to the development of Anabaptist communities. Anabaptists tried to convert entire cities, like Zurich, into Anabaptist settlements, or they just moved into communes. To complicate matters, many Anabaptists believed that, as Christians who were instructed not to be part of the world, they were not bound by civil authorities. It isn't hard to imagine why governments didn't want fringe religious groups who disregarded laws within their borders.

The Anabaptist movement grew throughout the 1500s, thanks in no small part to the scores of missionaries the Anabaptists sent throughout Europe. As the Anabaptist ranks grew, both Catholics and Protestants grew concerned. Both believed the Anabaptist message could potentially threaten the status quo in Europe. To combat the Anabaptists, both sides took shots at them. Zwingli denounced them. Several leaders across Europe found themselves in prison; many more fell victim to execution by means of torture, drowning, burning, choking, and more. The powers-that-be never killed the Anabaptist movement, but they slowed it significantly.

In the 1530s, a gentleman named Menno Simons (1496–1561) took the lead in the Anabaptist movement. He helped strengthen the movement, then organized many Anabaptists throughout Europe into small communities. These communities of Anabaptists eventually took the name Mennonites. Unlike many of the more radical Anabaptists before them, the Mennonites generally obeyed civil authority. Very much pacifists, they refused to take up arms for any reason. The Mennonites influenced several other denominations of Protestantism, including the Quakers, Baptists, and the Amish.

> ### Would You Believe?
>
> Perhaps a quarter-million Mennonites currently reside in the United States. That number represents roughly half the Mennonites in the world today.

The Amish and the Quakers

The Amish developed much later than the early Anabaptists. Jacob Amman (1644–1720), an Anabaptist elder in the 1600s, called for a number of reforms the Mennonite leaders of Switzerland did not like. The disagreement grew until Amman decided it would be best for him and his followers to part ways with the Mennonites. The new offshoot became known as the Amish.

Like so many other Anabaptist groups, the Amish believed in the supremacy of the Bible and they interpreted it literally. In addition to the strict laws of the Bible, the Amish upheld a set of unwritten moral guidelines known as the "Ordnung." Like many other Anabaptist groups, the Amish practiced shunning those with unacceptable lifestyles; they went a step further than traditional Anabaptists and even shunned those who married outside their church. When the Amish faced severe persecution in the 1700s, many left for the United States.

The founder of the Quakers, George Fox (1624–1691), found himself drawn to religion from an early age. While in his twenties in England, Fox preached with such passion and authority that he was often sentenced to beatings. Among Fox's early followers were 60 men and women who helped him spread his message. By the late 1660s, Fox's small group of followers had grown into tens of thousands of faithful. As the movement grew, the society endured increasing persecution from the English government because of its members' refusal to attend and pay tithes to the Anglican Church. (We'll discuss the formation of the Anglican Church shortly.) Because of the increased persecution, the Quakers began a widespread immigration to North America, where they settled in the colonies of New Jersey and Pennsylvania, which was named for Fox's friend William Penn. The Quakers, like their Anabaptist ancestors, placed great emphasis on lay leadership and on moral standards. They emphasized the goodness of man because of the presence of God in all humans, and they promoted absolute nonviolence.

As a Matter of Fact

The Quakers originally were known as the Religious Society of Friends. The society became known as Quakers when an angry English judge referred to the group as such. In 1677, a few hundred Quakers settled in North America with the help of William Penn, who, though he stayed behind in England, drew up a charter for the new settlement. Years later, King Charles II granted Penn a large tract of land which Penn called Sylvania, Latin for "woods." In honor of Penn's father, Charles renamed the land Pennsylvania.

The English Reformation Soap Opera

Historians have long argued that much of the success of the Protestant Reformation can be traced to the political and economic motivations of some of the princes and monarchs who chose Protestantism. There can be no argument about the motivation behind the English Reformation. More so than any of the other Protestant movements, the English Reformation owes its beginning to the political and economic interests of a monarch—and from the lust and desire of that monarch, who had one of the largest egos in modern European history. To give King Henry VIII sole credit for the English Reformation would be erroneous, however. There were reformers—real reformers—who came before Henry delivered the decisive blow to Catholicism in England.

The Torch is Passed in England

After Wycliffe, William Tyndale (c.1490–1536) took over as the leader of the reform movement in England. Like Wycliffe, Tyndale placed his trust in the Bible rather than in Church tradition and the words of the papacy. While working on his education, Tyndale wanted desperately to study the Bible but his instructors made him study theology instead. Tyndale decided then that his mission in life was to make the Bible available for Englishmen. At the time, English law forbade the translation of the Bible into English, so Tyndale sought permission for his project. When it was denied, Tyndale worked out of his home in secret. The secret quickly spread and Tyndale fled to Germany to continue his work.

Would You Believe?

Whereas Wycliffe used the Latin translation of the New Testament, the *Vulgate*, for his English translation, Tyndale used the Greek. The *Vulgate* was full of translation errors from the original text, so Tyndale's turned out to be much more accurate.

Tyndale completed his translation in 1525 and had it smuggled into England. Despite the best efforts of the Catholic officials there, the Tyndale Bible, actually just the New Testament, found its way into the hands of many, many Englishmen. Tyndale paid a heavy price for his efforts. Eleven years after the completion of his translation, Tyndale fell into a trap set by the pope. A group of men mugged Tyndale and took him to a prison where he later was hanged and then burned.

Tyndale's New Testament served as the basis for the work of Miles Coverdale (1488–1569), the author of the first complete English Bible. Upon Coverdale's completion of the Bible, English reformers pushed for the Bible to be made available to churches across England. One of the biggest supporters of this movement was Thomas Cranmer, the Archbishop of Canterbury and advisor to King Henry VIII.

I'm Henry VIII I Am

Henry Tudor became King Henry VIII (1491–1547) in 1509. Henry was a Catholic king in a Catholic nation. There were reformers in England, but the nation had not yet turned away from the Church. Henry's wife was Catherine of Aragon (1485–1536), a devout Catholic. Matters seemed to be in order in Henry's life and England seemed to be in great shape to resist the Protestantism that swept over Europe. Henry blasted Martin Luther and provided the Church with undying support as the movement got underway. The pope even gave Henry the title of Defender of the Faith.

All Henry needed was a male heir to carry on his Catholic legacy in England. He and Catherine tried and tried, but Catherine failed to give him the male heir he so desperately wanted. The only child from their marriage to survive was a daughter named Mary. Henry decided that since Catherine could produce no male heir and basically no healthy children, something had to be wrong with her; being the king, he never would have imagined that it might actually have been his fault.

Henry loved women and had any number of conquests throughout his marriage to Catherine. However, Henry found one woman, Anne Boleyn (c.1507–1536), whom he could not conquer. In fact, Henry became smitten with young Anne and decided he'd like to add a notch for her on his bedpost. Henry had to have Anne, so he set out to find a way to get rid of Catherine. Thus began the real-life soap opera.

Henry would have liked a simple divorce from Catherine, but the Catholic Church did not allow divorce. After all, when two souls joined in marriage, they were bound together in a permanent union by God. What God joined together, no man could undo. Therefore, Henry didn't have the option of a divorce. Henry found a loophole, though, and hoped he could be granted an annulment. Catherine had actually been Henry's brother's wife before she married Henry. According to Catholic law based on a passage in the Old Testament, a man could not marry his dead brother's wife but Henry did anyway. Since the marriage never should have occurred in the first place, Henry argued, an annulment would fix the whole problem. He wrote to the pope and requested an annulment but the pope didn't want anything to do with it. As it turned out, the pope feared the Holy Roman Emperor, whose troops had occupied Rome, and the Holy Roman Emperor's aunt was none other than Henry's wife, Catherine.

Henry's advisors were split over what to do. One group led by Thomas More persuaded Henry not to do anything to damage the relationship between England and the papacy. More, a staunch defender of Catholicism, had opposed the distribution of Tyndale's Bibles. Thomas Cranmer (1489–1556), on the other hand, who had supported the distribution of Tyndale's Bibles, found himself again opposed to More. Cranmer suggested to Henry not to wait for Rome but to go ahead and marry Anne—in secret, of course.

Most pleased, Henry did just that. He also appointed Cranmer as Archbishop of Canterbury, the highest ecclesiastic position in England. Before long, Henry's marriage to Catherine had been annulled and his marriage

Would You Believe?

Henry VIII required a public oath of support as a way to enforce the Act of Supremacy. Thomas More, defender of Catholicism to the end, refused to take the oath. Henry arrested, tried, and executed More on charges of treason.

to Anne declared valid. When the pope found out about Henry's shenanigans, he threatened to excommunicate Henry. Henry responded by making Anne the Queen of England. Needless to say, this horrified the papacy and many hard-line Catholics in England, including Thomas More. Just a few months after Henry's marriage to Anne, she gave birth to a bouncing baby … girl. Once again Henry, or rather Henry's wife, had failed to produce a male heir; this daughter would be named Elizabeth.

The Reformation Parliament

The English Parliament, or Reformation Parliament as it later would be called, went to work right away and officially broke ties with the Catholic Church. In 1533, Parliament passed the Statute in Restraint of Appeals which made all legal matters in England subject to the authority of the crown rather than the papacy. These legal matters included appeals, wills, ecclesiastical grants, and, most importantly, marriages. This technically allowed "the King's Great Matter" to be handled by the English rather than by the papacy.

Drafted by one of Henry's closest advisors, Thomas Cromwell (1485–1540), the statute made it illegal to appeal to the pope on any matter. Parliament followed up in 1534 with the Act of Supremacy, legislation that declared the king the true head of the Church in England, or in Parliament's own words, "Protector and only Supreme Head of the Church and the clergy of England." Cromwell took the lead in moving this through Parliament, too. Basically, Parliament declared the pope officially irrelevant.

The English Reformation had begun not because of passionate preaching or heartfelt convictions. Henry just wanted out of his marriage with Catherine. But there were other good reasons for breaking ties with Rome. The Church owned perhaps more land and wealth in England than the king himself, and the break with Rome gave Henry the opportunity to confiscate that land. Beginning in 1535, Cromwell, who disapproved of monastic life anyway, visited numerous monasteries and abbeys throughout the land. The following year, Henry and his advisors closed the monasteries and sold the lands to nobles in what became known as the dissolution of the monasteries. This worked well for Henry. Those opposed to monasticism were pleased that monasteries were gone. Henry made a ton of cash, and nobles increased their holdings.

The Church of England

Despite the break with the papacy and the creation of a national church in England (called, of course, the Church of England), Henry's new church was still very Catholic. Other than no longer recognizing the pope as the head of the Church, there weren't many dramatic theological changes made to the new church. The Church of England, also known as the Anglican Church, still held most Catholic beliefs including *apostolic succession*. The Anglican Church even practiced a very high-church, liturgical service much like the Catholic Church. The Anglican Church was so Catholic that Henry passed the Six Articles in 1539 reaffirming many traditional Catholic beliefs. Strongly opposed by the pretty-much-Protestant Thomas Cranmer, the Six Articles reaffirmed the Catholic doctrines of transubstantiation, clerical celibacy and chastity, and the importance of confession. Cranmer and Cromwell both wanted more change in the new Church, but Henry did not. Therefore, the Reformation in England initially amounted to little more than a transfer of power from Rome to the English throne.

Define Your Terms

Apostolic succession is the belief by the Catholic, Lutheran, Anglican, and other churches that Christ is still with the Church through the ordination of bishops. Christ chose and ordained the apostles who ordained the next generation and so on through history so that all current bishops can trace their ordination to the apostles and, therefore, to Christ.

Protestant, Catholic, and Protestant Again

All that notwithstanding, Henry still didn't have the male heir he needed to carry on the line. As it became apparent something was wrong with Anne Boleyn, because she couldn't produce a male heir, either, Henry lost interest in her. Henry and Thomas Cromwell trumped up charges of witchcraft, adultery, and treason, then tortured some poor fellow to obtain a false confession against Anne. In 1536, England executed Anne. Less than two weeks later, Henry married Jane Seymour (1508–1537), the woman who eventually would give Henry the male heir for which he longed.

Henry died in 1547 and left the throne to his 10-year-old son, Edward. Edward's uncle, the Protestant Edward Seymour (1506–1552), became protector, or the real ruler, until Edward matured. With that, the Protestants finally got their wish. Cranmer instituted big changes in the Church of England that made the church more Protestant. The Protestants reformed the Lord's Supper and allowed priests to marry. They repealed the Six Articles and introduced the *Book of Common Prayer*. The *Book* served as a guide for the liturgy in services as well as a guide for morning and evening prayers. It combined traditional theology with ideas from other reformers such as Luther and Zwingli. Protestantism surely would have become even more pervasive in England had young King Edward not died at the age of 16.

Would You Believe?

Few people know that after Edward died, Lady Jane Grey became queen and "ruled" for nine days. Jane was placed precariously on the throne to continue Protestantism. Unfortunately for Jane, Mary took the crown from her, imprisoned her, then had her executed when she refused to convert to Catholicism.

All the while Edward "ruled" as Edward VI (1537–1553), Henry's first child, Mary (1516–1558), was gathering support from Catholics in England. She was determined to take the throne and return England to the true faith. Mary and her right-hand man within the Church, Cardinal Reginald Pole (1500–1558), made their number-one priority restructuring the Church and undoing the things that Henry and Edward had done. Mary declared previous reforms null and void. Many Protestant leaders saw the writing on the wall and fled the country. Those who did were wise because Mary and Cardinal Pole persecuted Protestants mercilessly, earning Mary the nickname "Bloody Mary." Many, including Thomas Cranmer, were executed under

Would You Believe?

Mary offered Cranmer his life in exchange for recanting his Protestant beliefs. Cranmer recanted but was sentenced to death anyway. He had the last word, though, when he recanted on recanting just before he died.

Mary's regime. England returned quickly and relatively easily to Catholicism, perhaps indicating that England wasn't so ready to leave the Catholic fold in the first place. Upon Mary's death, her half-sister, Elizabeth, daughter of Henry and Anne Boleyn, ascended to the throne of England as Elizabeth I (1533–1603).

Elizabeth I (see Chapter 7) took the throne and returned England to Protestantism once again. In 1559, Parliament undid the Catholicism of Mary and reinstated the *Book of Common Prayer*. Parliament adopted the Thirty-Nine Articles, the fundamental theological beliefs of the Anglican Church. Elizabeth also brought back the Anglican Church as the official church in England. A shrewd politician, Elizabeth learned from the mistakes of her predecessors. Rather than being aggressive with her policies toward Catholics the way Mary was toward Protestants, Elizabeth took a middle-of-the-road position concerning religion within her realm. Basically, she declared that Protestantism would be the official religion and then ignored Catholics as long as they kept quiet and didn't make a scene. She made sure not to make enemies with Catholics at home and she tried to stay out of the way of the pope. Nevertheless, the Church tried to do away with her and return England to Catholicism. One pope excommunicated her and another gave his blessing for assassination attempts. Neither tactic worked. England grew angry with Rome and drifted farther and farther away. Elizabeth had successfully chosen a religion for her kingdom and made it stick without much resistance.

> **Would You Believe?**
>
> Elizabeth's moderate religious policies, known as the Elizabethan Settlement, pleased neither extreme Catholics nor extreme Protestants. However, most of the country and many people in Europe accepted the arrangement.

The Least You Need to Know

- John Calvin established a theocracy in Geneva, Switzerland, where the city council kept its citizens in line with a strict moral code.

- Calvin published his theology in *Institutes of the Christian Religion*; central to his theology was the belief in predestination.

- John Knox, influenced greatly by Calvin, founded the Presbyterian Church, the official church in Scotland.

- Reformers across Europe started smaller reform movements and ultimately created Protestant denominations like the Amish and the Mennonites.

◆ Reformers like Wycliffe and Tyndale laid the foundations for the English Reformation, but Henry VIII actually broke with Rome and created the Church of England.

◆ "Bloody Mary" Tudor returned England to Catholicism and her half-sister, Elizabeth, restored the Anglican Church for good after Mary's death.

5

The Catholic and Counter Reformations

In This Chapter

- ◆ Reformers within the Church call for change
- ◆ The Protestant Reformation forces the Church's hand
- ◆ The landmark meetings known as the Council of Trent
- ◆ New orders and societies form to slow Protestantism and win souls back for the Church
- ◆ The Inquisition searches for heretics and other enemies of the Church

Few would argue that the Protestant Reformation sneaked up on the Church and caught it off guard. As far back as Wycliffe and Hus, individuals noticed things about the Church and about its hierarchy that moved them to speak their minds and call for change. As time went on, more and more people echoed the sentiments of the early reformers, challenging the Church on matters of theology and practice and calling for an end to

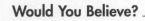

Would You Believe?

In the three centuries before the climax of the Protestant Reformation, several Church councils conducted by leading Church scholars and theologians convened to discuss reform and change. However, the overwhelming majority of problems pointed out by reformers were never dealt with in any significant way.

Define Your Terms

The **Catholic Reformation** was the movement within the Catholic Church to end corruption and abuses and address once and for all the theological issues raised both by reformers and Protestants. The movement can also be referred to as the Counter-Reformation, because at this time the Church also slowed the spread of Protestantism and reclaimed many former Catholics.

corruption and abuses. When no changes occurred, some reformers simply cut their ties with Rome and did their own thing.

Initially, the Church could dismiss the reformers as troublemakers and denounce their teachings. The Church dealt with some instigators by applying political pressure and with others by arresting or imprisoning them. On some occasions the Church tried to quiet the outspoken ones by executing them; this rarely had the desired effect, though. By the time of Luther, Calvin, and some of the other Protestants who broke away from the Church, Catholics were leaving the Church in large numbers.

The Protestant Reformation may not have been entirely responsible for the Church's decision to look inward and to address the issues raised by reformers and Protestants alike, but it did put the Church in a position where it really had no other choice. From a Protestant perspective, the *Catholic Reformation* began in response to the rise of Protestantism and ended about the time the Thirty Years' War ended (see Chapter 8). From the Catholic perspective, the Catholic Reformation predates the Protestant Reformation because of the early calls for reform by Catholic leaders. Furthermore, because the Church considers itself in a state of perpetual introspection and always strives to deal with issues that arise, the Church would argue that the Catholic Reformation is never-ending.

Renewal and Reform

The earliest, and some of the loudest, reformers from the Church, such as Wycliffe and Hus, had genuine concern for the well-being of the Church and wanted to see changes made that would bring the Church back in line with what they believed was God's design. But because the Church denounced them and their loyalty to the Church wavered, they hardly can be considered part of the Catholic Reformation.

Many other reformers within the Catholic Church, though, remained devoutly Catholic.

The Catholic Reformation was a grass-roots, bottom-up movement begun by both laymen and clergy. It climaxed with the papacy taking action, but the papacy resisted calls for reform for centuries. The papacy certainly feared the possible consequences of admitting that problems existed or that the theology of the Church was not sound, but loyal Catholics who called for a renewal of Biblical and Christian values had no desire to challenge the pope, make the papacy look bad, or diminish the status of the Church. Rather, they felt deep convictions to help correct the shortcomings that had hindered the Church from realizing its full potential.

Let's Get Fired Up

In the years following the Catholic Reformation, the Church officially attributed much of the corruption and abuses in the late-medieval Church to *humanism* and *secularism*. Ironically, two of the most passionate figures of the Catholic Reformation were also two of the greatest humanists, Thomas More and Desiderius Erasmus.

Define Your Terms

Humanism is the glorification of man and his potential.

Secularism is the emphasis on material things of this world rather than on things related to the afterlife and spirituality.

The humanists (see Chapter 2) were well read in the classics and in the original texts of the Bible. They recognized that something was amiss in the Church and called for reform. The approach was an intellectual one. Thomas More wrote the famous work *Utopia* as a satire on the problems he saw in society. More stayed loyal to the Catholic Church even after Henry VIII broke away and formed the Anglican Church; More truly was devoted more to the Church than to his king. His passionate defense of Catholicism cost him his life, but his martyrdom drew attention to his message.

One of More's close friends, the Dutch humanist Erasmus, also used the power of the pen. Also like More, Erasmus never feared conflict or confrontation. In Erasmus's *Praise of Folly*, he satirically ripped the papacy. He, too, remained loyal to the Church and always recognized the authority of the Church. Erasmus risked telling the truth, no matter how uncomfortable it was for him or the pope, because he cared about the Church.

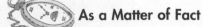

As a Matter of Fact

Thomas More and Desiderius Erasmus became lifelong friends while Erasmus spent time studying in England. They shared a common passion for the Catholic Church and they wanted to see the Church institute some amount of reform. Though they respected Luther, they wanted institutional reform, not doctrinal changes to Catholicism. Because of their love for the Church, neither hesitated to comment on the state of the Church. Erasmus's most famous and important work, *Praise of Folly*, was dedicated to his friend Sir Thomas More.

A well-known group made up of less well-known individuals emerged in the early sixteenth century in Rome. The group, known as the Oratory of the Divine Love, consisted of both clergy and laymen and most were humanists. The members sought to live as the apostles lived, in an attempt to restore the holiness of Christ and the apostles to renew and reform the Church. They hoped to emulate the apostles' exemplary lives by preaching to and caring for the sick and the meek—actions they no longer saw from the Church. As some of its members traveled from Rome to other places and founded new chapters, the piety of the Oratory found its way across Italy and eventually into other parts of Europe. Other members founded new orders, such as the Theatines Clerks Regular, or Theatine Regular Clerics. A few of the members of the Oratory went on to be high-ranking bishops and even popes.

Time for a Tune-Up?

One of the most influential members of the Oratory turned out to be Gasparo Contarini (1483–1542). Contarini served as an advisor to Pope Paul III (1468–1549) when Paul wanted a report on just what the problem seemed to be in the Church. After an investigation, Contarini compiled a report that said basically the same thing Erasmus said: perhaps the biggest problem in the Church was the papacy. Though it was a bitter pill for the pope to swallow, he acted wisely and calmly. Paul knew the Church, and even the papacy, needed to change. Despite resistance from several powerful Church leaders, Pope Paul III began to revamp some aspects of the papacy. Among other things, Paul ended the practice of simony, one of the things early reformers complained about the most. In keeping with promises he had made before

Would You Believe?

Pope Paul III excommunicated Henry VIII for his divorce from Catherine and supported the Holy Roman Emperor in his war against German Protestants, who wanted religious independence from Rome. While he wanted to reform the Church, he wanted to slow Protestantism as well.

he became pope, Paul tried to gather together a Church council to discuss reform and to clarify Church doctrine. However, Paul III never succeeded in getting Church officials to agree on a time and place for such a council to convene.

Who's Trent?

Finally, after much negotiation with the Holy Roman Emperor, in 1542 Pope Paul III called the council, which would meet in Trent, a city just on the Italian side of Alps. Finally, three years later, the council began the first of several sessions: 1545–1547, 1551–1552, and 1562–1563.

The pope and the Holy Roman Emperor hoped the Council of Trent would accomplish a number of things. First, they hoped to reconcile, at least to some extent, with the Protestants. Second, they hoped for true reform of the abuses prevalent among many of the clergy. Finally, they hoped to create definitive doctrines that would carry the Church forward for centuries to come. The first meeting of the Council was not very well attended, and, interestingly, spent much of its time discussing what it would discuss. At times the meetings were cordial, but at other times they deteriorated into heated shouting matches and arguments. Nevertheless, after 17 years of debate, the Church had what it needed.

Reconcile? Inconceivable

One of the first disagreements that arose at the first session was whether or not the rift between Catholics and Protestants should or even could be reconciled. There were those who hoped that the Council might make some theological concessions to the Protestants in hopes of winning them back. More conservative clergy wanted nothing to do with reconciliation: the Protestants had made their decision and chosen the path of heresy. Those opposed eventually won control of the proceedings, and reconciliation no longer had any real chance.

Another obstacle between Catholics and Protestants was the lack of Protestants at the Council. When the idea for the Council first made its way to the leaders of the Protestant Reformation, they demanded the meetings be held in Germany. Rome demanded they be held in Italy. Trent was controlled by the Holy Roman Emperor but located very close to Italy. A few Protestants showed up for the second session of the Council, but had little or no effect on the proceedings.

Reformed or Reaffirmed?

Perhaps the first order of business for the Council was to outline the major differences between Catholic doctrine and Protestant heresy. The Protestants raised a number of issues over the course of the Protestant Reformation and the Council intended to address those issues. For example, one of the major points of contention for the Protestants was the supremacy of the Bible over all, including *Church tradition* and the papacy. The Council reaffirmed the Church's position that while the scriptures are important, Church tradition must be held as equally important.

The Council also dealt with the translation of the scriptures. Many reformers either spoke against the *Vulgate*, a fifth-century translation of the Bible by St. Jerome written in common Latin, or created new translations from the original texts. In response, the Council recognized St. Jerome's *Vulgate* as the official and authorized version of the Scriptures. The Council also addressed Protestant concerns over the interpretation of the scriptures. Protestant reformers often argued that each believer had not only the right but the responsibility to read and interpret the scriptures for themselves—without the Church. The Council rejected that, saying that only the Catholic Church had the authority to interpret the scriptures.

Define Your Terms

The phrase **Church tradition** generally refers to the writings of the early Church fathers, or those who lived in the first several centuries after Christ, the declarations of the papacy, and the findings of ecumenical councils such as the Council of Trent.

Another of the most significant issues dividing the two sides was that of salvation. Most Protestants claimed that salvation came through faith in God's grace alone. The Council rejected that claim and upheld the assertion that good works through the Church were as necessary for salvation as faith.

The Council then tackled the Protestant idea that there existed only two sacraments, rather than the seven held by the Church. The Council debated each sacrament and reached the conclusion that there were in fact seven. One sacrament, the Lord's Supper, caused much disagreement between Catholics and Protestants. The Council rejected the Protestant views of the bread and the wine and upheld the doctrine of transubstantiation. The Council also confirmed that the wine should be withheld from the laity and taken only by clergy.

The Council of Trent also reassessed a number of doctrines held by the early and medieval Church that had come under fire. The Council reaffirmed the doctrines of the belief in purgatory, the veneration of the saints, clerical celibacy, apostolic succession, and the liturgy. Skeptical Protestants pointed to these "findings" as being exactly what they expected.

The Council of Trent did do a few things that should have satisfied at least some Protestants. Although the Council did not dismiss the practice of selling indulgences, it did demand that the wide-scale use of indulgences be reduced and that the abuse of the sale of indulgences be curtailed completely. The Council also found that, as many early reformers claimed, the local clergy had serious issues, including lack of theological training and, even worse, illiteracy. The Council mandated that seminaries be built for the education of priests, a huge step toward cleaning up the clergy. The Council addressed claims of absenteeism and required that bishops actually visit or reside in their dioceses.

The Council of Trent has been evaluated from both the Protestant and the Catholic perspective. To Protestants, the Council of Trent reformed very little and brought about only a few institutional changes. They had always expected the Council to merely go through the motions and uphold everything the Church believed all along.

As a Matter of Fact

While the Catholic Reformation culminated with the Council of Trent, the Council of Trent certainly was not the first such reform-minded gathering of Church scholars. In fact, the Council of Trent was actually the nineteenth meeting of an ecumenical council. The first such meeting occurred in 325 A.D. with the First Council of Nicaea, where the Church adopted the Nicene Creed. The 21st and last such council occurred in the 1960s with the Second Vatican Council. The ecumenical councils hold great importance in Catholicism because the Catholic Church holds Church tradition equal to the importance of the scriptures.

To Catholics, though, the Council accomplished two of its main goals: it found flaws within the Church and addressed them. The Council very easily could have found nothing at all to change and declared the Church to be in good working order. To its credit, the Council concurred with public opinion and required action on some issues. Additionally, the Council solidified the Church's position on a number of issues, thereby confirming several

Would You Believe?

When the Council of Trent finally wrapped things up after nearly 20 years, the pope issued a decree officially confirming all the Council's findings, which then became part of official Church tradition.

very important Church doctrines. The Council of Trent became the guiding light of Catholicism for several centuries because it put in writing exactly what the Church believed on many vital issues.

Order, Order

It was one of the ironies of the Catholic Reformation that monasticism played such a role in the renewal of the Catholic spirit. After all, numerous Protestant reformers had denounced monastic life and claimed that it had no basis in the scriptures. Because the Catholic Reformation began largely as a bottom-up movement, much of the commitment to a new and better Catholic Church came from within the monasteries, specifically from common monks and nuns. Monasteries and *convents* originally were founded on the principles of obedience, poverty, and chastity. Those principles, according to Protestant and Catholic reformers alike, had gone missing from many of the clergy. In order to return those principles to the Church and draw people back to Catholicism, several new orders, or groups of clergy, most of them monks, appeared during the Catholic Reformation.

> **Define Your Terms**
>
> A convent is a community of nuns, or women who have taken the vows of obedience, poverty, and chastity; it is comparable to a monastery.

The Somaschi Order of Regular Clerics, so named for its place of origin in Somasca, Italy, started with the work of Jerome Emiliani (1481–1537). Emiliani began with just a handful of followers who formerly had brief affiliations with other orders. They formed their own order and made their life's work caring for the poor, the sick, and the orphaned. Only a few years after the founding of the Somaschi, the Capuchins branched away from the Franciscan Order of monks founded by St. Francis of Assissi (c.1181–1226). The Capuchins adhered to the Franciscan monastic rules and even dressed like Franciscan monks with their brown, hooded robes. Soon after that, Anthony Zaccaria (1502–1539) founded the Barnabites, the first order named for St. Paul. The Order of the Barnabites counted among its members priests, uncloistered nuns, and even married couples. Eventually, the Barnabites created the Angelice, a female branch of the order. The Barnabites, like other orders, were committed to living pious lives.

> **Continental Quotes**
>
> One of the mottos of the Barnabites shows their dedication to helping their fellow man: "Let us run like madmen, not only toward God but toward our neighbor as well."

The Society of Jesus—No Girls Allowed

Perhaps the most influential of all the orders that grew out of the Catholic Reformation was the Society of Jesus, or the Jesuits, founded by Ignatius of Loyola (1491–1556). Born in Spain, Ignatius went into the military and served there until he was wounded in battle in 1521. During his period of recuperation he spent time reading about the saints. His readings so moved him that he began a new life of meditation, prayer, and *flagellation* in a cave. After a year in the cave, Ignatius traveled to Jerusalem and back and then enrolled in school. After he finished his university program, he gathered together a few followers and formed the Society of Jesus, or Jesuits.

The small Society of Jesus traveled here and there, tending to the poor and gathering more followers. Ignatius used great discretion in whom he allowed into the order but the numbers grew anyway. In 1538, Pope Paul III recognized the Jesuits as an official order within the Catholic Church. The Jesuits built their order on a set of very strict rules for living and developing spiritually.

Would You Believe?

In the mid-sixteenth century, Jesuit numbers hovered around 1,000. Less than 100 years later, the Jesuits numbered more than 10,000.

Ignatius and the Jesuits had a passion for education and for the Church. The decision to educate youth through the Church came naturally for the Jesuits. Ignatius believed that he could give children one of the finest educations anywhere and at the same time create loyal Catholics. Because the Jesuits set such high standards for those admitted into the order, the Jesuits maintained a membership highly suited to teach the children of Europe and to model for the children exemplary lifestyles. With considerable funding from Rome, the Jesuits founded schools and colleges across Europe. In no time, the Jesuit educational institutions earned outstanding reputations.

The Jesuits also placed great emphasis on missions. Jesuit priests traveled with explorers across the Atlantic to the New World. Other Jesuit priests traveled throughout Europe and even to Asia. Everywhere they went they successfully won souls for the Catholic faith. Perhaps the Jesuits' greatest success, though, occurred in Brazil. In each place, the Jesuit missionaries ministered to the people and taught them about Christianity.

The Jesuits are due much credit for the success of the Catholic Reformation. The Jesuits effectively spread Catholicism not just in Europe but all over the world. They brought countless non-Catholics to Catholicism, and they brought many former Catholics back to the Church.

The Ursuline Order—No Boys Allowed

While the Jesuits were out teaching all over the world, a woman in Italy, in the midst of the Renaissance, wanted women to be able to teach the way the Jesuits did. There were plenty of orders for women, but women who became nuns were forced to be cloistered; because unmarried women could not be sent out into the world by themselves, nuns were forced to live in convents.

In 1535, Angela Merici (1474–1540) decided to change that tradition, so she founded the Ursuline Order for women in Brescia, Italy. The Ursuline Order was to be a teaching order, and the Order's number-one priority was the education of young women. The women in the Order were not nuns and they did not hide behind the cloistered walls of a convent. Rather, they met in various homes and then went into the world to do their work.

At the time of the founding of the Ursuline Order, women were expected to be beautiful and to inspire. They were not given the chance to be educated. Angela wanted girls, rich and poor, to have that chance. In much the same manner as the Jesuits, the Ursulines hoped to Christianize their students. More specifically, Angela wanted to Christianize her young women through education so that the homes and families they might one day begin would already have a solid religious foundation. The Ursuline Order did such great work that the pope praised Angela. He offered her the chance to be the head of an order of nuns, but Angela refused. She chose to stay with the Ursulines and in the world.

> **Would You Believe?**
>
> Angela Merici named the order for St. Ursula, the saint famous for her 11,000 virgin companions.

Visions of Avila

> **Define Your Terms**
>
> In Spain, a **converso** was one who had been converted to Catholicism. The Church still kept a close eye on conversos because they rarely trusted them, particularly the converted Jews.

Women in Spain got the chance to be part of the Catholic Reformation, too, but in a more traditional manner. Theresa of Avila (1515–1582), the daughter of a *converso* family in Spain, read letters of St. Jerome and decided to become a nun. She entered a convent in Avila at the tender age of 20, where she grew very ill over the next several years. She left the convent to recover.

Upon returning to her devout religious life filled with prayer and meditation, she received visions. Her visions evoked deep emotions and feelings of religious ecstasy. She traveled across her native country forming new convents called Carmelites of the Strict Observance. Teresa advocated strict rules for pious living and deeply personal religious experiences for believers. Teresa was part of a movement known as mysticism. The Carmelites, like the Jesuits, Ursulines, and other orders, played huge roles in renewing and reforming the Catholic Church.

Expect the Inquisition and the Index

Plenty of officials within the Church cared more about stopping the spread of Protestantism than reconciling with them. Many such officials, Cardinal Carafa (1476–1559) being a perfect example, viewed Protestants as heretics who had strayed away from the Church and turned their backs on God.

For Carafa, these heretics did not deserve the chance to reconcile, they deserved punishment. Carafa and others like him urged Pope Paul III to bring back the medieval tool known as the Inquisition. Two other major inquisitions had occurred prior to Pope Paul III, one in 1231, and the other in Spain in 1478, so there were precedents for such a tool. Pope Paul III probably didn't need too much convincing, appalled as he was by the influx of Protestant and secular ideas in his homeland of Italy. In 1542, Paul created the Congregation of the Inquisition, also known as the Holy Office and as the Roman Inquisition. The Congregation included six cardinals, one of whom was Carafa, who became known as Inquisitors General. The primary job of the Roman Inquisition was to find heretics, especially in Italy, and deal with them.

> **Would You Believe?**
>
> The Spanish Inquisition under Ferdinand and Isabella earned particular notoriety for the Church's brutal treatment of Muslims and Jews. Many non-Catholics fled the country in fear for their lives. Many who stayed behind paid with their lives. A few Jews and Muslims did convert to Catholicism, though.

Hunting for Heretics

The primary targets of earlier inquisitions were Jews, Muslims, witches, and the garden-variety heretics. During earlier inquisitions, there were no rabble-rousers like the Protestants or astronomers who wrote nonsense about the universe (see Chapter 11). The first two inquisitions frequently used torture to extract confessions, true or otherwise, from "heretics." The first two inquisitions also frequently executed those found guilty of heresy.

The Roman Inquisition under Pope Paul III differed in two major ways. First, the Roman Inquisition targeted heresy related mostly to the orthodoxy of the Church. In other words, the Congregation generally targeted people for academic and theo-logical reasons. The Congregation didn't bother with no-name individuals running around in the country-side of Italy. Second, the Roman Inquisition didn't resort to nearly the same level of brutality. Public trials often concluded with the accused making a public recantation and then doing public penance. This way, the public saw that the Catholic Church and its teaching were true and right and even merci-ful. This remained true for several years, or at least while Pope Paul III was pope.

Would You Believe?

The courts of the Roman Inquisition used a fourteenth-century inquisition handbook called the *Directorium inquisito-rium* as the guide for correct inquisition procedures.

When Carafa became Pope Paul IV, the Roman Inquisition took on a new personal-ity. He stepped up the fervor with which the Congregation sought out heretics or "suspects" as he called them. He also turned the Congregation loose on the Church. Under Paul IV, bishops and even cardinals found themselves under fire. Paul IV was perhaps a little less reluctant to use force, too. It was against the Church law for the Church to execute someone, but once heretics were convicted, they could be handed over to secular authorities for execution.

Bad, Bad Books

The Roman Inquisition targeted academics and leaders of the Protestant movements, so it was no surprise that the papacy also targeted the writings of the "heretics." As both literacy and the availability of the printed word spread quickly throughout Europe in the fifteenth and sixteenth centuries, thanks to Gutenberg (see Chapter 2), Europeans read more and more tracts, pamphlets, and books.

The papacy feared that most who read the printed word couldn't distinguish between writings that were good and those that were evil. The papacy also feared that those who could distinguish between good and evil writings would be tempted, then cor-rupted, by the evil writings. The papacy called for a list of the bad, bad books. Known as the *Index librorum prohibitorum*, the Index of Prohibited Books listed heretical or potentially heretical books which were officially outlawed by the Church in all Catholic lands. The Index also included a list of authors and printers who were banned. The Council of Trent produced a similar list called the Tridentine Index.

The Index actually banned most things currently in print at that time. As the years went by, the pope and the Congregation could and often did add books, authors, and printers to the naughty list. The list of authors banned by the Index proved to be distinguished, including such writers as Hus, Wycliffe, Zwingli, Calvin, Servetus, Luther, Coverdale, Cranmer, Machiavelli, and even Erasmus. As the centuries passed, the Church added such famous writers as Descartes, Pascal, Voltaire, Montesquieu, Locke, Mill, Hugo, Dumas, and Swift. The Church actually maintained the Index until 1966 when it was dismissed.

Would You Believe?

In addition to all unauthorized versions of both the New Testament and the Bible, the Index banned Catholics from reading the Koran and the Talmud.

Though its efforts were varied, the Church did accomplish its goals with the Catholic Reformation, or Counter-Reformation. The Church initiated some institutional reform and reasserted certain doctrines thereby strengthening the Church and the office of the papacy. The Church, with the help of new religious orders, reinvigorated Catholicism and created a renewed sense of interest and pride in the Church and the theology of the Church. The Church also countered the spread of Protestantism and won back some of those Catholics who explored Protestantism. Thanks also to the Roman Inquisition and the Index, controversial though they may have been, the Catholic Reformation was a success for the Church. After the Protestant and Catholic Reformations, Europe stood squarely divided into two camps that would find themselves at odds for centuries to come.

The Least You Need to Know

- Reformers as far back as Wycliffe and Hus called for reform in the Church. Some reformers broke ties with the Church while others remained loyal and worked for reform within the Church.

- The Council of Trent reaffirmed many doctrines, such as transubstantiation, purgatory, and the authority of the papacy and Church tradition. The Church did initiate some reform in the areas of indulgences and the training of priests.

- New Catholic orders, particularly the Jesuits and the Ursuline Order, played significant roles in slowing Protestantism and winning people for Catholicism.

◆ Pope Paul III started the Roman Inquisition to find heretics and slow the spread of anti-Catholic literature, ideas, and theology.

◆ On the whole, the Catholic Reformation successfully slowed the growth of Protestantism. Additionally, the Catholic Reformation cleaned up the Church some. Most importantly, though, the Catholic Reformation redefined Catholicism for the next four hundred years.

Part 2

Might Makes Right, Right? (c.1450–1750)

This part tells of an era when those in power had the luxury of imposing political and religious ideas on the people of Europe. Explorers and conquerors spread European ideas to the New World. France struggled to establish one religion, faced battles over religion, and ultimately made a great compromise to save the country. Here you'll find the strange but true story of the great witch hunts. This section also details the rise of two of the most powerful political forces in European history. First, the Holy Roman Empire rises to greatness and controls a continent, at least in the minds of the Holy Roman Emperors. Second, Louis XIV of France rises to the status of Sun King and rules longer than any other monarch in European history. His legacy, too, was unlike any Europe had ever seen. Other rulers tried to rule like Louis XIV, but no one even came close.

Chapter 6

God, Gold, and Glory

In This Chapter

- ◆ Europeans' interest in the other side of the ocean
- ◆ New technology helps with exploration
- ◆ Why explorers risked life and limb
- ◆ The explorers' hall of fame
- ◆ The Spanish Armada dominates the seas

"In fourteen hundred and ninety-two, Columbus sailed the ocean blue." True enough. However, the story of European exploration is much greater and begins centuries earlier than Christopher Columbus.

Europe Looks Beyond the Horizon

Throughout the Middle Ages, Europeans traveled extensively through-out North Africa and Asia. Niccolo and Maffeo Polo, not to mention Niccolo's slightly more famous son Marco Polo (1255–1324), traveled all the way to China and even spent time in the court of the legendary Kublai Khan. Before the Polo expeditions, the pope sent emissaries to the Mongol capital of Karakorum.

Those who traveled abroad brought back many fantastic stories of fascinating far-off places. Polo, in his book *Travels*, told of his difficult journey to China and back and of his time in such places as Sri Lanka and Sumatra. More fantastic tales were spread in a book titled *The Travels of Sir John Mandeville* written in the early fourteenth century. Its author tells of finding giants, headless humans, and more in his travels to the Far East. These stories stayed with Europeans and eventually helped spark some interest in what else might be found abroad. These travelers weren't traveling just for the sake of traveling, though. They were trading, and trade was good for quite a while.

> **Would You Believe?**
>
> Although Marco Polo is famous for his travels to China, as chronicled in his book *Travels*, some historians doubt the authenticity of his stories. Furthermore, some historians doubt he even made it all the way to China!

Especially while the Mongols controlled the lands between Europe and China, profitable trade routes existed as far east as India and even into parts of China. The Crusades opened up many trade routes in North Africa for Europeans who demanded silks, spices, mirrors, and other luxury items crusaders took back to Europe. Both during and after the Crusades, European traders profited greatly from these trade routes.

For the most part, these trade routes were over land. Very little sea travel occurred at this time, for a few reasons. Shipbuilding and *cartography* had hardly reached zeniths during the Middle Ages, so traders tended to be land lovers. With the rise of the Islamic Ottoman Turks in southwest Asia and the decline of the Mongol Empire, Europeans, not known for their friendly relations with the Muslims, found it more and more difficult and dangerous to trade in Ottoman-controlled lands. It was thanks to the Ottomans, then, that Europeans started looking for safer and more profitable trade routes.

> **Define Your Terms**
>
> **Cartography** is the science of mapmaking.

Europeans Begin Overseas Exploration

Europeans had been trading in exotic and often dangerous places for centuries, but European overseas exploration began in the early fifteenth century. The fact that Muslims were making travel and trade by land difficult for Europeans did not make Europeans launch immediately into the Atlantic Ocean in search of a new world, though. Europe had to ease into this new form of exploration.

European sailors of the fifteenth century did not believe the world was flat, so that wasn't what kept Europeans close to the shore. Rather, the technology that eventually would make ocean voyages possible simply wasn't available prior to the fifteenth century. Ships weren't built and equipped for ocean voyages, maps weren't extensive enough, and a body of knowledge of open-sea travel simply did not exist. Thanks to Portugal, though, that was about to change.

Portugal sat virtually isolated on the outer edge of the Iberian Peninsula, so it was only natural that Portuguese traders and explorers took to the seas. Early in the fifteenth century, Portugal conquered the Muslim town of Ceuta in Morocco. On that expedition was the young son of Portugal's King John I (1357–1433). Prince Henry (1394–1460), also known as Henry the Navigator, later led the Portuguese southward from Portugal to the Canary Islands and to the Azores. Henry also sponsored expeditions southward along the African coast where the Portuguese established a lucrative gold and slave trade. With each journey, the Portuguese explored a little more, learned a little more, tweaked their maps, and gained valuable information for use on the next journey.

Would You Believe?

Although there is some debate about the authenticity of the stories, Prince Henry "the Navigator" is said to have founded Europe's first navigational school where students learned skills such as navigation and cartography.

Cutting-Edge Technology

In the decades prior to the launch of overseas expeditions, Europeans made improvements in a number of areas and fine-tuned some instruments and equipment that allowed their expeditions to become increasingly successful. Although some famous explorers claimed that maps were practically useless to them, maps played a large role in the boom in overseas exploration.

Before the fourteenth century, most "world maps" relied on classical maps and descriptions of the world along with information from travelers, which proved to be shaky, at best. Most maps included only the Mediterranean region and many had the city of Jerusalem at the center. Few people had any idea how inaccurate these maps really were.

In 1375, Abraham Cresques created the *Catalan World Atlas*, a much more useful map of the Mediterranean than anything before it, complete with sailing instructions and compass readings. From here, maps continued to improve, with every expedition adding to the body of knowledge. Cartographers also added grids to some of the newer maps in this era, grids that eventually would become latitude and longitude lines.

Maps certainly weren't the only things that received upgrades during the age of exploration. Ships, too, received overhauls. The medieval galleys of Europe did well along the European coast, but they weren't built for seafaring. Hull construction changed at some point during the age of exploration, allowing for more storage and more stability.

Would You Believe?

Historians have very few details about how ships were constructed during this time. Most of the information about these ships has been reconstructed based on models, journal entries, and a very few preserved examples of the ships.

Another change was sails. Most ships of the day were equipped with both sails and oars because ships couldn't always count on the winds and the currents to be favorable. The *caravel* helped fix this problem. The caravel was a ship with large square sails for moving forward and small triangular sails for sailing diagonally into a headwind. The caravel made it possible to sail into the wind. The caravel didn't sail straight into the wind; simple physics prevents that. However, the triangular sails allowed the caravel to travel across the wind in a zig-zag pattern. Caravels also benefited over the years from stronger sails and ropes, which allowed for smaller crews, better decking, better rudders, and more.

The basic compass had been around for at least a few centuries in Europe and for much longer in China. However, a new and improved compass emerged that had a disk displaying degrees beneath the compass needle. As the maps became more precise, the new compass became more important. Another navigational tool that improved during this time was the *astrolabe*. The astrolabe measured the distance of the sun and stars above the horizon and allowed for fairly accurate calculations of a ship's distance above and below the equator. For example, if the North Star measured 25° above the horizon, the sailor knew his ship was 25° above the equator, and so on. This system worked pretty well as long as the ship wasn't too close to the equator; when the readings became inaccurate, the sailors used the sun instead of the North Star. The astrolabe, like the compass, became more useful as maps became more precise.

Going East by Sailing West

Much of the "information" and "knowledge" of the world and the oceans during the Middle Ages was based on the science and philosophy, or speculation, of Greek scholars. While many classical calculations were remarkably accurate, many weren't. The same holds true for the more modern works like Pierre d'Ailly's *Image of the World* from 1410.

Pierre d'Ailly (1350–1420) believed that oceans covered only about one fourth of the earth's surface and that the Atlantic Ocean was not very wide at all. In his treatises, d'Ailly uses ideas from Ptolemy, Aristotle, and others, including Aristotle's reasoning that West Africa must be close to East India because elephants existed in both places. This information helped convince people that a new route to Asia, which by land lay geographically east of Europe, could be found by sailing west.

The importance of this idea was not that it was possible to do so—after all, everyone knew the earth was round—but that it was reasonable and even practical. If d'Ailly was correct, ships could sail west from Europe and reach Asia in a matter of days, especially if the winds were favorable. By the calculations of Columbus and others, Asia lay only about 5,000 miles to the west.

In reality, the estimate was about 7,000 miles off. But this not-so-sound logic eventually would lead to one of the greatest discoveries (or blunders, depending on your perspective) in all of history.

Would You Believe?

Pierre d'Ailly was also a high-ranking Church official and conciliarist who worked to heal the wounds of the Great Schism (see Chapter 1).

What's Your Motive?

The explorers and the financiers were curious about what lay across the sea. So were the intellectuals of the day. That wasn't enough, though. Ocean voyages were dangerous and expensive. Why did explorers risk their lives to brave the uncharted waters of the world? Why did kings and queens finance expeditions to unknown places with no guarantee of a return on their investment? Simply put, for God, gold, and glory—not necessarily in that order.

Would You Believe?

The motives of the explorers greatly resembled the motives of the Crusaders: go on a mission for God, keep whatever gold you find, and bask in the glory.

God

Two religious factors helped motivate European explorers and financiers to explore overseas. First, many Europeans believed that somewhere far away from Europe there existed a Christian land. Some Europeans hoped to make contact with other Christians. Likewise, many were eager to make contact with uncivilized, heathen lands. Many Europeans, including Columbus, believed that by making contact with these heathen lands beyond the seas, the conversion of the entire world to Christianity would soon be underway.

While this would certainly be the manifestation of God's will, the conversion of newly discovered lands had another implication. Not only would a soul be added to the Kingdom of God with each conversion, but a soul would also be added to the earthly kingdom of Spain, Portugal, or whatever country sponsored the expedition. Who knew how many potential souls could be added to the kingdom of Spain or Portugal? And, of course, to the Kingdom of God.

Gold

There was no way to be sure what would be found across the ocean but the explorers and those who sponsored them were banking on finding something of value. Europeans knew what could be found in Asia and they were hoping to find a sea route to Asia to replace the land routes that had been pinched by the Muslims. This was one of the primary reasons for sailing westward.

The more exciting possibility was that there were new, unexplored lands that would yield great hordes of gold and treasure as well as trade goods. Classical texts tantalized Europeans who dreamt of finding lost gold. Even Columbus believed he knew approximately where he could find King Solomon's gold mines. The sponsors of the overseas expeditions stood to gain the most, since they endured the greatest financial risk, but if a caravel full of gold and exotic wonders sailed into port, the leader of the expedition would have been rewarded handsomely.

Glory

Both the explorers and the financiers of the expeditions put themselves in the position to be either wildly famous or shamefully infamous. Should an expedition actually find Asia by sailing west, all involved would be known throughout Europe and throughout history. Should an expedition fail or turn up no treasure, all involved would be the laughingstock of the courts of Europe. Like Crusaders from preceding centuries, explorers hoped they would find and conquer some far-off land over which they would one day rule. Lands, titles, and power surely awaited any explorer who could bring glory to his sponsor.

Guys Who Sailed the Ocean Blue

From the beginning, the Portuguese took the lead in overseas adventures. They were the first to work their way down the western coast of Africa, and they were determined to be the first to find a sea route to Asia, but they had no intention of heading west to get there.

Dating back to the days of Prince Henry the Navigator, the Portuguese pushed farther and farther down the African coast. In 1487, a sailor named Bartholomew Dias (c.1450–1500) followed the same course as other Portuguese sailors before him along Africa's west coast. Dias encountered difficult winds and currents so he turned his ships west and went with the flow. Dias took his ships so far west he easily could have gone on to what is now South America, but he was determined to travel around Africa. Dias caught a ride on the westerlies and rode them past the southern tip of Africa. Once around Africa, Dias turned north. He had done it; he had sailed around the southern tip of Africa. Dias paved the way for other Portuguese to make their way to Asia, including Vasco da Gama.

Would You Believe?

Dias named the southern tip of Africa the "Cape of Storms" only to have it renamed the "Cape of Good Hope" by the King of Portugal.

Vasco da Gama (c.1460–1524) used the knowledge gained by Dias to make his way southward from Portugal, around the Cape of Good Hope and ultimately all the way to India. Da Gama's voyage brought a fortune back to Portugal, but it was the establishment of a route to India that made it a great success. The Portuguese remained a force to be reckoned with in the Indian Ocean for centuries, going on to establish many trading posts along the route to India. Trading in spices like cinnamon, peppers, and ginger, along with dyes and textiles, the Portuguese made quite a living in the Asian markets.

Because the Portuguese got in on the ground floor of the overseas business, the pope issued a statement in 1481 granting Portugal all land south of the Canary Islands and west of Africa. Of course, the pope had no knowledge of what actually lay west of Africa. After all, the Americas technically fall into the category of "west of Africa."

As a Matter of Fact

Vasco da Gama played a vital role in establishing the Portuguese as one of the premier powers in trade during the sixteenth century. Da Gama's first voyage impressed upon the Portuguese crown the importance of establishing trade routes and building trade ports in the East. Vasco da Gama is so highly regarded and esteemed in Portugal that he is the subject of the most important piece of Portuguese literature, *Os Lusiadas*, an epic similar to Virgil's *Aeneid*.

The early voyages of the Portuguese were not intended to be so-called voyages of discovery, though. As Spain got the bug for exploration, Spain appealed the papal decision and ultimately ended up with a compromise called the Treaty of Tordesillas. The 1494 treaty drew a vertical line of demarcation through what is now South America. Spain got rights to everything west of the line while Portugal received rights to all land east of the line. For Spain the treaty was rather timely, because Spain had launched the first expedition of Spanish explorers just two years before the Treaty of Tordesillas was finalized.

Columbus—Hero or Hack?

Originally from Genoa, Christopher Columbus (1451–1506) remains the poster boy for European exploration and expansion 500 years after his death. Undoubtedly, Columbus possessed tremendous naval skills and a passion for sailing. He began his career working for Castile (part of Spain) and for Portugal before his life changed forever in 1492.

Based on his study of both contemporary and classical texts, Columbus became convinced of the theory that Asia could be reached quickly by sailing west from Europe. He took this idea to the king of Portugal, but the king wasn't interested. At the time, Portugal was interested in trade expeditions, not expeditions that might or might not discover something new. So Columbus presented his case to Ferdinand and Isabella of Spain. They were interested, but only enough to grant Columbus a measly three ships, 90 men, and a handful of supplies. Truly, the king and queen of Spain kept their enthusiasm in check and their expectations low.

Continental Quotes

"And the sea will grant each man new hope …."
—Christopher Columbus

Columbus set sail with great anticipation in August of 1492. In October, Columbus finally sailed into what are now the Bahamas, then Cuba, and finally the island of Hispaniola, or what is today the Dominican Republic. Unfortunately for Columbus, he believed he had landed in a group of islands not far from Japan, a group of islands known as the Indies. Believing such, Columbus named the inhabitants "Indians," a name that in many ways has endured to this day.

Would You Believe?

Columbus's initial expedition included three ships. The *Niña* and the *Pinta* were caravels. The *Santa Maria* was a slow, fat-hulled ship called a *nao*, which simply means "ship" in old Spanish.

Down to only one ship because one of his ships sank and one of Columbus's captains took the other, Columbus decided to leave 40 of his men on Hispaniola until he could return. Columbus eventually met up with his rogue captain and the two made their way back to Spain where Columbus was greeted with a hero's welcome. Columbus was granted a title and a government position in the newly found land; he also was to receive a share of the land's wealth. Columbus returned to the islands three additional times over the next 10 years. During his later visits, Columbus made excursions to the coast of modern-day Central America.

Ferdinand and Isabella must have been excited about the reports Columbus gave them. He told them about the peaceful people he found in the islands, people who were open to prayers and the sign of the Cross and who could be converted. He told of a variety of crops produced on the island. He explained that he surely would have discovered more valuables had his ships been at his disposal the entire time, valuables that his men back in the islands probably had discovered already. Ferdinand and Isabella believed him and gave him command of 17 ships and 1,500 men.

Columbus returned to find that the men he left behind had found no great treasures. Worse, many of the men had managed to fall victim either to each other or to the natives. Apparently, some of his men went on a wild search for gold and left many natives in their wake. The Spaniards who returned to the islands with Columbus settled in and established a cruel pattern of behavior not unlike the original Spanish settlers left behind by Columbus. They forced the natives to work the land and rewarded them with brutal treatment; Columbus had virtually no power to stop the madness. Columbus never got his settlements under control and he certainly never managed to produce the fortunes he believed he would find. Columbus's administration and his treasure hunt were a flop, his geography was more than a little inaccurate, and his treatment of the natives, whether directly or indirectly, was nothing less than exploitation. Once his biggest supporters, Ferdinand and Isabella took away nearly all they had given Columbus and refused to sponsor any further expeditions.

Would You Believe? _____

A geographer from Florence named Amerigo Vespucci (1451–1512), who happened to be on a Spanish ship exploring the coast of modern-day Brazil, determined in 1501 that in fact Columbus landed nowhere near Asia but rather he had stumbled upon a continent that no one in Europe knew existed, a "New World" so to speak. The continent later was named "America" in honor of Vespucci.

The Conquistadors

Some of the most important expeditions ever launched by Spain were led not by sailors but by *conquistadors*. The conquistadors led military forces and conquered land that Spain, or the conquistadors themselves, wanted. Whereas Columbus claimed land and established Spanish presence through administrative means, the conquistadors established Spanish presence through the use of force. The conquistadors claimed, and then took, more land for Spain than any other Spanish explorers. The two most successful of all the conquistadors were Hernán Cortés and Francisco Pizarro.

Define Your Terms _____

Conquistador is Spanish for "conqueror," and refers primarily to the Spaniards who conquered territory in the New World.

In the years following the Spanish settlement of Hispaniola and Cuba, the Spanish population grew rapidly. Settlers poured into the area faster than it could support the population. Spanish administrators turned their attention toward the mainland whose coast had been only minimally explored. Natives of the New World with whom the Spaniards had contact told of a civilization on the mainland that interested Spain.

The Spanish Governor of Cuba, Velasquez, chose an ambitious young Spaniard named Hernán Cortés to lead an expeditionary force inland to seek out the civilization. Velasquez later changed his mind about Cortés, but it was too late. Cortés stayed a step ahead of Velasquez and took off for Mexico with around 500 men. Upon his arrival in 1619, Cortés met native tribes who were enemies of the mighty Aztec Empire, a civilization ruled by the rich and powerful Montezuma. The tribes weren't too interested in converting to Christianity but they sure were excited about fighting with the Spaniards against the Aztecs.

Cortés and his men made their way to the capital of the Aztec Empire, Tenochtitlan, and met the ruler, Montezuma. Montezuma and the Aztecs believed Cortés and his men to be ancient gods returning to the Aztecs, so Montezuma welcomed Cortés and showered him with gifts. Over the next two years, Cortés thanked Montezuma by destroying the entire Aztec civilization, razing many of their cities including their capital, and stealing unimaginable wealth. Cortés managed such a feat with only about five hundred of his own men, less than two dozen horses, a few pieces of artillery, some native allies, and a secret biological weapon: smallpox. The immune systems of the natives of the New World had no defense against the diseases brought from Europe. Columbus and his expeditions took disease to the Bahamas, too, but the destruction paled in comparison to that in Mexico.

Would You Believe?

Upon landing on the Mexican coast, many of Cortés's men feared what lay inland. To strengthen his troops' resolve and to prevent his troops from having any thought of retreat, Cortés emptied his ships' supplies and burned his ships.

Francisco Pizarro (1470–1541) followed a pattern similar to that of Cortés. He had spent time in Panama City and other places, but had not discovered the gold and glory he so badly wanted. Pizarro headed to South America in search of the Inca Empire, a civilization rumored to be vast and wealthy. Pizarro arrived in Peru to discover a land taken with smallpox and desperate to overthrow the Inca. Pizarro allied with natives, much like Cortés had done, and used the natives to overthrow the mighty Inca Empire. Pizarro took huge amounts of gold and silver and established a capital at Lima on Peru's coast. The silver trade from the former Inca lands eventually would become a major part of the economy of Spain.

While Cortés and Pizarro were by far the two most successful conquistadors, the term became synonymous with explorers who used the armed forces to conquer land for Spain. After all, conquering land was as legitimate a way to acquire new land as through diplomacy. The conquistadors were successful for a number of reasons. They used natives to help with battle and they had the benefit of iron weapons and armor. The conquistadors also played by different rules than the natives they conquered. The Aztec and Inca used battles to take captives who would be sacrificed later; the Spaniards used battles to kill as many people as possible. The greatest advantage the conquistadors had,

Would You Believe?

While the conquistadors possessed artillery and some guns, they used these modern weapons more to scare and to awe the natives than to kill them.

though, was the unwitting use of biological warfare. European diseases killed millions upon millions of natives in North, Central, and South America.

More Who Explored

In the decades following Columbus, literally dozens and dozens of explorers made their way across the Atlantic to the shores of the Americas. Others attempted more dangerous and exciting endeavors. Some found great wealth and fame while others met an early demise.

One of the most dramatic voyages was made by Ferdinand Magellan (c.1480–1521) and his crew. The Spaniard set sail for South America in 1519 and then sailed along the South American coast until he reached the southern tip. He carefully navigated the straits at the southernmost tip of the continent, now known as the Strait of Magellan, and made his way into the Pacific Ocean, which had been discovered by fellow Spaniard Vasco de Balboa (1475–1519) in 1513. Four months later, after a harrowing journey with practically no food, the expedition landed in the Philippines. Though natives there killed Magellan, two ships left the Philippines, sailed westward, and headed for the Spice Islands. Finally, in 1522, 15 of Magellan's original 260 men returned to Spain, having circumnavigated, or sailed around, the globe.

Would You Believe?

Ironically, after de Soto discovered the Mississippi River, he died of a fever and his men buried him in the river he discovered.

The Spaniards were all over the place during the age of exploration. In 1513, Juan Ponce de Leon (c.1460–1521) explored what is now Florida in search of the Fountain of Youth. Hernando de Soto (c.1500–1542) explored more of southeastern North America 30 years later and discovered the Mississippi River. About the same time, Francisco Coronado (1510–1554) scoured southwestern North America in search of gold.

The French and English, not to be outdone by their Spanish-speaking rivals, sent their share of explorers into the great unknown, too, although they did enter the game a little later than everyone else. In the 1530s, Frenchman Jacques Cartier (1491–1557) explored the St. Lawrence River in North America. In the early 1600s, Samuel Champlain (1567–1635) continued the exploration of the eastern coast of North America. Late in the 1600s, Jacques Marquette (1637–1675) and Louis Joliet (1645–1700) made their way along the northern part of the Mississippi River. Ten years later, René-Robert-Cavelier, Sieur de La Salle (1643–1687) explored the mouth of the Mississippi River and claimed it for France. Near the end of the fifteenth century, the Italian-born explorer for the English John Cabot (c.1455–1499) explored Newfoundland, Nova Scotia, and Labrador. In the 1570s, Francis Drake (c.1540–1596) became the first Englishman to sail around the world. Then in the first decade of the next century, Henry Hudson (1565–1611) explored the Hudson Bay and Hudson River.

> ### Would You Believe?
> La Salle met a most unfortunate death when his men, bent on mutiny, assassinated him in the middle of the Texas wilderness, where they left his body for the wild animals to devour.

For the Portuguese, Spanish, English, and French, exploration led to expansion through colonization, or the founding of colonies. These *colonies* were created to generate revenue for the mother country, as sources of new natural resources, and as new markets. Some of the colonies begun during this era disappeared or broke away early on, while others remained under control of the founding country even into the twentieth century.

>
> ### Define Your Terms
> A **colony** is a settlement established in a distant land by a country for trade purposes.

Going Dutch

While the other European powers were busy spending energy and money on exploration and colonization, the Dutch developed a unique business plan of their own. Because the Netherlands covered only a small geographic area and lacked the large populations of other European nations, the Dutch didn't have the resources to explore or colonize the world; their stint in colonizing the New World didn't last long.

Rather, the Dutch concentrated on trade. Through a combination of fishing and shipbuilding, the Dutch generated huge revenues. As the shipbuilding industry grew, the Dutch carried trade goods for other nations throughout the Baltic and North Sea regions and then throughout the world. By the beginning of the seventeenth century, the Dutch enjoyed amazing prosperity. As they branched out, the Dutch imported raw materials from other trade powers and redistributed the goods as finished and refined products. The prosperity attracted jewelers, financiers, and

> ### Would You Believe?
> The Dutch were such savvy businessmen that they managed to buy the entire island of Manhattan from the Native Americans for about $24 in beads and trinkets.

others from across Europe. For a while, Amsterdam, the Dutch capital, served as the financial capital of Europe.

The Making of the Armada

The Spanish explorers and conquistadors set in motion a series of events that changed both the Old World and the New World forever. The settlements established in the New World grew into colonies whose sole purpose was to bolster the Spanish economy. Perhaps more than any other nation, Spain benefited from the exchange of goods between the Americas and Europe as well as the influx of precious metals from the Americas. The colonists ravaged the lands surrounding the Spanish colonies in search of gold, crops, and anything of value that could be sent back to Spain. The colonies grew so prosperous that huge ships full of goods made journey after journey back and forth across the Atlantic. It didn't take long for others to realize what precious cargo was being hauled across the ocean.

The Booming Economy

Initially, the staple of the Atlantic economy, particularly for Spain, was importing precious metals like gold and silver. Ships took so much tonnage of the valuable metals back to Spain that many economists and historians blame the fall of Spain on the inflation caused by injecting so much gold and silver into the Spanish economy. For a while, though, Spain enjoyed a golden age, so to speak, because of the enormous wealth the gold brought with it. After all, gold was the common currency of Europe. Every nation desired gold and would trade anything for it. The nation with an endless supply of gold had the means to build palaces, armies, ships, colonies, roads, or whatever else it wanted or needed. Such was the case with Spain.

At first, the Spanish administrators in the New World, known as *encomenderos*, were charged with overseeing land, resources, and natives. Many of these encomenderos used the Native Americans to mine precious metals. Likewise, encomenderos who ran plantations of sugar cane and other crops used natives to work the fields. When the majority of the natives succumbed to the dreaded European diseases, black Africans were shipped to the Americas to provide labor. The slaves were strong and able and the economy flourished.

The New World contained many fascinating new crops like maize and potatoes that were sent to Europe to improve the diets of Europeans. Likewise, though, plants and animals were sent from Europe to the New World to help support colonists there. Animals like sheep, goats, cattle, and horses were introduced to the New World from Europe. Fruits and vegetables like apples, peaches, clover, and grains also traveled to the New World from Europe. This exchange of goods between Europe and the New World came to be known as the Columbian Exchange.

Would You Believe?

Historians also include among the things traded in the Columbian Exchange the numerous diseases that wiped out so many natives of the New World. Smallpox proved deadly, as did diseases like the plague, chickenpox, measles, and flu.

The Finest Fleet

As the Spanish economy boomed, others took notice. Both rival nations and pirates drooled over the booty that Spanish treasure ships, or *flota*, carried across the ocean year after year. Caravels initially did fine, but they could not carry the huge, heavy cargoes produced by the colonies in the New World. Spanish shipbuilders modified the caravels a number of times and finally settled on a large-hulled ship, called a *galleon*, designed specifically for carrying cargo. As pirates and rival nations intercepted the galleons, Spain added guns to the treasure ships. Some galleons had as many as 30 or more large guns mounted on them. As threats to the precious cargo increased, Spain modified the galleons to hold both soldiers and treasure. These escort ships traveled alongside the regular treasure ships to offer some protection. The threat of hostile ships, though, still had not been thwarted.

The Spanish got wise and adopted a convoy system of large numbers of ships, both treasure galleons and guard ships, making the voyages together. The theory of strength in numbers proved to be watertight. To further protect their precious cargoes, the Spanish built fortified ports in places like Cuba, Mexico, and Panama in which their treasure fleets could safely dock. With the new convoy system and fortified ports, the Spanish fleet lost fewer ships than ever. Even when attacked, ships rarely sank. Attacks from enemy ships usually damaged sails and masts rather than critically damaging the massive hulls. By working to protect its cargoes from ports around the world, the Spanish had created the world's largest and most powerful fleet, a fleet that Spain believed to be invincible.

Would You Believe?

Two of the most famous attacks on Spanish galleons occurred when Sir Francis Drake attacked and captured, on two separate occasions, ships carrying gold, spices, ivory, exotic foods, and more. The combined booty probably totaled nearly 100 million dollars.

The Least You Need to Know

◆ A sense of curiosity about the world around them, along with other motivations, created in Europeans an interest in exploring the lands that existed overseas.

◆ The development of such things as the astrolabe and the caravel enabled Europeans to make long voyages never before possible.

◆ The Portuguese took the lead in overseas travel but their voyages were for trade and not so much for exploration.

◆ Columbus, determined to find a sea route to Asia, sailed west and landed in the Bahamas, a group of islands he believed to be in Asia.

◆ Conquistadors like Cortés and Pizarro contributed to the disappearance of indigenous populations in the New World through military endeavors and the introduction of diseases.

◆ The Portuguese, Spanish, French, and English all sponsored voyages of discovery that resulted in the formation of colonies.

Our Religion Is Better Than Your Religion

In This Chapter

- ◆ Royal and religious tensions nearly tear apart France
- ◆ The Netherlands cause some serious headaches
- ◆ The aftermath of the English Reformation
- ◆ The invincible Armada
- ◆ The great witch hunts

The sixteenth century proved to be a time of both political and religious turmoil in France. In many instances, politics and religion were virtually indistinguishable. As France tried to recover from the plague and the Hundred Years' War (see Chapter 1) that devastated the country less than a century earlier, the monarchy worked hard to centralize power under the crown and away from the nobles, creating tension between the monarchy and the aristocracy. To further complicate matters, many noble families in France jumped on the Protestant bandwagon, known in France as the Huguenots, which began as a small, fringe group but eventually numbered as many as two million souls despite persecution from the French government.

As if France didn't have enough trouble on its hands, it spent the first half of the century embroiled in a conflict with the Habsburgs and eventually with the Holy Roman Emperor. Throughout these conflicts, the French economy teetered on the brink of disaster.

The Habsburgs and the Valois

The Habsburgs and the Valois were two of the most important and influential families in all of Europe. The Habsburg family traced its roots to medieval Switzerland. Over the few hundred years following the beginnings of the family's local rule, the Habsburgs managed to take control of what is now Austria and parts of Germany. In the thirteenth century, electors chose a member of the Habsburg family as German king. The throne stayed in the family on and off for centuries, and by the fifteenth and sixteenth centuries the Habsburgs had control of the Holy Roman Empire, which in theory was the secular kingdom that included all Catholics in Europe. The family's sphere of influence split in 1556 when Emperor Charles V, also Charles I of Spain, gave his Austrian holdings to his brother, Ferdinand, and Spain to his son, Philip. After this, there existed the Austrian Habsburgs and the Spanish Habsburgs.

 As a Matter of Fact

> The Habsburg Empire lasted in one form or another even into the twentieth century. Though the Habsburg family split into two groups, the Austrian Habsburgs and the Spanish Habsburgs, in the early sixteenth century, only the Austrian Habsburgs proved to have significant longevity. Despite the effective fall of the Holy Roman Empire after the Thirty Years' War, the Habsburg family remained intact in Austria and did not collapse until the family was deposed at the end of World War I.

The Valois family traced its roots back to Charles of Valois, whose descendants claimed the French throne ahead of the English King Edward III (see Chapter 1). The dispute over the French throne, won by the Valois, resulted in the Hundred Years' War. The Valois succeeded the Capetian Dynasty in France, the first modern dynasty in France dating back to the Middle Ages. The Valois remained in power in France until 1589, when they gave way to the House of Bourbon.

The Habsburgs and Valois found themselves at odds beginning in 1494 when King Charles VIII of France invaded Italy, parts of which the Habsburgs asserted claims to. Italy took the physical brunt of these wars, which took place across Italy and left destroyed governments of Italian states in their wake. France suffered defeat after defeat and crushing treaty after crushing treaty. After more than 50 years of war, the fighting finally drew to an end in 1559 with the Treaty of Cateau-Cambrésis, which basically reaffirmed Spanish control over most of Italy and French ownership of Calais.

In the midst of the Habsburg-Valois Wars, a number of interesting things happened that set the stage for huge problems later in France. Young Francis I (1494–1547) took the throne in 1515. Unlike the two kings before him, Francis embraced the Renaissance ideals that had made their way out of Italy. Francis also did not seem to be obsessed with fighting in Italy the way his predecessors had been. That would change, though.

Francis had his eye on the Church in France and in 1516 signed the Concordat of Bologna with the pope. The concordat, or agreement, supported the pope against any conciliar movement (see Chapter 1), and in return the king of France got to appoint the high-ranking members of the clergy in France. This was good for the Church because it solidified the French stance for Catholicism and assured that the French wouldn't become Protestant. It was good for France because the French king was assured the loyalty of those who made up the Church; he also maintained some independence from the pope. Unfortunately, the clergy he appointed were not interested in ministering or in spiritual affairs, so the Church in France entered a state of spiritual decline.

In the years following his ascension to the throne, Francis vied for the position of Holy Roman Emperor, the secular ruler of Catholic lands in Europe. To become Holy Roman Emperor, one needed to receive votes from electors, or the German princes who had been designated to choose the Emperor (see Chapter 8). Charles I of Spain received the votes and became Holy Roman Emperor Charles V. After the election, Francis and Charles were archenemies. Both wanted the Empire, both had interests in Italy, and they were neighbors. Francis followed in the footsteps of those before him and became obsessed with defeating Charles in Italy. While he carried on in France, Francis also allied with Protestants in Germany fighting against Charles V and with the young Henry VIII in England.

Would You Believe?

Francis and Henry VIII held a tournament to celebrate their alliance. The tournament was such a spectacle, with so many expensive tents erected, that the place became known as the Field of the Cloth of Gold. While the tournament was a smashing success, the alliance turned out to be practically meaningless.

The Many Wars of Religion

While Francis I occupied his time fighting in Italy and competing with Charles V, Protestantism made its way into France. While Lutheranism did have some followers within French borders, Calvinism had the bigger impact in France. Francis unquestionably opposed Protestantism, but he was too busy to do much about it. Twice he followed the pope in declaring Protestant preaching and literature illegal in France, but he never actively persecuted the Protestants in France.

Francis died in 1547 and Henry II (1519–1559) took the throne. Henry pursued the Huguenots much more aggressively. Furthermore, Henry's wife, Catherine de' Medici (1519–1589), who would eventually become Queen Mother and regent of France,

Continental Quotes

Nostradamus, the legendary predictor of future events, predicted the death of Henry when he said, "He (Henry) will pierce his eye through a golden cage ... then he dies a cruel death."

really went after the Huguenots, persecuting them with imprisonment, torture, and even execution. Interestingly, Catherine was the great-granddaughter of Lorenzo the Magnificent, one of the great Florentine Medicis of the Renaissance. Henry died in 1559 shortly after the signing of the Treaty of Cateau-Cambrésis. Henry enjoyed tournaments, so he took part in one celebrating the treaty. In a joust, a splinter of his opponent's lance pierced his eye and went into his brain. He died shortly thereafter. Catherine became regent and ruled for her son, who was not yet old enough.

Beginning in 1562, France found itself embroiled in what has come to be known as the Wars of Religion. While fighting certainly took place many times during the 32 years or so of the Wars, actual warfare was only intermittent during the era. The Wars of Religion were more like a longstanding feud between dynastic houses. Catherine led the Valois against the intrigues of the House of Guise, all of whom were Catholics. Also in the mix was the House of Bourbon led by Antoine de Bourbon, King of Navarre. Antoine had little interest in Protestantism but his wife and children supported the Huguenots. Catherine found herself in a sticky situation: the Huguenots posed a religious threat but the Guises posed a political threat. Catherine had to balance the two threats in such a way that her children remained in line for the throne.

In 1562, the first War of Religion broke out when Catherine, acting as regent, issued an edict that gave some toleration to Huguenots by allowing them to gather in open fields; she hoped to garner some support from Huguenots against the hated Guises. The Duke of Guise, in response, burned a building that housed probably hundreds of Huguenots. The Huguenots responded and the fighting went on until the following year. Such "wars" continued for 10 more years. Just as one side seemed to have the upper hand, the other would win momentum and then fortunes were reversed. The historical context of these wars helps explain the high tensions on the part of both Catholics and Huguenots in France during the latter half of the 1600s. England had just become Protestant and Protestantism swept over Europe. Likewise, Catholic monarchs were clamping down on the rise of Protestantism across Europe. Neither side was sure who ultimately would come out on top.

As a Matter of Fact

The House of Guise and the House of Bourbon were two of the most powerful families in France during the sixteenth century. They often vied for power in and around the royal court. The Guises were staunchly Catholic while the Bourbons were Protestant. The two families eventually become entangled in the affairs of Catherine de' Medici. Though Catherine was Catholic, she despised the Guises more than Protestantism.

War of the Three Henrys

Following a Huguenot victory over Catholic forces in 1570, Catherine made a calculated move in her continuing battle against the Guises. She agreed to marry her daughter to the Protestant Henry of Navarre (1553–1610), son of the now-dead Antoine de Bourbon, in hopes that this would create an anti-Guise alliance. Henry married Margaret de Valois in August, 1572, in Paris. At the time of the marriage, both Catholic and Huguenot forces had gathered in Paris just in case trouble broke out between the Catholics and Huguenots.

Just days after the marriage, an attempt was made on the life of a Huguenot noble, Admiral Gaspard de Coligny. The Huguenots blamed the Guises and demanded that something be done. In an interesting move that dashed whatever peace she hoped to make with the marriage of Henry and Margaret, Catherine convinced her son, the young King Charles IX, to finish off Coligny and act against the Huguenots for fear that the Huguenots would stage a revolution in Paris. As a result, Coligny was stolen from his room, stabbed, and then flung into the streets. Catherine had turned on the Huguenots she once used as allies against her enemy, the House of Guise.

In the minds of the Parisians, the king had just declared war on the Huguenots and Parisians were more than happy to lend a hand. In what became known as St. Bartholomew's Day massacre, Catholics found and executed thousands of Huguenots.

Catholics took Henry of Navarre prisoner. Massacres broke out all over France. This led to a war in the following decade known as the War of the Three Henrys.

The War of the Three Henrys marked the final chapter in the French Wars of Religion. The war dragged on and on between three contenders: King Henry III (of the House of Valois) of France, who had ascended to the throne in 1573 on the death of Charles IX; Henry of Guise; and Henry of Navarre, the only Protestant among them.

The war brought chaos down on France. The rivals had allies of all sorts and from places outside France. The Catholic League and Habsburg Spain supported Henry of Guise, the Huguenots and other Protestant nations supported Henry of Navarre. Almost no one supported King Henry III. The frightening possibility arose that Spain could invade France to "liberate" the Catholics. Henry III managed to have Henry of Guise murdered, but the Catholic League still opposed Henry III and so did many Frenchmen.

When Henry III realized that he was on the brink of defeat, he joined forces with Henry of Navarre against the Catholic League. A friar stabbed Henry III, who, just before he died, said that Henry of Navarre should be king, provided he would become Catholic. Henry of Navarre still had fighting left to do, but he eventually won the throne.

Paris Is Worth a Mass

A Catholic nation that had been fighting against Protestants for years now had its very own Protestant king. That presented all sorts of religious and political problems. In 1593, in a momentous ceremony at St. Denis, Henry of Navarre, now King Henry IV, converted to Catholicism. Henry knew that he had no choice if he were to rule a nation united instead of a nation divided. He reasoned, "Paris is worth a mass." Although he feared his Huguenot supporters would turn on him and that the pope would make life difficult for him, he did what he believed would be best for the people of France. For the most part, France accepted Henry right away. Some of his followers did turn away, but not all of them.

> **Continental Quotes**
>
> "I want there to be no peasant in my kingdom so poor that he cannot have a chicken in his pot every Sunday."
>
> —King Henry IV of France

In a show of good faith and in an attempt to end any further civil war, Henry issued the Edict of Nantes in 1598. The Edict extended some limited toleration to Huguenots. Huguenots were allowed to worship and were allowed to live in certain cities. In return, the Huguenots were to stay quiet, leave Catholics alone, and basically stay out of trouble. Henry IV worked to rebuild the nation, both physically and economically, during his reign. He worked hard for his people and he possessed a genuine concern for their welfare. He is remembered in France even today as *le bon roi Henry*, or "the good King Henry."

Would You Believe?

Henry IV fell victim to a crazy assassin named Ravaillac. For his crime, Ravaillac suffered horrible torture including be burned by hot sulphur and boiling oil before he was drawn and quartered, or pulled apart by horses. Ravaillac's family was forbidden to ever use the family name again.

The Naughty Netherlands

In the late fifteenth century, an area known as the Low Countries passed from Mary of Burgundy to the Habsburgs. The Low Countries consisted of 17 medieval fiefdoms, or lands that belonged to a lord. Emperor Charles V united these provinces with the Pragmatic Sanction in 1549 and made the Seventeen Provinces an entity under Habsburg Rule. When Charles abdicated and split his empire, his son Philip received the Seventeen Provinces, or the Netherlands. The people of the Netherlands, or the Dutch, enjoyed relative peace and prosperity. They were masters of trade and commerce. They worked hard to stay on good terms with everyone and as a result did business with many nations. The Dutch exported finished goods made from imported raw materials, they exported herring, they built ships, and they shipped goods for other nations. The Netherlands was a highly valued commodity, especially the city of Antwerp, and quite a gift for Philip.

The Rule of Philip II

Philip II of Spain (1527–1598), son of Holy Roman Emperor Charles V, inherited quite an empire when his father gave up his title in 1556. Philip enjoyed the fruits of the laborers who before him had established colonies and trading posts in the Americas and trade routes back and forth from there. About the time Philip took over in Spain, shipload after shipload of American gold and goods arrived in Europe regularly and made Spain a financial powerhouse. The Netherlands became vital to Spain's financial success because of the many goods and services available there.

While each province of the Netherlands had its own government, the provinces recognized and paid taxes to a central government in Brussels headed by Margaret of Parma (1522–1586), Philip's sister-in-law.

The system of government worked well for the Netherlands but Philip insisted on increasing Spain's influence there. The Dutch were not happy. Furthermore, when Philip signed the Treaty of Cateau-Cambrésis, the Dutch expected relief in taxes and an increased role in Philip's administration. Neither happened. Philip couldn't conceive of allowing the Netherlands to continue doing their own thing without his micromanagement. Philip had his hand in the government and economics of the region. Furthermore, a staunch Catholic, Philip was determined to keep the open-minded Dutch strictly Catholic, too. This inflexibility led to big problems for Philip in the Netherlands.

The Revolt of the Netherlands

The Netherlands had been impacted by a force that also had influenced France at about the same time. Calvinism spread to the Netherlands and many, including the nobility, embraced the religion. Being a staunch Catholic and believing himself to be the defender of the Catholic faith, Philip launched an attack on heresy in the Netherlands. Philip targeted many Calvinists, including some of the more prominent citizens of the Netherlands. Punishments for heresy under Philip's inquisition included execution and confiscation of the heretic's property. Because many in the Netherlands perceived Philip's actions as unfair, local governments refused to uphold Philip's laws. In 1566, townspeople stormed Catholic churches and destroyed statues and stained glass windows in what became known as the "iconoclastic fury." Then in 1567, Calvinist rebels seized a few small towns; Philip had had enough.

Philip sent the Duke of Alba, Fernando Alvarez de Toledo, into the Netherlands with 10,000 troops who established themselves in towns, arrested thousands, and executed at least 1,000 people. Additionally, Alba created new laws and imposed new taxes. He basically did everything Philip had done, only worse. In response, rebellious Protestants escaped some of the towns and began forming a military force. They gathered in the northernmost provinces and organized a resistance to the Spanish. Joining the resistance was an exiled group of pirates called the Sea Beggars who attacked Spanish ships and Spanish ports. The Sea Beggars allied with William of Orange (1533–1584) who helped finance the resistance.

The Duke of Parma, Alexander Farnese, eventually persuaded the southernmost provinces to remain loyal to Philip. It took plenty of money but they were convinced. On the contrary, the northern provinces pulled together and formed the Union of

Utrecht in 1579. The Union served as a defensive alliance against Spain and against the southern provinces. Elizabeth I of England threw her support, both financial and military, behind the United Provinces, as the northern union became known. After all, Elizabeth wanted the United Provinces as a buffer between the Spanish Netherlands, or the southern provinces, and England just across the English Channel.

Finally, in 1609, an exhausted Spain signed a 12-year truce and the United Provinces, though not officially recognized as a nation, were left alone while the southern Spanish Netherlands remained under Spanish control. The economic superiority of Antwerp then shifted to Amsterdam in the north. The Netherlands issue proved to be costly for Spain and for Philip, who died in 1598 and left his son, Philip III, to carry on.

Protestants vs. Catholics in England

While plenty of people in England already wanted to break with Rome, there were also plenty of Englishmen who never imagined themselves as anything but Catholic. Therefore, whether the monarch required everyone to be Protestant or Catholic, there always existed a group who wanted option B. This helps explain why the country never really broke into civil war or even unrest when the national religion went from one to another seemingly overnight.

After Henry VIII's "reformation" in England, the nation flip-flopped back and forth between Protestantism and Catholicism. When Henry died, his son Edward VI, 10 years old, took the throne. Henry's first daughter, Mary Tudor, started licking her lips because she knew it wouldn't be long before she had her chance to return the country to Catholicism. Edward died as a teenager and Jane Gray ruled as long as it took (nine days, to be exact) for Mary to gather her troops and take control of England.

Bloody Mary

Mary Tudor was determined to take the throne and return England to the true faith. Despite Protestant efforts to stop her from becoming queen, Mary and her supporters took control of the English court. The new queen and her advisors set out to return Catholicism to England and to squelch all Protestant voices. Mary's ruthless persecution of the Protestants in England, including high-ranking Protestants like Thomas Cranmer (see Chapter 4), earned her the nickname Bloody Mary. With surprising ease, Mary succeeded in restoring Catholicism in England. If Mary hadn't died when she did, England likely would have remained Catholic.

Would You Believe? ___

Mary had to make one major compromise when working with Parliament to fully restore Catholicism in England. Parliament agreed to fully commit to Catholicism only if Mary agreed not to restore all monastic lands that Henry VIII had taken from the Church and distributed amongst the English nobility.

Mary's life as queen was arguably a sad one. She deeply loved her husband, Philip II of Spain, but he never returned the affection. His absence left Mary deeply saddened if not depressed. The issue of children further complicated her life. It was common knowledge that Mary desperately wanted a child; not once but twice Mary believed she was pregnant. Each time, Mary's court took her away into the countryside where all anxiously awaited a baby, yet she never delivered. After her second "phantom pregnancy," as the condition often was called, Mary grew very ill. She never fully recovered and grew weaker and weaker. One of her dying wishes was that her half-sister would keep England Catholic. Upon Mary's death, her half-sister Elizabeth, daughter of Henry VIII and Anne Boleyn, ascended to the throne as Elizabeth I (1533–1603).

The Virgin Queen

Elizabeth I took the throne—and returned England to Protestantism once again. In 1559, Parliament undid the Catholicism of Mary and reinstated the *Book of Common Prayer*. Parliament adopted the Thirty-nine Articles, the fundamental theological beliefs of the Anglican Church. Elizabeth also brought back the Anglican Church as the official church in England.

A shrewd politician, Elizabeth learned from the mistakes of her predecessors. Rather than being aggressive toward Catholics the way Mary was toward Protestants, Elizabeth took a middle-of-the-road position concerning religion. Basically, she declared that Protestantism would be the official religion and then ignored Catholics as long as they kept quiet and didn't make a scene. She made sure not to make enemies with Catholics at home and she tried to stay out of the way of the pope. She also made sure that theological debates were left to scholars, not politicians.

Would You Believe? ___

Known as the "Virgin Queen" because she never married, Elizabeth probably did not want to sacrifice any of her authority as queen to a husband. The cunning queen also dangled her eligibility to suitors to keep them in line—potential suitors were not likely to cause problems for her politically.

Nevertheless, the Church tried to do away with her and return England to Catholicism. One pope excommunicated her and another gave his blessing for assassination attempts. Neither tactic worked.

England grew angry with Rome and drifted farther and farther away. Elizabeth had successfully chosen a religion for her kingdom and made it stick without much resistance. Elizabeth's moderate religious policies, known as the Elizabethan Settlement, pleased neither extreme Catholics nor extreme Protestants, but most of the country and many people in Europe felt pretty good about the arrangement.

Down with the Armada

Surely one of the main reasons Philip II wanted so desperately to hang on to the Netherlands was so he could use the ports to stage a major invasion of England once the opportunity presented itself. Shrewdly and wisely, Elizabeth I offered her support to the northern provinces partly to keep Spain occupied and partly to keep the provinces free of Catholicism for the good of England. Philip, who had been married, pretty much in name only, to Elizabeth's sister Mary, never really had much of a problem with Elizabeth even after she took the throne, until she helped the provinces. He also resented the fact that Elizabeth appeared sympathetic to the Sea Beggars. As tensions mounted between Spain and England, Elizabeth authorized attacks on Spanish ships. Philip decided to send his Armada to help with the invasion of England in 1588.

Philip's plan was for his invincible Armada to rid the English Channel of all English vessels and clear the way for the Duke of Parma to invade from the Netherlands. The Spanish battle plan was, like Philip, traditional and uncreative. The Armada planned to pull alongside the English ships, grapple the enemy ships, and fire upon them with artillery. The Spanish vessels, loaded with Spanish troops, planned to board the English vessels once the Spanish guns disabled the English ships. The English had other plans.

On July 29, 1588, the Armada, numbering about 130 ships, entered the Channel. English artillery were there to welcome them. Many of the Armada ships were relatively cumbersome supply and cargo ships designed more for the open waters of the ocean. The smaller, faster English vessels sailed circles around the Armada and sent them into disarray. Furthermore, because they had better artillery, the English could keep a safe distance and take advantage of their superior guns. The English fleet damaged a number of ships right away.

Unfortunately for the Spanish, the Duke of Parma wasn't quite ready to invade when the Armada arrived in Calais, so the fleet had no choice but to anchor offshore of the Netherlands. Seeing a perfect opportunity for some mischief, the English launched several fireboats, or boats set afire to set enemy ships ablaze, toward the immobile fleet. As the fireboats drifted toward the fleet anchored in a secure formation, many of the Spanish captains took off with their ships. Those who didn't flee were left exposed to the floating fireballs. The next morning, only a few Spanish ships remained to face the English fleet. Seeing the futility of fighting, the remaining Spanish ships fled to the North Sea. The English, completely out of ammo, bluffed and chased the Spaniards away. The English had defeated the invincible Armada, the most powerful navy in the world; less than half of Philip's ships made it home. There would be no invasion of England.

> **Would You Believe?**
>
> The defeat of the Spanish Armada in 1588, coupled with the loss of the United Provinces, pretty much made Spain increasingly irrelevant in European affairs for the next four centuries. Spain had risen to "superpower" status by creating the world's premier fleet, so the loss of the Armada caused Spain's prowess to plummet.

It was during the Spanish retreat and subsequent return to Spain by circumnavigating the British Isles that the remaining ships of the Armada encountered yet another dangerous foe. Rather than facing more ships, the Armada faced a brutal storm that virtually finished off the remaining vessels. The English, upon learning of the storm and its effects on the Spanish ships, declared the winds an act of God.

How to Find Witches

The period from the end of the Middle Ages to the end of the Reformation marked a period of intellectual unrest. For the first time in a very, very long time, the world as Europe knew it appeared somewhat unstable. Theology fell victim to pluralism. The scriptures drew challenges from theologians that the Church called heretics. The world seemed not quite as black-and-white as the Church had always made it seem. This unrest seemed particularly high in those places where the Church seemed to be losing its grip. For example, Spain and Italy experienced far less hysteria than places like Germany, France, and England. This intellectual unrest and hysteria often manifested itself in the form of witch hunts.

While there had always been suspicions of witches and witchcraft in Europe, the concerns never got out of hand until around the end of the Middle Ages, when the economic, social, and religious landscape of Europe underwent rapid changes. Generally, even as the number of trials of "witches" began to increase in the fourteenth and fifteenth centuries, the greatest increases in panic coincided with economic hardships, crop failures, social unrest, or tragedy. After all, if all was well, there probably were no witches at work. Conversely, if a cow dropped dead for no apparent reason, if crops failed, or if an epidemic broke out in a village, then there probably were witches or witchcraft afoot.

The Changing Status of Women

While not all accused witches between 1450 and 1650 were women, certainly most were. Some regions of Europe actually tried more men than women, but those regions were exceptions. Perhaps the root of the witch hunts was *misogyny*.

Misogyny has existed throughout history, perpetuated by male-dominated, patriarchal societies. The evidence is easy to see even in ancient cultures. In many ancient religions, mysterious, mystical powers and the unpredictable forces of nature were identified with women. Goddesses of the ancient pantheons often possessed these powers. Even in Christianity, it was Eve, the woman, who was seduced by Satan and, in turn, lured Adam to do evil in the Garden of Eden. Historically, men have blamed the female gender for the Fall of Man. With misogynous tendencies already, men didn't need much imagination to believe that women were potentially evil.

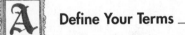

Define Your Terms

Misogyny is the hatred of women.

Conflicts over the social status of women played a significant role in the witch craze that swept over Europe. During the Dark Ages or the Low Middle Ages, when barbarian kingdoms dominated the continent, women were considered little more than property. In fact, barbarian chieftains and warlords often measured wealth and worldly success according to the amount of land and the number of cattle and women they possessed. Women had nowhere to go but up. Though they didn't climb high on the social ladder, women's status did improve somewhat during the Middle Ages. Because women often were left at home to manage affairs while the men were at battle or on Crusades, there were many examples of women managing and owning property, particularly after their husbands died. It may not seem like much, but that was a huge leap from just a few hundred years before. As the years passed, not many but a few women actually became educated. Again, not much of an improvement, but an improvement nonetheless.

While the Renaissance did see a few women achieve notable status, the resurgence of humanist ideals probably did more harm than good for women. Traditional humanism, not to mention traditional Christian doctrine, portrayed women as the "weaker vessel," man's less-than-equal partner, the inspiration for art, not the creators of art. Any progress women had made was set back by this ideology. As society and religion seemed to come undone after the Middle Ages, the antithesis to the traditional patriarchal Christian society seemed to be the matriarchal society governed by the devil.

One of the greatest detriments to the status of women was the publication in 1485 or 1486 of the *Malleus maleficarum*, or *The Hammer of Witches* by Heinrich Kramer and James Sprenger. The equivalent of *The Complete Idiot's Guide to Finding and Identifying Witches*, the *Malleus* served as the leading authority on witches for centuries to follow. According to the *Malleus*, women were "by nature instruments of Satan" and "by nature carnal." Because the *Malleus* was endorsed by the Church, the handbook became as good as law. In fact, the *Malleus* became practically irrefutable. For those who did not believe in witches and witchcraft at the time of its publication, the book made them change their minds. The *Malleus* states that "people who hold that witches do not exist are to be regarded as notorious heretics." The language couldn't be more clear about the Church's position on the existence of witches. This opinion and this book, combined with the misogyny that already existed in Europe, fueled many fires upon which witches were burned.

> **Continental Quotes**
>
> Note the misogynous nature of the text of *Malleus maleficarum* as the authors consider women and their "addiction to evil": "Therefore, let us now chiefly consider women; and first, why this kind of perfidy is found more in so fragile a sex than in men."

The Great Witch Hunt

With the status of women in a dismal condition, with copies of *Malleus* floating around in great numbers, and with difficulties around every corner, Europe was primed for a feeding frenzy. Belief in witches far predated the fifteenth century but never before had there been so many accusations, trials, and subsequent executions of "witches." As economic hardship, agricultural struggles, and health issues gripped Renaissance Europe, the unscientific common people needed an explanation for things that happened around them. In much the same way many people feared that the Black Death was caused by a vast Jewish conspiracy that sought to eliminate Christendom by poisoning wells, Europeans looked to witches for the explanation for unexplainable events. More often than not, women were the accusers in cases of witchcraft. Also, more often than not, the reason for the accusation was something as simple as the death of cow, the disappearance of a pig, the appearance of a rash, or the illness of a child.

Those targeted most often weren't the beautiful, seductive young girls who tantalized men and put husbands under the influence of their charms. Rather, those most frequently accused were older women, often widowed, who lived by themselves in relative seclusion. Those unfortunate women made easy targets because they had few dealings with everyone else in the communities and perhaps lived outside community norms. Those who had never had children found themselves at a higher risk of being accused. Women of all ages did end up on trial across Europe, but men did, too, so no one really ever was safe from the witch hunts.

Once someone was accused of witchcraft, or having relations with the devil, he or she was tried in court, usually a secular court but sometimes a Church court. The Inquisitors often used torture to extract "confessions." They searched the body of the accused for marks of the devil, or birthmarks. Other deformities, including scars and third nipples, were dead giveaways that the accused had had relations with the devil at some point. Birth defects in children also indicated that the mother had had relations with the devil. Unfortunately for the accused, rules of evidence were pretty lax and almost nonexistent. As a result, convictions weren't too hard to come by. About half of all convictions ended in execution, often by hanging, burning, or drowning. Once one or two people in a community were tried, a frenzy often ensued and before long one or two turned into 10 or 20.

As a Matter of Fact

An often misunderstood fact about the Great Witch Hunt in Europe centers on the execution of witches. While "witches" faced a variety of possible forms of execution, the most common form of execution for the guilty was not burning at the stake. In fact, though many were burned or drowned or broken on the rack, most executions were hangings. Those not executed were sometimes mutilated, locked in stocks, dunked or beaten. The misconception about the burning of witches may result from the large number of dead "witches" whose bodies were burned by authorities to prevent any further evil from being carried out.

Between 1400 and 1700, the years the Great Witch Hunt peaked, as many as 100,000 Europeans were tried as witches. Some countries tried and executed tens of thousands while other countries tried and executed only a few. While the Church did endorse the *Malleus*, the phenomenon of the Great Witch Hunt should not be interpreted as an institutional phenomenon but rather as a widespread local phenomenon. The societal stigmatization of women made it easy for common men and women to accuse others, particularly women.

Would You Believe? _____

Even children fell victim to the witch hunt craze. The following was taken from a 1629 letter of a high-ranking official in Wurzburg, Germany: "there are children of three and four years, to the number of three hundred, who are said to have had intercourse with the Devil. I have seen put to death children of seven, ten, twelve, fourteen, and fifteen."

The Least You Need to Know

◆ Religious tensions in France between Catholics and French Protestants, or Huguenots, led to the Wars of Religion. Ultimately, after the War of the Three Henrys, the Catholics remained in control while the Huguenots received some limited tolerance.

◆ The Low Countries, or the Netherlands, believed they were being oppressed by the staunchly Catholic Philip II of Spain. As a result, the northern provinces broke away and fought for their independence. The Protestant northern provinces became known as the United Provinces, while the Catholic provinces in the south were known as the Spanish Netherlands.

◆ After the English Reformation led by Henry VIII, Mary Tudor returned England to Catholicism. Upon Mary's death, Elizabeth I adopted a moderate and tolerant religious policy, returned England to Protestantism, and maintained domestic peace.

◆ Philip's invincible Spanish Armada fell to a smaller, faster English fleet in the English Channel in a 1588 attempt to invade England. One of Philip's motivations was the Protestant Elizabeth I and her aid of the Protestant northern provinces of the Netherlands.

◆ Fueled mostly by misogyny and social and economic uncertainty, Europeans tried approximately 100,000 men and women between 1400 and 1700. Just over half of those convicted of witchcraft were executed.

◆ While religion didn't necessarily sponsor the Great Witch Hunt, religious denominations certainly didn't mind and they didn't preach tolerance.

Chapter 8

The Rise and Fall of the Holy Roman Empire

In This Chapter

- ◆ What exactly is the Holy Roman Empire?
- ◆ The union of church and state
- ◆ It's good to be a Habsburg, most of the time
- ◆ The Thirty Years' War
- ◆ The end of an empire, sort of

Just as the sixteenth century in western Europe proved to be a time of both political and religious turmoil, the seventeenth century proved to be equally tumultuous for central Europe. And, just like in England, France, and the Netherlands in the century before, the disputes over religion in central Europe in the seventeenth century usually served as thinly veiled disguises for political issues, territorial disputes, and concerns over land and boundaries.

As nations jockeyed for political power and the title of "Europe's Premier State," monarchs did whatever was necessary to improve their position, expand their borders, and further their interests. Some monarchs sided with traditional enemies for their own gain and some even supported other religions to get what they wanted for themselves and their nations. One of the major players in the drama that unfolded during the seventeenth century was not a state per se but was an empire, sort of.

The Holy Roman Empire

The Holy Roman Empire, that centuries-old entity that played such a pivotal role in so many political and religious affairs throughout European history, once again found itself in the thick of things during the seventeenth century. The Holy Roman Empire, although a political and religious force, didn't really qualify as a European nation. It had no real geographic boundaries, no official census records for its population. Historians have debated when the Empire began and what its true nature was; there have been debates on the nature and responsibilities of the Emperor and the extent of his political powers. In short, the Holy Roman Empire and the position of Holy Roman Emperor were as much theoretical as practical.

The origins of the Empire trace back to the year 800 or a few years before. When Pope Leo III (d.816) became pope in 795, quite a few opponents, especially among the nobility, worked to have him removed and finally deposed him. Pope Leo III appealed to Charlemagne (c.742-814), or Charles the Great, who was the King of the Franks and the undisputed greatest secular power in Europe.

Charlemagne's advisors suggested that no men could question the authority of the pope, and Charlemagne agreed. He traveled to Rome and put down the rebellion against Leo. On Christmas Day in the year 800, Pope Leo III crowned Charlemagne *Imperator Romanorum*, or Emperor of the Romans. Legend says that Charlemagne never would have entered the church where Leo crowned him had he known that Leo was going to give him such a crown and title.

Historians disagree over the nature of the title; some argue that the title was meant as an honorary title with no real power, while others maintain that the pope created a new secular arm of Rome with the title. Either way, the first *Imperator Romanorum* since the fall of Rome in 476 was back in action. Interestingly, though, Charlemagne never referred to himself as "Holy Roman Emperor" or even as "Emperor of the Romans." Rather, Charlemagne considered himself *Imperator Romanorum gubernans Imperium*, or Emperor Ruling the Roman Empire.

Whether the Holy Roman Empire actually began in 800 could be debated, but the foundation had at least been laid. Several Frankish kings after Charlemagne used the title but exercised little "imperial" authority. Then, after the assassination of an emperor in 924, the title remained unused for about 40 years. Probably the actual and practical beginning of the Holy Roman Empire came in 962 when Pope John XII (c.937-964) crowned the German king Otto I (912-973) as emperor.

Like Charlemagne, Otto traveled to Italy to save the pope and Rome from political unrest and instability. The pope crowned Otto emperor, then signed the *Diploma Ottonianum* which made the emperor the protector of the Papal States, one of the independent states in Italy. With title and power in hand, Otto saved the Papal States from its would-be conquerors.

Would You Believe?

Though Pope John XII gave the crown to Otto "the Great," John changed his mind later and actually tried to get rid of Otto. As it turned out, Otto returned to Italy and deposed the very pope that crowned him emperor.

Neither Holy nor Roman nor an Empire

The eighteenth-century philosopher Voltaire (see Chapter 12) once commented that the Holy Roman Empire was neither Holy nor Roman nor an empire. In many ways, Voltaire couldn't have been more right. Dating back to the earliest days of the empire, the right to rule had nothing to do with holiness, piety, religious devotion, or anything of the sort.

Beginning with Otto, the right to rule as emperor was a perk of being the German king. Germany was not yet a nation but rather a kingdom comprised of smaller principalities. The German princes occasionally exercised the power to choose a king, but more often than not they merely approved the succession of the next in line. Regardless, once on the throne, the German kings also staked their claim as the next emperor. Most German kings ultimately were crowned emperor, though popes occasionally chose not to crown a German king emperor because of disputes regarding a king's ascension. The designation of both the emperor and the empire as "holy" had nothing to do with the spiritual nature of the emperors themselves; it simply implied an alliance with the Church and the fact that the emperors were to be defenders of the faith and the Church.

In 1338, the German electors declared that they and they alone had the right to choose the emperor—without the input of the pope; the pope did still perform the coronation of the emperor, though. This system prevailed until the coronation of Charles V in 1530, after which all such coronations took place in Germany rather than in Italy. While that might seem to finally make the use of the term "Roman Empire" somewhat problematic, the "Roman" part of the title had never had anything to do with the German kings being chosen by or crowned in Rome. Beginning with Charlemagne's family, or the Carolingian dynasty, as it was known, the kings maintained that the Roman Empire had not ceased to exist in 476 when Augustus Romulus abdicated to barbarian invaders. Rather, the Carolingians argued, the Empire had simply been suspended for several hundred years. Although that reasoning made the Holy Roman Empire "Roman" in their minds, the Empire actually was not Roman per se.

In theory, the Holy Roman Emperor ruled an empire comprised of all western Christians. This wasn't too much of a stretch, initially, because Charlemagne had his Franks organized into a kingdom, the only organized state in Europe. Only after he centralized the government in Germany did other modern states form across the continent. These states were far more cohesive than any empire perceived by the Emperor or the pope, and the monarchs weren't always excited about recognizing someone else's authority over their lands. The loyalties of these peoples did not lie with the emperors unless the nobles were granted titles within the empire.

As the centuries passed, the Holy Roman Emperors found themselves granting more and more land, titles, and rights to nobility all over the continent. As the emperors gave away these things, the strength of the empire decreased. A true empire the Holy Roman Empire was not.

Church and State

In theory, the relationship between the emperor and the pope seemed mutually beneficial. By stroking the ego of a German king and bestowing a title, the pope gained a powerful ally with an army committed to defending the Church, the papacy, and the Papal States. Furthermore, the pope had a far-reaching political arm with which he could enforce all things papal throughout Christendom.

The emperor, in exchange for a vow of loyalty and a commitment to be the defender of the faith, received a nifty crown, a great title, and secular authority over all of Christendom, even in places where he wasn't the actual hereditary king. Additionally, the emperor received not only funding but also papal authority for the use of his armies. In reality, though, the emperor's influence remained limited largely to Germany and the surrounding areas—in other words, to his own kingdom.

In theory, the pope handled all spiritual matters that affected Christendom while the emperors handled all things secular or political. The cooperation, though not exactly the union, of Church and state seemed very promising for both parties. However, the line between political and secular issues frequently blurred or disappeared altogether. Popes often failed to see eye to eye with the emperors. Emperors occasionally appointed Church officials in a practice known as investiture (see Chapter 3) and that never went over well with the papacy. Disputes over secular authority in Italy caused concerns. German emperors often found themselves in conflicts of interest when trying to balance ruling Germany as king and ruling Christendom as emperor.

To say that the relationship between Church and state was tenuous at times would be an understatement. On the other hand, imperial and papal interests occasionally fell neatly in line, particularly during the Reformation and the Catholic or Counter Reformation.

Would You Believe?

On more than one occasion, the conflict between pope and Emperor intensified to the point that the pope actually excommunicated the Holy Roman Emperor.

Europe's Most Powerful Family

The Habsburgs may not have won any popularity contests during their day but they certainly had everyone's attention. Though they began with a relatively small sphere of influence (see Chapter 7), the Habsburgs grew into perhaps the most influential family in all of Europe outside of the Medici family of Italy. The power of the Habsburg family culminated with Charles, son of Philip Habsburg and maternal grandson of Ferdinand and Isabella.

Charles was arguably the first true king of Spain, since previously Spain had actually consisted of the smaller states of Aragon and Castile. Charles went on to become Holy Roman Emperor Charles V. While Charles V was a Habsburg by birth, he wasn't German. In fact, it's hard to say *what* nationality Charles was. Regardless, Charles put the Habsburg family in a position to be powerful in Spain and Germany *and* claim the title of Europe's Most Powerful Family.

Continental Quotes

Born in Madrid but not truly having a place to call home, Charles V once said, "I speak Spanish to God, Italian to women, French to men, and German to my horse."

Most family trees of European ruling families after the Middle Ages were intertwined with those of other ruling families, and the Habsburgs were no exception. Ruling families often arranged marriages between their children, creating political and economic unions that, in theory, would be beneficial for both families. A family who ruled one country often had children, grandchildren, and cousins permanently linked to other countries all over the continent. The Habsburg family tree epitomized the family tree linked to other families and other countries.

Both Charles V and his brother, Ferdinand, who later became Holy Roman Emperor Ferdinand I, were grandsons of Ferdinand and Isabella, who sponsored Columbus. When Charles, who was old and tired, abdicated, he gave his brother Ferdinand the empire and he gave Spain to his son Philip. Ferdinand's son, Maximilian II, as well as two of Maximilian's sons, Rudolf and Matthias, upheld the family tradition and went on to become Holy Roman Emperor, too. Literally everything stayed in the family as Maximilian II married Maria, a daughter of his uncle Charles V. After Maximilian's two sons became emperor, his third son, Maximilian III, helped another Habsburg, the intensely Catholic Ferdinand of Styria, become Holy Roman Emperor Ferdinand II. The son of Ferdinand II also ascended to the throne of the Holy Roman Empire and became Ferdinand III. One of the daughters of Maximilian II married Philip III of Spain, grandson of Charles V and son of Philip II. Later, Philip IV of Spain married the daughter of King Henry IV of France (see Chapter 7).

As a Matter of Fact

One of the individuals found in the Habsburg family tree, Philip IV of Spain, made an amazing discovery shortly after the beginning of the Thirty Years' War. In 1622, a young painter named Diego Rodriguez de Silva y Velazquez painted a portrait in Madrid that caught the attention of Philip's chief minister. In 1623, Velazquez painted a portrait of Philip and impressed Philip so much that Velazquez became the only artist allowed to paint the king, a status Velazquez maintained his entire life; the current whereabouts of the painting are unknown. A master of the Spanish Baroque period, Velazquez's greatest work was *Las Meninas*, a beautiful painting that in 1985 was named the world's greatest painting.

In the grand scheme of European history, the lives of some of these people were of little importance historically, while others had great historical impact. However, the family tree with many far-reaching branches illustrates how complex and how interconnected the lives of the individuals and families of this era were. In the case of the Habsburgs, their importance can hardly be overstated. The family collectively controlled Spain, Spanish holdings in the New World, and parts of Italy and the Netherlands, along with Germany, Austria, Bohemia, Hungary, and more in central and western Europe. Furthermore, the Habsburgs had ties to other countries through marriage and through Catholicism. If an international incident occurred in Europe after the Middle Ages, the Habsburgs more than likely were involved either directly or indirectly.

The Thirty Years' War

At the height of its power, the Holy Roman Empire, ruled by the Austrian Habsburgs, and its ally Spain, ruled by the Spanish members of the Habsburg family, dominated European politics. A number of developments in the sixteenth and seventeenth centuries, however, made life more difficult for Europe's most powerful family.

First, the Holy Roman Empire could only rule effectively when it had the cooperation of those local and provincial officials the emperor put in power. As the empire's power peaked, though, many princes simply waited for the opportunity to break with it.

Second, nations such as France and Sweden were waiting for the chance to take shots at the empire—and take land. Finally, the Reformation (see Chapters 3 and 4) drove a wedge between the electors within the empire, some Lutheran and some Catholic. The Peace of Augsburg of 1555 was to help maintain a balance between the two religious groups. In the years prior to the war, though, a few of the electors had converted to Calvinism, a religious denomination not legalized at Augsburg. Religious tensions in Germany built as some of the German princes chose Calvinism. What started arguably as a German civil war between Ferdinand and Prince Frederick of the Palatinate soon escalated into an international war of politics and religion that manifested itself in four distinct phases.

Out the Window

The Protestants in Bohemia took great exception to the appointment of Ferdinand II as King of Bohemia, and later as Holy Roman Emperor. Ferdinand reneged on the tolerance shown to Protestants by his predecessors including Holy Roman Emperor Rudolf. Catholic authorities stopped the construction of a number of Protestant houses of worship. The Protestant nobility of Bohemia was on the verge of a revolt. At the castle in Prague, a number of prominent Protestants seized two

Define Your Terms

The term **defenestration** comes from the Latin meaning "out the window." The 1618 defenestration, although considered *the* defenestration, actually was the second significant event of its kind. The first involved followers of Jan Hus.

Catholic officials along with their trusty secretary and flung the three from a window high in the castle. Remembered as the *Defenestration* of Prague of 1618, this event helped spark the Thirty Years' War.

The Protestant and Catholic accounts of the defenestration vary greatly. In reality, the three Catholics not only survived the fall but also escaped with only their pride damaged. They landed in a ditch beneath the window filled with a trash heap, most probably piles of manure, that helped break their fall. According to the three men (and thus the official Catholic version), they called out to Jesus and Mary on their way down and angels swooped down from the heavens, caught the righteous men, and sat them gently on the ground unharmed—with no piles of manure involved.

The Bohemian Phase (1618–1625)

Occasionally historians subdivide the Bohemian Phase into two smaller phases, the Bohemian Phase (1618–1621) and the Palatinate Phase (1621–1624 or 1625). The first of the fighting erupted in Bohemia in 1618 at least partly as a result of the defenestration. Archduke Ferdinand, of the House of Habsburg, of course, became king of Bohemia in 1617. Wanting to exercise his power and defend his faith, King Ferdinand took away some of the religious liberties the Bohemians had enjoyed for generations. The Protestants organized a resistance movement comprised mostly of Czechs against Ferdinand and his oppressive Catholicism and deposed him. In his place, they chose Frederick V of the *Palatinate*, a Calvinist.

Define Your Terms

The **Palatinate** was an area of Germany along the Rhine River which prior to 1356 was ruled by a count palatine, originally a permanent representative of the king of the Franks, and after 1356 by an elector, one of the princes who elected the Holy Roman Emperor.

Imperial forces of the recently elected Holy Roman Emperor Ferdinand II quickly descended upon the resistance; the Catholic League and the Spanish Habsburgs subsidized the expense of building a military. The combat came to a screeching halt when imperial forces crushed the Protestants near Prague at the Battle of White Mountain. The emperor then used Jesuit missionaries to work over the noncombatants. Rather than giving up, as the imperial forces hoped, the Protestants' will for self-determination only increased. Despite the increased efforts of the Protestants, the imperial forces prevailed and Bohemia eventually lost its Protestant identity.

As the first phase of the war unfolded, private mercenary armies formed hoping to cash in on the fighting. Among the more dynamic and ambitious leaders of these mercenary armies was Albrecht von Wallenstein (1583–1634). Although Wallenstein was born a Czech Protestant, he offered his services to the emperor; after all, he was a mercenary. After much pressure from those around him, the emperor gave in and commissioned Wallenstein and his army of 125,000 men. Wallenstein and his troops had their way with Germany; they pillaged and plundered at will. Because Wallenstein built his army, his troops were loyal only to him and not to the emperor. Though Wallenstein rose to power during the Bohemian Phase of the war, he would leave his indelible mark during the second phase.

The Spanish seized the opportunity to successfully invade Frederick's holdings along the Rhine River while Frederick was busy in Bohemia. After the invasion, Frederick, with the aid of other Protestants, tried to free his lands from the Spanish. Despite their best efforts, the Protestants failed to wrest them from the Spanish.

The Danish Phase (1625–1630)

Enemies of the Habsburgs from around Europe, Protestants and Catholics alike, watched in terror as the imperial forces, led by Wallenstein, razed the Protestant resistance in Germany. In an effort to end the imperial push through Germany and aid fellow Protestants, the King of Denmark, Christian IV (1577–1648), invaded northern Germany. While Christian certainly invaded as the champion of the anti-Habsburg cause, he had every intention of exerting his influence on the region in the process. Onlookers from as far away as the Netherlands and England cheered Christian, but to no avail. Out-manned, he fell to Wallenstein as had so many other challengers in places like Silesia, Schleswig, and the Baltic region.

Encouraged by Wallenstein, the emperor issued the Edict of Restitution in 1629. The edict outlawed Calvinism and other sects of Christianity and allowed only Catholicism and Lutheranism in the empire. The Peace of Augsburg, 70 years earlier, had allowed Lutherans to keep all lands confiscated from the Church during the Reformation. The Edict of Restitution required that all lands previously confiscated from the Church by Protestantism be returned.

This marked the pinnacle of Habsburg power in Europe. Protestants across the continent now feared both Wallenstein and the emperor: Wallenstein because of his armies and ruthless tactics, and Ferdinand because he seemed close to unifying and giving the Holy Roman Empire actual power. Concerned that Wallenstein had grown too strong and no longer represented their interests, the leaders of the provinces within the empire and the Catholic League pressured the emperor to relieve Wallenstein of his duties.

The Swedish Phase (1630–1635)

While religion remained the ostensible reason for the continued fighting, politics emerged as the real reason for the war during the Swedish Phase. Since the first champion of Protestantism had failed to thwart the Habsburgs, Europe desperately needed another. The Swedes had been busy in northern Europe grabbing land for trade purposes for some time when the Protestant King of Sweden, Gustavus Adolphus (1594–1632) announced his plan to enter the fight against the Habsburgs.

While his 100,000-man army had the potential to seriously damage the imperial forces, Gustavus Adolphus also hoped to expand his holdings in his foray into Germany. Subsidized by France, the Swedes won major victories that probably prevented Ferdinand from uniting all German states under the control of the Holy Roman Empire. While it might seem strange for France, a Catholic nation, to support the Protestant Swedes against fellow Catholics, France saw an opportunity to weaken the Habsburgs and to tip the balance of power away from them. With a confident and successful Gustavus Adolphus in the north, the emperor found himself in the unenviable position of inviting Wallenstein to rejoin the cause.

The French Phase (1635–1648)

Unfortunately for the Swedes and the Protestants, Gustavus Adolphus died from a battle wound in 1632. Then the Swedes were, for the most part, defeated in 1634. In an unsurprising turn of events, Wallenstein turned on Ferdinand, in anger over his first dismissal and with hopes of creating a kingdom of his own. Ferdinand declared Wallenstein guilty of treason and had him murdered by his own troops. As the tides turned against the Protestant princes, some of the princes offered peace in exchange for the rejection of the Edict of Restitution. The timing couldn't have been better, and Ferdinand welcomed the prodigal sons back into the fold as allies.

Continental Quotes

"The Lord God is my armor!"

—Gustavus Adolphus, spoken before his final battle in which he refused to wear armor because of a wound he received in the previous battle.

With the Swedes no longer able to do France's dirty work, France officially entered the war on the side of the Protestants days before news of the peace between the empire and some of the princes went public. Just as France supported the United Provinces against the Spanish Habsburgs, France supported the Protestants against the Habsburgs.

The weaker the Habsburg family, particularly in neighboring Spain, and the Holy Roman Empire, the greater France's status was in European political affairs.

Because neither the empire nor the Protestants could deliver the knockout punch, the fighting dragged on and on. There were virtually no decisive battles in the final phase of the war. Casualties mounted on the battlefields with no victors, and civilians away from the battlefields

Would You Believe?

Because the French Phase of the Thirty Years' War involved Germans, French, Dutch, Scots, Swedes, Spanish, and even Finns, historians often refer to it as the International Phase.

suffered heavy casualties, too. The non-Germans who rushed to the aid of the Protestants in Germany burned and looted every place they went in Germany in an attempt to weaken their opponents. In the long run, this tactic proved devastating for all Germans. As was typical of seventeenth-century warfare, the armies and the weapons were larger and more deadly than ever before in European history. However, war tended to drag on as each side bludgeoned the other without ever delivering the

final blow. Finally, after 30 years of long, drawn-out fighting, the two sides started winding down in 1643. With all involved exhausted, the Thirty Years' War officially ended in 1648 with the Peace of Westphalia, one of the most significant settlements in all of European history.

Would You Believe?

The French and Spanish did not wrap up their fighting with each other until the Treaty of the Pyrenees in 1659.

Aftermath and Fallout

The Peace of Westphalia, actually treaties signed at Münster and Osnabrück, had religious and political ramifications that lasted for centuries. First, the peace recognized the sovereignty of the German princes, all 300 or so of them. Each prince was free to choose the religion for his principality. Furthermore, the papacy could no longer intervene in German religious issues. The Church's practical influence on European affairs took a major hit. The Peace of Westphalia also upheld the Peace of Augsburg, added Calvinism to the short list of religions allowed in German states, and made the Edict of Restitution null and void. As it turned out, even after all the fighting and subsequent diplomacy, the states of northern Germany remained mostly Protestant while the southern German states remained mostly Catholic.

Would You Believe?

The Catholics and Protestants refused to meet face to face so they agreed to use two cities to formally end the war. The Catholics signed in the city of Münster and the Protestants in Osnabrück.

Would You Believe?

The Peace of Westphalia is often looked to as the first example of modern diplomacy, diplomacy where matters of state take precedence over religion.

As for the political aspects of the peace, the United Provinces finally won recognition as an independent state. Switzerland, too, won recognition as a state. The German princes, as part of their sovereignty, won the right to make alliances and form treaties as long as they didn't declare war on the Holy Roman Empire. Sweden received a nice wad of cash and control over land along the Baltic. The biggest winner politically, though, was France. France received the region of Alsace, an area of land that would be hotly contested between France and Germany even as late as World War II, and in a later treaty received part of the Spanish Netherlands and land along the Pyrenees. France's international meddling had paid huge dividends. Spain no longer stood as the most powerful nation in Europe. That distinction, after the Peace of Westphalia and the Treaty of the Pyrenees, belonged to France and France alone. Spain officially lost the United Provinces while France grew larger. France also benefited from the fragmentation of the Holy Roman Empire.

The End of an Empire

The Holy Roman Empire arguably reached its zenith with the Edict of Restitution and stood on the threshold of becoming a permanent, powerful fixture not only in Germany but also in all of Europe. Then, just 20 years later, the Peace of Westphalia rendered the empire virtually irrelevant. With the German states now sovereign, the empire had no control over the states collectively. There existed among the German states no central government, no central court system, and no checks on princes or nobles who might fall out of favor with the empire. The cession of territories to France and Sweden and the acknowledgement of the independence of the United Provinces and Switzerland shrank the geographic area over which the empire could possibly have any influence. For all intents and purposes, the Holy Roman Empire lost nearly all power after the Peace of Westphalia.

Would You Believe?

The Holy Roman Empire, though basically a powerless, nostalgic institution, did not cease to exist until 1806 after a defeat by Napoleon.

While the empire seemed to crumble, the Habsburg family emerged from the war in remarkably good shape. The war had not finished off the family along with the empire. Ironically, the Austrian Habsburgs found themselves in a great situation even though their attempts to strengthen the Holy Roman Empire and eliminate Protestantism had failed. The Habsburgs controlled Austria and Bohemia and were on the verge of extending their control eastward into the Balkans and southward into Italy. Even after the Holy Roman Empire fell, the Habsburgs ruled what became known as the Austrian or Austro-Hungarian Empire, a formidable multiethnic empire that was considered a European power.

Agricultural, Economic, and Population Disaster

Spain and the Holy Roman Empire lost in a big way as a result of the Thirty Years' War. The biggest losers, though, were the Germans. Because the overwhelming majority of fighting during the war took place on German soil, Germany suffered terribly in a number of ways. Soldiers and looters destroyed countless farms and estates and wiped out both crops and livestock in the process; the mercenary troops by far did the most damage. Even after the war, the farmland was in no shape to begin productive agriculture and the livestock had been drastically depleted. The supply of food might have been enough to support the German population alone but the huge numbers of foreign troops who occupied areas of Germany added an enormous strain.

As a result of the food shortages, Germans suffered not only from malnutrition but also diseases such as dysentery, typhus, the plague, and even scurvy. The diseases already present in Germany prior to the war worsened during and after the war. Wherever the troops went, disease was sure to follow. The lack of food and supplies caused innumerable refugees to flee their homes in search of food and shelter. These population displacements, along with casualties from the fighting, often left entire towns or rural areas completely depopulated.

The German economy took blow after blow over the course of the war. Because of the dramatic influx of gold and silver into Spain from the New World, Europe saw significant inflation. This inflation was compounded in Germany by the shortages that raised prices of food and supplies to often ridiculous levels. Inflation rose higher in Germany than anywhere else in Europe. Trade and commerce practically ceased in many areas because of the fighting and because of the lack of people necessary to support trade routes.

Interestingly, though, the economies in a few cities actually boomed, due to the floods of refugees who sought safe harbor within the city walls. The depopulation of so many areas created labor shortages similar to the years following the Black Death (see Chapter 1). Many landowners were forced to pay high prices for laborers to work the land. Some lacked the resources to start again and were forced to sell to wealthier landowners. The scores of peasants forced to sell their property eventually became serfs in many parts of eastern Europe.

While the economic and agricultural losses were enormous, the population losses were staggering. Historians and economists estimate the total cost of the war in human life at somewhere in the range of several million. Several hundred thousand lost their lives on the battlefields; the balance died as a result of poor agricultural conditions or epidemic diseases. Some figures, though debated by many historians, showed the population of the German states shrinking by as much as 30 percent because of the war. If those numbers were conservatively cut to 20 percent, that would still estimate the German population dropped from over 20 million to around 15 million over 30 years. Estimates indicate that both urban and rural areas suffered heavy population losses so there were very few safe havens for refugees. It should be no wonder that the Thirty Years' War remained the greatest disaster in German history until the twentieth century.

As a Matter of Fact

The inhumane actions of the mercenary armies during the Thirty Years' War caused great loss of life not only because of their destruction of farms and livestock but also because of their brutal enforcement of imperial laws and their lack of loyalty to the imperial cause. The poor showing of the mercenaries in this war contributed to the demise of mercenary armies and the rise of national armies.

The Least You Need to Know

- ◆ The Holy Roman Empire, theoretically, dealt with all secular issues concerning Christendom, while the pope handled all the religious issues. Realistically, the empire's influence remained mostly over the German states.

- ◆ The Holy Roman Emperor often quarreled with the pope over territorial issues, issues concerning limits on imperial power, and over pseudo-religious issues like investiture.

◆ The Habsburgs, by virtue of controlling Spain at its peak and the Holy Roman Empire at its peak, could be considered Europe's most powerful family during the sixteenth and early seventeenth centuries.

◆ The Thirty Years' War actually started when some Protestants threw three Catholics out of a castle window into a dungheap.

◆ The Thirty Years' War began as a war of religion and ended as an international war of politics involving German states, the Holy Roman Empire, Spain, France, Denmark, Sweden, and others.

◆ The Thirty Years' War resolved little with regard to religion, the original cause of the war, yet it cost Europe millions of lives. The Thirty Years' War effectively ended the Holy Roman Empire.

Am I in Charge? Absolutely!

In This Chapter

◆ The origins of absolutism

◆ The rise of the Sun King

◆ The English absolutists

◆ Civil war rocks England

◆ A revolution that was glorious?

The early years of the seventeenth century featured economic and agricultural events that shaped the politics of the seventeenth century, particularly in western Europe. The economies of many countries slowed. The harvests across Europe yielded less food than usual because of climatic changes and because of war-related damage to farmland. These changes left many people unhappy, hungry, and financially strapped. Politically, all classes jockeyed for position in western Europe. Peasants demanded rights, nobility demanded more power, and monarchs demanded that the peasants and nobles fall in line. The time was right for the rise of the absolutists.

Absolutism was a form of government, usually within a monarchy, in which the ruler exercised absolute power over virtually all facets of his or her kingdom. In other words, absolute monarchs controlled government and law, religion, economic policy, the military, and in some cases the culture of the country. In order to be an absolutist, the monarch needed to eliminate all competi-

Define Your Terms

Some historians prefer the term "administrative monarchy" to "absolute monarchy."

tion within the country: no courts to overrule his or her decisions, no armies to threaten stability, and no nobles powerful enough to successfully scheme against the crown. Absolutism served to streamline the governing of a nation and reduce the time it took to make and act on decisions. From the perspective of the ruler, absolutism was ideal in times of crisis, war, or revolution.

The absolute monarchs of the seventeenth century took a page out of the proverbial book written by the New Monarchs of the fifteenth century. The New Monarchs included such rulers as Henry VII of England; Louis XI, "the Spider King," of France; and even Ferdinand and Isabella of Spain. These New Monarchs centralized power, reduced the power of the nobility, and streamlined and revitalized the economy. Ferdinand and Isabella went a step further and took control of religion by chasing Jews and Muslims from Spain. The New Monarchs were Machiavellian and often strict, if not brutal, as was Louis XI.

Planting the Seeds of Absolutism

As the seventeenth century rolled around in France, the situation seemed bleak. The harvests were poor, the economic situation was terrible, and religious tensions still plagued the nation. Peasants throughout France were hungry and the nobility desperately wanted political stability. Simply put, France needed strong, creative leadership to restore order and develop new methods of governing and stimulating the economy.

France got a taste of that leadership with King Henry IV and his chief advisor; unfortunately, Henry's rule didn't last long enough. Soon after his passing, one of France's greatest minds found himself in a position of power from which he could move France forward and turn it into the dominant nation in Europe. But the man who masterminded the transformation of France wasn't a king but a cardinal. What this cardinal accomplished, though, had its beginnings during the reign of Henry IV.

Henry IV

King Henry IV took over following a dreadful series of religious wars that tore the country apart (see Chapter 7). In 1598, only nine years after he took the throne, Henry IV converted to Catholicism to placate the French Catholics and issued the

Edict of Nantes to allow the Huguenots to live in relative peace. Unlike so many French monarchs before him, Henry cared deeply for France and the French people. Henry also appointed a Protestant, Maximilien de Bethune, Duke of Sully (1560–1641), to be his chief minister. Henry could hardly have made a better choice.

In only a dozen years, Henry, who once promised "a chicken in every pot" for the people of France, turned the nation around and put France in a position to benefit from the strategic moves made by his successors. Had Henry not been murdered by a madman in 1610, there is no telling how much farther he could have taken France.

Sully and Richelieu

The Duke of Sully proved to be invaluable during the reign of Henry IV. Under Sully's leadership, France lowered the taxes for the French peasants. Traditionally, peasants were expected to bear the greatest tax burden in France because there had always been more peasants in France than any other demographic group. The percentage of a peasant's wages that were eaten up by taxes usually left that peasant in dire straits. To compensate for the drop in revenue, Sully created a fee for officers of the court to guarantee that the royal officials were able to pass the office down through their families. Sully also leased the collection of some taxes to tax collectors.

In one of his most brilliant and progressive moves, Sully helped finance the Company for Trade with the Indies, a company specializing in overseas trade. Sully saw the potential for generating endless revenues by overseas trade, as well as increasing revenues by making domestic trade quicker and easier. To bolster domestic trade and commerce, Sully began work on a national system of highways to speed up the transportation of goods. He also drained swamps, began construction of canals, and worked to prevent deforestation. Much of Henry's success as king must be attributed to Sully.

Would You Believe?

For all he did to improve France, Sully never won any popularity contests. Catholics disliked him because he was Protestant and Protestants disliked him because he remained loyal to Henry IV. Furthermore, contemporary accounts paint Sully as rude and stubborn. Sully's political career ended abruptly with the assassination of Henry IV.

Upon Henry's death, the boy-king Louis XIII (1601–1643) took the throne. Because Louis was too young to rule, his mother, Marie de' Medici, headed the government as queen-regent. She may have held the title, but Marie didn't do much; the real power lay with the nobles of the royal council. In 1628, though, everything changed with the appointment of Armand Jean du Plessis, Cardinal Richelieu (1585–1642) as the chief minister to the king. Richelieu had plotted against the former chief minister, La Vieuville, and, upon the arrest of La Vieuville, the king moved Richelieu into the vacant position.

Richelieu had two main goals for France and he set out immediately to accomplish each. Richelieu wanted to centralize power and he wanted to weaken the Habsburgs. Richelieu took power away from many of the nobles by creating new positions within the government called *intendants*. He divided France into 32 regions and placed *intendants* in each region to carry out royal orders, collect taxes, preside over judicial hearings, and recruit soldiers. The *intendants* were appointed by the king and were not allowed to serve where they had any family ties or financial interests; Richelieu insisted on this to prevent corruption and conflicts of interest. This system greatly weakened the nobility because the *intendants* performed many of the tasks previously performed by the nobility. As the nobility lost power, the king gained power.

Richelieu believed that a strong national government could only be achieved after local governments had the backing of Paris. Uprisings, violent protests, and riots had been common for years. Richelieu made it possible for local authorities to respond quickly and severely, with the full support of the French military. An example occurred at the Protestant stronghold of La Rochelle in the 1620s. In the mind of King Louis XIII, the Huguenots there had nearly established political and military independence and the city needed to be brought back in line. Richelieu led the siege of the city himself and won a decisive victory over Protestantism. He destroyed the city walls, dealt with city officials, then celebrated mass in the city. This strong show of force set an example for all of France to see; the national government would not tolerate insubordination of any kind, political or religious.

Would You Believe?

On one occasion, Richelieu learned of a conspiracy against the government led by a high-ranking and powerful duke. Without a second thought, he had the duke beheaded. Richelieu hoped to intimidate his enemies with his harsh example.

Richelieu's biggest domestic challenge probably was the financial situation. Richelieu's larger, more powerful central government and army cost more money than France had. The government was stronger than ever before, yet it still lacked the power to tax any way it wished. Much of the nobility remained exempt from taxation and many local economies still had the power to vote on taxation. While Richelieu managed to use local governments to help bolster the economy through revenue sharing, the national government still had not reached a state of absolutism.

As for foreign policy, Richelieu recognized the danger in having Spanish Habsburgs to the north and south of France and the Austrian Habsburgs controlling Germany to the east. His sole foreign policy goal was to weaken the Habsburgs. He did this by supporting the enemies of the Habsburgs, even though they were Protestant, in the Thirty Years' War (see Chapter 8). Richelieu even entered the war on the side of the Protestants. Through his unorthodox and often ruthless tactics, Richelieu succeeded in strengthening the French government, weakening the Habsburgs, and laying the foundation for real absolutism in France.

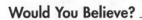

Would You Believe?

Richelieu justified his strict policies by claiming that God would allow certain actions by the state that would not otherwise be allowed by private citizens.

Mazarin

As Richelieu approached his final days, he convinced Louis XIII to name Jules Mazarin (1602–1661) as his next chief minister. The king took his advice. Mazarin, an Italian-turned-French-citizen, worked closely with Richelieu and knew his political philosophy well. Soon thereafter, Louis XIII died and a new boy king took the throne. Under Louis XIV (1638–1715), whose mother acted as queen-regent, Mazarin quickly moved into a position of authority. Mazarin worked to continue Richelieu's anti-Habsburg policy and his centralizing domestic policy.

Mazarin was successful in his foreign policy. He negotiated France's position in the Peace of Westphalia and in the Treaty of the Pyrenees. He successfully added territory to France and set an expansionist precedent his young king eventually would follow.

As for Mazarin's domestic policy, he tried to do things the way Richelieu did, but met with little domestic success. Mazarin failed to control the nobility. He also faced a backlash over rising taxes and a failing economy, especially after a period of peacetime. Ultimately, the French rebelled in civil wars known as the Fronde. The king and Mazarin prevailed, but not before Mazarin was chased from France twice. These uprisings, witnessed firsthand by Louis XIV, made an indelible impression on the young monarch.

Mazarin died in 1661 and thus the kingdom was turned over completely to Louis XIV. Historians have argued that Mazarin, perhaps because he was Italian, concerned himself more with foreign policy than with helping the people of France. Regardless, he helped pave the way for the reign of Louis XIV, the likes of which Europe had never seen.

The Sun King

Few men in history have been more suited to be king than Louis XIV. Under the tutelage of Mazarin, the young Louis received on-the-job training for a job he would do longer than any other monarch in European history; he ruled France from 1643 until 1715. Louis read diplomatic papers, learned geography, and watched those around him as they conducted affairs of state. Of all the lessons he learned while watching the administration of Mazarin, the one that had perhaps the greatest impact on his reign was that the nobility could not and should not be trusted.

Louis learned from Mazarin, who learned from Richelieu, the importance of being a grand and powerful monarch, and the role suited him well. Louis loved being the king. He basked in the grandeur and he craved the attention he received as courtiers competed for his time. Mazarin impressed upon the religious king that God placed monarchs on thrones and they were intended to be God's earthly rulers. Louis embraced that idea as well as the opportunity to further the Catholic cause. During his reign, Louis redefined the European monarchy and drew the blueprint for absolutism.

Would You Believe?

Louis XIV called himself the Sun King and he surrounded himself with statues of the Greek god of the sun, Apollo.

Becoming an Absolutist

Without a doubt, Richelieu and Mazarin helped mold Louis and his ideas about the monarchy. Richelieu believed that a strong nation needed a strong government with as much power as possible in the hands of those who govern from the capital. He believed in intimidating those who opposed the government. Richelieu believed in doing whatever was necessary to further the cause of the nation both at home and abroad.

Though he was unable to produce the same results, Mazarin passed the ideas along to Louis during his formative years. However, the effect of the Fronde on Louis can hardly be overstated. Louis witnessed the chaos up close and personal; a mob once broke into his bedroom and scared him out of his wits. Louis was convinced that a strong central government had to be his number-one goal. Rather than confronting the nobility and trying to subdue them, Louis decided to convince the nobility to work with him. In doing so, he could control the nobility without the nobility realizing that they were being controlled. Louis convinced the wealthy nobles on more than one occasion to support measures that benefited both the nobility and the monarchy. Eventually, Louis convinced the nobility of his grandeur and nobles would do anything simply to be in his presence.

Using Versailles

The amazing palace at Versailles went a long way toward achieving that end. Louis XIII began construction of a hunting lodge in a small town just a few miles outside Paris, which Louis XIV turned into one of the most expensive palaces ever conceived.

Louis' plan was to create a getaway where nobles and foreign dignitaries could be entertained. Furthermore, Louis wanted all who laid eyes on Versailles to be awed. He wanted foreign visitors to see Versailles and imagine the immense wealth France surely possessed. He wanted all visitors to be intimidated by his grandeur, his majesty, and his opulence.

He succeeded. Tens of thousands worked every year until Louis' death to turn the hunting lodge into the grandest chateau ever built. Louis devoted between 10 and 20 percent of his entire national budget to the construction of his palace. The grounds spanned 2,000 acres and 12 miles of roads inside 12 miles of enclosing walls. The 26 acres of rooftops covered 700 rooms and 67 staircases that were decorated by 6,000 paintings, 2,100 sculptures, and thousands more drawings and engravings. Mirrors, gold leaf, and the finest furniture anywhere adorned the entire palace. It is estimated that Versailles could host as many as several thousand guests along with a few thousand full-time staff. Louis used Versailles to impress and intimidate visitors and to magnify his image and that of France.

Would You Believe?

Louis XIII wasn't particularly fond of his wife, and hoped to use the lodge at Versailles as a retreat from her. Louis XIV "fell in love" with two of Mazarin's nieces. To protect one of them from the womanizing monarch, Mazarin sent her out of the country.

He also used Versailles to keep the nobility in check. Louis XIV required all of the uppermost nobles to spend at least part of the year at Versailles. Perhaps the nobles took exception to such a requirement at first, but it didn't take long for the nobility to consider it an honor just to be invited. Once at Versailles, the nobles found themselves in the lap of luxury and they certainly didn't mind the stay. The king threw lavish feasts and balls. The king put on plays and ballets, including some of his own work. It became quite the social event.

For those fortunate few, the king himself would allow them into his presence, even allow them in his bedchamber to watch him rise from bed or help him put on a coat. Louis, a master manipulator, convinced the nobility they were fortunate to be with him in his palace. Louis, however, had an ulterior motive. By requiring, or inviting, the nobles to stay at Versailles, he managed to have all his potential advocates and opponents in one place. He and his officers could keep close tabs on the nobles. Louis' agents often eavesdropped and intercepted correspondence just to be sure there were no plots against the king. It has been said that Louis "domesticated" the nobility. While that may be an overstatement, there is no doubt that Versailles proved an invaluable tool in keeping them in check.

One French Religion

Louis had always been taught that a king was God's ruler on earth. As such, Louis firmly believed that he had a duty to defend his faith. Though Henry IV showed remarkable leniency toward the Protestants, Louis wasn't prepared to do the same. He, like Richelieu and Louis XIII, believed there really was no room in France for more than one religion. Louis first sought a Protestant-like group of Catholics called Jansenists. Louis forced the Jansenists into hiding until after his death. Next, he turned his attentions toward the Huguenots. In 1658, Louis revoked the Edict of Nantes and stripped the Huguenots of all rights they had enjoyed previously. Louis closed the Calvinist churches, burned and banned their literature, and exiled any who refused to convert to Catholicism. In what turned out to be bad economically for France, thousands of hardworking Huguenots fled to other countries; with them they took a large tax base that France desperately needed.

> **Would You Believe?**
>
> One of the great mathematicians of European history, Blaise Pascal, was a well-known Jansenist.

Colbert and Mercantilism

Louis used the bureaucratic system of *intendants* just as his teacher and his teacher's teacher had done. He also placed great trust in particular ministers who helped him make important decisions. Perhaps the most influential of all his ministers was Jean-Baptiste Colbert (1619–1683). A former trainee under Mazarin, Colbert worked his way up to the position of minister of finance.

Under the leadership of Colbert, France adopted an economic policy of *mercantilism.* Although a mercantilist bureaucracy created an increase in the number of government officials necessary to keep the economy going, the benefits were huge. Colbert's strategy manifested itself most in overseas trade, colonization in places like Canada and the Mississippi Valley, and the creation of trading companies; in mercantilism, the profits from these all went to the state.

Define Your Terms

Mercantilism is an economic system in which all economic activity has the aim of making the national economy stronger.

To aid this endeavor, Colbert helped France expand its navy. Colbert also created industries and regulated the quality of the goods produced. Colbert encouraged the formation of guilds, or groups of craftsmen from the same profession, to aid the development of master craftsmen. The mercantilism encouraged by Colbert would have gone a long way toward making France prosperous had it not been for Louis' deficit spending on Versailles and on the military.

Louis on the Battlefield

For all of Louis' interest in art, music, and culture, few if any monarchs of his day had such an interest in the military. Louis poured obscene amounts of money into his military, and he got his money's worth. Louis created the largest and most formidable professional, standing army Europe had ever seen. With this army, he launched a campaign to expand his borders. Unfortunately for those within his borders, Louis taxed his people heavily. Furthermore, he diverted funds away from hunger relief and other benefits for the French people and diverted those funds to the military budget.

He began in 1667 and in 1668 and captured towns in the Spanish Netherlands. From 1672 until 1678, he fought to win a few more towns in the Spanish Netherlands. As Louis kept fighting and conquering, other European nations grew tired of his expansionist tendencies. Louis had already engaged the English, Dutch, Spanish, and the Holy Roman Empire. Undeterred by former alliances against him, Louis continued to expand, this time eastward into German territory as far as Strasbourg. Fed up, a coalition of the Dutch, the Spanish, the English, the Swedes, the Austrian emperor, and even some German princes finally put a stop to Louis and his army. The fighting ceased with the 1697 Peace of Rijswijk. Louis returned all the land he had taken over the past 20 years, with the exception of Strasbourg.

War suited Louis and his absolutist government. Though the military expenditures wracked the economy, Louis used the military to flex muscles at home and not just abroad. Taxes, conscription, and displays of military prowess all were methods of controlling those around him. Despite his magnificent army and his military expenditures, Louis had affected the life of virtually every Frenchman through the military. The French paid heavy taxes, fed soldiers, and gave their lives—only to lose most of the lands that Louis wagered so much to conquer.

Continental Quotes

"Why do you weep? Did you think I was immortal?"
—King Louis XIV of France, reportedly spoken on his deathbed.

Would You Believe?

A major patron of the arts, Louis XIV used his coffers to support artists and playwrights and to finance academies for art, music, dance, and even architecture.

"L'etat, c'est moi"

The seventeenth century has been called the Golden Age of France as well as the Age of Louis XIV. Louis XIV defined an era, a nation, and a culture. Both during his rule and after, the man Louis XIV was synonymous with France the nation. Louis once remarked, "L'etat c'est moi," or "I am the state." What he meant was that he was the embodiment of France and vice versa. Louis didn't just rule France—Louis XIV *was* France, a phenomenon attributed partly to his greatness as a king and partly to his longevity.

By controlling nearly every aspect of France, Louis XIV determined how the world saw France and how the French saw France. He was the trendsetter in art, music, fashion, and French culture. He redefined the monarchy; Louis was the seminal French monarch. He redefined the modern military; the French army was Louis' army. Though he bankrupted the country, Louis left such a legacy that seventeenth-century France is defined by Louis XIV.

Absolutism in England

Absolutism in France during the seventeenth century grew out of a need for strength and order from the government, and survived into the eighteenth century. In England, just across the English Channel, absolutism lacked the same intensity and longevity.

Some historians argue that the English monarchs of the seventeenth century were not absolutists at all because they never fully controlled one of their major competitors, Parliament, and their attempts to establish absolute monarchies resulted in epic battles with Parliament. Nevertheless, several monarchs certainly *wanted* to be absolutists; furthermore, the example of English absolutism gave way eventually to a model known as constitutionalism.

The English monarchs, probably more than any other absolutists, used the doctrine of the divine right of kings to justify their attempts at absolutist rule. According to the doctrine of the divine right of kings, God's will placed the monarch on the throne. Therefore, questioning the legitimacy or the authority of the king equated to questioning God. The desires of the people were irrelevant, and they had no right to rise up against a poor ruler.

King James

Queen Elizabeth chose as her successor James Stuart, her cousin, who had long been King James VI of Scotland and would become King James I of England (1566–1625). Unlike his cousin, James probably wasn't the best person for the job at the time.

The English weren't too fond of the Scots, and James did nothing to help matters. Once when his advisors asked him to wave to a crowd, King James threatened to drop his pants instead, so they could, well .... To make matters worse, the new king subscribed to the doctrine of the divine right of kings. He even wrote an essay and lectured Parliament about the subject. James wrote, "The state of monarchy is the supremest thing on earth" and kings "sit upon God's throne." He went on to argue, "as to dispute what God may do is blasphemy, so is it sedition … to dispute what a king may do."

James spent vast amounts of money on his court and on his favorites. He needed more money, but the Parliament, particularly the House of Commons, stood in his way. The members of Parliament didn't mind paying more taxes, but they demanded a say in how the revenue was to be spent. The king and the Parliament butted heads over and over again. James may have wanted to rule absolutely, but the Parliament had other ideas.

Religion also plagued the reign of James I. Though England had been Protestant for some time, many Protestants believed the Anglican Church still had too much lingering Catholicism. Many of the Protestants in England were Calvinists; the most radical were known as Puritans. The Puritans wanted to get rid of

Would You Believe?

The King James Bible, first published in 1611, was commissioned by James I to settle a number of disputes and to make sure the Bible supported the Church of England. The majority of James's translation is identical to Tyndale's translation.

several things in the Anglican Church, including bishops. James and his son, Charles, were Protestant, but their refusal to get rid of bishops made them seem loyal to Catholicism. Many people believed the nation was sliding down the slippery slope toward Catholicism again; this would create huge problems later in the century.

Charles I and the English Civil War

James's son, Charles I (1600–1649), followed as King of England. James wasn't the kindest man who ever sat on the throne, but Charles was worse. His contemporaries considered him rude and untrustworthy. Charles had a difficult time getting along with most everyone, especially the Parliament. Complicating Charles's early years as king was a Parliament that had become very defensive during the years of James I. In the first years of Charles's rule, he wanted to go to war with Spain to help his brother-in-law, Frederick V of the Palatinate, regain his lands in the Thirty Years' War.

Parliament didn't like the idea of raising taxes for Charles's vendetta, so in 1628 they made Charles agree to ask for their permission to levy taxes each year. Seeing a chance to further his absolutist intentions, Charles decided to rule without calling Parliament at all the next year, or the next, or the next. Charles didn't call Parliament into session, or summon the representatives to meet together, again until 1640. In the meantime, Charles did things like fine people for not attending his coronation and collect ship money, a tax levied against coastal counties during wartime to help defend the English coast; Charles, though, required it of all counties and during peacetime.

Religion once again aggravated an already tense situation. Puritans had been lobbying for changes in the Anglican Church. Charles, married to a French Catholic, had the Archbishop of Canterbury make Anglican services more and more Catholic. Those Puritans who opposed these measures were tried before the notorious court called the Star Chamber and then tortured. The archbishop tried to enforce his new ideas in Scotland, but the Scots not only rebelled but also invaded the northern part of England. Charles, financially out of options and desperate to fight a war against the Scots, called Parliament in 1640 in hopes of finding the necessary funds. What Charles got, though, was not exactly what he had in mind.

Parliament saw Charles as an absolutist on the rise and believed he needed to be held in check. Parliament removed the Archbishop of Canterbury, shut down the Star Chamber, repealed a number of taxes, and passed a provision called the Triennial Act that guaranteed a session of Parliament at least every three years. Fed up with the insubordination, Charles and an armed force loyal to him stormed Parliament in

1642 to arrest the leaders of the movement against him. When that plan failed, Charles regrouped and built an army.

Charles and his army, called the Cavaliers, found support for the crown in the northern and western parts of the kingdom. The Parliamentary forces, called the Roundheads, found support in the southeast. People of England picked sides and civil war erupted in 1642. The Parliamentary army consisted almost entirely of Puritans, but they were divided over religious concerns. The Puritans finally put their quarrels aside and reorganized under a member of the House of Commons named Oliver Cromwell (1599–1658).

Cromwell led his New Model Army to a decisive victory over the Royalists in 1645 and the king surrendered the following year. The war was not over, though. The Puritans continued fighting with other sects and finally ran all the Presbyterians out of Parliament, leaving what became known as the "Rump Parliament." This Rump Parliament tried Charles I and sentenced him to death by beheading. After the execution of the king in 1649, the Rump Parliament abolished the monarchy altogether, disbanded the House of Lords, and established a Puritan commonwealth under the leadership of Oliver Cromwell.

Would You Believe?

The execution of the king, known as regicide, was taken far more seriously than the execution of common criminals. After the beheading, Charles was not declared a traitor and Cromwell allowed Charles's head to be reattached for the sake of Charles's family.

Cromwell and the Protectorate

Although Cromwell never desired to be a king, he turned out to be far more absolutist in nature than either of the two absolutist kings before him. He proved to be a good military leader, but he was harsh, strict, pious, and often brutal. He had no tolerance for opposition to his ideas. While the government under Cromwell was called a commonwealth, or a republican form of government, the resulting government was a military dictatorship called "The Protectorate." Power should have been in the hands of Parliament, but Cromwell controlled the army so he held the power.

In 1653, the Instrument of Government, a codified constitution prepared by the army, called for regular sessions of Parliament and gave Parliament alone the power to tax. Cromwell tore up the document and placed England under martial law, or rule by the military. Cromwell censored the press and used spies to intercept mail. Though many in England initially welcomed Cromwell because he restored order, England grew tired of the self-proclaimed Lord Protector. Cromwell even disbanded Parliament in 1653 when it tried to take away his army.

As for religion, Cromwell despised Catholicism, so much that he saw it as seditious, but he proved to be surprisingly tolerant toward Jews whom he allowed to return to England for the first time in hundreds of years. He treated Catholics mercilessly as evidenced by his inhumane massacre of Irish Catholics in Ireland in 1649 shortly after coming to power. To this day the Irish refer to the resentment of the English as "the curse of Cromwell."

Economically, Cromwell and Parliament, before he disbanded it, adopted a mercantilist philosophy similar to that of Colbert. The Navigation Act of 1651, which had as its goal the undermining of the rival Dutch fleet of trading ships, required that all English goods be carried only by English ships. When that strategy didn't ruin the Dutch, Cromwell resorted to a naval war against them. When Cromwell died in 1658, of malaria, oddly, rather than on the battlefield, the fear of chaos spread through England. However, not many mourned Cromwell's death. Most of England was ready to have a king again and to give up the dream of having an entire nation of pious Puritans.

After Cromwell died, his son Richard Cromwell (1626-1712) ruled as Lord Protector for roughly eight months. Richard's two older brothers had died before their father so Richard inherited the title and position, which he abdicated without a fight when the Rump Parliament insisted he do so. Richard's opposition often referred to him as Tumbledown Dick.

As a Matter of Fact

Three years after Cromwell died, his body was exhumed for a bizarre practice known as posthumous execution. On the twelfth anniversary of the execution of Charles I, Cromwell's dead body was hung from the gallows, then beheaded. Cromwell's head was then displayed for some 20 years before it fell off the pole on which it was displayed. After remaining in private ownership for centuries, scientists in the 1930s determined that the head purported to be Cromwell's was, in fact, Cromwell's. When the owner died, the head was given to Sidney Sussex College, Cambridge, where it was buried in 1960.

The Restoration

In the Restoration of 1660, a newly elected and very much Anglican Parliament invited the exiled son of King Charles I to return as king. Parliament, both houses, returned to its former state. The Anglican Church was reaffirmed, as were the courts and the agents of local government. Luckily for Parliament, Charles II (1630–1685) proved to be relatively easy to get along with. Charles had no intentions of hunting heretics or engaging in theological debates. Likewise, he intended to get along with Parliament rather than fight with them. To encourage cooperation between the king and Parliament, Charles created a council of five members who were to act as his advisors; this council is the predecessor of the modern cabinet in government.

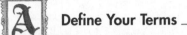

Define Your Terms

The period of time between 1649 and 1660 is known as the **Interregnum,** or time between kings.

The Anglican Parliament passed a number of laws, including the Test Act of 1763, that required Englishmen to receive the Eucharist of the Anglican Church in order to vote or hold office. While these laws seldom were enforced, they showed the Parliament's sincerity about returning England to the Anglican Church and keeping diversity out of England. This determination to be Anglican led to major upheaval near the end of Charles's reign.

Define Your Terms

Charles's council was known as the **Cabal.** Its name came from the initials of its members: Clifford, Arlington, Buckingham, Ashley-Cooper, and Lauderdale).

The Death of English Absolutism

James I and Charles I really wanted to be absolutists, and with Cromwell the title certainly seemed to fit. However, absolutism, to whatever extent it did actually exist in England, faced extinction. Not all Englishmen were ready to see absolutism go, though. Thomas Hobbes (1588–1679) witnessed the horrors of the English Civil War, albeit from France, and became convinced that an absolute government was necessary.

Hobbes didn't care if absolute power rested with king or Parliament, but he argued that absolutism was necessary to control man, who is driven by self-preservation. Man, he argued, would resort to greed, corruption, and worse in a competitive environment not dominated by authority. An absolute government offered man a sense of security so that he would not be forced to resort to such violent and barbaric behavior. Unfortunately for Hobbes, his ideas displeased everyone and absolutism never appeared in England again.

The Glorious Revolution

Charles did get along with Parliament but he believed his income wasn't enough to run the country. In a dangerous move, Charles made a secret deal with Louis XIV of France. In exchange for slowly converting himself and England back to Catholicism, Charles would receive a huge annual stipend from France. News of the treaty leaked and panic struck England. Charles's lack of any legitimate heirs complicated matters because the English feared his Catholic brother would take the throne and restore Catholicism to England. Parliament began work on legislation that would not allow the throne to pass to a Catholic but Charles dissolved Parliament before the law passed.

Would You Believe?

Royalists disliked Hobbes because he denounced divine right and Parliamentarians disliked him because they didn't believe anyone, not even Parliament, should have limitless power.

England's worst fears were realized when James II (1633–1701) became king in 1685 and appointed Catholic officials to all sorts of positions in direct defiance of the Test Act. James's actions were heard in court—but by judges he had appointed. James's actions were upheld. James then granted religious freedom to anyone and everyone. It seemed as though absolutism might be making a comeback in England.

When the wife of James II had a son, the possibility of a new Catholic dynasty in England seemed unavoidable. A number of prominent Englishmen extended an invitation to James's daughter, Mary, and her husband, Prince William of Orange, both of whom were Protestant. Reportedly, a group of seven English nobles, known as the Immortal Seven, sent William an invitation to depose James, an invitation that may have even been in code. James II realized that he was about to be replaced at least and possibly even executed. Fearing for their lives, James II and his family fled to France. The following year, in 1689, William and Mary were crowned King and Queen of England.

The events leading up to the coronation are remembered as the Glorious Revolution. The events were glorious in two ways. First, the flight of James II marked the death of both absolutism and the idea of divine right of kings in England. Second, the "revolution" replaced one king with another with no bloodshed.

The English philosopher John Locke (1632–1704) argued for such a turn of events. He believed that all men had natural rights—the right to life, liberty, and property. He believed that it was the duty of the government to protect those rights. When a government failed to do so, according to Locke, the people had a right to rebel against the tyranny.

Would You Believe?

Locke's ideas were fundamental in the creation of the fledgling government of the United States.

Limits on the Crown

The way William and Mary became regents held great importance for England and for the development of the English system of government thereafter. Parliament offered them the crown, and William and Mary accepted the terms and conditions established by Parliament. There was no fine print. William and Mary knew that the rules applied not to them but the crown. They understood that they were acknowledging the supremacy of Parliament, and essentially the English people, over the crown. In other words, the monarchs from this point forward ruled only with the consent of the governed.

Parliament put in place a number of safeguards against future tyranny, largely in reaction to the Stuart kings (James I, Charles I, Charles II, and James II) and Cromwell. Laws were to be made in Parliament and were not to be undone by the monarch. Parliament would convene every three years and the crown could not meddle in Parliamentary affairs. Monarchs could not threaten judges in order to get favorable rulings. All monarchs were to be Protestant, and nonmainstream Protestants were granted some religious freedoms.

England had, in one century, gone from a monarchy in which the king and Parliament were always at odds to a government that started to look more and more like a constitutional monarchy. In other words, by the end of the seventeenth century, the law reigned supreme over the monarchy rather than the monarch ruling above the law.

The Least You Need to Know

◆ Absolutism is a form of government in which the ruler, usually a monarch, exercises control over most areas of the government and eliminates or controls any institutions that might compete with him for power.

- The best example of absolutism was France's Louis XIV. Cardinal Richelieu and Jules Mazarin laid the foundations of French absolutism.

- Louis XIV dominated France like no other monarch ever had. He defined French politics, religion, and culture for the second half of the seventeenth and early eighteenth centuries.

- Absolutism in England never developed as fully as it did in the French model. The Stuart kings fought against Parliament for control and against Puritans who sought to purify the Anglican Church of any remaining Catholic elements.

- During the *Interregnum*, the victor of the English Civil War, military dictator Oliver Cromwell, kept England in a state of martial law. He showed no mercy to Catholics, especially those in Ireland.

- The Glorious Revolution in England put the nail in the coffin of absolutism in England and paved the way for constitutional monarchy.

Chapter 10

The Eastern Absolutists

In This Chapter

- Austria on the rebound
- Prussia becomes a powerhouse
- So many Fredericks
- Russia comes into its own
- For Pete's sake
- The overblown art of the Baroque

After about 1300, and particularly after the onset of the Black Death, history took a much different course in eastern Europe than it did in western Europe. Things didn't go so well for peasants in eastern Europe.

The Plight of the Peasants

In western Europe, peasant conditions generally improved (see Chapter 1) as the centuries passed. A shortage of labor after the plague meant better economic conditions, and the common people slowly earned more and more rights and freedoms. Though the peasants still were at the bottom of the food chain, serfdom, that state of being legally bound to one's lord similar to the way a slave might have been, declined in western Europe and by the sixteenth century most peasants were free.

During roughly the same period, landlords in eastern Europe were using their political power to clamp down. They passed laws that restricted peasant movement and took away what little land the peasants owned and worked. Furthermore, the lords increased the feudal obligations of the peasants. Peasants were reduced to forced laborers who often worked the majority of the week with little or no compensation; the yield from the land went almost entirely to the lord to meet the peasants' feudal obligations. While economic and agricultural factors surely played some part, historians point to the political factor as the greatest reason for the rise of serfdom in eastern Europe. That political factor in eastern Europe was that the common people had no representation like the commoners of England with the Parliament and France with the Estates General, for example. After all, the same economic and agricultural situation in western Europe led to the opposite result for the peasants.

Would You Believe?

Runaway peasants were to be returned to their lords in eastern Europe. Often a runaway had his ear nailed to a post and was then given a knife to free himself; runaways probably didn't try to leave a second time.

The course of history proved different for the monarchy in the east and west, too. During the centuries after the Middle Ages in western Europe, monarchies grew powerful, often at the expense of the nobility. In eastern Europe, though, the landed nobility once again came out on top. There occurred so much political intrigue, war, and so many disputes over succession that those who hoped to be monarchs frequently had to bribe and barter with the nobility to win their support. Basically, these compromises reduced eastern monarchs to being "first among equals" rather than superior to the nobility. Finally, after about 1600, strong monarchs emerged in eastern Europe, monarchs who helped lay the foundation for eastern absolutism. The greatest examples of such rulers rose in Austria, Prussia, and Russia.

Austria After the War

The Thirty Years' War left Germany physically and emotionally exhausted, facing a devastated economy and a depleted population. Politically, there existed no real unity because Germany existed as a region of more than 300 independent principalities that would not unite until the nineteenth century. The war decimated the Holy Roman Empire and left it virtually powerless over the German states. As emperors, the

Habsburgs were out of luck; all the German-speaking provinces, including those hereditarily belonging to the Habsburgs, were in bad shape.

One of the German-speaking provinces, Austria, held by the Habsburgs, would eventually vie for superiority in eastern Europe. Austria represented the heart of Habsburg power; from here the Habsburgs sought to centralize and expand their power after the dust settled from the war. Austria faced challenges, threats from the Turks and competition from Prussia, but it carved out a niche in the European political and military landscape that remained until the twentieth century.

More Serfs and Fewer Protestants

The first challenge for the Habsburgs after the Thirty Years' War involved shifting gears. The Habsburgs no longer held imperial power but they did hold land in eastern Europe. Ferdinand III (1608–1657) worked to centralize power in Austria, Bohemia, Styria, Moravia, parts of Croatia, and the region of the Tyrol.

Austria belonged to the Habsburgs already. Bohemia, as a result of the war, owed much allegiance to the Habsburgs. The Czechs who lived in Bohemia prior to the war were mostly Protestant. When the Protestants rebelled early in the 1600s, the Catholic and imperial forces crushed them. The emperor, who still had power then, took vast holdings from the Protestant nobility and turned the land over to Catholic nobles. In return, the nobles owed loyalty to Ferdinand and to the Habsburgs. Furthermore, the virtual elimination of Protestantism helped create a sense of religious unity; the opportunity for a split over religion had been removed. After the war, the Bohemian nobles were mostly foreign and very few were Bohemian. The Habsburgs killed two birds with one stone as they permanently secured the nobles' loyalty and tightened the grip on Bohemia. The growing ranks of serfdom unwittingly strengthened the bond between nobles and Habsburgs. The serfs were made to work more for less compensation and the tax burden fell on the peasants; both made the nobles very happy and very loyal. Bohemia belonged to the Austrian Habsburgs.

Habsburgs After the War

Ferdinand III formed a standing army to keep domestic trouble to a minimum; with an army, Ferdinand III had no challenges from within his own borders. The Habsburgs prepared for the next challenge, moving eastward into Hungary, which the Turks had controlled for centuries. The Islamic Ottoman Empire had competed with the Habsburgs of Austria time and again; the Ottoman Turks nearly captured Vienna in the sixteenth century.

In the late 1600s, the Turks decided to take one last stab at the Habsburgs. With financial support from the Hungarian Protestants, who enjoyed Muslim tolerance, and from the Habsburgs' archenemy, Louis XIV, the Ottomans set their sights on Austria. They marched on Vienna in 1683 and for two months laid siege to the city. Just as the city was prepared to capitulate, reinforcements arrived and forced the Turks to retreat. As the Habsburg and allied troops battled the Turks over the following years, the Habsburgs conquered most of Hungary and Transylvania.

The Austrian holdings were growing into an Austrian Empire. The Habsburg monarch controlled three main areas that included Austria, Bohemia, and Hungary. To be sure, though, the lands of the Habsburgs were in no sense a nation. The three areas had different histories, different languages, different legal systems, and different cultures. As the Habsburgs added land, they attempted to institute a somewhat absolutist government. For example, in Hungary as in Bohemia, the Habsburgs attempted to wipe out Protestantism and promote Catholicism. This resulted in a number of revolts by the Hungarian nobles who wanted not only religious tolerance but also political freedom from the Habsburgs. Habsburg ruler Charles VI (1685–1740) ultimately compromised with Hungary. Hungarian nobles received some privileges in return for their acceptance of Habsburg rule. Tied up with affairs elsewhere in Europe, Charles had no choice.

The War on Louis

By the eighteenth century, the troublesome Louis XIV of France had been gobbling up land and upsetting the rest of Europe for years. When the king of Spain died and left the throne to the grandson of Louis XIV, the rest of Europe couldn't stomach the idea of Louis basically inheriting Spain and all of its holdings. Everyone knew who would call all the shots if Louis' grandson were on the throne in Spain, and Europe found itself in the War of the Spanish Succession.

For a dozen years, the Grand Alliance of the Austrians, Prussians, Dutch, and English fought Louis. When the nations finally signed the Peace of Utrecht in 1713, Louis' grandson got the throne but had to agree not to unite the two nations under one crown. Furthermore, Louis gave away French holdings such as Newfoundland and Nova Scotia to the English, as well as the Spanish Netherlands to Austria. The timing turned out to be pretty good for Austria. By 1715, Austria held the former Spanish Netherlands, Austria, Silesia, and Bohemia, along with Sardinia and Naples in Italy.

The Pragmatic Sanction

The Habsburgs held the reins of a nice-size and growing empire, but they knew the whole thing could fall apart at any time even under their pseudo-absolutist rule. They had seen what happened elsewhere—in Spain, for example—when succession problems threatened to destroy generations of political efforts. Charles VI took the initiative to solve this problem by issuing the Pragmatic Sanction in 1713.

The Pragmatic Sanction declared that the Habsburg lands were never to be split up but rather passed to the next heir completely intact. Charles, the last of the male Habsburgs, even included a provision that allowed for a female to become heir to Habsburg holdings if necessary. Unfortunately for Charles, who spent three decades trying to sell the Pragmatic Sanction to everyone else, few others shared his enthusiasm for the idea.

Prussia (with a P!)

Located on the Baltic just northeast of Poland lay Prussia (with a P that *is* pronounced). Just west of Poland lay Brandenburg. In the days of the Holy Roman Empire, electors of the same family governed the two provinces, even though they were not geographically connected. As the Thirty Years' War raged in Europe, Brandenburg and Prussia fell victim to the same devastation and destruction as other German states. The population of both states declined and agriculture struggled to feed those who survived. The governing bodies, known as estates, in Brandenburg and Prussia as well as in other states suffered huge losses in power and numbers because of the war, opening the door for an opportunistic and ambitious young leader to take the fate of these two lands into his own hands.

The Hohenzollerns

The Hohenzollern family ruled as first among equals in both Brandenburg and Prussia at the time of the Thirty Years' War. The Brandenburg Hohenzollerns were electors of the Holy Roman Empire while the Prussians were just nobles. When the Prussian Hohenzollerns went by the wayside in 1618, the Brandenburg Hohenzollerns inherited Prussia. For just over 20 years, Brandenburg and Prussia, along with some other scattered German holdings inherited about the same time as Prussia, suffered through the war. Because of the war, the estates rarely met, though they did theoretically retain some power.

In 1640, Frederick William (1620–1688) became the elector of Brandenburg. Frederick decided to stop being the whipping boy of Germany and create a powerful state by uniting his holdings under one central government. Standing in his way were the estates. The estates of Brandenburg and Prussia consisted of *junkers*, who were the only

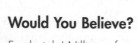

Define Your Terms

The **junkers** were landowning nobility in Prussia.

ones allowed to levy taxes. The junkers, especially after the war, resisted Frederick William's efforts to unite the states and exert his control. After 20 years of back and forth between the estates and Frederick William, the estates gave in, first in Brandenburg and then in Prussia. Frederick William eventually won power over the estates.

Fredericks, Fredericks Everywhere

Using the same technique Ferdinand III used in Austria after the war, the Great Elector built a standing army to maintain control over his three holdings. To pay for the army, the Great Elector needed to raise taxes. Using the threat of his military, he forced the estates to approve his taxes, then used his military to collect the taxes and

Would You Believe?

Frederick William, formerly known as the elector of Brandenburg, adopted for himself a name more becoming of an up-and-coming leader: Frederick William the Great Elector.

punish those who didn't pay. That confrontation marked the beginning of the end for the estates. With the estates no longer a problem, Frederick William the Great Elector raised taxes again and again. The income under the Great Elector tripled and the army grew to nearly 10 times its original size. Frederick William created a military state in which he controlled the military and the finances. To keep the nobles from revolting against him, the Great Elector kept the tax burden with everyone but the landed nobility.

The Great Elector's successor, another guy named Frederick, proved to be less interested in the military. Elector Frederick III "the Ostentatious" (1688–1713) was an artsy ruler interested more in copying Louis XIV than expanding his borders; he took the name Frederick I of Prussia upon becoming King of Prussia. The Ostentatious succeeded in building a lavish palace and patronizing the arts. As a result, the Prussian state was in for a rude awakening when Frederick William I (1688–1740) took over in 1713.

Arguably the greatest of the Hohenzollerns, Frederick William I "the Soldiers' King" returned the Prussian state to one dominated by the military. The Soldiers' King poured money into the military but he took a special interest in the way the army was put together. He sent his recruiters into all the cities, towns, and villages of his lands looking for tall boys and young men to be a part of the Prussian army. Frederick believed that tall soldiers possessed special qualities that other soldiers didn't. He even created a regiment called the Grenadiers composed of giants, or soldiers who stood at least six feet tall.

Frederick's obsession not just with soldiers but also with the military led to the development of one of the finest militaries in all of Europe. He took an army of less than 40,000 and grew it to more than 80,000, making Prussia's one of the largest in Europe. Frederick actually had a hand in training his military. He dressed in a military uniform and personally drilled his troops. A stickler for detail, Frederick brutally punished those who broke rank or otherwise made mistakes. His absolute control over the military carried over into his politics.

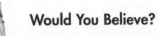

Would You Believe? ___

Frederick William "the Soldiers' King" had a deranged fascination with and weakness for tall, uniformed soldiers. He confided that beautiful young girls had nothing on tall soldiers. Interestingly, he remained completely faithful to his wife.

The military has historically offered commoners a chance at social mobility. Frederick applied that principle to civil service during his reign and allowed numerous common Prussians to work their way to up prominent positions in his administration. The junkers resented the changes brought by Frederick, but Frederick had a solution. Rather than destroying the junkers, Frederick enlisted them and gave them command of his troops. The junkers for the most part enjoyed the opportunity to control the peasants in both the army and in civilian life.

Like the disciplined army he created and ruled with an iron fist, Frederick's government proved efficient, effective, and free from corruption. Even the Prussian society grew to be highly structured and militaristic. He ruled with no major backlashes against him from within his government. The Prussian state, the military, and spirit reminded many of the militaristic Sparta.

Would You Believe? ___

Perhaps the most militaristic of all his contemporaries, the Soldiers' King kept his mighty Prussian state at peace during most of his years as the leader of Prussia.

Russia on the Rise

A great state once existed in Russia, a state centered on the capital of Kiev. Not exactly European and not exactly Asian, Russia spanned immense territory and included a people known as the Slavs. The name Slavs came from an ancient word meaning "slave."

In the thirteenth century, the great Golden Horde, or the armies of the Mongols, conquered all of China, then Hungary, then Russia. Once the Russians grew strong enough and the Mongols weak enough, the Russians withdrew their loyalties and created their own state. The Russians, though independent, remained geographically isolated from the rest of Europe and never advanced at the rate of other European nations. Finally, in the seventeenth and eighteenth centuries, the Russians made strides to catch up.

No More Mongol Yoke

While the Mongols frequently destroyed entire cities along with the people who lived there, they also left many cities. The Mongols then used local princes to collect taxes. The Mongols were too busy sacking other places to hang around and collect tributes. Each year the local princes that the Mongols allowed to stay in power paid tribute and gave slaves to the Mongols. Those who tried to rebel against the Mongols soon suffered their wrath. As long as the prince continued to pay, the Mongols let him stay. This unpleasant arrangement has been called the Mongol Yoke.

Beginning in the thirteenth century, the great prince in Moscow took the initiative to put down popular uprisings so the Mongols didn't have to, and grew powerful and wealthy under the so-called Mongol Yoke. The most significant of these early princes in Moscow grew enormously wealthy, so much so that his nickname was Ivan Moneybags. Ivan I (1288–1340) put down a rival's uprising and reaped great rewards from the Mongols. Over the next century, the Prince of Moscow became a powerful, hereditary position. By the time of Ivan III (1440–1505), Moscow not only collected taxes from but also controlled all of the Russian lands. Though still technically under Mongol control, the prince of Moscow had absolute control over all the major cities of Russia and the Slavic peoples. As Ivan III conquered land, he kept half and gave half to his *service nobility*. Because there was nowhere for the nobility to turn for help, they were forced to do as Ivan said. Ivan eventually grew wealthy and

Define Your Terms

Nobles who were granted land and titles on the condition that they serve in the army were called **service nobility**.

powerful enough to renounce his loyalties to the Mongols and ceased payments. The Mongols had spread themselves too thin throughout their holdings and lacked the military might to challenge Ivan, who began calling himself Ivan the Great. Russia had officially rid themselves of the Mongol Yoke.

Hail Czar

The position of the Prince of Moscow had gained so much power that Ivan the Great began to see himself as the same kind of all-powerful ruler as the Roman Caesars, hence the title *czar* (also frequently spelled *tsar*) for Russian rulers. In a sense, Ivan claimed the divine right of kings as justification for his power. Furthermore, because the leaders of the Eastern Orthodox Church in Russia took up residence in Moscow, the Orthodox clergy began to speak of Moscow as the "third Rome"; Constantinople, capital of the Byzantine Empire of old and birthplace of Eastern Orthodoxy, was thought of as the second Rome. Ivan even married the daughter of the last of the Byzantine emperors. The Russians developed a superiority complex and looked at the Eastern Orthodox Church as the only true church. All others in Europe were heretical. All that was left for the czars of Russia was to create an empire that rivaled that of Rome.

Define Your Terms

An Orthodox clergyman remarked after the Muslim sack of Constantinople, "Two Romes have fallen, but the third stands, and a fourth there will not be."

Was Ivan Really Terrible?

The centuries-long struggle for power and for land by Russian princes culminated in Ivan IV (1530–1584). In 1533, at the age of 3, he became Prince of Moscow and then, in 1547, Czar of All Russians. Not long after his ascension he launched attacks on the fading Mongol empire in the east and on lands to the west.

To say that the mentally unstable Ivan ruled as an absolutist would be an understatement. Ivan used terror, torture, and the threat of execution to enforce his will in every part of Russia. Ivan really flipped when his wife, Anastasia, died. He had already been struggling to subdue the *boyars*, those nobles who traditionally inherited lands and titles. Being the paranoid psychotic he was, Ivan blamed them for Anastasia's death. Ivan turned on the boyars in a horrifying display. Ivan used a secret police force called Oprichniks, men in black clothes riding black horses, to arrest and execute the boyars, take their lands, and terrorize their families.

Ivan forced the nobles to serve in the military to keep their titles. He forced the peasants to serve in the military to keep their lives; the peasants who didn't serve were bound to the land by serfdom. Ivan took over trade and commerce so that all craftsmen, artisans, and businessmen essentially worked for the czar. He practically enslaved all of Russia and no one dared challenge his authority. The people's fears were justified: Ivan the Terrible once sent his thugs to execute as many as 50,000 in the city of Novgorod.

As a Matter of Fact

Some peasants fled into the frontier wilderness to escape the reaches of Ivan's police forces. These outlaws, who joined other warriorlike peoples in the wilderness, became known as Cossacks. The Cossacks made their living, and their reputation, by pillaging lands held by the Ottomans and land held by the vassals of the Ottomans including Russian lands. An Ottoman official once informed the Grand Duke of Russia that the Cossacks would not respond to Ottoman threats because "The Cossacks do not swear allegiance to me, and they live as they themselves please." The Cossacks eventually played a large role in the expansion of Russia north into Siberia and south into the Caucasus.

To Modernize or to Westernize? That Is the Question

When Ivan died in 1584, perhaps by poisoning, Russia faced hard times known as the "Time of Troubles." Family members of the dead Ivan warred and intrigued amongst themselves in hopes of becoming czar. Finally, in 1613, Michael Romanov, grand-nephew of Ivan, became czar. The next 70 years, though, were filled with social, political, and religious instability. The nobles worked to take back some of their lost powers and further oppressed the peasants. Scandal rocked the Eastern Orthodox Church as reformers targeted corruption. A rebel named Stenka Razin led a Cossack rebellion that threatened to overthrow the Russian government.

Things looked bleak in 1689 when Peter took over as czar. Not only was Russia being torn apart by internal strife, it also lagged behind the rest of Europe in many areas. Peter had quite a job ahead of him.

Peter the Great

Peter the Great (1672–1725) made strengthening the Russian military his primary goal, so he could continue the expansionism of his predecessors and keep the rowdy peasants in check. Peter inherited an army that paled in comparison to some of the other European armies of his day. The Russian army was not a full-time professional standing army like the army of Prussia or France, and it relied heavily on the service nobility. In his early days, Peter didn't do much with his obsolete army. He watched from the sidelines more than he participated. Then Peter became interested in modern weapons and military strategy and decided he needed to upgrade his military.

Historians like to debate whether Peter the Great upgraded his military, and eventually his country, in order to *modernize* or in order to *westernize*. On a year-and-a-half tour of western Europe, disguised as a common Russian and not dressed as czar, Peter found many ideas he later used in Russia. He visited the courts in the capital cities and the schools and workshops of the leading academic cities. In truth, Peter wanted to become more modern, especially in the field of military science, and used the western example to do so.

Reforming Russia

After his tour—and a humiliating defeat at the hands of the Swedes—Peter shook up the military. He tightened his hold on the nobles by carefully enforcing the program of service nobility. Since his nobles were required to serve in the military, he required all nobles to first attend five years of schooling and imported the best teachers from western Europe. They taught his future officers languages, science, math, engineering, and medicine.

Peter created a bureaucratic meritocracy to handle both military and civilian affairs. He created a professional standing army that numbered more than 250,000 and consisted of noble officers and peasant foot soldiers. He also created a navy practically from scratch. Peter eventually tied up more than three-fourths of his country's revenues in his military. To finance his army, Peter changed the primary tax from a land tax to a soul tax, or a tax paid for each person rather than on the land that people owned; after all, not every Russian owned land.

In the process of modernizing his military, Peter infused his entire country with western, and modern, ideas. Peter encouraged Russians to dress like western Europeans. He even required nobles to shave their beards or pay a beard tax. Peter encouraged the nobles to hold tea parties and socialize the way westerners did. He changed the calendar from the traditional Russian to the Julian calendar, with January 1 as the first day of the year and years counted from the birth of Christ. He encouraged education, began a state-sponsored newspaper, and also instituted reforms in the church hierarchy.

At first glance, it would seem that Peter's list of reforms had far-reaching effects in Russia. While some reform did occur, particularly in the military, Peter's reforms required a huge bureaucracy to enforce them. The 14-level bureaucracy Peter created was such a managerial nightmare that many reforms never went into effect simply because there weren't enough administrators to make sure the reforms were carried out.

As a Matter of Fact

Russia's Peter the Great towered over most every one of his contemporaries. He possessed amazing athletic abilities and, interestingly, an inclination for tinkering with things. He built numerous models of buildings, ships, and more. This knack for working with his hands led to an interest in dentistry and even minor surgery. Peter experimented with dentistry and often "practiced" on those around him. He kept many of the teeth he pulled and they are still on display in a museum in St. Petersburg. Also on display in St. Petersburg are many of the medical and dental instruments Peter used for his hobby.

The City in the Swamp

Peter dreamed of having a warm-water port on the Baltic from which he could launch his mighty navy. To gain the territory to build such a city, Peter engaged the Swedes in the Great Northern War, a long, drawn-out war that finally ended with Russia gaining what is now Estonia and Latvia.

On land gained in the war, Peter built his city—actually starting work long before the war was over. Named St. Petersburg, not for Peter but for his patron saint, St. Petersburg was to be his capital.

For his new city, Peter chose a plot of land in the middle of marshland. Peter and his army of engineers and serfs drained the marshland and erected a magnificent city.

Would You Believe?

As many as 30,000 or more serfs and other laborers lost their lives to the harsh conditions during the construction of St. Petersburg.

Peter, so impressed with Versailles, modeled his palace and his city on western stylings. To make his city modern, like everything else he created in Russia, his engineers constructed straight streets, straight city blocks with houses in straight rows, drainage canals, and even street lights. All construction conformed to rigorous standards set forth by the government. To jump-start the population of

St. Petersburg, Peter ordered nobles to move to the city and build expensive homes. Likewise, he ordered craftsmen to move to the city. The serfs, of course, were already there doing the manual labor. To finance the city, Peter taxed the wealthiest Russians. When Peter died in 1625, St. Petersburg boasted thousands of residents and a style that was at once uniquely western and uniquely Russian.

If It Ain't Baroque ...

After the Council of Trent, the Catholic Church decided that artwork should stir the emotions. The Church wanted art to tell stories and convey feelings to parishioners, particularly the illiterate and the uneducated. The style of art that developed a few generations later became known as Baroque, a term that applies to both the era and the art of the era. Baroque style began in Italy and spread throughout Europe. Baroque style manifested itself in painting, sculpture, music, and even architecture. The Church used the Baroque style to do just as it intended. The absolute monarchs of the late sixteenth and seventeenth centuries also found a use for the Baroque.

Baroque Art

Baroque art has been called everything from gaudy to overblown to flashy to ornate. All of those descriptions have some amount of truth. Because Baroque art was intended to stir the emotions, artists used big strokes and vivid colors to paint stirring or sensual scenes. Most Baroque artists had a flair for the dramatic. The Italian painter Caravaggio created stirring images with unusual perspective and poses. The sculptor Bernini created sculptures with religious themes that were deeply emotional and passionate. The Flemish painter Peter Paul Rubens painted sensual works featuring plump, full-figured nudes—a first in European art. The Baroque art of Italy often featured religious themes. The Baroque art of the Flemish and the English, though, featured portraits and still life because their Protestant faith prohibited religious iconography. The Baroque music of such masters as Bach and Liszt were as detailed and ornate as the art. For the absolutists, however, the greatest contribution of the Baroque masters was the architecture.

Continental Quotes

"The aim and final end of all music should be none other than the glory of God and the refreshment of the soul."

—Johann Sebastian Bach

Using the Baroque to Bolster Absolutism

What the cathedral was to the Catholic Church the palace was to the absolute monarch. Just as Louis XIV used Versailles to impress and intimidate visitors, so did other absolutists use Baroque architecture to flaunt their wealth and convey their power. The Catholic Church wanted Baroque art to convey emotion and drama. So did absolutists.

Examples of Baroque architecture intended to awe visitors and celebrate the grandeur of the absolutists appeared in Paris at Versailles, in Vienna, in Stockholm, in Ludwigsburg, in London, and in St. Petersburg. These palaces featured enormous gardens, huge pillars or columns, fabulous staircases, and opulent decorations everywhere. In order to leave visitors overwhelmed, architects designed the palaces so that visitors walked from one entry way to another to another, each room increasing in splendor and magnificence until they finally reached the throne room or some other important room. Often the walls were adorned with huge murals, some portraying the monarch winning great battles.

Just as important as the construction of the absolutist's palace was the construction of the towns or cities that inevitably grew up around the palace. Cities featured wide streets to allow troop movement and the use of carriages. Often the streets spanned outward from the palace. The buildings along the straight streets were Baroque in style. The most modern absolutist cities even featured upscale stores where the elite could shop. The absolutists made sure that even visitors who never saw inside the palace still left with a sense of awe and a sense of the king's magnificence.

The Least You Need to Know

- ◆ Although not as extreme, Austria attempted absolute rule after the Thirty Years' War to unite Austria, Bohemia, Hungary, and its other holdings.

- ◆ Prussian absolutism resulted in one of the finest militaries in all of Europe, particularly under the leadership of Frederick William the Soldiers' King.

- ◆ Once Russia rid themselves of the Mongols, they expanded their borders and established absolute control over the Russian people. Beginning with Ivan III, Russia believed Moscow to be the third Rome and Russian rulers to be the equivalent of Roman Caesars.

- ◆ Peter the Great used western European ideas, and absolute authority, to modernize his military as well as Russian society.

◆ Highly emotional and ornate Baroque art and architecture grew out of the Church's desire for a way to use art to speak to the masses.

◆ Absolutists used the Baroque, particularly Baroque architecture, to flaunt their wealth and convince visitors of the crown's power and grandeur.

Part 3

Revolutions Galore (c.1500–1800)

This part tells the story of change and how Europe dealt with that change. Traditions, dogmas, accepted doctrines, and even absolute truths were literally shattered. Scientists approached the universe from different angles and came to conclusions different from anyone who observed the world before them. The thinkers who came later applied the same rational process to analyzing problems of society and came up with conclusions that affect each of us today, contributing greatly to the foundations of modern government, modern science, and even modern religion. Agricultural innovators and hungry peasants developed new ways of producing food for an undernourished population. Over time, their discoveries and inventions produced remarkable results. This part also tells the fascinating and tragic story of the French Revolution: class struggle, economic hardship, and civil liberties, all playing a role in one of the most important events in all of European history.

Chapter 11

Revolt of the Scientists

In This Chapter

- The changing view of the world
- Copernicus: the center of controversy
- The mounting evidence against Ptolemy
- Newton puts it all together
- Dogmatic religion and science don't mix
- The making of the scientific method

The sixteenth and seventeenth centuries proved as unsettling for science and philosophy as for religion. Just as Luther, Calvin, and others led a theological revolution that shook the very foundations of Christendom, a number of scientists beginning in the sixteenth century led a revolution of sorts in science that challenged everything humans thought they knew about the world and universe around them. The work of the scientists made waves not just in the academic and scientific worlds but in the world of religion, too.

Each scientist who contributed to the body of knowledge built upon the work of his predecessors. By the turn of the eighteenth century, ancient scientific flaws had been revealed, new discoveries had been made, and the approach to science had been changed forever. Also like the revolution in religion, the revolution in science initially was met with much skepticism and loud outcries from many who refused to accept that what they had always believed may have been inaccurate. The Scientific Revolution was revolutionary only in the sense that an old way of doing things was replaced by a new way; the term "revolution" in no way implies that the changes took place quickly.

A New Worldview

Historians often refer to the post–Scientific Revolution concept of the universe as a "new worldview." This new outlook involved accepting new ideas and rejecting, or at least being open to skepticism about, old ideas. For many academicians, "out with the old and in with the new" was uncomfortable and disconcerting.

The new worldview eventually extended to many areas of science but it began in the field of astronomy, which experienced a resurgence following the Renaissance. Not only had the Renaissance fostered curiosity and discovery, it had encouraged the study of classical texts. Among the ancient texts dusted off for research were those of classical philosophers and astronomers like Aristotle and Ptolemy. The work of such philosophers and astronomers made up the core of what Europeans believed about the universe for more than a millennium.

Would You Believe?

Governments patronized scientists the way that rich individuals and the Church patronized the arts.

The Renaissance fascination with classical texts wasn't the only factor in the renewed interest in astronomy. The fifteenth and sixteenth century emphasis on navigation, cartography, and exploration necessitated new and better techniques for viewing and mapping the stars. These factors, combined with the intellectual curiosity that grew out of the universities of the Middle Ages, made the conditions prime for a revolution in scientific thought.

The "Old" Worldview

Prior to the Scientific Revolution, the scientific and religious communities placed a great deal of faith in the work of the classical minds of Aristotle and Ptolemy, who studied the heavens, speculated about the night sky, and made calculations.

Their observations seemed to indicate that the heavenly bodies they observed in the sky orbited the Earth in circular patterns. They calculated the orbits of the stars and the sun with no real problem, but the orbit of the planets gave them fits. Rather than following circular orbits, the planets seemed to be all over the place. Ptolemy explained this by saying that the planets traveled in *epicycles* within their orbits around the Earth. The belief that the heavenly bodies orbited around the Earth was known as the geocentric view of the universe, that the Earth is the center.

Define Your Terms

An **epicycle** is a smaller orbit within a larger orbit.

Aristotle compounded the confusion by maintaining that the heavens and the heavenly bodies were composed of different matter than the Earth. The combination of Aristotle and Ptolemy's ideas produced the concept known as the Ptolemaic universe. The Ptolemaic universe consisted of a series of crystal spheres containing the orbits of the sun, moon, stars and planets. The Ptolemaic universe placed the stationary Earth in the center of the crystal spheres. Beyond the crystal spheres was heaven, where God and the angels resided.

This suited the Church just fine. According to the scheme of the Ptolemaic universe, the universe was finite and heaven and God were in an absolute location. This made everyone feel secure about things that could not be seen. The spheres of the old worldview, though, were soon to be shattered.

The Copernican Hypothesis

Nicholas Copernicus (1473–1543) was a brilliant scholar with a background in church law, math, medicine, and astronomy. He studied astronomy in Poland after receiving a clerical position.

Copernicus believed that Ptolemy's system was flawed. He didn't necessarily doubt the idea about the spheres or about perfectly circular orbits, but he wasn't sold on Ptolemy's rules explaining the orbits of the heavenly bodies. Copernicus was interested in an old theory that dated back to the ancient Greeks and placed heavenly bodies in orbit around the sun rather than around the Earth. Copernicus worked with this theory for more than 20 years.

Afraid that he would be the laughingstock of the world of astronomy, Copernicus did not publish his work, *On the Revolutions of Heavenly Bodies*, until 1543. A devout Catholic, he dedicated the work to the pope. Copernicus did not declare the heliocentric theory that the sun is the center of the universe to be truth in his book, but rather offered the theory for speculation and for mathematical consideration.

The heliocentric theory challenged a number of ideas besides just the geocentric nature of the universe. If Copernicus's theory were correct, the size of the universe would actually be exponentially larger than under the Ptolemaic system. The stars in the Copernican theory stayed still while the Earth moved, a huge departure from Ptolemy. One of the biggest points of contention arose over the position and make-up of the Earth. According to the old worldview, the Earth was the center of the universe, and everything else, made of different matter, revolved around it. The Copernican theory took the Earth out of the center of the universe and made it just like any other planet flying through space. It meant that the heavenly bodies were made of the same matter as the Earth. It reduced the importance of Earth in the universe God created. It also took heaven off the map.

Copernicus's theory was revolutionary only in that it made everyone stop and think a little differently. Copernicus proved little except that the geocentric universe didn't exist. After all, the sun isn't the center of the universe. It would be up to the astronomers who followed to take Copernicus's ideas and prove them. Copernicus died shortly after he saw the first copy of his published book in 1543.

Brahe, Kepler, and Galileo

One of Europe's leading astronomers, a Dane named Tycho Brahe (1546–1601), put himself on the map when he studied a new star that appeared in the night sky in 1572. After becoming renowned, Brahe reaped the rewards of his fame. The Danish government financed a huge observatory for Brahe. Since Brahe believed that the planets revolved around the sun and the sun and planets together revolved around the Earth, his theories weren't his greatest contribution to science. But Brahe studied the heavens, both with the naked eye and with an expensive telescope funded by the Danish government, for more than 20 years, amassing more data than he could ever synthesize. The amazingly accurate data that he collected was to be Brahe's legacy.

Would You Believe?

Tycho Brahe lost part of his nose in a duel and replaced the missing part with an alloyed metal made of gold and silver.

Brahe's apprentice, Johannes Kepler (1571–1630), kept the data collected by Brahe and used them to work on Copernicus's theory. For 10 years Kepler applied Brahe's work to Copernican thought. A gifted mathematician, Kepler believed the key to understanding the universe was to be found in mathematics. He believed that a mathematical relationship existed between all the heavenly bodies in the universe.

Finally, Kepler produced three fundamental laws of planetary motion. First, Kepler proved that the planets traveled in elliptical orbits and not in circular orbits with epicycles. Second, Kepler showed that a planet's speed increases as it gets closer to the sun and then slows down as it moves farther away from the sun. Third, Kepler demonstrated a direct relationship between a planet's distance from the sun and the time it takes that planet to orbit the sun. Kepler's laws proved what Copernicus speculated: the Ptolemaic system was wrong.

 As a Matter of Fact

Johannes Kepler belonged to a Lutheran family but he disagreed with Luther's stance on the Eucharist. As a result, the Lutheran Church refused him the sacraments. In spite of the fact that he could not receive the sacraments within the Lutheran Church, Kepler refused to convert to Catholicism. On another interesting note, near the beginning of the Thirty Years' War, Kepler defended his mother against charges of heresy and witchcraft.

About the same time Kepler pored through Brahe's data, Galileo Galilei (1564–1642) explored ideas about motion. Galileo, also a brilliant mathematician, helped revolutionize science in a number of ways. Rather than speculating about motion, Galileo experimented with it. After his experiments, Galileo concluded that objects were in a state of motion until a force stops the motion. This idea flew in the face of the physics of Aristotle and other classical philosophers, who said that rest was the natural state of objects.

Would You Believe?

Galileo conducted his motion experiments by rolling balls down grooved pieces of wood and not by dropping the balls from atop the Leaning Tower of Pisa. These experiments resulted in the law of inertia.

Galileo learned about the invention of a telescope and built one himself. With his telescope, Galileo, already a supporter of the Copernican hypothesis, got himself into trouble. He discovered that Jupiter had moons, that the sun had sunspots, and that the moon had craters everywhere. These discoveries further debunked the old worldview that the planets were embedded in crystal spheres and that the heavenly bodies were made of a perfect matter different from that which composed the Earth.

As Galileo wrote more and more, he caught the attention of theologians in Europe who reported him to the pope and to the Inquisition. The pope granted Galileo permission to write about his theories as long as he didn't hold them as truths. Furthermore, the Inquisition determined that the Copernican idea of nonstationary Earth was heretical. As Galileo aged, he worked on his most important work, *Dialogue on the Two Chief Systems of the World*, which was published in 1632. Galileo often wrote in an arrogant, condescending tone and such was the case with this work. It was also a little more forward-leaning than the pope had hoped it would be. As a result, Galileo found himself on trial for heresy. (More on that later.)

On the Shoulders of Giants

Sir Isaac Newton once said, "If I have seen further, it is by standing on the shoulders of giants." Newton spoke of those intellectual giants who went before him—Copernicus, Brahe, Kepler, and Galileo, among others. What the scientists before Newton had done was nothing short of incredible. Taking one step at a time, they shattered over a thousand years of philosophical, religious, and scientific "truths." Without the work of any one of these "giants," the scientific community would have had to wait much longer to prove what Copernicus hypothesized.

However, the "giants" failed to put it all together in one organized and accurate system that explained the universe. Scientists had worked with planetary motion, motion of objects on Earth, geocentric versus heliocentric systems, and more. What was missing, though, was a synthesis of all of those things. That synthesis would appear less than 50 years after the death of Galileo.

Continental Quotes

"Trials are medicines which our gracious and wise Physician prescribes because we need them; and he proportions the frequency and weight of them to what the case requires. Let us trust his skill and thank him for his prescription."

—Sir Isaac Newton

Sir Isaac Newton

Perhaps the most brilliant of all the minds of the Scientific Revolution, Sir Isaac Newton (1642–1727) was an Englishman who had already achieved more by the age of 24 than most scientists achieve in a lifetime. Many of the theories Newton developed in his life regarding physics remained unproved for over 200 years because the math needed had not yet been invented.

A devout Anglican, Newton hoped to bring together science and religion. Newton worked with mathematics and physics and also did extensive work in the field of optics, a field in which he experimented extensively. He believed that the universe operated according to a set of rational, mathematical principles and that these principles could prove the existence of God, a rational being. Newton believed that God was the cause of all motion and matter, but he didn't believe God was responsible for the behavior of matter.

Newton studied and thought and formulated and determined that the behavior of matter was due to certain principles of physics that governed the universe. It was this belief in certain laws of physics that led him to develop his theory of gravity, particularly as it applies to the motion of heavenly bodies. Newton was on the verge of something truly remarkable.

Would You Believe?

Newton also spent time studying the science of alchemy. Alchemists searched for a mysterious substance that would turn ordinary metals into gold.

Principia

Finally, in 1687, Newton put it all together in his landmark masterpiece, *Philisophia Naturalis Principia Mathematica* or *Mathematical Principals of Natural Philosophy*. He boasted that while he had demonstrated certain laws before, his *Principia* would demonstrate "the frame of the System of the World."

His *Principia* indeed did just that and so laid the foundations for physics that lasted until the twentieth century. In his book, Newton outlined three main laws concerning motion, then proved that these laws could be applied to heavenly bodies in motion. Newton's synthesis of the work of those before him and his own work presented a picture of the orderly universe ruled by laws and principles he believed existed. After the publication of *Principia*, Newton grew famous, particularly in England; his ideas took a little longer to become popular on the continent.

Would You Believe?

Newton became so popular after *Principia* that he was made president of the Royal Academy of Sciences and was knighted.

The Reaction of Religion

The hypotheses presented by the Scientific Revolution created quite a stir within organized religion. The Copernican universe challenged the accepted idea about the universe, the location of heaven and Earth, and the importance of Earth in the grand scheme of things. The Ptolemaic system with a stationary Earth at the center of the universe allowed clergy and laymen alike to know exactly where heaven lay and Earth's location in the universe relative to heaven. It would be easy to chastise the dogmatic religious leaders of the sixteenth and seventeenth centuries for clinging to the ancient ideas of Aristotle and Ptolemy, but there was scriptural evidence that indicated the classical ideas were correct.

For Christians who did not emphasize the literal translation of the scripture, the scientific hypotheses posed no tremendous threat. For others who believed in a strict literal translation of the Bible, the Copernican theory seemed heretical. Several verses in particular gave credence to the belief that the Earth stood still while everything else moved around it. Joshua 10:13 and Habakuk 3:11 tell of how the "sun stood still, and the moon stopped" and how the "sun and moon stood still in the heavens." 1 Chronicles 16:30 and Psalm 93:1 both say, "The world is firmly established; it cannot be moved."

Luther and Calvin Sound Off

The Catholic Church didn't respond nearly as quickly to the Copernican hypothesis as did the Protestant leaders. There are probably two main reasons for this. First, Copernicus dedicated his work to the pope, and his work was used as the basis for the reform of the Julian calendar into the current Gregorian calendar. Second, because the Catholic Church placed as much emphasis on Church tradition as on the scripture, the Church didn't really want to be bound to a strict literal translation of the Bible. Protestants like Martin Luther and John Calvin, though, showed less restraint.

Martin Luther in 1539 said, "People gave an ear to an upstart astrologer who strove to show that the Earth revolves, not the heavens or the firmament, the sun and moon …. The fool wishes to reverse the entire science of astronomy; but sacred scripture tells us that Joshua commanded the sun to stand still, and not the Earth." John Calvin jumped into the fray, too, writing in reference to Psalm 93:1, "Who will venture to place the authority of Copernicus above that of the Holy Spirit?" Though these two had scorned Copernicus, their chastising had no real effects. The same could not be said after the Church had its say on the matter.

The Church Chimes In

The Catholic Church didn't weigh in on the Copernican hypothesis until 1616, when the Holy Office officially banned *On the Revolutions of Heavenly Bodies* more than 70 years after its publication. The Holy Office added Copernicus's work to the Index of

Prohibited Books because the doctrine of the "motion of the Earth and the immobility of the Sun" was "false and altogether opposed to the Holy Scripture."

Eight years after the Church officially took a stand on the Copernican theory, the Inquisition and the pope found themselves forced to deal with Galileo. The pope warned Galileo, allowing him to write about Copernicus only as long as he didn't present the hypothesis as truth. Galileo didn't heed the pope's warning. His *Dialogue on the Two Chief Systems of the World* literally made fun of the old worldview, and the Church didn't appreciate it.

Continental Quotes

"It is surely harmful to souls to make it a heresy to believe what is proved."

—Galileo

Galileo was brought before the Inquisition and tried for heresy. Galileo, an old man at the time of his trial, was imprisoned and threatened with torture and execution before he finally recanted. His recanting was recognized by most simply as a formality, so nobody believed he had really changed his mind. In reality, the harsh position of the Inquisition did more harm to the Church than to Galileo's theories or his legacy. Galileo lived out his days under house arrest.

As a Matter of Fact

Although it probably did not happen, legend says that, as he left the courtroom, the arrogant and frustrated Galileo defiantly uttered, "*E pur si muove,*" or "But it moves," referring to the earth. If Galileo had actually gone back on his recantation, he could have faced the death penalty. In 1737, nearly 100 years after his death, Galileo's remains were moved from their original resting place to a mausoleum at the Church of Santa Croce. At that time, the middle finger of Galileo's right hand was removed and placed in a bowl in which it is displayed today at the Institute and Museum of the History of Science in Italy. On the marble base that holds Galileo's finger is a Latin inscription by Tommaso Perelli that reads:

This is the finger, belonging to the illustrious hand that ran through the skies, pointing at the immense spaces, and singling out new stars, offering to the senses a marvelous apparatus of crafted glass, and with wise daring they could reach where neither Enceladus nor Tiphaeus ever reached.

Cooking with Bacon and Descartes

The importance of the Scientific Revolution lay not just with the invention of the telescope, the advancements in medicine, the acceptance of the Copernican hypothesis, or the laws of motion. Arguably more important than the knowledge gained during the Scientific Revolution was the change in the methodology used to gain new knowledge: the development of the modern scientific method, the same method used today to test hypotheses and to gain new scientific knowledge.

No single thinker published a book or an essay outlining the new methodology. Rather, it was a fusion of the ideas of two of the great thinkers of the seventeenth century, Sir Francis Bacon and René Descartes.

Sir Francis Bacon and Inductive Reasoning

The Englishman Sir Francis Bacon (1561–1626) advocated the use of the experimental method for gaining knowledge, the same method used by Galileo. Often considered a philosopher, Bacon contributed profoundly to the Scientific Revolution.

> **Continental Quotes**
>
> "Knowledge is power."
>
> —Sir Francis Bacon

> **Would You Believe?**
>
> Francis Bacon desired to serve his country and he worked his way through many positions within the administrations of Elizabeth and James I. However, a black cloud followed him from office to office; he could not stay out of debt. Furthermore, his homosexual practices offended many around him. He finished his career in government service when he took bribes, almost certainly to pay debts.

Bacon believed true knowledge could be gained only through observation, specifically of experiments. Reasoning based on observation, called *inductive reasoning*, was a fundamental part of *empiricism*, the use of empirical evidence to gain knowledge. Bacon believed that the logic and reasoning used by Aristotle and other thinkers of old to develop scientific theories had serious flaws, because several factors could affect human reasoning and taint the resulting "knowledge." Speculation, according to Bacon, usually did not produce accurate or useful knowledge. If a scientist wanted to gain knowledge of the planets, he should observe, record, and then analyze the data the way Brahe and Galileo had done. Rather than working backward from a generalization, Bacon recommended observing, then making a conclusion, then generalizing once the conclusion is proved. Bacon criticized those who relied on thinkers like Aristotle who didn't use the empirical method but relied only on reasoning.

Bacon advocated government funding for science and argued that the scientific discoveries of the future could make the leading scientific nations rich and powerful; he hoped one such nation would be England. On a number of occasions Bacon found himself in a position to influence the government of King James I to patronize science, and served in several high-ranking positions. In a strange turn of events that really has had no bearing on his scientific legacy, the English government indicted Bacon on more than 20 counts of corruption and dismissed him from office.

René Descartes and Deductive Reasoning

Frenchman René Descartes (1596–1650) approached science from a different angle than Bacon. Like so many other figures of the Scientific Revolution, Descartes ranked among the great mathematicians of all time. In the middle of the Thirty Years' War, Descartes realized the relationship between algebra and geometry; later he would invent analytical geometry.

Descartes disagreed with the dogma of the Church based on obsolete ways of thinking. Descartes believed that the universe was based on mathematical and logical relationships. In his famous *Discourse on Methods* in 1637, he proposed that the key to nature lay in mathematics, which could also be used to understand humans and human institutions, such as political units.

Because human senses, used in observation of experiments, can be deceived, observation is fallible. To prove his point, Descartes used what was known as the wax argument. He noted, with his senses, the size, shape, texture, and feel of a piece of wax. As he moved the wax toward a flame, the size, shape, and texture changed, but the wax remained wax. That simple experiment, for Descartes, proved that the best judgment was the one made by the mind and not by the senses.

Descartes believed in a good God who had no desire to deceive man and thus bestowed on man a keen mind capable of great things. Such was Descartes' faith in the power of the human intellect that only logic, or deductive reasoning, can be trusted. Descartes' approach to knowledge was nothing like Bacon's. Descartes' approach involved doubting everything that could be doubted and then making generalizations based on obvious truths. Descartes took his scientific approach, considered a philosophy by many, to the extreme and formed what has become known as Cartesian dualism. For Descartes, doubting everything and applying reason causes everything to fall either into the category of matter or of mind; in other words, everything is either physical or spiritual. He even used logic and reason to prove, at least to himself, not only his own existence but also the existence of God. His famous quote, "I think, therefore I am," summarizes his proof of his own existence. Unfortunately for

Descartes, he never really found great support from either the government or the Church. Descartes had always rejected the Aristotelian view of the universe, the view held by the Church throughout the Middle Ages, and he refused to allow religion to influence his philosophy. He based his philosophy on pure reason, even his philosophy dealing with God and truth, and as a result drew the ire of the Church. His works were officially banned in 1663.

Consequences of the Scientific Revolution

The Scientific Revolution resulted in new information about the world and the universe, new information about medicine, new techniques for navigation, and the creation of an international scientific community. The greatest consequence of the Scientific Revolution, though, was the new worldview that replaced the old one. No longer was Europe bound by tradition, classical texts, and superstitions. Europeans were free to question the status quo, search for verification of traditions, and think outside the box.

Foundations of the Modern Scientific Method

Both Bacon and Descartes put forth diametrically opposed theories concerning the best way to obtain scientific knowledge. Bacon discounted logic and reasoning in building a body of knowledge. Descartes, on the other hand, undervalued the benefits of observation and experimentation.

The two mutually exclusive theories were of little value independently, and scientists following Bacon and Descartes didn't see eye to eye for some time. For about a century, the English relied heavily on the experimental method, while the French placed great emphasis on the deductive model and mathematics. However, over the course of the next hundred or so years, European scientists began to fuse inductive and deductive reasoning. The combination resulted in what scientists call the modern scientific method. The scientific method was, and still is, important because it freed scientists from the dogmas, traditions, and ancient ideas and texts that dominated medieval thought. It encourages curiosity, creativity, and trial and error.

Though the modern scientific method can vary somewhat, the accepted form contains all of the following:

- **Observation**—Taken directly from Bacon, observation includes the collection and recording of data.

- **Hypothesis**—The hypothesis is the theory that will be tested.

- ◆ **Prediction**—Taken directly from Descartes, prediction or deduction involves making a logical estimation of the outcome of the experiment based on generally accepted truths.

- ◆ **Experiment**—The actual experiment or testing results in the availability of empirical data from which the researcher can draw a conclusion.

Today researchers from elementary students to Nobel Prize-winning scientists in billion-dollar labs use the scientific method to guide their experiments. Furthermore, the modern scientific method is the backbone of thesis and dissertation programs at most universities.

A Community of Science

The Scientific Revolution left a legacy that still exists today. During the Middle Ages, the university system in Europe produced mostly lawyers and clergymen. With the advent of the Scientific Revolution, universities became the training grounds for many of Europe's greatest minds. Nearly all of the Scientific Revolution's most influential figures either studied or taught at the university level. As science, particularly astronomy, became more and more important in Europe, science faculty positions were added to many universities. Professors and students alike earned more and more esteem in the intellectual community.

As interest in science among intellectuals grew, the scientific community grew, which led to the formation of scientific groups like the Royal Society of London, which gave lectures, published papers, and contributed to the body of scientific knowledge. Universities and colleges received funding from governments to pursue scientific advancements and to build observatories; the observatory at Nuremburg and Brahe's Danish observatory are great examples. Governments often invested in the sciences with hopes that the investments would pay financial dividends.

Science Saving Lives

The Scientific Revolution, almost entirely an intellectual movement, produced practically nothing tangible and useful for the common European. The exception to that, thankfully, was in the medical field, where the Scientific Revolution provided several breakthroughs that translated to better health and many lives saved.

Like the rest of science, medicine in the sixteenth century relied heavily on tradition and ancient texts, especially those of the classical Greek physician Galen. Sixteenth-century scientists Andreas Vesalius (1514–1564) and Theophrastus Bombastus von Hohenheim, also known as Paracelsus (1493–1541), revised and then rejected Galen. Rather than teaching and working with medical theory, they actually practiced medicine.

Would You Believe?

For many years the use of cadavers was forbidden by the Catholic Church, so William Harvey's work definitely was cutting-edge.

Later, an Englishman named William Harvey (1578–1657) dissected cadavers and made tremendous strides gaining knowledge in the specific area of the human circulatory system. He noted that the body operated as a machine and was subject to certain laws and principles in much the same way that other scientists noted the world around them.

The Least You Need to Know

- Europe was dominated by the old worldview throughout the Middle Ages, founded in the classical texts of philosophers and astronomers like Aristotle and Ptolemy, which theorized a stationary Earth and a finite, geocentric universe. The first sign of trouble for the old worldview came when Copernicus hypothesized about a heliocentric system.

- After the work of Brahe and Kepler, Galileo wrote about the Copernican hypothesis and made discoveries with his telescope that disproved the Ptolemaic system. Galileo ultimately found himself on trial for heresy.

- Sir Isaac Newton's synthesis of all his predecessors' work, including much of his own work, in *Principia* explained laws of motion and gravity as they applied to the Earth and to heavenly bodies.

- The fusion of Bacon's inductive method and Descartes' deductive method resulted in the modern scientific method.

Chapter 12

Enlightening the Public, Not the People

In This Chapter

- ◆ Who's enlightened and who needs enlightening
- ◆ Skepticism and reason
- ◆ Were the philosophes really that smart?
- ◆ The crème de la crème
- ◆ Absolute rulers embrace the Enlightenment

The Scientific Revolution did more than simply remove the earth from the center of the universe: it permanently changed the way Europeans thought and looked at the world around them. it impressed upon them the importance of examining everything, asking questions, observing, and experimenting. This way of thinking and looking at the world reached its peak among intellectuals in the eighteenth century in a movement known as the Enlightenment.

Linking the Revolution and the Enlightenment

Most events or movements throughout history wait for later generations to name them. The Renaissance waited hundreds of years to be identified as such. It was intellectuals in their own era, however, who declared their movement to be the Enlightenment, their purpose being to enlighten Europe, to shed light on its intellectual darkness.

The Enlightenment was a direct result of the Scientific Revolution, but its roots actually go back much farther. The ancient Greek philosopher Aristotle invented formal logic; the Renaissance thinkers rediscovered his methodology (see Chapter 2); and then the thinkers of the Scientific Revolution built upon his deductive reasoning. The writers and intellectuals of the eighteenth century embraced the new worldview and the new way of thinking produced by the Scientific Revolution and the Enlightenment was born. These writers and intellectuals placed great value on the concept of reason, or the combination of logic with common sense and empirical evidence. The Enlightenment thinkers believed that the methodology of science, the union of inductive and deductive reasoning, could be applied to all sorts of problems outside the field of science, and that the scientific methodology could lead to the betterment of society.

Science Chic

The Enlightenment thinkers were the intellectual elite, and represented a small fraction of society. They found an audience, small though it was, among the social elite, the aristocracy, and the wealthy middle class. As the new way of thinking developed, scientists and the scientific community grew in esteem and influence. All things scientific became increasingly popular among the aristocracy, who attended lectures to hear scientists speak about the natural world. As Europe moved deeper into the Enlightenment, book production and book sales soared across Europe. The Enlightenment would have a profound effect on the reading public of the eighteenth century.

Applying What We've Learned

The intellectuals of the Enlightenment maintained that the scientific method could be applied to issues and problems that were not scientific in nature: that the new way of thinking could be used to gain insight into the human condition. These thinkers believed that there was much to be learned about humanity, society, and the laws that govern society through the application of the scientific method, to create better humans and better societies. The Enlightenment called this concept *progress*.

As a Matter of Fact

A Frenchman named Bernard de Fontenelle (1657–1757) wrote a revolutionary book, *Conversations on the Plurality of Worlds* (1686), that went a long way toward making science interesting and comprehensible for nonscientific readers. Fontenelle used a conversation between two wealthy aristocrats to explain the Copernican system and other aspects of the natural world. The success of Fontenelle's book served as a sign of things to come.

Whereas the humanists of the Renaissance sought to recreate and equal the great feats and achievements of classical Greek and Roman society, the Enlightenment thinkers believed that humans had the potential to get better and better, that the examples of Greece and Rome could be surpassed. The idea of progress, the advancement of man and society for good, remained a key tenet of Enlightenment thought throughout the eighteenth century, and the improving economic and social conditions for most of Europe during the eighteenth century lent some credibility to the Enlightenment's claims. The Enlightenment thinkers touted the betterment of society as their ultimate goal, and indeed conditions for most western Europeans improved simultaneously with the rise of things like more tolerant and less repressive representative governments.

Why So Skeptical?

It should not come as a surprise that the new way of thinking caused problems for guardians of the established religious and social order during the eighteenth century. The Scientific Revolution proved the necessity of questioning tradition and dogma, developing and testing hypotheses, and generally being open-minded and creative.

After an era of absolute rulers and religious warfare and persecution, it made sense to Enlightenment thinkers to question the authority and oppression of absolute rulers. It made sense to question the absolute truth on which religions based their absolute claims to absolute authority over absolutely everyone. In other words, the Enlightenment thinkers were skeptical of anything that was "absolute." Just a few centuries earlier, the absolute truth was that the Earth was the center of the universe, heaven lay in a location just outside the finite universe, and the Catholic Church was the only true religion. The Scientific Revolution and the Reformation shattered all those absolute truths. Enlightenment thinkers wondered how anything could be absolute if those things were proven to be not necessarily the truth.

Skepticism didn't begin with the scientists. Skepticism dates to the ancient Greeks, but more concretely to the sixteenth-century Frenchman Michel de Montaigne (1533–1592). Montaigne spent much of his life mediating between Catholics and Protestants (see Chapter 7), and he experienced much turmoil as a result of the religious differences among his fellow Frenchmen. Montaigne disapproved of the conflict over religion and wondered if either side actually held a monopoly on the truth. Montaigne observed and questioned many other things about human nature and recorded his thoughts in his progressive *Essays*. Montaigne in fact invented the literary form known as the essay, in which he pondered a topic, usually pertaining to himself or to human nature in general. Montaigne grew to believe in man's inability to attain certainty. He also hinted at cultural relativism, or the lack of a universal truth; in other words, truth varied from culture to culture. Montaigne suggested that example and experience carried far more weight and value than abstract knowledge and tradition. These beliefs made Montaigne a skeptic, or a proponent of skepticism.

Would You Believe?

Montaigne believed in marriage but personally he preferred not to give in to romantic feelings because of the way that romantic love stifles freedom.

Skepticism questions established truths. Is knowledge true? Are perceptions true? Can one ever have absolute knowledge about anything? Scientifically, skepticism leads to the practice of the scientific method. Philosophically, skepticism leads to questioning religion, politics, the social order, and the authority on which current practices are based. Critics of skepticism claimed that skeptics denied truth, but skeptics merely questioned the existence of truth.

Another Frenchman continued the tradition of skepticism. Pierre Bayle (1647–1706), a Huguenot who fled to the safe haven of the Dutch Republic to escape the oppression of Louis XIV's Catholic government, wrote the *Historical and Critical Dictionary* (1697) that showed his skepticism of religion. He pointed out the errors of historical and contemporary religious writers and theologians, citing examples of how human beliefs about religion had been diverse or wrong and arguing for open-mindedness. Because in France his works would have landed him in prison, or worse, he remained in the Netherlands and published his works there. They were then smuggled into France, where they found their way to the bookshelves of many, many French intellectuals.

Skepticism of the status quo even appeared in an unlikely place: the writings of travelers to foreign lands. Travelers often documented what they saw as they traveled to foreign lands, such as the New World and China. Travelers noted primitive and ostensibly uncivilized peoples living in harmony without strict governments, oppressive laws, state religions, or other features of modern European states. If these peoples lived in harmony and peace and prosperity without the "truth" of European religions and states, skeptics asked, then are the current values and traditions of European states and churches absolutely true? Just as the Scientific Revolution shook the foundations of science, the Enlightenment was about to undermine the status quo of religion and society.

The *tabula rasa*

Another major blow to the status quo and the idea of universal, absolute truths came in the wake of the 1690 publication of John Locke's *Essay Concerning Human Understanding*. Locke (1632–1704) shed serious doubt on the Cartesian and ancient Greek idea that humans are born with certain innate knowledge that can be drawn out through questions, logic, and deductive reasoning. Locke's theory proposed that all knowledge was based on experience, that humans are born a blank slate, or *tabula rasa*, on which all knowledge is written as they live. Universal truths didn't exist because each person's knowledge and version of truth were based solely on his or her own experiences.

This theory fell perfectly in line with the Enlightenment idea that man and society could be improved. Education and social institutions could have a positive impact on humans if they carried no *a priori* knowledge, or knowledge independent of experience, but rather were a blank slate waiting to be filled.

The Philosophes

The Enlightenment as an intellectual movement truly came together during the mid-eighteenth century when the philosophes united for the common cause of educating the public. The philosophes had a number of interests and backgrounds, but they shared the common belief that they were intellectual beacons whose responsibility it was to enlighten the public. To the philosophes, common Europeans had no real use for the message of the Enlightenment because they would forever be preoccupied by their own survival. The philosophes believed in the value of questioning traditions, in the possibility of improving humanity, and in the possibility of progress. They were philosophers in the sense that they exercised their intellects but they had little interest

Define Your Terms

Philosophe is the French word for philosopher. The philosophes were the intellectual leaders of the Enlightenment.

in abstract thought. They had a concrete, practical purpose: to free the public from the dogmas of tradition, superstition, and false medieval ideas that never seemed to go away.

One way the philosophes hoped to free people from superstition and dogma was to expose the fallacies of organized religion. The philosophes believed, as Newton did, that a rational God created a universe bound by rules and laws and then set the universe in motion like a clock. They believed that because God was rational, he could be understood through reason. There was no need for the superstitious teachings of the various denominations, nor for the ceremonies and mysticism that accompanied organized religion. The philosophes called this new view of God and his creation *deism*.

The philosophes were reformers, but their "reform movement" was a top-down and not a grass-roots movement. The philosophes believed the only way society would change was through the education of those who ruled, the aristocrats and even the monarchs. Only they had the power to change existing laws and societal conditions.

Intellectual Freedom in France

For the philosophes, the few years before and after 1750 was when the most important early works were published. The unofficial headquarters for the philosophes was France. France didn't allow the philosophes total intellectual freedom, but in the years after Louis XIV died, repression and aggressive actions against intellectuals eased up a little. During the reign of Louis XIV, intellectuals who challenged the government or the Church generally found themselves tied to a post about to be burned to death. In the post-Louis years, intellectuals rarely faced the death penalty. They might have had their works banned and burned, and they might have been jailed or exiled, but they didn't really fear for their lives.

Even though they didn't fear for their lives necessarily, the philosophes often made their statements against the Church or against the state in a veiled form. They often wrote novels where the characters bad-mouthed other characters who represented the establishment. Some philosophes used the dictionary or encyclopedia format to express their views. Still others used satire to disguise what they really wanted to say.

Another reason the Enlightenment flourished in France had to do with language. French served as the polite language of the elite and the diplomatic language of politicians throughout Europe, and because French culture dominated Europe, French ideas easily spread with the language.

As a Matter of Fact

Charles-Louis Secondat, baron de Montesquieu (1689–1755), attacked the French government even though he was a high-ranking official. In 1721 Montesquieu published a satire called *Persian Letters* in which two Persians visited France during the reign of Louis XIV and made many unfavorable observations, compared the French government to their own harsh Persian government, and took shots at the pope. Besides the obvious satire, the *Persian Letters* explored government and morality. Montesquieu later applied the scientific method to problems of government in *The Spirit of the Laws* in 1748, comparing governments and examining factors such as geography and history as they influenced governments to discern which conditions promoted liberty and prevented tyranny. It didn't take long for Montesquieu's work to end up on the *Index* (see Chapter 5).

A French phenomenon that contributed greatly to the spread of Enlightenment thought took place in the homes of wealthy aristocrats. Gatherings of philosophes often hosted by wealthy, educated women were known as salons. The salons offered the intellectual elite of France places to gather to discuss politics and religion free from the control of the universities, the Church, and the government. One of the most famous salons was in the Paris home of Madame Marie-Thérèse Geoffrin (1699–1777). The greatest of France's intellectuals met in Geoffrin's salons. Eventually, as Enlightenment ideas spread to other European states, so did the idea of salons. Prominent European cities including Berlin, London, and Warsaw hosted salons as well.

As a Matter of Fact

The salons of Paris, and later of other cities, served as the breeding ground for much intellectual activity during the Enlightenment. However, the free-thinking philosophes could not speak in public the way they did behind closed doors in the salons. Therefore, in order to get their ideas into the hands and minds of the world outside the salons, the philosophes used a variety of letters. The philosophes made copies of letters, they published letters, and they even began writing letters to the editors of various pamphlets and periodicals. Much of the success of letter writing for intellectual and political purposes can be attributed to the salons of the Enlightenment. Salons weren't popular with all the Enlightenment thinkers. A number of intellectual men resented the power and influence of the women who hosted salons.

The Encyclopedia

Arguably the greatest work of the Enlightenment came in 1751 with the appearance of the first volume of the *Encyclopedie*, or *Encyclopedia: The Rational Dictionary of the Sciences, the Arts, and the Crafts*.

Although Denis Diderot (1713–1784) and Jean le Rond d'Alembert (1717–1783) edited the *Encyclopedie*, over a hundred intellectuals in fields such as mathematics, religion, law, and industry contributed thousands of articles to the manuscript that eventually reached seventeen volumes. The two editors hoped to do two things with the *Encyclopedie*. First, by making vast amounts of knowledge available, they hoped to promote the greater good of mankind. Second, they hoped to change Europeans' way of thinking. They believed the *Encyclopedie* would cause people to question dogmas and abandon superstitions, thus leading to the formation of a more educated public.

Would You Believe? ___

Because the *Encyclopedie* openly challenged religious intolerance and the Catholic Church while praising Protestant thought, the work in its entirety was banned by the Church. However, for those who subscribed to the work and paid the steep price, the volumes were delivered secretly upon completion.

By 1780, the 35 volumes contained over 70,000 articles and over 3000 illustrations. The articles covered every imaginable topic from science to math to religion to morality to manufacturing to the arts. Diderot firmly believed that every topic should be examined and explored regardless of what anyone thought or felt, and that this examination ultimately would lead to progress. For 15 years, Diderot and the others labored to produce the volumes, despite pressure from Rome and efforts by the publisher to dilute the contents. The *Encyclopedie*, which openly questioned the intolerance of religion and government, made a huge impact on all of Europe.

Tolerance: A Reasonable Expectation

The philosophes pushed hard for education, the exchange of ideas, the use of reason, and especially tolerance. They argued that a society benefited humanity only if tolerance existed not only in government but also in religious institutions.

The philosophes generally didn't mind absolute rulers as long as those rulers displayed some amount of benevolence and tolerance. What the philosophes despised most of all were intolerant religious institutions, factions, and individuals. History's greatest crimes and most devastating wars, many philosophes observed, had been committed in the name of religion. For the philosophes, organized, institutionalized religion led to conflict among denominations and to superstitious rituals. They routinely criticized all churches, not just the Catholic Church, for their resentment and harsh treatment of anyone who dared think differently. It was despicable to the philosophes that Christians killed other Christians in the name of Christianity.

The deism they taught allowed and encouraged tolerance of others who claimed to be Christians. For the philosophes who practiced the deism they preached, the most important things about Christianity were the acknowledgement of God the creator and a reasonable, rational approach to the search for that creator. Among the most outspoken of the lot against organized religion was François Marie Arouet (1694–1778).

a.k.a. Voltaire

One of the most famous of all philosophes, Voltaire, which was Arouet's pen name, had an interesting early career that greatly influenced his work as a philosophe. In 1717, Voltaire insulted the regent of France and earned himself nearly a year in Paris's infamous Bastille prison (see Chapter 14). Ten years later, Voltaire popped off about a powerful nobleman and earned himself more jail time and a good thrashing. The French finally let Voltaire out of jail after he promised to leave France.

True to his word, Voltaire left for England, where he pondered his unfair treatment in France. When he returned, he found his way into the company of one of France's greatest female minds, Gabrielle-Emilie Le Tonnelier de Breteuil, marquise du Châtelet (1706–1749). The aristocratic Madame du Châtelet, who had a deep interest in science and mathematics, allowed Voltaire to live on her property while he studied and wrote.

Would You Believe?

The Royal Academy of Sciences refused membership to Madame du Châtelet simply because of her gender. This spurned woman, however, translated Newton's *Principia* into French.

In his many works, Voltaire argued for tolerance and justice. He wrote that a good monarch was a good thing because most people weren't capable of governing themselves. He tried to convince the French rationalists that they needed a good dose of English empiricism. He glorified England and the English system of government and he slammed the French government. Voltaire reserved his harshest criticism for the Catholic Church, however. He disapproved of what he saw as its intolerance, oppression, and hypocrisy. Voltaire certainly believed in God but his religious beliefs centered on deism.

As a Matter of Fact _____

Voltaire wrote extensively about philosophy, social issues, and religion, but his most famous work turned out to be *Candide*, a racy, rip-roaring satire that lambasted oppression, the Church, the papacy, the violence of war, and even other philosophers. Voltaire, a pessimist by nature, had as his main purpose in writing *Candide* to rebut the optimistic philosophy of the contemporary philosopher Leibniz, who maintained that the world was the best of all possible worlds and was just as God intended it to be.

Voltaire's crusade against the oppression of the Catholic Church and all organized religion stemmed largely from the religion-related violence he witnessed throughout his lifetime. Likewise, his crusade against political oppression and intolerance resulted mostly from his personal experiences in French jails. However, the event that turned Voltaire into a lifelong advocate for political justice and fairness occurred not in his life but in the life of another.

In 1762, French courts executed a Frenchman named Jean Calas. An innocent man, Calas had been accused of murdering his son. Despite being tortured before his execution, Calas never confessed to the crime. This case cut Voltaire to the quick, and he became obsessed with it. In 1763, Voltaire published *A Treatise on Tolerance*, a powerful and timeless work that decried the intolerance exhibited by the government and the Church. Voltaire argued that governments should hold secular values in higher esteem than religious values, because state-imposed religion always results in violence and injustice.

The Later Enlightenment

The German philosopher Immanuel Kant (1724–1804) said in his 1784 essay "What Is Enlightenment?" that the spirit of the Enlightenment was embodied in the Latin phrase *sapere aude*, or "dare to know." Kant meant that the Enlightenment encouraged people to boldly ask questions, to seek knowledge, and to dare to think independently. He couldn't have been more right, particularly about the Enlightenment in its later years before 1789.

As if the early Enlightenment thinkers hadn't been bold enough, the later intellectuals made even bolder assertions than their forebears. The later thinkers of the Enlightenment lacked the unity of the philosophes of the mid-eighteenth century, formulating their own systems of thought that typically were much more dogmatic, exclusive, and inflexible than those of the early philosophes. In fact, some of the later philosophes created divisions in the Enlightenment movement. The rigid and determined Baron d'Holbach serves as a perfect example.

Baron d'Holbach, Atheist

The German Baron Paul d'Holbach (1723–1789), who was educated in France, took Newton's idea about the universe operating as a clock or as a machine to the extreme. D'Holbach argued that even humans are machines that have no free will. According to d'Holbach, forces and laws of nature governed the lives of humans, not humans themselves and certainly not God. He aggressively argued against the existence of God and even against the existence of human souls. After all, why would human machines have a need for souls?

From the safety of the Netherlands, d'Holbach published *System of Nature* (1770), a work that deeply troubled many of the philosophes. The philosophes had worked hard for tolerance and for the acknowledgement of the existence of God, regardless of how God was approached, and d'Holbach aggressively pushed his atheism in the name of the Enlightenment. D'Holbach often hosted formal dinners with other intellectuals to discuss their atheism, a relatively new development for Europe.

David Hume, Also an Atheist

One of the most influential of all d'Holbach's dinner guests was the Scottish skeptic David Hume (1711–1776). Hume combined skepticism and empiricism into a carefully formulated world-view that would have long-lasting effects on Europe. For Hume, Locke's ideas about human learning and the human mind made a great deal of sense. All knowledge was sensory, just impressions made on the mind by the senses. Anything that could not be experienced with the senses, through experimentation for example, could not be known.

The logical extreme of Hume's philosophy, which he laid out in *The Natural History of Religion* (1775), was that the belief in God equaled superstition, since God could not be experienced with the senses. Hume's philosophy also implied a great deal of relativism. One person's truth or knowledge wasn't necessarily the truth or knowledge perceived by another. For Hume, beauty was in the eye of the beholder.

Rousseau's Different Take on Society

The most influential political philosopher of the later Enlightenment turned out to be one of the stranger, more interesting individuals. The paranoid Jean-Jacques Rousseau (1712–1778), of Swiss origin yet influenced by Diderot and Voltaire, began his intellectual career by arguing in the mid-eighteenth century that the new emphasis on science and intellectualism had led to a decay in morals in Europe. He followed that essay with works ranging from fiction to essays on education and politics. Though his novel *The New Heloise* proved to be the most popular French work of fiction in the second half of the eighteenth century, Rousseau made his mark with his political philosophy.

Would You Believe?

Rousseau's distaste for society and his paranoia led him to spend his final days secluded in the countryside far away from his contemporaries.

While so many other philosophes believed that a better, progressive society would lead to better lives for mankind, Rousseau was wary of society and civilization. He believed the relationship between man and society was more strained than other philosophes did. Rousseau once remarked, "Man is born free and everywhere he is in chains." This statement shows Rousseau's distrust of society and civilization.

Rousseau's *The Social Contract*, written in 1762, proved to be his most significant political work. Rousseau argues that man will be best served by entering into a social contract, an agreement to be governed. Those who give their consent to be governed agree to live by certain moral standards that place the general will of the people above individual interests. The general will, difficult to define, can be described as that which is in the best interest of the collective.

Rousseau also emphasized popular sovereignty, or the people's ownership of true political power. These ideas undermined the political authority of rulers and governments who placed no importance on the power of the people. It is no wonder that the French government banned Rousseau's work. Despite the ban, Rousseau's ideas, particularly about the general will and popular sovereignty, would be the guidelines for many revolutionaries in the years of the French Revolution (see Chapter 14).

As a Matter of Fact

Rousseau made a significant impact on education with his manuscript *Emile*. In the book, Rousseau described the rearing and education of a young boy, Emile, in the natural world rather than in the urban world. Through his writing, Rousseau stressed the emotional needs of students and persuaded the reader to consider the whole person of the student rather than just the intellect of the student. Furthermore, Rousseau emphasized that children are greatly different than adults, have different needs than adults, and should not be treated like adults.

The Oxymoron of Enlightened Absolutists

At first glance, the use of "enlightened" and "absolutists" in the same sentence may seem very strange. Actually, a few absolute rulers did embrace aspects of the Enlightenment movement and considered themselves enlightened, even if contemporaries and later historians did not. The absolutists of eastern Europe seemed particularly interested in the message of the philosophes.

The philosophes welcomed the interest in the enlightenment from absolutists. They sought change from the top down for two reasons. The rulers had the power to change things, and the people couldn't be trusted to do so. Even Voltaire remarked that a benevolent ruler, even an absolute one, might be just what the people needed. Absolutism was a way of life for much of Europe, so the replacement of absolute governments with democratic or republican governments never really seemed like a possibility. Rather, the philosophes shared their ideas with the absolutists partly because the absolutists of the east would listen and partly because the philosophes believed they could help bring about reform. To some extent they did.

Frederick the Great

Frederick II of Prussia (1712–1786), also known as Frederick the Great, hardly was cut out of the same mold as his father, Frederick William I (see Chapter 10). Frederick despised the military and enjoyed literature and the arts as a young boy. He rejected his father's militaristic lifestyle and his religion, Calvinism. Frederick even embraced all things French, something that drove his father crazy.

By the time Frederick inherited the throne from his father in 1740, he had resolved to change his rebellious ways and use the mighty military he inherited. He invaded Silesia and took vast lands and population from Maria Theresa of the House of Habsburg, practically doubling Prussia's land and population. Frederick soon found himself bogged down in the Seven Years' War, in which France, Russia, and Maria Theresa tried to knock Prussia out and divvy the land up between them. On the verge of defeat, Frederick's Prussia survived only because the new leader of Russia called off his attack.

Frederick had always had a fondness for the Enlightenment, but he had never instituted any of its ideals in Prussia because of his incessant warring. After the brutal war, a kinder, gentler Frederick decided to concentrate on a more efficient, tolerant, and humane rule of Prussia. He created a fair and efficient judicial system, perhaps the best of its day in Europe. He got rid of torture tactics within the system and ensured that his officials were free from corruption. He allowed his subjects to worship as they pleased. Once the host and good friend of Voltaire, Frederick encouraged education, the advancement of knowledge, and philosophical activity. Many of the philosophes, including Immanuel Kant, fought for freedom of the press, or the freedom to publish philosophical and scholarly findings, and Frederick heard their pleas. Frederick worked hard to improve the lives of his subjects by promoting education, agriculture, and the economy in general. He had become the benevolent ruler of which Voltaire had written.

Catherine the Great

Catherine the Great of Russia made her way from relative obscurity up the political food chain to achieve true greatness. Catherine (1729–1796) married Peter III, the nephew of Peter the Great's daughter, in 1744. From the beginning of the relationship, Peter, pock-marked in appearance and with brainpower to match, was no competition for the brilliant and cunning Catherine. Catherine spent her time reading the works of the philosophes. She had absolutely no interest in her husband, but she did have a desire for his crown. Patiently she waited for her opportunity. Less than a year after Peter took the throne in 1762, Catherine's lover, an officer in the Russian military, led a revolution in the palace. After they deposed Peter, who had squandered the loyalty of the military when he decided not to continue attacks on Frederick's Prussia, the brothers of Catherine's lover murdered the hapless Peter. Catherine the Great had the crown she wanted.

Catherine was the sweetheart of the philosophes. Because she had so engrossed herself in the writings of the philosophes, Catherine ruled from day one as an enlightened monarch. As Peter the Great had done, Catherine imported westerners to infuse western culture into the still-backward country of Russia. She brought in both art and the written word to introduce the nobility to the glory of the West. She sponsored many of the philosophes when no one else would and she corresponded extensively with the likes of Voltaire. She offered to publish the *Encyclopedie* and subsidized it on occasion.

As a Matter of Fact _____

Catherine certainly will be remembered as a woman of letters. In addition to her devotion to the development of the French *Encyclopedie*, Catherine worked diligently to establish herself as a patron of literature in Russia. The famed Hermitage Museum in St. Petersburg began as Catherine's personal collection of art and literature. Catherine also did her part to contribute to the body of literature by writing a manual on education in which she used many of the ideas put forth by John Locke.

Just as Peter the Great upgraded the Russian military, Catherine upgraded the Russian culture. Catherine hoped to overhaul the justice system, much the way Frederick had done in Prussia, but her goal was never fully realized. She did abolish torture and grant some religious tolerance, though. Catherine might have granted other freedoms, perhaps even to serfs, had it not been for a rebellion led by a Cossack named Pugachev. After she crushed the rebellion, she realized she needed to keep the peasantry in check and keep the social status quo. This, along with generous grants of conquered lands such as Poland to her nobles, kept the nobility happy and loyal.

Would You Believe? _____

Throughout her reign, Catherine had many lovers upon whom she always lavished gifts. Even as a sixty-plus senior citizen, she had lovers as young as twenty-two.

Maria Theresa and Joseph II

The two remaining enlightened absolutists lacked the Enlightenment fervor that Frederick and Catherine possessed, but they nevertheless ruled as enlightened monarchs. The Empress Maria Theresa (1717–1780) of Austria limited the Church's influence, strengthened the bureaucratic system, and eased up on the peasants a little by limiting the power of the landlords.

When her son, Joseph II (1741–1790) of Austria, came to power in 1780, he picked up where his mother left off and initiated his own enlightened reforms. He placed the Church under more restrictions than his mother had and extended religious tolerance to both Protestants and Jews. Like Catherine and Frederick, Joseph sought to overhaul the bureaucracy and make it a more efficient governing machine. Joseph abolished serfdom altogether and, in doing so, created a backlash among his nobles. He also required that the peasants' remaining obligations be converted to cash debts. The peasants hated this because they didn't have any cash. In a move designed to make his society better, Joseph inadvertently angered everyone. Needless to say, when Joseph died, Habsburg Austria was a mess.

The Least You Need to Know

- ◆ The Enlightenment was an intellectual movement in the eighteenth century that grew out of the new way of thinking created by the thinkers of the Scientific Revolution.

- ◆ The Enlightenment, though it had some political effects, was an intellectual movement among the elite of Europe.

- ◆ The leaders of the Enlightenment were intellectuals who called themselves philosophes and who saw themselves as the intellectual beacons in a dark and gloomy Europe.

- ◆ The philosophes, and indeed the Enlightenment, embraced and championed such things as skepticism, reason, deism, and political and religious tolerance.

- ◆ Some of the leading minds of the Enlightenment included Bayle, Locke, Montesquieu, Voltaire, Hume, d'Holbach, and Rousseau.

- ◆ The themes of the Enlightenment found popularity among the aristocrats of Europe and with the absolutists of eastern Europe.

- ◆ Absolute rulers including Frederick the Great of Prussia, Catherine the Great of Russia, and Maria Theresa and Joseph II of Austria instituted reforms in their lands and ruled as enlightened monarchs.

Chapter 13

The Agricultural Revolution and an Expanding Europe

In This Chapter

- ◆ Exciting new agricultural techniques
- ◆ More food equals more and more and more people
- ◆ The beginnings of industrialization
- ◆ Mercantilism and colonization go hand in hand
- ◆ The introduction of slavery into the Western Hemisphere

For all the intellectual and scientific progress made in Europe prior to the eighteenth century, the common people of Europe benefited little. In fact, for the common people of Europe, the vast majority of whom worked in agriculture, life had hardly changed at all in a thousand years.

Seeds of Revolution

The peasants of the early eighteenth century found themselves stuck in the doldrums of everyday life the way their ancestors and their ancestors' ancestors had. Day in and day out, peasants went into the fields to till or to plant or to harvest. Their lives were tied to land that offered little more than subsistence regardless of how much labor they put into the land. Even in the most fertile regions of Europe, an acre of land offered but a few bushels of yield, scarcely more than the same acre would have produced a hundred or even a thousand years earlier.

As if the fickle nature of the land didn't cause enough hardship, the peasants of Europe also had to face the possibility of such agricultural disasters as drought, flood, harsh winters, and crop failure. Peasants generally tried to harvest enough grain to use some immediately and keep a reserve. However, reserves were only available after bountiful harvests and often spoiled from moisture or rats. When harvests were poor or reserves failed to meet the needs of the peasants, people took drastic measures in order to survive. Records indicate that the consumption of grass and bark was quite common in villages where food supplies ran short. There's almost no telling what other famine foods, as they were called, became part of the diets of hungry Europeans over the centuries. Poor diets led to weakened peasants with weakened immune systems. Diseases such as dysentery ravaged villages. Famine years in some villages meant that as many as one third of the inhabitants would not survive the winter.

Fortunately, between 1700 and 1750, centuries-old agricultural methods and ideas started to change, leading to what historians call the Agricultural Revolution. In recent years, it has become popular among historians to discount the importance of any one person or development in the Agricultural Revolution. Some historians claim that no revolution occurred at all, mostly because the advancements came slowly and took a great deal of time to impact all of Europe. There can be little debate, though, that the improvement of land, its more efficient use, the development of new agricultural devices, the use of selective breeding, and the use of innovative crops all led to the availability of more and better food for Europe. Furthermore, the amount of labor needed to produce the larger amounts of food actually decreased and freed up laborers to work in other industries besides agriculture.

Open and Closed

In the Middle Ages, desperate but clever peasants developed a new method of managing the land they worked that proved to be the biggest agricultural advance of that era. They instituted the open-field system, a way of using all available land in and around a village for the good of the entire village while retaining some sense of ownership over the land. As time passed, farmers fine-tuned the open-field system so that the land produced more crops. Eventually, though, the small landowners were strong-armed by wealthy landowners into selling their small plots of land. It didn't put every peasant farmer out of work, as many feared it might, but there were consequences from selling the land to the wealthy landowners, who fenced off the land and did away with the open-field system.

The Open-Field System

Under the open-field system, the land in and around a village was divided into large, open fields that were then subdivided into long, narrow strips of land. The community of peasants worked the open, unfenced fields year in and year out. While this system was actually an improvement over the primitive farming methods used before the Middle Ages, there were serious drawbacks. The peasant farmers had no true understanding of how nutrients like nitrogen had to be in soil in order for crops to grow and be productive. But, although they didn't know that planting the same crop in the same field year after year exhausted the nutrients that crop needed, they did know that, eventually, that crop would fail.

Eventually, the peasants developed a system of crop rotation, often called the three-field system and then the four-field system. In the three-field system, farmers planted two different crops in two different fields and left the third field fallow. After a few years, the farmers would rotate the crops through the fields so that a new field would be left fallow, the previously fallow field would be planted, and the remaining field would be planted with a different crop.

Crops most frequently planted in the fields included grains like wheat or rye and then perhaps beans. There were problems inherent in the system. For example, even though fallow fields didn't need to be tended the way other fields did, they still needed to be plowed several times each year to keep the weeds under control. Also, because animals like horses and oxen were necessary for working the land, some common fields were set aside for pasturing the animals; the commons, or large tracts of centrally located land, were accessible to everyone not only for grazing but for gathering firewood and the like.

In many cases, because of the pastureland and the fallow fields, scarcely more than 50 percent at a time of the arable land was actually used for farming. The acres that were farmed produced pathetically little yield relative to the energy put into the land, which explains why so many peasants went to bed hungry. It's important to note, though, that the open-field system combined with crop rotation was a welcome improvement over any farming methods used in Europe before.

Enclosure

Owners of relatively large amounts of land, particularly in England, forced many poor peasants to sell their strips of land. The impetus for the large landowners to begin the enclosure movement, in full swing by the mid-eighteenth century, was the noticeable increase in yield compared to the previous centuries. The causes for the increase were the innovations to which the Agricultural Revolution is largely attributed. The consolidation of land formerly scattered throughout the larger fields

proved to be efficient and also contributed to higher yields. By enclosing large tracts of land, managers of the enclosed crops were able to keep unwanted grazing down, practice selective breeding, prevent the spread of crop disease from one field to another, and employ progressive techniques with entire fields. To be fair, even though the large landowners moved forward with enclosure and people other than common farmers led the way in innovation, the tenant farmers were the ones who put the innovations into practice and made them work.

The peasants were coerced to sell their land not by force but through a legal system dominated, of course, by the large landowners. Peasants resisted as long as they could, but the pressure became too great. As the landowners amassed vast amounts of land, the fields were fenced or enclosed and access to the commons restricted. The peasants weren't kicked off the land completely, though, because the wealthy landowners certainly weren't going to till and sow and harvest the land themselves! The landowners rented the lands back to the peasants.

The peasants resented enclosure for a number of reasons. First, peasants lost access to the commons. Second, the peasants who were forced to give up their land were suddenly landless, the worst possible state of existence in Europe. Third, the peasants had no choice but to pay the rents, which often seemed unfairly high.

Revolutionary Agricultural Technology

One reason historians like to discount the degree to which the Agricultural Revolution was truly revolutionary is the length of time it took for all the developments to be widely used and to pay dividends.

One of the earliest advancements came as early as the seventeenth century in a seemingly unlikely place. In the Low Countries, much of the land lay below sea level and was covered with marshes and swamps. Because the population of the Netherlands grew so rapidly in the fifteenth and sixteenth centuries, drawing the maximum yield from the land was vital.

The ingenious Dutch drained the swamplands, enclosed fields, practiced crop rotation, and used manure to fertilize the fields. They maximized the land they had, and their techniques served as the model first for England and then for the rest of Europe. In the seventeenth century, the Dutch engineer Cornelius Vermuyden (1595–1683) traveled to England where he led a land reclamation project that eventually drained tens of thousands of English acres that became valuable farmland. It was on just such land that English farmers, and later farmers in other parts of Europe, experimented with new crops, new gadgets, and new methods of farming.

As a Matter of Fact

The land reclamation project of Cornelius Vermuyden in the low marshlands of England, land known as the Fens, proved highly successful in providing new, arable land for English farmers. However, the project ran into a major snag before completion. Vermuyden, a Dutchman, employed Dutch laborers and engineers for the project. Furthermore, the Fensmen who lived off the land were stripped of their livelihoods during the reclamation process. In response, the Fensmen attacked Vermuyden and the Dutch workers. Vermuyden, in order to finish the project, had to employ English workers and had to pay the Fensmen for lost wages.

Nitrogen Replenishing Crops

The word nitrogen would have meant absolutely nothing to Europeans in the eighteenth century. Little did they know that nitrogen, and the crops that put nitrogen into the soil, played a major role in the Agricultural Revolution. The revolutionary crops that changed the way Europe farmed were legumes. Legumes, also called nitrogen-fixing plants, converted nitrogen from the air and put nitrogen into the soil in a form usable by other vegetation.

Europeans had used legumes such as beans and peas for centuries, but sometime in the late seventeenth or early eighteenth century, the farmers of the Netherlands used them in a revolutionary way. They planted turnips and clover in fields that had traditionally been left fallow. After a few years of the turnips and clover, the wheat and other grains planted in those fields exceeded expectations. As an added bonus, the turnips and clover made great fodder for the animals, rather than using other resources to feed the horses and oxen. The manure produced by the animals could, in turn, be used to fertilize the fields.

One of the biggest advocates of the use of turnips was a wealthy English statesman named Charles "Turnip" Townsend (1674–1738). Townsend discovered the revolutionary effects of turnips and clover while serving as an ambassador across the English Channel. It was said that Turnip Townsend spoke of little else but turnips and their benefits. On his large estate, Townsend abandoned his fallow fields in favor of turnips; he used plenty of manure and reaped huge rewards. His obsession, and more importantly his willingness to be innovative, inspired many other aristocratic landowners to try new agricultural methods.

New Agricultural Techniques

Just as innovators and new crops helped improve the bottom line, so did new devices and techniques. One of the more interesting innovators was Jethro Tull (1674–1741). Tull, another Englishman, set out to be a lawyer but his health prevented him finishing his studies. Tull reportedly disliked manual labor, and liked his laborers even less because of their inability to do things the way he wanted.

Tull realized that his laborers were inefficient when spreading seeds by hand, so he invented a seed drill. The drill created evenly spaced holes drilled at precise depths and had a funnel that sent a precise amount of seeds into the drilled holes. It took quite a while and several revisions for the drill to catch on, but it finally did years later as the aristocracy became fascinated with innovative agriculture.

For all of Tull's innovative ideas, he often was thought of as a quack and the stereotypical crazy inventor. Not all his ideas were as on target as his seed drill. For example, he thought the use of manure in fields was overrated. Instead of using manure, he pounded and crushed the soil to release nutrients. He certainly deserves credit, however, for thinking outside the box, for not relying on tradition, and for using the typical English empirical approach to problems.

Another innovative Englishman whose contributions were important was Robert Bakewell (1725-1795). Bakewell worked in animal husbandry and is often called the father of animal breeding. Bakewell set out to breed certain characteristics into and out of lines of sheep, cattle, and horses. The medieval practice of allowing the village animals to graze the commons often resulted in random breeding. The males and females were allowed to intermingle and breed as they pleased.

Bakewell changed that and allowed males and females to breed only when he wanted them to breed. Furthermore, he ignored the medieval taboos of inbreeding, or breeding animals from the same family. Bakewell bred two animals together to reproduce certain traits. One example of such breeding was a particular line of sheep he perfected with fatty shoulders to accommodate the taste of the English for fatty mutton. The practice of selective breeding led to improvements in livestock that, in turn, led to better milk-producing animals, better work animals, and hardier animals in general.

People, People Everywhere!

The combination of new farming techniques, new crops, new devices, and better livestock contributed to a population explosion in Europe during the eighteenth century, particularly after 1750. However, there was more at work than just agricultural and dietary factors.

War, famine, and disease had always kept the European population in check, but all three declined in the eighteenth century. The construction of roads and canals throughout the seventeenth and eighteenth centuries reduced the significance of crop failure by allowing more access to surplus resources from other locations. Each of these factors set off a chain reaction that resulted in population increases in many if not most European nations.

The Chain Reaction

Historians and population experts agree on only general factors that contributed to the population boom. Agricultural advances led to a higher yield per acre. More and better food in the European diet led to improved immune systems. Better immune systems, along with the decline of deadly diseases and catastrophic warfare, contributed to lower death rates. Better immune systems coupled with a lower marriage age for some women resulted in higher birth rates and perhaps lower infant mortality rates. Some historians have speculated that the draining of marshes and swamps led to a decrease in the number of disease-carrying insects such as mosquitoes. Others have pointed to improved sewage systems.

Taking all these factors into consideration, two conclusions have been made over and over. First, the single most important contributor to the population boom was simply the *drop* in the mortality rate across Europe. Second, as much as humanists would like to credit humans with the boom, the population explosion was a combination of man-made and naturally occurring phenomena.

Limiting Population Growth

Dating as far back as classical Greece and Rome, thinkers have worried about over-population. In nature, overpopulation results in sick, weak animals that eventually die off leaving only the strong as survivors. Those concerned about overpopulation have always feared the same result in the human population. For eighteenth-century con-temporaries, that fear was very real.

In reality, the population boom probably contributed greatly to the birth of industri-alization (see Chapter 17) in Britain. While historians can see that in retrospect, contemporaries like Thomas Malthus could not. Malthus (1766–1834) expressed his concerns in *Essay on the Principle of Population* in 1798. Malthus, an ordained Anglican minister and a pessimist by nature, believed that if not checked, the human pop-ulation would continue to expand at a greater rate than the supply of food. Malthus feared that war, famine, and disease were nature's, and therefore God's, ways of keeping population in check.

> **Continental Quotes**
>
> "Hard as it may appear in individual cases, dependent poverty ought to be held dis-graceful."
>
> —Thomas Malthus

If man hoped to keep these checks to a minimum, he must work to keep the popula-tion down. According to Malthus (the second of eight children), the best way to do this was to limit human reproduction, preferably through abstinence but also through marrying later in life. The pessimist in him blamed the poor for most of society's woes and he doubted that the poor were capable of showing the restraint necessary to do as he prescribed. If Malthus and his followers had gotten their way, British leg-islation would have prevented the poor from marrying and having kids altogether.

The Cottage Industry

The growth of the rural population in the eighteenth century in many ways led to the growth of rural industry, too. The population boom created more rural peasants in Europe who needed work, and agricultural work wasn't always available. Even rural residents who did have work on the land always welcomed the opportunity to supple-ment their income; since farming was largely seasonal, even those with full-time employment on farms had extra time to earn extra income.

Capitalists in the cities took notice of the labor surplus and saw an opportunity to employ rural workers at a price usually lower than urban workers earned. The primi-tive industry that resulted would later become known as the *cottage industry*.

Rural Industry or the Putting-Out System

Even in the Middle Ages, rural peasants participated in some amount of industry, although it had nothing to do with factories and manufacturing. Industrious peasants with hand tools produced all kinds of small objects, from wooden shoes to articles of clothing to lace to crafts. Prior to the eighteenth century, the peasants didn't produce or earn much. As capitalists from the cities moved business into the countryside, the opportunities for the rural peasants to work increased rapidly. The move from occasional work to steady work for peasants in the countryside was the result of the putting-out system, a system that began in England and later spread to the continent.

A number of workers and their families were involved in the putting-out system. The system involved an entrepreneur and a circuit of households. The entrepreneur would invest in raw materials such as wool purchased from a rural farmer. The entrepreneur would then take the wool first to one home, then to another and another. The family of each household would perform each step of processing the wool. When the entrepreneur picked up the final product at the last home on his circuit, he had finished cloth or even clothing, which he could sell in the city or export. Often the entrepreneur would drop off a new load of raw materials as he picked up the processed materials.

This basic plan had countless variations as the entrepreneurs used any number of raw materials and had them processed to different stages of completion. The system worked well for all involved and the industry grew quickly. The entrepreneurs could pay the rural workers less than urban workers who had some protection from guilds, and the entrepreneur didn't have to worry about the guilds' quality-control measures in the countryside. The rural workers often had no other steady income, so they were happy to get whatever work came their way.

Proto-Industrialization and Textiles

Though a number of products fell under the umbrella of the cottage industry, the goods produced most often were *textiles*. The textile industry proved to be quite lucrative for the entrepreneurs who fronted the capital, and provided a stable income for the weavers and spinners. This system can be seen as proto-industrialization, the forerunner of work that took place in mills and factories.

The homes of workers who participated in the textile industry often contained little else but

Define Your Terms

A **textile** is a type of material made from thread or yarn that is woven, matted, knotted, or formed in a similar matter.

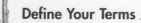

Define Your Terms

Unmarried and wid-owed women who made their living by spinning thread for weavers were known as **spinsters.**

the loom and a few pieces of furniture. The entire family had work to do. One member spun the wool or cotton into thread or yarn, another wove the thread, and even children helped by combing or cleaning the wool or cotton. The weaver with his or her loom could work so quickly that several spinners were needed just to keep up. Often the weaver would recruit others in the village, in addition to his family members, to spin thread for him.

Despite the benefits for all involved, problems arose in the rural textile industry. While the guilds had no control over the rural workers, they also had no control over the entrepreneurs. This meant that there was no one to enforce a system of standard weights and measures, no objective person to make sure the bales were the proper weight or that the workers turned in the proper amount of finished product. Disputes were commonplace. Quality suffered sometimes, too, especially because of the work-ers' work habits. It was common for workers to work hard all week and then take a day or two off after payday. Then, as the deadline approached, the workers kicked it into high gear to finish on time. Almost certainly the quality suffered as a result.

The Atlantic Economy

As the population grew in the eighteenth century, Europe looked beyond its borders to meet the ever-increasing demands of its ever-increasing consumers. Overseas ex-pansion provided a plethora of goods and allowed some of Europe's population to migrate overseas to relieve the population pressure in the British Isles and on the continent. In the eighteenth century, as with proto-industrialization, Britain led the way in building an economy centered on trade and colonization across the Atlantic Ocean. Other countries eventually followed suit in the prosperous Atlantic Economy.

The Atlantic Economy grew out of the spirit of overseas exploration and colonization and the economic policy of mercantilism, both of which began long before. Britain wasn't the only nation that sought to expand across the Atlantic. The French, Dutch, and Spanish also had interests there dating back two or three hundred years. So many hands in the pot was bound to create conflict. Over the seventeenth and eighteenth centuries, the desire for control of the Atlantic Economy, particularly land in North America, resulted in a number of armed conflicts.

In the second half of the seventeenth century, three separate armed conflicts between the English and Dutch dealt setbacks to the Dutch, including the English capture of

New Amsterdam, which was renamed New York. After the War of Spanish Succession (see Chapter 10), Britain won from France parts of Canada and it won from Spain control of the slave trade. Then in 1763, at the end of the Seven Years' War, a virtual world war that was fought in Europe and in North America, Britain won the rest of the French holdings in North America. Little did Britain know that in just a few short years, all their hard work in the North American colonies would go up in smoke (see Chapter 14).

Would You Believe?

The Seven Years' War was known in North America as the French and Indian War.

Colonies as a Function of Mercantilism

The basic economics of mercantilism dated back to French advisors like Colbert. French mercantilism involved government regulation of the economy so that everything within the economy benefited the national economy. The roads, the laws, and especially the colonization were intended to strengthen the national economy. The English take on mercantilism, though, varied slightly. While the French never considered sharing the wealth with private interests, the English mercantilists believed both the government and private interests could benefit from mercantilism.

The Navigation Acts served as a great example of such thinking. The Navigation Acts required that imported goods be carried on British ships. The same policy applied to goods heading in and out of British colonies. These laws gave British shipping companies a monopoly on overseas trade. Eventually these laws would offend the colonists; all their goods had to go to England, even when they might have commanded higher prices elsewhere.

One of the most significant manifestations of mercantilist ideas was colonization. The French typically sponsored the colonies abroad so that the financial rewards would go directly into French coffers. The English, on the other hand, allowed private investors to back the colonization efforts. These investors, through joint stock companies, provided the capital needed to establish trade colonies. With groups of investors, no single investor faced financial ruin if a colony failed.

The English crown benefited because it, along with the investment companies, reaped the rewards of the goods imported from the colonies—and it could tax the colonists. The mercantilist ideas, though seemingly restrictive and arguably oppressive, were based on the idea that the colonists would be guaranteed a market for their goods. In spite of the arguments against mercantilism, the system allowed English colonists in North America to enjoy tremendous prosperity relative to other people of equivalent social status in other parts of Europe.

Adam Smith

As the mercantilist policies filled the treasuries of the English, French, and even the Spanish, some opposition arose over the oppressive nature of mercantilism. Small merchants were bullied out of business by the large trading companies. The small merchants wanted their fair share; they argued against the monopolies created by mercantilism and in favor of free trade. Perhaps the loudest voice for such things came from the Scottish professor and philosopher Adam Smith (1723–1790).

A great lecturer of philosophy at the university in Glasgow, Smith was heavily influenced by the economic theory of the physiocrats. The physiocrats were philosophes who applied Newton's mechanistic view of the universe to economics. They believed that physical laws governed economics just like the universe. According to these laws, the economy would benefit from individuals being allowed to compete for their own self-interests. Physiocrats were not fans of mercantilism because it repressed the individual and did not allow competition.

 **As a Matter of Fact**

It has been said that Adam Smith often seemed scatter-brained and absent-minded, particularly at the beginning of lectures, but that he possessed the gift for gab and could really speak well once he got going. Even though Smith advocated free trade and competition, he considered humans to be greedy, selfish, and generally untrustworthy. Nevertheless, he believed the unhindered economy driven by competition would tend to benefit society.

Adam Smith published his landmark economic philosophical work, *Inquiry into the Nature and Causes of the Wealth of Nations*, in 1776. Often called *Wealth of Nations*, Smith's work called for economic liberalism and described mercantilism as oppressive, restrictive, and unfair. Smith argued that individuals had no chance to profit unless they were favorites of the government. Smith proposed a *laissez faire* economic policy instead, in which the government stayed out of the way and let the economy play out. He disapproved of most government restrictions on trade and commerce, including tariffs.

According to this ideology, the economy would benefit from competition among individuals. Prices would be lower because of competition and products would be better because people would be free to pursue the skills they were best at. Smith argued that a government's responsibility was to protect its citizens from foreign threats, keep order within its borders, and maintain public works. Beyond that, Smith maintained, if the people were allowed to pursue their own self-interests, an "invisible hand" would move the economy toward that which is best for the nation. While Smith's work was initially dismissed by many, it became one of the most influential works ever in the field of economics and is still studied by economists and economics students today. Smith's work helped establish economics as a systematic discipline in its own right and led to the dismissal of many earlier economic schools of thought.

Slavery

Many of the settlers who made the journey to the colonies of North America did so as indentured servants. In exchange for their paid passage across the Atlantic, they agreed to work for a period of years. After a while, an interesting problem developed in the colonies. Labor to work the vast amounts of land was hard to find and expensive. The large plantations of cotton, tobacco, and sugar cane faced the same problems.

The practice of importing slaves from Africa to the New World dated to the sixteenth century when the Spanish and the Portuguese first brought slaves to the New World. The Dutch followed suit later and so did the English. By the turn of the eighteenth century, the use of African slaves in the Caribbean islands had spread to the large plantations in the southern colonies like Virginia. After the introduction of African slaves into the British colonies in North America, production skyrocketed. The slaves proved so popular that landowners bought more and more and more. By the end of the eighteenth century, slaves represented almost one fifth of the population of the colonies.

Would You Believe?

The Europeans turned to Africa for slaves because the Native Americans who were used first as slaves died quickly in bondage.

The Triangle Trade

Over the course of the more than four centuries that African slaves were transported to the Americas, a general pattern of trade existed, known as the Triangle Trade. Manufactured goods including fabric, liquor, and guns were used by European slave traders to acquire African slaves from along the west African coast. Many of the Africans exploited by the slave traders were actually captured in the African interior by other Africans and sold to the traders in coastal ports. The slaves then made the difficult journey across the Atlantic to the Americas, where they were traded for raw materials such as sugar, cotton, and tobacco. The ships then headed back to Europe where they unloaded the raw materials for refinement and processing. A new shipment of manufactured goods was loaded onto ships and the cycle began again. The Triangle Trade proved lucrative for all involved—except the humans who were enslaved.

It has been estimated that millions upon millions of Africans were uprooted and shipped against their will to the Americas. For many, the hardships began long before they arrived in the New World; many died en route in what is referred to as the Middle Passage, the route from Africa to the Americas. Slaves were packed into ships like sardines and barely fed and watered. Almost immediately, slaves found themselves ill from lack of sanitation and from exposure to European diseases. Those who died were simply tossed overboard. The Middle Passage alone claimed perhaps millions of slaves who never even made it to the Americas.

The slave trade eventually slowed, but not until the end of the eighteenth century did the slave trade finally end. Of course, so many slaves lived in the Americas by that point that trade across the Atlantic was no longer necessary. Most European nations had emancipated the slaves in their overseas colonies by the mid-1800s.

The Least You Need to Know

- The Agricultural Revolution was revolutionary in that new techniques, crops, and devices allowed Europeans to increase the total amount of food produced and the amount of food produced per person.

- Crop rotation, enclosure, draining swamps, the use of nitrogen-fixing plants, and selective breeding were among the innovative ideas used to produce record amounts of crops. The increase in food started a chain reaction that contributed to a population explosion.

- The population boom precipitated a need for more goods and more jobs. The surplus of rural workers made it possible for entrepreneurs to employ the rural workers in cottage industries, particularly in the production of textiles.

- Mercantilist governments used colonies to bolster both national economies and private interests. Opponents of mercantilism, including the physiocrats and Adam Smith, argued for *laissez faire* economic policies.

- The slave trade sent millions of Africans across the Middle Passage as part of the Triangle Trade to the Americas. The slaves were traded for raw materials that were then sent to Europe for manufacturing.

14

The French Revolution

In This Chapter

- ◆ Those troublesome colonies in America
- ◆ Louis XVI and his no-win situation
- ◆ Tennis courts, a minimum security prison, and thousands of angry women
- ◆ Seriously—the Committee of Public *Safety?*
- ◆ The Madness is finally stopped

Between 1776 and 1815, Europe experienced a political revolution that can be traced directly to the ideas of the philosophes. The philosophes didn't start the revolution in politics, and they certainly didn't start the fighting, but their ideas were the rallying cry of those who did revolt.

The philosophes' calls for human rights, also called liberty or freedom, inspired men in the British colonies of North America and in France to take up arms against their oppressors. Ideas such as popular sovereignty made people believe that political power should rest in their hands, not in the hands of the oppressive monarchs. The revolutionaries also demanded equality—not economic or gender equality, just equal protection under the law. The American colonists demanded to be treated as Englishmen and not as third-class citizens. The people of France demanded the old social order be done away with so that everyone was equal under the law.

These ideas may not seem radical in the twenty-first century, but they were indeed revolutionary concepts for eighteenth-century Europe. Those liberals, or men who advocated change in favor of human rights and equality under the law, faced stiff challenges from the conservatives, or men who desired to maintain the status quo. Ultimately, the liberals won out in the colonies and in France—but at a tremendous price.

Trouble for the Brits

The colonies in North America had always been a good investment for the British. They were, for the most part, pretty low-maintenance. The colonies were self-sufficient, they made their own laws, and they didn't require too much attention from the British government. As such, the colonists felt a sense of separation from the British.

There were no serfs or nobles in the colonies. No oppressive government forced a state church on the colonists. Although technically the colonists were British, over time many came to think of themselves as American. When Britain went to war against the hated French in the French and Indian War, as the Seven Years' War was called in North America, the British flooded the colonies with soldiers.

After successfully pounding the French in 1763, the British decided to leave their soldiers in the colonies to defend against anybody else who tried to trespass. The war basically doubled the British national debt, and now, faced with the possibility of leaving the soldiers in America long-term, the British government had no choice but to raise the colonists' taxes. The colonists paid some of the lowest taxes in the world, just a fraction of the taxes that the English paid. Nevertheless, they didn't appreciate it.

The Colonies Get Mad

The new British taxes came in the form of the Stamp Act, a new tax on all sorts of printed material including legal documents, newspapers, pamphlets, even playing cards. The Stamp Act struck a nerve with the colonists. Protests and riots broke out and Parliament eventually gave in and repealed the tax. The colonists, who the British government believed were being terribly unreasonable, maintained that Parliament had no authority to change laws and levy taxes. They began to see the British government as a potential threat to their comfortable way of life.

Things hit the fan again in 1773, when the
British government went to the aid of the
East India Company, a trading company that
shipped tea, and effectively cut colonial merchants out of the picture, helping to boost the
business of a British company rather than contributing to the economic well-being of the
colonists.

Would You Believe?

The Stamp Act required
that small stamps be affixed to
paper documents to show that
taxes had been paid on items.
The English had been paying
stamp taxes for many years when
Parliament decided to levy the
tax in the colonies.

The colonists were furious, so a group of men
dressed as Native Americans and threw themselves a tea party. Actually, they sneaked into
Boston Harbor and dumped massive amounts of the company's tea overboard. Such
rebellious and lawless behavior left the British government with no choice but to
tighten its grip on the rowdy colonists. Parliament passed the Coercive Acts, limiting
colonial political freedom and strengthening royal power in the colonies.

The assemblies or lawmaking bodies from several colonies officially denounced the
actions. A continental congress, a meeting of representatives from the various colonies, met in 1774 and decided they would not give in to the oppressive measures of
the British government. Back in England, Parliament met and decided it wouldn't
budge either. As tensions between the two sides mounted, fighting broke out in 1775.

The Colonies Declare Independence

Throughout 1775 and 1776, many of the best and most influential colonial politicians
worked to sway public opinion against the British government, even arguing in favor
of independence from Britain. On July 4, 1776, the Second Continental Congress
signed the Declaration of Independence, a document that listed the atrocities of King
George III (1738-1820) and claimed the colonies were no longer subject to British
rule. The colonists had officially drawn their line in the sand.

The British government could not allow colonies in which it had so much time and
money invested to break away from the empire, so it responded with force. The fighting escalated between the professional British armies dressed in fancy red coats and
the rag-tag militia of the colonists, many of them farmers or craftsmen. The British
soldiers were aided by some colonists, called Loyalists, who remained loyal to the
crown. All things being equal, the British would have and should have crushed the
colonial armies. However, the colonists had allies across the Atlantic who were more
than happy to undermine the British.

The Colonies Get Help from France

The French didn't want to openly declare war on the Brits, but King Louis XVI (1754–1793) did want to avenge the humiliating defeat of the Seven Years' War. Before the French officially threw their weight behind the rebellious colonists, the French government allowed the politician and playwright Beumarchais (1732–1799) to create a fake company called Roderigue Hortalez et Cie, through which the French and Spanish governments funneled aid to the American independence movement. By 1777, French troops were headed to America, and by 1778 approximately 15,000 French troops were added to the colonial forces.

With the entrance of French troops in the war against the British, the scales tipped in favor of the Americans. French and colonial forces actually numbered more than British forces, not including the Hessian mercenaries employed by the British. The Americans got a huge boost when France granted the former colonies, now calling themselves states, favored nation status in 1778. The French followed that treaty with another that created an alliance for the purpose of maintaining the independence of the United States. Britain soon found itself at odds not only with France but also with the Spanish, the Dutch, and even the Russians.

The British couldn't afford such entanglements, so they granted independence to the rebellious Americans in 1783 at the Treaty of Paris. Were it not for the efforts of the French—including the sacrifice of more than 2,000 soldiers—the colonies' rebellion may very well have been squashed.

The French Get an Idea

Many in Europe watched with great anticipation as the events across the Atlantic unfolded. When the dust settled and the Americans stood victorious, the significance was not lost on Europe. An oppressed people championing liberty and equality had taken up arms against the government and had made their own destiny. If it could happen in America, it could happen in Europe.

> **Would You Believe?**
>
> Many of the ideologies of the founding fathers of the United States derived directly from Enlightenment thinkers. Locke's belief in natural rights, or the right to life, liberty, and property, was of monumental importance in the drafting of the American system of government.

Many of the French who served, including the heroic Marquis de Lafayette (1757–1834), had gone just to fight the British—and then found themselves fighting for ideals like liberty and democracy. They returned to France fired up by what they experienced in America. French thinkers examined the events and the documents of the revolution, documents like the U.S. Constitution. The revolution in America didn't cause the revolution in France, but it definitely influenced French revolutionaries.

Louis XVI's Dilemma

Much like the revolution in America, the French Revolution had its roots in economics, but the French Revolution and its causes are much more complicated than simple economic turmoil. Social factors, class tensions, and class struggle certainly played a role in the outbreak of the revolution. Many revolutionaries had political reform as their primary concern; others wanted political power for themselves. Many French revolted simply because they were hungry and the mob mentality proved too hard to resist. Historians have hotly debated the causes and nature of the revolution but probably all agree that there was no single cause. Most also probably agree that, on the eve of the revolution, King Louis XVI was in a no-win situation.

Thanks, Sun King

Louis XIV left a legacy that defined French culture and set a new standard for European militaries. He also left an insurmountable debt that crippled the French economy. His expenditures for constructing his military, fighting his wars, and building his palace at Versailles were staggering. His spending in these areas left little money for less important things—like the people of France.

When Louis XIV died in 1715, the throne passed to five-year-old Louis XV (1710–1774), his great-grandson. The Duke of Orleans ruled as regent until 1723 and restored vast amounts of power to the *parlements*, the high courts in France, in an attempt to please the nobles. The parlements had the power to check any decree of the crown before it became law. Later in his reign, the young King Louis XV turned his attention away from the ladies just long enough to take the power away from the parlements. When King Louis XVI took the throne in 1774, probably hoping he would be appreciated, he restored power to the parlements.

Trouble over Taxes

King Louis XVI inherited a nation burdened with tremendous debt not only from Louis XIV but also from Louis XVI's Seven Years' War. He inherited a power struggle between the crown and the parlements. Louis XV's efforts to raise taxes had been met with resistance from the parlements, and Louis XVI's efforts were met with the same. The parlements, nobles who had long had exemptions to certain taxes, resisted all efforts to tax the wealthy.

In 1776, Louis XVI tried to increase taxes to fund the Americans' fight for independence, but his request for new taxation was denied. He was forced to borrow money to help the rebellious Americans. The economy could hardly stand it. The debt soared as the government practiced dangerous deficit spending. Louis and his ministers decided to call an assembly of notables, a meeting of wealthy and powerful nobles and clergymen from around France. Louis presented a plan for a new tax, but the assembly wasn't impressed, informing Louis that his far-reaching taxation could be approved only by the Estates-General, the legislative body of France.

The problem was, the Estates-General hadn't met in over 150 years. Louis ran off the notables and decreed a new tax anyway. It didn't last long because the parlement in Paris disallowed the new tax. Enraged, Louis tried to dismiss the judges of the Paris court but the public did not react favorably to that idea. Realizing that he really wasn't the absolutist he thought he was, Louis XVI conceded and called for a meeting of the Estates-General.

The National Assembly and Revolution

Calling the Estates-General opened a can of worms for Louis XVI that no one expected. The process of electing the representatives created a stir among all the social classes. Suddenly everyone looked to the future, a future perhaps without an absolutist and a future with at least considerable change. Each social group in France had its own ideas about what needed to be changed and how. The clergy had ideas about church reform, the nobility had ideas about taxation, and the common people had ideas about all kinds of social and political reform. Each of these groups made up the legal social classes of France called the estates.

The Three Estates

At the time Louis XVI called for a session of the Estates-General, France had three legal classes or orders of citizens. Though they were legal classes they certainly were not distinct. Each of France's twenty-five million or so inhabitants fell into one of the three estates.

The clergy, all one-hundred thousand of them, made up the first estate. The Church owned about 10 percent of the land in France but paid relatively little in the way of taxes. The second estate consisted of several hundred thousand nobles and accounted for about 25 percent of the French land. Membership in the second estate had nothing to do with wealth; they had hereditary claims to membership because their ancestors were nobles. Members of the second estate often were wealthy, though, because of their holdings of land or because of the age-old right to tax peasants for their own benefit. The second estate also enjoyed a variety of tax exemptions, many dating back generations. Even those who possessed little wealth believed themselves superior to the third estate and at least equal to the first estate.

More than twenty-four million French, everyone who was neither clergy nor nobility, fell into the third estate. It made no difference whether a person was a wealthy businessman or a poor urban worker, a well-to-do lawyer or a rural peasant. If a Frenchman was neither clergy nor nobility, he was a commoner.

Historians have long debated the source of the social tension leading up to the French Revolution. Some historians emphasize the tensions between the three estates. In many cases, members of the third estate were wealthier than some of the members of the second estate and, therefore, resented being treated like the other commoners. Other historians have emphasized the differences between the individuals within the estates. The wealthiest members of each of the three estates had very different economic and political interests from the poorer members of each estate. Even though many lawyers and merchants were members of the third estate, their interests were nothing like the interests of the peasants and the urban poor. Though the classes were divided legally, many members of the second and third estates had more in common with one another than with other members of their own estates.

Becoming the National Assembly

After their election to the Estates-General, the delegates made their way to Versailles in 1789. The majority of delegates from the first estate were not wealthy. The second estate's delegates were split economically and politically, but most were wealthy nobles and only a few were liberals seeking real change. Most of the third estate's delegates were lawyers and government officials whose interests lay in social advancement. For the most part, the poor had no representation.

Though the delegates came from different estates, there were a few things that nearly all wanted to see changed. Nearly all the delegates wanted to move away from absolutism, to have the Estates-General meet regularly, and to give them power over the monarch with regard to taxes and laws.

When the Estates-General last met in 1614, the three estates met separately and votes were counted by estate. In other words, the first and second estates often voted 2 to 1 against the third estate, thereby maintaining power over the commoners. For the 1789 meeting, the third estate's number of representatives was increased to equal the first and second estates' delegates combined. The change came by royal decree largely in response to the rather vocal demands of the members of the third estate and an army of pamphleteers who championed the cause. The third estate's delegates were excited about the possibilities until they learned that the estates were still going to meet separately, just like in the old days. From virtually the first day of the meetings, the estates locked horns in a stalemate. The third estate refused to meet unless Louis XVI agreed that all the estates meet as a single assembly. Six weeks later, some of the liberal priests left the first estate and went to meet with the third estate.

On June 17, the members of the third estate decided to call themselves the National Assembly. A few days later, the National Assembly showed up to meet in their regular meeting place and discovered that the meeting hall had been "closed for repairs." They smelled a conspiracy against them, so they found an indoor tennis court where they could meet. It was there, led by Abbé Emmanuel Sieyès (1748–1836), that they swore the famous Tennis Court Oath, a vow that they would not leave until the National Assembly had written a new constitution for France. Sieyès had written the influential pamphlet *What is the third estate?*, in which he argued that the third estate, not the other two, truly represented the French people. Days later, the king ordered the three estates to meet together. However, on the heels of that order, he changed his mind and decided to try absolutism once more. Louis dismissed some of his liberal advisors and he ordered troops to Versailles to disband the Estates-General.

Would You Believe?

The most influential painter of this time, Jacques Louis David, painted a stirring scene of the Tennis Court Oath. In the painting, a brewing storm can be seen outside through an open window. Indeed, a storm was brewing in France.

Bastille and the Great Fear

Louis XVI couldn't have picked a worse time to try to flex his muscles. Economic conditions were terrible in France, especially around Paris. Awful harvests resulted in exorbitant bread prices, prices the poor could not afford. As prices spiraled, workers lost their jobs at astounding rates. While the king, and those before him, *had* made decisions that adversely affected the economy, the poor people believed that the king and the nobles were directly responsible for the shortages, the high prices, the unemployment, and the general state of despair.

In mid-July of 1789, the poor of Paris, who began to gather in crowds demanding food, caught wind of troop movement; they feared the king had dispatched the troops to disband the crowds and attack the city. In a panic caused by misunderstanding, the mobs descended on a prison called the Bastille, believing it housed massive supplies of weapons and gunpowder that could be used to defend the city against the attacking royal troops.

The mob demanded entry but the prison's governor refused. When the mob tied to force its way in, the guards opened fire and killed almost 100 Parisians. The mobs continued until the prison surrendered. They killed some of the guards and the governor, and put the governor's head on a pike; the mayor of Paris met the same fate. The crowds then appointed the Marquis de Lafayette commander of the "army" in Paris. The poor of Paris had begun the armed revolution and had effectively taken control of the city away from the king.

The chaos didn't remain isolated in Paris for long. In the days and weeks that followed the storming of Bastille, peasants throughout France, also suffering from hunger and high prices, rebelled against their feudal lords. Throughout the French countryside, peasants attacked their masters, pillaged their estates, and burned the paperwork that bound them to their lords. They destroyed the fences that enclosed fields and had their way with the forests and the farmland. The Great Fear, as it was known, terrified the nobles. In reaction, an assembly gathered at Versailles and abolished serfdom and many of the unpleasant fees and fines that went with serfdom. The peasants had brought about change and established themselves as a force to be reckoned with in the revolution.

Would You Believe?

Shortly after they abolished serfdom the nobles reneged somewhat, but the peasants paid no attention. The French peasants never again paid the fees and fines of feudalism to their former masters.

The National Assembly Takes Over

The storming of the Bastille proved crucial to the survival of the National Assembly. Had the popular uprising not occurred, Louis' troops would have forced the National Assembly to disband. Instead, the National Assembly continued to meet. In August it produced a timeless document and over the next two years enacted changes that seemed destined to put France on course for becoming the liberal state desired by so many prior to the revolution. When the rest of Europe realized what had happened in France, some nations joined forces and tried to undo what had been done. As if the domestic turmoil weren't enough for the French people, they faced the threat of foreign invasions bent on restoring the monarchy.

Declaration of the Rights of Man

In August 1789, the National Assembly produced *The Declaration of the Rights of Man*, a document that embraced Enlightenment ideals like liberty, equality, freedom from oppression, freedom of the press, and the right to property. The document even used Enlightenment phrases like "the general will." The *Declaration* also emphasized popular sovereignty, another Enlightenment ideal.

Much like the documents of the American Revolution, the document declared, "Men are born and remain free and equal in rights." The document clearly identified the ideals for which the revolutionaries were working. However, the *Declaration* proved much easier to complete than any written plan for the government. As profound as the document was, it left out one major group of French—the women.

What About the Women?

Women received no equality. This exclusion prompted writers like Olympe de Gouges (1748–1793) and Mary Wollstonecraft (1759–1797) over the next few years to call for equality for women. De Gouges' *Declaration of the Rights of Woman* in 1791 called for men to end the oppression of women. Wollstonecraft, an Englishwoman, wrote *A Vindication of the Rights of Man* in 1790 and *A Vindication of the Rights of Woman* in 1792. Wollstonecraft wrote of the intellectual potential of women and of the potential contributions of women to economics and politics. Both writers were convinced that women could be a powerful force in the world. After all, women had played a major role in the early days of the revolution.

In October 1789, thousands of hungry, angry women of Paris, fed up with high prices and bread shortages, marched 12 miles to Versailles to express their frustrations to the National Assembly and the king. Upon arriving at Versailles, the mob stormed the palace, killed guards, and demanded that the king and his queen, Marie Antoinette (1755–1793), return with them to live in Paris. Most commoners, forced to live on practically nothing, hated Marie Antoinette, who was famous for her extravagance. The next day, the mob escorted the royal family back to Paris where they were to remain. Likewise, the National Assembly left Versailles and returned to Paris.

> **Continental Quotes**
>
> "Dear God, guide and protect us. We are too young to reign."
>
> —Marie Antoinette

National Assembly Makes Some Changes

The National Assembly wanted to create a constitutional monarchy, or a monarchy limited by written laws, and forced Louis XVI to accept the new government in 1790. The National Assembly also did away with the legal order of nobility. The National Assembly created uniform districts throughout France of roughly equal size and introduced a standard system of weights and measures for all of the districts.

The Assembly extended tolerance to Protestants and Jews and, in a shocking move, nationalized the Church, confiscating all Church property and closing monasteries. It then issued a paper currency, called *assignats*, backed, in theory, by the property taken from the Church. Eventually, France sold the Church's property to help fund the government.

In another controversial move, the Assembly abolished guilds and workers groups. The Assembly didn't forget about women but they didn't do anything drastic, either. It extended some property and divorce rights to women, but not voting rights. Though well intentioned, many of the moves of the Assembly divided France. In particular, the moves against the Church and against workers divided the elite and the working classes.

Would You Believe? __

In 1791, a lawyer named Robespierre observed all that had occurred thus far and declared the revolution over. He was wrong.

Europe's Response to Revolution

The conservative monarchs of Europe were horrified that liberalism had practically removed the French monarch from the throne. Although Louis XVI remained head of state, his power was subject to the constitution and the National Assembly. Fearing that such revolutionary ideas might spread across the continent, and after learning that an attempted escape by Louis XVI had been thwarted, the leaders of Austria and Prussia issued the Declaration of Pillnitz.

Basically, the declaration threatened foreign intervention in French affairs. The declaration was supposed to intimidate the French and slow the revolution in France. It had no such effect. The newly elected Assembly in 1792 thumbed its nose at the monarchs and declared war on the Habsburg ruler Francis II. Prussia joined Austria in the First Coalition. By 1793, France had also declared war on Britain, Holland, and Spain. Miraculously, the French outlasted the First Coalition, thanks in part to the rigid controls of yet another new government in France. France eventually amassed an army of approximately 800,000 men and gained control of all French land. The First Coalition had failed.

Off with His Head: The Reign of Terror

For the elections of the new Assembly in 1791, none of the members of the National Assembly were eligible to be elected. The Assembly took on a new character and personality. The new members proved to be more zealous about liberal Enlightenment ideals and more wary of the monarchy. Amidst the panic of impending war with Austria and Prussia, the poor of Paris stormed the royal gardens where Louis and his family lived. The Assembly stripped the king of all his powers and imprisoned him, then called for a popular election of a new legislative body called the National Convention.

This began what historians often call the "second revolution." The second revolution began immediately after the imprisonment of the king when mobs attacked prisons and massacred nobles who they believed were conspiring with their foreign enemies. These attacks were known as the "September Massacres." One of the main features of the second revolution was the work of the new National Convention. In 1792, the National Convention moved even further away from monarchy and declared France a *republic*, a radical break from the old France.

> **Define Your Terms**
>
> A **republic** is a form of government in which political power lies in the hands of representatives elected by the people.

The Girondists and the Mountain

The entire National Convention stood firmly committed to creating a republic and making it work. The convention's members despised the privileges of the aristocracy and they were dead set on fighting oppression. Most of the members of the convention were Jacobins, or members of the Jacobin political club in Paris. Despite many seemingly similar political and social views, though, the National Convention faced a rift as a result of two sides competing for power within the Convention.

The moderate and conservative Girondists, named for a region in France, and the radical Mountain, named for high-up seats in the assembly hall upon which they sat, fought bitterly for control. The Girondists believed that the Mountain would institute a dictatorship in France if they gained control. The Mountain believed the Girondists would sympathize with the king and the aristocracy. Though the National Convention easily convicted Louis XVI of treason, the next decision came less easily.

The Girondists wanted to imprison Louis, but the radical Mountain called for his head. In the end, the Mountain won the vote and Louis XVI paid for his "treason" on the guillotine in January of 1793. Marie Antoinette, after being carted through the streets like a common criminal, died upon the guillotine in October of the same year.

The deciding factor in the battle for control of the National Convention lay outside the Convention itself. The urban poor, known as *sans-culottes*, became involved in politics over the course of 1792 and 1793. They demanded radical changes that would result in a government guarantee of food for the poor. The Mountain seized the opportunity to join the *sans culottes* to prevent riots and to shift power away from the Girondists. After some sneaky politics, the Mountain had dozens of Girondists arrested for treason, leaving the Convention easily controlled by the Mountain.

Define Your Terms

Sans culottes means "without breeches." The urban poor often were called *sans culottes* because they wore pants instead of the breeches worn by the wealthy.

Robespierre and the Reign of Terror

During the crisis of war with the First Coalition, food shortages, and peasant uprisings around France, the National Convention created an organization known as the Committee of Public Safety, granting it dictatorial powers to effectively deal with the crisis. Ideally, the committee maintained order and provided for internal peace and stability. After the Mountain gained control of the National Convention, the radical Maximilien Robespierre (1758–1794) and his followers took control of the Committee of Public Safety.

Their first task was to fight off the foreign forces, which they did in commanding fashion by appealing to the nationalistic pride of the French people, particularly the *sans culottes*. They also instituted a controlled economy in which the committee fixed prices, regulated production, and enforced a system of rationing. The committee determined what craftsmen and artisans produced and when and where the products were shipped. Initially, the national economy was focused solely on supplying the military with its needs. This attempt at nationalizing the economy was the largest such endeavor in the history of Europe.

Would You Believe?

The committee outlawed white bread and pastries and ordered that all grains, including both high- and low-quality grains, be mixed together to create a "bread of equality"—a very mediocre bread barely suitable for consumption.

One of Robespierre's goals was to create a republic of virtue in France. He wanted to nationalize everything, and the more radical revolutionaries wanted to de-Christianize everything. Robespierre made sure that books, pamphlets, and even everyday items were branded with revolutionary messages. The government encouraged the creation of patriotic art and the staging of patriotic festivals. The government closed churches of all denominations and replaced Catholicism first with the Cult of Reason and then with the Cult of the Supreme Being. Once, the government sponsored the Festival of Reason inside the esteemed Notre Dame Cathedral.

The new religion had no foundations in former religions; it was created entirely by Robespierre and those around him. The bottom line of the cult was that all men possessed souls and that there existed one god, the Supreme Being. Robespierre, apparently proud of his new religion, declared, "Never has the world which He created offered to Him a spectacle so worthy of His notice." Ironically, the man who was directly responsible for tens of thousands of imprisonments and executions also declared, "He created men to help each other, to love each other mutually …."

As a Matter of Fact

In one of the most interesting moves of the de-Christianization movement, the new government even replaced the Gregorian calendar with a new French Republican Calendar consisting of 12 months of 30 days each. Each month consisted of three 10-day weeks. The months were given names that translated roughly as "snowy," "windy," "flower," "meadow," and "hot." Each day of each month was also associated with plants, animals, and tools. All these efforts show the new government's determination to eliminate anything that would remind the French of the old order and the old way of doing things.

Just as the Committee of Public Safety devoted much attention to foreign enemies, it turned its attention inward, too, and focused on the "enemies" at home. Led by the increasingly paranoid Robespierre, the committee launched what became known as the Reign of Terror. Robespierre used the committee as a tool to eliminate those who opposed either the republic or the committee, rounding up political enemies of the republic and trying them in special courts not bound by the usual laws of France. The committee's courts tried and convicted hundreds of thousands of French for treason and related crimes. Tens of thousands lost their lives under the Reign of Terror, while more than a quarter-million more found themselves in prison. The Reign of Terror targeted all enemies of the state, young and old, rich and poor, men and women. The oppressive king had been replaced by a ruthless, blood-thirsty dictatorship. The paranoid Robespierre even had some of the men within his circle executed.

The brutality and repression of the republic met with much resistance among the common people in France, especially women, who resented the changes in religion and in everyday life. Perhaps the best example of such resistance by women was the work of Charlotte Corday (1768–1793), a staunch supporter of the Girondists. Corday became repulsed by Jean-Paul Marat, a newspaper man who called for more violence and who was responsible for the arrests of numerous Girondists. Corday told Marat that she could provide him names of more Girondists and Marat finally gave her an audience. Marat had a terrible skin disease so he spent most of his time in the bathtub. She entered his bathroom and dictated several names to him. As he wrote, she pulled a knife and stabbed Marat in the chest. Corday paid for her efforts on the guillotine. The assassination was immortalized by the painter Jacques Louis David in his famous *Death of Marat*. The painting shows an assassinated Marat lying lifeless in his tub.

The Thermidorian Reaction

Those around Robespierre, and many others in the National Convention, began to fear they might be the next victims of Robespierre's Reign of Terror. Therefore, when Robespierre stood to address the National Convention on the ninth day of the month of Thermidor, or July 27, 1794, by the Gregorian calendar, his opponents grabbed him and arrested him. The next day, Robespierre met the same fate as tens of thousands of his victims. As the guillotine added the names of Robespierre and some of his followers to the list of casualties of the French Revolution, the Reign of Terror ended and the Thermidorian Reaction began.

The National Convention, controlled now by moderates, ended the terror, released many political prisoners, and removed Jacobins from scores of government positions. The new leadership also eased the economic restrictions and worked to make France more in line with middle-class values. The Convention's new policies were hard on the poor. Prices rose and shortages resulted from the wealthy buying things like crazy. In a strange turn of events, the wealthy women even reacted wildly by wearing lipstick and dresses made of revealing fabric that showed an unprecedented amount of cleavage. In contrast to such wildness, many people sought to reopen churches. The movements to bring back the Church were most often headed by women.

Things were good for the middle-class and bad for the poor. Eventually, the poor revolted again as a result of food shortages. Rather than granting concessions to the poor, the Convention used the army to crush the uprisings. The poor were effectively made irrelevant in politics for another generation. To solidify its hold on the government and economy, the middle-class-dominated Convention created a new constitution in 1795.

The Establishment of the Directory

The new constitution created the first bicameral legislature in French history, made up of the Council of Five Hundred and the Council of Ancients, and a new executive, a five-man body known as the Directory. The Directory relied on the military to maintain power and chase away the remaining Jacobins and Royalists. The Directory also used the military to sustain the economy. The Directory kept the army busy abroad adding lands to the holdings of the French republic. Under the Directory, the French armies marched all over Europe, especially in Italy and the Netherlands, even venturing into Egypt.

By 1799, the Directory had managed only to hang on to control in France. The wars abroad weren't going as well as they had in previous years and turmoil emerged at home. Some politicians wanted to revise the constitution and some generals seemed to be doing their own thing. Disunity prevailed, which provided the opportunity for a strong leader to step in and take control.

The Least You Need to Know

- The 13 British colonies in America rebelled against Britain. Aided by France, the colonies declared and eventually won their independence from Britain. Many of the French who fought in America took ideas about liberty, equality, and opposing tyranny back to France after the war.

- The enormous debt left by Louis XIV and Louis XV, coupled with the enormous expenses incurred during the Seven Years' War and American Revolution, left Louis XVI in a terrible financial mess.

- Three social orders, or estates, existed before the French Revolution and were represented in the Estates-General. Louis XVI called the first meeting of the Estates-General since 1614 because he needed to raise taxes.

- The poor of Paris played a major role in the revolution. First, mobs stormed the Bastille and later hungry women marched to Versailles where they captured the royal family.

- The National Convention, the leading body of the new French Republic, saw its power eventually go to the radical Mountain, led by Robespierre, whose Committee of Public Safety instituted the Reign of Terror, an attempt to rid France of all opposed to the new republic.

- After Robespierre was guillotined, a new constitution placed power in a bicameral legislature and an executive called the Directory.

Part 4

You Say You Want More Revolution? (c.1776–1900)

This part shows how struggle gave birth to strong rule which gave way to struggle which gave way to …. You get the idea. Napoleon seized power after the French Revolution and almost conquered Europe. After Europe's armies and the Russian winter finally defeated him, the leaders of Europe reinstated strict controls. Oppressed peoples struggled to revolt and create nations where they had some input, but the revolutions were shortlived. Brilliant politicians also harnessed that desire for nation status to create two modern nations, Italy and Germany. Competition increased among the European powers and that competition led to imperialism, entangling alliances, and plenty of tension. The rise of machines both simplified and complicated lives, resulting in an industrialized continent with new, work-related challenges. Socialists attempted to address these issues and, as a result, socialist thought would dominate Europe for the next 200 years.

A "Little" Guy Named Napoleon, a Big Wig Named Metternich

In This Chapter

♦ Napoleon climbs the ranks in the military

♦ Europe stands against Napoleon

♦ France gets a king again

♦ The Allies try to prevent another Napoleon

♦ Two dangerous political philosophies challenge the conservatives

♦ The Age of Metternich

The years 1795 to 1799 proved long and difficult for the Directory. Corruption, failing efforts abroad, and waning popularity caused the Directory to be less and less effective. Deserters from the French army protested the conscription laws, and the Netherlands were revolting. Finally, in 1799, France scored a series of victories against the Second Coalition, but the republic faced financial ruin and the Directory's popularity was at an all-time low. The French people no longer possessed the zeal that led to the revolution.

In October 1799, a fiery young general named Napoleon Bonaparte (1769–1821) returned to France from a campaign in Africa. Upon his return, Emannuel Joseph Sieyès (see Chapter 14) informed Napoleon of his plot to overthrow the corrupt Directory. The others involved were Charles Talleyrand, another of the Directors named Roger Ducos, and Napoleon's brother, Lucien. France, in turmoil once again, needed strong leadership and Sieyès hoped to provide it. Napoleon agreed to participate.

The Little Man with Big Plans

On November 9, 1799, or 18 Brumaire Year VIII, by the Revolutionary Calendar, Napoleon led troops that dispersed the Council of Five Hundred and the Council of Ancients. Only a rump legislature stayed behind to name Ducos, Sieyès, and Napoleon as *consuls* to run the government. The coup was supposed to leave Sieyès with the most power but Napoleon outdid him. Sieyès had his own carefully considered constitution that he hoped to install in the new government. Napoleon, however, created a new version of that constitution that made him First Consul in a new French government called the Consulate. He followed that up with another constitution that made himself First Consul for life.

In a sudden turn of events, Napoleon had basically taken control of France. In one month, he enjoyed a meteoric rise from Corsica on his way to becoming the most powerful man in the world.

> **Define Your Terms**
>
> The term **consul** was taken from the classical Roman government. The position of consul in Rome was the highest elected position in the government.

The Kid from Corsica

An understanding of Napoleon's early life and background is vital to appreciate who he was and what he accomplished. Napoleon Bonaparte was born into a noble family on the island of Corsica in 1769. His father served as a delegate from Corsica to the court of Louis XVI. At the age of 10, Napoleon began his education at a military school in France. He did well in math and geography; his performance in other subjects was not impressive. Upon completion of his first military school, Napoleon attended an elite military school in Paris called the École Militaire, founded by Louis XV. There he studied and excelled in artillery. He graduated faster than most cadets and earned a commission in the military. At 16, Napoleon began his career. He served his first years in the military in France in rather uneventful and unmemorable fashion. That changed with the outbreak of the French Revolution in 1789 (see Chapter 14).

Would You Believe?

Napoleon is often remembered as a short person, yet his height was not far below the average for Frenchmen of his day. His nickname *la petit caporal* referred to his relationship with common soldiers and not his physical stature.

Napoleon's Military Career

After spending some time in Corsica while on leave, Napoleon fled to France in 1793 after a conflict developed between him and a nationalist leader in Corsica. Upon his return to France he earned a position as an artillery commander. Napoleon was a brilliant military strategist and a master at using the artillery to his advantage. He also proved to be a clever adversary who employed spies and intelligence information to use the element of surprise against his enemies. He first won national recognition in the daring and brilliant capture of the French city of Toulon, which had risen up against Robespierre and then been occupied by British troops aiding the resistance. Napoleon again garnered acclaim in 1795 when he successfully defended the National Convention against waves of attacks by an angry mob. His maneuvers, using pieces of seized artillery, earned him particular favor from the Directory.

Napoleon followed those victories with a successful campaign into Italy and Austria in 1796 and 1797. City after city and region after region capitulated as he marched through. Napoleon grew powerful and influential in French politics. To get him out of the limelight, the Directory sent him to Egypt in 1798, ostensibly to protect French trade in the region. He met with mixed results; he defeated numerous armies, but he lost his fleet to the British. Just as things looked bad for Napoleon, he slipped out of Egypt and back to France.

Would You Believe?

Napoleon's expedition to Egypt included numerous scientists who discovered a tablet, named for the nearby town of Rosetta, that later unlocked the secret of Egyptian hieroglyphics. A popular myth, which is completely unfounded, blames Napoleon's expedition for the Sphinx's missing nose.

First Consul, Then Emperor

In 1799, after the coup of 18 Brumaire, France adopted a new constitution known as the Constitution of Year XVIII. By the terms of the constitution, Napoleon became the First Consul, with numerous powers resembling those of a dictator. Two years later, in 1801 or year X of the Revolutionary calendar, France adopted an updated Constitution of Year X, which made Napoleon First Consul *for life*. In each case, France adopted the constitutions by *plebiscite*. Clearly, the people wanted Napoleon.

Define Your Terms

A **plebiscite** is a national election in which the citizens accept or reject a proposal.

Three years later, Napoleon's men discovered a Bourbon plot against him. Using this plot as justification, along with heightened worries caused by war with the English, Napoleon proclaimed himself emperor in 1804. A popular myth has it that Napoleon took the crown from the pope and crowned himself, but that story remains just a myth.

Napoleonic France

France had been wracked by turmoil since 1789. Napoleon made the restoration of order his primary goal. He planned sweeping changes to the corrupt government, bringing all groups together for the common purpose of the betterment of France, and bringing the French people on board with his regime. His goals were lofty, but Napoleon would reach them. He created a Bank of France to tackle financial problems and over several years the economy started to turn around. He used the military to instill a sense of pride and patriotism in the French people. He improved France on many levels by building parks, canals, sewer systems, and highways.

In order to bring the common people of France in line with his regime, he worked out a deal with the pope known as the Concordat of 1801. The agreement recognized Catholicism as the religion of most of the French, coming just short of saying that Catholicism was the official religion of France, thus allowing Napoleon freedom from Church rule. The Concordat also made French clergy take an oath of loyalty to the state and provided that France would pay the salaries of the clergy. The papacy won the right to select the bishops in France.

The Concordat worked out well for all parties. The people won back the religion that had been taken from them during the revolution, the Church found a way back into France, and Napoleon made peace with both the people and the papacy. Furthermore, Napoleon united the clergy, which had experienced a rift during the revolution when some took an oath of allegiance to the revolutionary government. Such calculated moves demonstrate Napoleon's political savvy.

Changes in Government

Napoleon set out immediately to restructure the French government. He completely reorganized the administrative aspects of the government and the *departements*, or provinces within France. He created a vast bureaucracy with himself at the top. He centralized the government and brought people from all over France to fill his bureaucracy. By providing them with jobs, he created loyalty to France, or rather to himself, among the government officials and workers. Napoleon won the loyalty of thousands and thousands of royalists within France by granting them amnesty, making them take an oath of loyalty, and placing them in high positions. He created a meritocracy with special titles and privileges for those in the government who served him well. Napoleon also practiced nepotism, placing relatives in prominent government positions to further guarantee loyalty at all levels.

Civil Code of 1804

For all Napoleon's restructuring, the greatest and longest-lasting of his reforms in France was that of the French laws. Before the French Revolution, no single code of laws existed in France. Laws varied from place to place and class to class and were riddled with loopholes, exemptions, and privileges. Napoleon wanted to create a new system that made all men equal under the law.

Napoleon based the format of his *Code Napoleon*, or Napoleonic Code, on that of the Roman emperor Justinian. He had his scholars codify French law, or combine the laws of France into a single, usable, and public code that was organized systematically. The new code, which went into effect in 1804, made the law clearer, more straightforward, and accessible to all. The new code guaranteed property rights and protection under the law to all male citizens. Though the Code Napoleon wasn't the first codified law in Europe, it was the most comprehensive.

Would You Believe?

Unfortunately for women, the code set back any progress made during the revolution. Under the code, women were reduced to legal dependents of their husbands and fathers. Furthermore, divorce became much easier to get, which did nothing to elevate women's status in society.

Napoleon Can't Get Enough of Europe

Being the military guy that he was, Napoleon couldn't wait to use France's army. Napoleon had hardly been in power when in 1800 he headed back to Italy to reconquer lands that had been lost during his absence. After a series of battles, Napoleon defeated Austria and took most Austrian holdings in Italy.

Napoleon then signed a treaty with Britain in which France won Malta. The peace was tenuous and strained and destined not to last long. Napoleon had already redrawn Germany, annexed Piedmont, and taken Malta, but he had his eyes on Britain and he hoped in the future to invade. With war with Britain just around the corner, Napoleon sold French land in North America to the United States for a little over seven million dollars, land eventually called the Louisiana Purchase. Britain wasn't all Napoleon wanted. He also had his sights on Russia and Prussia. It remained to be seen whether he would realize his foreign policy goals—nothing less than the domination of Europe—the way he realized his domestic goals.

The Coalitions

In 1803, Napoleon positioned troops in French ports along the English Channel in preparation for an invasion of England. As Napoleon prepared for invasion, Europe prepared for Napoleon. Britain joined Austria, Russia, Naples, and Sweden in the Third Coalition against France, the first two having been formed against revolutionary France.

When Napoleon tried to bring his fleet to the English Channel from the Mediterranean in preparation for a possible invasion of England, he suffered a major setback. Britain's Lord Nelson crushed the French fleet at the historic Battle of Trafalgar, establishing the permanent dominance of the British navy and effectively preventing a French invasion. With his hopes for a naval invasion of England permanently squashed, Napoleon looked eastward. Napoleon's troops marched through Germany and engaged Coalition forces in Germany and Austria. In December 1805, at the Battle of Austerlitz, Napoleon used brilliant strategy to crush the opposing forces. He knocked Austria out of the war and kicked them out of Italy with a treaty. Russia temporarily retreated but at the cost of much land. Unopposed in Germany, Napoleon created a new German Confederation of the Rhine of which he was the protector. The Fourth and Fifth Coalitions likewise proved ineffective against Napoleon and suffered humiliating defeats.

The Grand Empire

Napoleon now saw himself as the emperor not just of France but of all of Europe. Those nations he hadn't beaten, he bullied. In his Grand Empire, Napoleon replaced monarch after monarch with his family members and he imposed his Code Napoleon on the lands he conquered. He often invaded under the guise of liberator rather than as conqueror; or so he wanted the people to believe. He planned to use his Grand Empire to defeat the one nation he couldn't defeat militarily: Britain.

> **Continental Quotes**
>
> "England is a nation of shopkeepers."
>
> —Napoleon Bonaparte

Napoleon used what was known as the "Continental System" to starve the British. He demanded that all his subjects and allies boycott Britain by not sending any shipments to the islands. Practically everyone participated in the system but Portugal; Britain never suffered the way Napoleon had hoped, though. Napoleon demanded that Spain help him invade Portugal but Spain refused. Napoleon invaded Spain and the Spanish opposition headed for the hills rather than engage him directly. In the meantime, Austria tried to break away, so Napoleon invaded and eventually defeated them, though many of his troops remained bogged down in Spain. At this point, Napoleon and his Grand Empire seemed virtually unstoppable. However, Napoleon had his sights set on one last big prize.

> **Would You Believe?**
>
> Napoleon's Continental System resulted in the demise of Amsterdam as a trade power and possibly in the delay of the Industrial Revolution's arrival in France—neither were expected results. The boycott and blockade of Britain also hurt the French badly.

The Original Waterloo

In 1811, Alexander's Russia stopped enforcing the boycott, which drew the wrath of Napoleon. Possibly Napoleon needed a whipping boy; possibly he'd heard that Russia was considering an invasion of Germany. Regardless, Napoleon ignored the advice of his advisors and started plans to invade Russia.

He amassed an army of 600,000 men and launched his offensive in June of 1812, defeating army after army as the Russians engaged him. But then the Russians began a retreat into the heartland of Russia. The Russians finally engaged Napoleon again outside Moscow. Historians estimate the battle resulted in between 50,000 and 70,000 dead in one day, making the Battle of Borodino one of the bloodiest battles in all of human history. The Russians abandoned the city and set it ablaze on their way out. Finally, after weeks in a burnt-out city, Napoleon began a retreat not only out of the city but also out of the country, often called sarcastically the Grand Retreat, back through frozen Russia. He had no supplies and had hoped to live off the land as he went, but the Russians had left nothing for him. Of the 600,000 French soldiers that entered Russia, only about 40,000 made it safely back to Poland and Prussia. Nevertheless, Napoleon headed immediately for Paris to raise another army.

As Napoleon gathered a new army, the Sixth Coalition smelled blood. Napoleon engaged the Coalition forces at Leipzig in the Battle of Nations. Outnumbered two to one, the French forces held out as long as they could but Napoleon eventually retreated to Paris. By April 1814, Coalition forces had converged on Paris. The mighty Napoleon was cornered. In mid-April, Napoleon agreed to an unconditional surrender and abdicated his throne. The Coalition agreed to let Napoleon keep the title of emperor—but he had to go be the emperor of the tiny island of Elba off the Italian coast.

> **Would You Believe?**
>
> France paid Napoleon an amazing two million francs yearly salary while he ruled his "empire" on Elba.

The Allies restored the monarchy in France, but it didn't last long. When Napoleon heard that the French monarchy had the nation in turmoil, he staged a daring escape from Elba early in 1815. He landed in France to find soldiers waiting to arrest him. In grand fashion, Napoleon convinced them to rejoin him instead. He took what troops he could muster and he marched on Paris. Upon hearing of Napoleon's return, the new French monarch, Louis XVIII, fled.

For a few months, a period often referred to as the Hundred Days, Napoleon ruled France again. He gathered more than 250,000 combined regular and citizen soldiers. In June, Napoleon engaged British and Prussian forces separately in an attempt to knock them out before they could join forces and defeat his new army. Although it seemed like a good idea at the time, things didn't work out according to plan. The Duke of Wellington finally defeated Napoleon's troops at the famous Battle of Waterloo in modern-day Belgium on June 18, 1815. After his defeat, Napoleon was banished to the island of St. Helena, in the middle of nowhere some 1,700 miles off the coast of Angola. Napoleon lived out his days there and died in 1821.

As a Matter of Fact

After he earned international renown for defeating Napoleon at Waterloo, Arthur Wellesley, the First Duke of Wellington, became a political star and rose through the ranks of British government. He eventually became British Prime Minister in 1828. The ultra-conservative Wellington, occasionally called "Old Nosey" because of his prominent nose, in not-so-conservative fashion led Catholic Emancipation in the United Kingdom. In other words, under his administration Catholics gained many civil rights in the UK. This action ultimately led to an anti-climactic duel between Wellington and Lord Winchilsea. In the duel, neither man fired at the other and Winchilsea eventually apologized to Wellington for accusing him of trying to destroy Protestantism.

Life After Napoleon and Balance of Power Politics

The years between 1789 and 1815 had been unsettling at best for most of Europe and for most European rulers in particular. The ideas of liberty and equality, neither of which sounded very appealing to the old regimes, took hold of France and led to both regicide and a bloody revolution. To make matters worse, outsiders tried to intervene in France but to no avail (see Chapter 14). As if the French Revolution and the war-mongering Directory weren't bad enough, the ambitious Napoleon Bonaparte marched his armies anywhere he pleased despite the best efforts of the rest of Europe.

After the Quadruple Alliance, which included Britain, Austria, Russia and Prussia, finally defeated Napoleon not once but twice, it seemed as though Europe might actually have some time to catch its collective breath. In one way or another, France had been stirring things up for some time and the four victorious nations, with some other minor nations riding their coattails, were determined to make sure France didn't cause problems again.

Maintaining a Delicate Balance

Renaissance Italy, a geographic region with a number of independent principalities, saw year after year of infighting and violent competition among the Italian states. Not until Italy adopted a system known as balance of power politics did the warring subside. The Italian states created a system of alliances and mutual agreements whereby the majority of the states would keep individual states in check in the case that any one state rose up and threatened the peace and harmony of the region.

After the turmoil of the French Revolution and Napoleon, the leaders of the predominant European powers decided it would be best for all of them to adopt such a system to prevent the same thing from happening in Europe again. Although their main goal was to keep France in check, the nations wanted a system that would prevent other nations from doing what France had done. Europe was tired of fighting and, with the promise of economic improvement as a result of the Industrial Revolution (see Chapter 17), Europe hoped for decades of peace and prosperity. With that in mind, the European powers set out to design a road map for continental peace.

The Bourbon Dynasty Restored

With Napoleon securely exiled, or so they thought, the victorious European nations of Austria, Russia, Prussia, and Great Britain decided it would be in the best interest of France, and frankly in the best interest of the other European monarchies, to reinstate the French monarchy. Louis XVI died during the revolution and his son, Louis XVII, died in prison in 1795. Therefore, the throne passed to Louis XVIII (1755–17824), the brother of Louis XVI.

King Louis XVIII was an unattractive choice for king on many levels. He was old and in poor health. He had little zeal for anything and he appealed to very few people. Upon the restoration of the monarchy in France, many of the *émigrés*, nobles who fled the revolution, returned to France with lists of demands. Likewise, many revolutionaries demanded a return to revolutionary ideals. In a show of good faith, Louis XVIII returned the government to a sort of constitutional monarchy, with a bicameral legislature that included the Chamber of Peers and the Chamber of Deputies.

Would You Believe?

Louis XVIII's feet and legs were crippled and disfigured from gout, a disease that commonly struck wealthy Europeans. Only they could afford to indulge in rich foods and alcohol, especially port, and they tended toward a sedentary lifestyle. Other famous gout sufferers included Henry VIII and Isaac Newton.

His government was weak, at best, and word of this prompted Napoleon to return, during which King Louis XVIII fled the country to Ghent fearing for his life. Upon Napoleon's second defeat and subsequent exile, this time for good, Louis XVIII returned to the throne where he ruled for about 10 more years. Upon Louis' death, the throne passed to his brother, who ruled as Charles X (1757–1836).

After Louis' restoration, violence had broken out against those suspected of supporting either the revolution or Napoleon. This violence resembled the violence that erupted after the Reign of Terror and was generally referred to as the White Terror. Louis did not support or approve the violence but he was powerless to stop it. The victorious Allies initially had decided to deal lightly with France because, after all, the nation had been oppressed by a dictator. However, after seeing the way the French people and soldiers rallied behind Napoleon upon his return to the nation he had supposedly oppressed, the allied nations decided not to go so easy on France after all.

The Congress of Vienna

The leaders of the Quadruple Alliance decided that the best way to reestablish order was to hold a congress, or a meeting of representatives, to decide the future of Europe. This meeting was to be held in Vienna in 1814 and 1815. Furthermore, they agreed to hold similar congresses every few years to maintain the order they established. This system of congresses, referred to as the Concert of Europe, helped maintain relative peace for another generation and helped prevent another continental war for about 100 years.

In addition to dealing with France and establishing a system of balance of power politics to keep the peace, the Congress of Vienna had the daunting task of deciding exactly what to do with all the states whose rulers had been unseated and whose borders had changed as a result of revolutionary and Napoleonic expansion. Too much had changed in Europe for the Congress to say, "As you were," and return every state on the continent to the way it was in 1789. Parts of Europe altered by Napoleon included Poland, the Netherlands, Saxony and other German states, as well as various parts of Italy. The Congress did, however, return France to its 1789 borders.

The states represented at the Congress of Vienna included Austria, Russia, Prussia, Great Britain, and France. Everyone present had to agree on the terms, even the big loser, France. The leading negotiator of the Congress was Prince Klemens von Metternich of Austria. Britain's prime minister, Robert Castlereagh (1769–1822), also played a major role in the negotiations. Charles Talleyrand represented France, Karl von Hardenburg represented Prussia, and Count Karl Robert Nesselrode (1780–1862) officially represented Russia, though Czar Alexander I did much of the negotiating.

Everyone agreed on a few major issues. First, France had been bothering the rest of Europe since 1789 and, if you wanted to get technical, since the reign of Louis XIV; nothing in its recent history suggested France would behave unless something were done. Second, everyone agreed that to the victors should go the spoils for all the time, effort, money, and lives wasted on the conflict with France. Third, everyone agreed that no single state should be rewarded so greatly as to upset the balance of power the Congress so desperately sought. Finally, all states of Europe were to be

Would You Believe?

Because the delegates from the major powers did the majority of the negotiating, the delegates from nations like Spain, Sweden, and Portugal had little to do. The host of the Congress often threw extravagant parties to keep them busy. It was said, "The Congress does not walk; it dances."

secure, stable states with permanent borders, states not likely to be preyed upon by other more powerful ones.

Because of the brief return of Napoleon and a major disagreement over the settlement, the Congress almost failed to accomplish its goals. In addition to returning France to its 1789 geographic size and restoring the French monarchy, the Congress forced France to pay a sizable remuneration. Furthermore, the Congress forced France to allow allied troops to be stationed within French borders for five years, just in case. Those were terms that everyone could agree upon, even Talleyrand.

Britain retained many holdings it had gained over the years in its many battles with France. Austria ceded territory it had won from France in exchange for land in Venetia and Lombardy and along the Dalmatian coast of the Adriatic Sea. Compensating Russia and Prussia didn't go as smoothly. The Russian czar, Alexander I (1777–1825), wanted to reestablish the kingdom of Poland, which would naturally be under Russian control. Prussia agreed to that idea provided it could have Saxony.

Metternich and Castlereagh feared that if those two states acquired so much wealthy and populous land the balance of power would be tipped in favor not only of Russia and Prussia but also in favor of the region of eastern Europe. The disagreement over this nearly led to more fighting; the treaty allowed for war if necessary. Fortunately for Europe, cooler heads finally prevailed. In the end, Prussia and Russia each took a smaller portion of the land they wanted.

Would You Believe?

Castlereagh and Metternich opposed the Russian annexation of Poland and the Prussian annexation of Saxony so much that they actually signed a secret treaty with France against the Russians and Prussians. Though nothing came of the threat of war, the precedent for secret treaties and alliances had been set.

As for other states around Europe, Belgium and Holland were combined to form the kingdom of the Netherlands, a larger state capable of defending itself. The three hundred-plus German states were consolidated into thirty-nine states which formed a loosely united German Confederation (see Chapter 19). Sweden received Norway from Finland. Spain and Portugal each got their old rulers back, whom Napoleon had knocked off their respective thrones, and the pope was restored as the ruler of the Papal States in Italy. Clearly, the Congress of Vienna was a major turning point in nineteenth-century Europe.

Many contemporaries criticized the conservative measures taken by the Congress, arguing that the Congress repressed the sense of nationalism and liberalism that was beginning to blossom in parts of Europe. Considering that the negotiations were influenced most by the conservative Metternich, perhaps the contemporary critics were correct. However, many later historians consider the work of the Congress to be a watershed because such broad, sweeping changes were instituted with the agreement of all involved.

More Isms

The decades following the Congress of Vienna saw a renewed intellectual movement. The themes of nationalism and liberalism didn't originate during the years after the Congress but they began to receive much attention. Intellectuals were intrigued by the ideas and how they affected people so much that they would take up arms and fight for them. The interest in these ideas and the open discussions about them kept the ideas of nationalism in the minds of everyone and fueled later revolutions against the efforts of the conservatives.

Nationalism

The first true example of nationalism in Europe dates to the fifteenth century and the Hundred Years' War (see Chapter 1). The two kingdoms of England and France fought for generations, initially out of a sense of feudal obligations to the king, but over the course of the war something new developed. The war turned into a war of English versus French rather than the English king versus the French king. The nationalism that developed gave birth to the modern concept of a nation-state, a concept that certainly was not lost on nineteenth-century Europe.

Nationalism can be defined as a sense of belonging or a sense of duty to a nation. Nationalism throughout history has been both fostered and enhanced by factors that would become increasingly important for the European people over the hundred years following the Congress of Vienna. First, nationalism is fostered and enhanced by a sense of a common culture: common language, history, religion, customs, and values. A common culture is vital to nationalism because people feel a sense of alikeness and belonging. The Irish and Scots serve as a great example. For centuries, the Irish and the Scots resented rule by the English and desired sovereignty mostly because they were different from the English and they didn't have much in common with the English.

Second, a common geography among a people fosters and enhances nationalism. When people live in close proximity to one another they are able to feel a sense of unity that people far away usually cannot. A common geography often ensures that the people within a given area have a common history and language, both of which are vital to nationalism. The influence of geography on nationalism can be seen in the example of the British colonies in America. Many of the colonists prior to the revolution had no sense of English nationalism because they did not have a common geography with the English; most had never even been to England. Even though the United States did not yet exist, many colonists had a sense of American nationalism much deeper than any sense of English nationalism.

Third, common political beliefs and goals greatly enhance nationalism. If a people who share common culture and geography also possess a belief in or a desire for republicanism, for example, the sense of nationalism will be such that the people probably will be inspired to take up arms. This can be seen over and over, especially in the instances of the British colonies in America and in France prior to the French Revolution. This sense of common political beliefs and political goals can be a major force in making changes in the status quo or in resisting change.

Because nationalism relies so much on commonalities among people, a sense of us-versus-them often results. This powerful force can be used to resist oppression or to resist outside influences, just as the French government under Robespierre did. However, this us-versus-them mentality often manifests itself in unhealthy ways, too. By emphasizing the differences between "us" and "them," people often objectify or dehumanize "them" to the point that the respect for human life is lost. Robespierre's Reign of Terror serves as just one of many perfect examples of such a mentality. This mentality also has social manifestations. The deep sense of nationalism among nineteenth-century Germans, for example, eventually led to the idea among Germans that they were superior to all other European peoples.

Liberalism

Most of the nationalists of the nineteenth century possessed a love and desire for liberalism, too. Liberalism, or advocating the ideas of liberty, equality, and human rights, first rose to prominence during the Enlightenment. The revolutions in America and in France serve as examples of the realization of liberal ideas. Central to liberalism was the belief in a democratic or republican government, as opposed to an authoritarian or monarchial government. Embraced by Enlightenment thinkers and revolutionaries throughout Europe, liberalism advocated the right to vote, freedom of expression, freedom of the press, and universal justice within the legal system. Liberalism advocated limitations on government by written constitutions. Basically, liberals wanted as little government intervention in the lives of the people as possible. As such, liberalism extended beyond politics into economics and even into religion.

While liberalism seems at first like the hope of all people everywhere, nineteenth-century liberalism certainly was not. Initially, nineteenth-century liberalism did not embrace fully democratic ideas like *universal suffrage* or even universal male suffrage. In fact, liberals most often supported republican forms of government with limitations on who could vote. Because many liberals actually believed that voting rights should go hand in hand with ownership of property, liberalism increasingly became identified with the privileged middle class. Intellectuals, in particular, often argued that liberal ideals should be extended to all people, or at least to all males, regardless of property ownership.

Define Your Terms

Universal suffrage is the right of all citizens to vote.

For the liberals who rested comfortably among the property-owning middle class, democracy seemed rather frightening. First, democracy would mean a reduction in the power of the middle class and, second, democracy would mean that the masses of uneducated people would be allowed to participate in the government. Those who embraced full-blown democracy were seen even among liberals as radical. Those radicals who embraced democracy often were the first to take up arms and resort to violence.

Conservatism

The Europeans most disturbed by the rise of nationalism and especially liberalism were those who embraced the idea of conservatism. According to the classical definitions, liberals advocated change while conservatives advocated the status quo. For the most part, that describes the conservatives of nineteenth-century Europe.

The conservatives of Europe were the landed aristocracy, the monarchists, and the privileged nobility. They didn't resist change just to spite the liberals and the nationalists or to be oppressive. From the perspective of the conservatives, Europe had always been ruled by the privileged. The monarchs of the west and east alike, though they had different relationships with the nobility of their nations, still were superior to most of the people they ruled. The ruling classes historically had been educated and had had experience in business and diplomatic affairs. They simply were the best suited to rule.

Conservatives looked in horror at the results of nationalistic and liberal movements: revolution. Aside from the fact that both nationalism and liberalism threatened the aristocracy's monopoly on power, the two ideals threatened the safety of everyone. Conservatives pointed to the violent, bloody French Revolution as the perfect example of what happened when liberals got the idea that they were capable of changing the status quo. Furthermore, most conservatives hated the idea of making the common people frenzied by spreading notions of democracy. Conservatives also feared the nationalism that so often accompanied liberalism. Many leading conservatives of the early nineteenth century ruled multinational empires. If each of the peoples ruled by the conservatives were stricken with nationalism, the conservative empires were doomed as each of the subjugate peoples would desire independence. No conservative of the nineteenth century epitomized this more than Metternich.

Prince Klemens von Metternich

Klemens Wenzel Nepomuk Lothar Fürst von Metternich-Winneberg-Beilstein, or simply Prince Klemens von Metternich, influenced the first half of the nineteenth century in Europe more than any other individual. Just as the years of Napoleon's rule are remembered as the Napoleonic Era, the years between 1815 and 1848 are commonly referred to as the Age of Metternich. Interestingly, though, Metternich influenced Europe without ruling.

Born into a noble family in 1773, Metternich grew into one of the finest diplomats and politicians in European history. One of his first political moves was his marriage to the granddaughter of the wealthy and influential Count Wenzel von Kaunitz in his early twenties. Metternich quickly climbed the social and political ladder using his skills as a politician.

Metternich possessed amazing confidence, which others usually perceived as conceit and arrogance. He possessed a genuine sense of social and intellectual superiority over most with whom he came in contact. Metternich trusted his own abilities to the extent that he never sought approval from peers or the masses. Indeed, he recognized the danger in seeking popularity. He despised nationalism and liberalism and believed that they led to chaos like revolutions, which he regarded as generally illegitimate. His ideas certainly were reflected in his political moves.

Metternich became an ambassador for the Austrian government and then received a promotion to the position of Austrian Foreign Minister after Napoleon crushed Austrian forces in 1809. Metternich went to work right away in an attempt to appease and befriend Napoleon. He even arranged a marriage between Napoleon and Marie-Louise, the daughter of the Holy Roman Emperor Francis II. After Napoleon's defeat in Russia in 1812, Metternich became less pro-France. As the war against Napoleon wore on, Metternich became convinced that there would be no successful negotiations with Napoleon and he ceased diplomatic relations with him altogether. Metternich focused on restoring the monarchy in France instead. It was after Napoleon's defeat and exile that Metternich began his influential role in European politics.

Would You Believe?

Metternich, a master politician, was also a notorious womanizer. He often mixed his two specialties by making friends with women who could offer political information either voluntarily or as pillow talk.

The Epitome of Conservatism

Metternich dominated the Congress of Vienna and set the tone for the meetings. Under his direction, the Congress redrew many boundaries so that liberalism and nationalism would have no safe places to develop. It was Metternich who directed the Congress to reinstate several ousted monarchs, since they were ousted illegitimately, in an attempt to reinstate the old regime in Europe. Not all European leaders shared Metternich's anti-liberal views, though. Russia's Czar Alexander I, for example, thought of himself as a generally enlightened proponent of liberal ideals. Metternich went to work on Alexander and his work paid off.

In 1820, Metternich knew for sure that Alexander had abandoned his liberal ideals when Austria, Prussia, and even Russia supported what was known as the Troppau Protocol. Metternich had put down liberal rebellions in Naples, and his actions had raised eyebrows, particularly Alexander's. At the Congress of Troppau in 1820, largely a result of the rebellions in Naples, the leaders of the three nations agreed in principle that states whose governments were in power because of illegitimate revolutions would no longer be recognized as members of the European Alliance, also known as the Holy Alliance. They effectively agreed that they would not recognize governments created by illegitimate, liberal revolutions. Metternich's conservatism also showed when he and Alexander refused to aid Greece in its attempts to overthrow the Ottomans.

The Holy Alliance

Although the Holy Alliance didn't officially result from the Congress of Vienna, it was an indirect result. Czar Alexander had the idea to form a peacekeeping organization of sorts known as the Holy Alliance to promote Christianity in Europe. Members of the Alliance were to conduct themselves in accordance with Christian ideals. In reality, the charter members of Russia, Prussia, and Austria used the Holy Alliance as a way of keeping liberal ideas in check.

Eventually, most of the rulers of Europe joined the so-called Holy Alliance except for the pope, the Ottoman sultan, and the King of England, George IV, who was bound by his constitution. However, prominent delegates to the Congress of Vienna, including Castlereagh and Metternich, discounted the Alliance as worthless. Ironically, the Alliance eventually became associated with Metternich, mostly because he and the Alliance both had an interest in the repression of liberalism.

Would You Believe?

England's Castlereagh called the Holy Alliance "sublime mysticism and nonsense."

Long Live the Status Quo

Metternich had much reason to fear the spread of both nationalism and liberalism throughout Europe. Even though he did not rule in Austria, he had a passion for tradition and for keeping things the way they had always been. The Austrian Empire ruled a variety of lands and peoples including Germans, Czechs, Hungarians, Italians, and more. The peoples ruled by Habsburg Austria had little in common with one another, other than being subjugated by the Habsburgs; they generally had no sense of national loyalty or unity. Metternich knew that the lands he helped govern would be ripe for nationalism and liberalism if those ideas were allowed to creep in. In order to keep them out of Austrian holdings, he tried to keep them out of Germany, too.

In 1819, he persuaded the Austrian-dominated German Confederation to adopt the Carlsbad Decrees. The Carlsbad Decrees required the German states to seek and destroy all ideologies that the conservative Metternich believed to be dangerous. The Decrees specifically targeted universities and newspapers, notorious havens of liberalism. The decrees required the removal of any teacher whose teachings were found to be hostile or subversive to the existing order. The decrees outlawed student associations and even planted spies among the students. The decrees proved equally repressive toward the press. Basically, everything that was printed in newspaper or pamphlet form had to be approved by state officials. The decrees also created a group of investigators who sought out violators of the decrees.

Practices like these helped the conservatives hang on a few more years. However, by 1848, the conservatives faced their most serious challenge yet: a wave of revolutions that swept Europe (see Chapter 18).

The Least You Need to Know

- Napoleon Bonaparte, a Corsican by birth, rose to prominence in the French military and eventually won the favor of the Directory. After staging a coup, Napoleon seized control of France by becoming First Consul in the new government.

- Napoleon reformed the French government by creating a bureaucracy and by reforming the legal system. His Code Napoleon remained in France, and in other countries he occupied, for years after his defeat.

- Napoleon conquered basically all of Europe except for Britain and Russia before finally suffering defeat at the Battle of Waterloo.

- The powers of Austria, Russia, Prussia, and Britain met at Vienna to redraw the map of Europe and to establish a system of balance of power politics.

- The Congress of Vienna, and subsequent international politics, reflected the conservative policies of Klemens von Metternich. Metternich constantly worked to keep the rise of nationalism and liberalism in check both in Austria and in Europe.

Chapter 16

The Industrial Revolution

In This Chapter

- ◆ Britain gives birth to another revolution
- ◆ Better wages—but at what cost?
- ◆ Children and factories don't mix
- ◆ The awful side of city life
- ◆ Nineteenth-century romance—sort of

As France struggled with a revolution during the late eighteenth century, Britain enjoyed a revolution of its own. The Industrial Revolution began in the late eighteenth century in Britain, then spread to the continent after the warfare subsided. Like the Agricultural Revolution, the Industrial Revolution changed the economy of Europe, the social structure, demographic patterns, and the way people lived. Unlike the Agricultural Revolution, no one set out to revolutionize industry. As the ancient Greek philosopher Plato said in his *Republic*, "the true creator is necessity, who is the mother of our invention." In other words, when a need or problem arose, an inventor devised a way to deal with that problem. When another arose, another creative person developed another solution, and so on. Such was the case with the Industrial Revolution.

Shop Britain First

The process of industrialization arguably grew out of the textile industry. For example, several yarn spinners were necessary just to keep one weaver busy on his loom. Often a weaver waited while the spinners produced more yarn. Then in 1733, John Kay (1704–c.1780) invented the flying shuttle, a device that allowed weavers to easily produce wider pieces of cloth at faster speeds than ever before. This created a need for more thread and yarn than ever before. To deal with that problem, James Hargreaves (1720–1778) invented his cotton "spinning jenny," which allowed spinners to produce more yarn than weavers could use. Now the need arose for better methods of weaving the vast amounts of yarn that were produced. Each step resulted in better, faster, or cheaper production.

Would You Believe?

The inventors responsible for many of the Industrial Revolution's early advances were not inventors by trade. Kay was a clockmaker, Arkwright was a wigmaker, Hargreaves was a carpenter and weaver.

Continental Quotes

"Were we required to characterise this age of ours by any single epithet, we should be tempted to call it, not an Heroical, Devotional, Philosophical, or Moral Age, but, above all others, the Mechanical Age."

—Thomas Carlyle

As the eighteenth century drew to a close, Britain produced a number of products, particularly textiles, at a faster rate and at lower prices than the traditional manufacturing centers. Output grew faster in the last part of the eighteenth century than ever before, but production skyrocketed between 1800 and 1830, after industrialization had really set in. The same rate of production hit the continent much later. Therefore, markets for industrial goods looked to England first because of the quantities and lower prices. Although the Industrial Revolution resulted from no planning or scheming in advance, it was no accident that industrialization sprang forth from Britain's bosom before that of any other nations.

Why Britain?

Several factors coincided at just the right time and amidst just the right conditions to allow Britain to give birth to industrialization. The first factor, though not necessarily the most important, was the mercantilist economic system and colonial empire. The overseas colonies provided England with all the raw materials it needed for booming industries. The colonies were also a captive market that guaranteed consumers for manufactured goods. Furthermore, the fleet used in the colonial empire could also be used to transport both raw materials and manufactured goods.

Second, agriculture played a major role in the development of British industrialization. The Agricultural Revolution saw major progress in England, and the English farmers reaped the rewards of abundant harvests. More and better harvests resulted in healthier and eventually more numerous people. The surplus of people made a new industrial workforce available. The surplus of people also created more consumers who demanded more goods. Because the bountiful harvests lowered the prices of food, the consumers weren't forced to spend every last penny to feed themselves. The small amount of extra money could be spent on luxury items, like leather instead of wooden shoes, an extra blanket, or even underwear.

Britain's isolation from Europe also played a major role. The constant wars of the continent did not interfere with the development of the textile industry or with innovation. British forces participated in wars during the late eighteenth and early nineteenth centuries, but the fighting and destruction occurred on foreign soil. And England didn't have to deal with trade wars, trade restrictions, and tariffs within its own borders the way places like France and Germany did.

Would You Believe?

Had Nelson not defeated Napoleon at Trafalgar, things might have been different for Britain. War with the French on British soil would have slowed, if not halted, industrialization.

The availability of natural resources in England also played a pivotal role in industrialization. Though the English had used up their forests, and thus their firewood, in the centuries before, Britain had plenty of coal, which would be especially important. Furthermore, the geography of the British Isles was such that a merchant never had to go far to get his wares to a waterway or to a port. Transportation over water routes often proved more efficient than ground transportation, especially before the advent of rail transportation. Unless waterways were frozen, boats could travel under most any conditions day and night. The same certainly was not true of heavy, horse-drawn wagons that often broke down or got stuck in soft ground. Easy transportation of both raw materials and finished goods greatly aided in the process of industrialization.

The First Factories

Industrialization didn't actually occur until the machines switched from manpower to some other source of energy. That switch took place sometime around 1771, when Richard Arkwright (1732–1792) invented the water frame.

The water frame, invented in 1771, was a machine used to spin yarn or thread that made stronger yarn faster than the spinning jenny. The water frame was too large to operate by hand, so the inventor and his investors experimented with horsepower. That proved ineffective so they settled on water power, hence the name. They constructed their first water frame in Derbyshire, England. Now these textile machines could no longer be operated out of homes; they were so large that they had to be constructed in special buildings. There also arose the problem of a labor shortage. There weren't enough available workers, so Arkwright built cottages and brought in workers and their families.

Just a few years later, Samuel Crompton (1753–1827) combined the spinning jenny and the water frame to produce a clever machine, the spinning mule. His first mule could be operated by hand at one's home. However, by 1800 the largest mules had hundreds of spindles and required large buildings like Arkwright's water frame.

In 1784, Edmund Cartwright (1743–1823) created a power loom. Weavers had always operated their looms by hand and foot power, even in water-powered factories, so Cartwright set out to fix the problem. Although his first model functioned rather poorly, he eventually used a steam-powered machine to operate his loom. Just after 1800, a better power-loom received a patent and the textile industry took off. As the years passed, the power-looms got better and better. Entrepreneurs often claimed that the power looms could produce many times the amount of finished product as the best hand weavers, and their claims were justified.

Would You Believe?

The nineteenth-century textile boom made cotton clothing a reality for millions. No longer did poor Englishmen have to wear wool clothing year-round.

By 1850, factories all over England contained perhaps as many as 250,000 such looms. England's ability to mass-produce textiles in factories had amazing effects. The cost of production dropped by as much as 75 or 80 percent in some cases, which translated into much lower prices for consumers on all sorts of textiles. With prices so low, nearly everyone in England could afford textile products like underwear. The rise of factories gave England many tangible and intangible benefits—but not everyone was happy about the new technology.

The Luddites

Near the turn of the nineteenth century, a Manchester company purchased hundreds of Cartwright's power looms for a factory. Disgruntled workers, fearing that their jobs were in jeopardy, burned the factory to the ground. Unfortunately for Cartwright, who really needed the money, the incident in Manchester discouraged other factory owners from purchasing Cartwright's product. Only 12 years later, the isolated incident in Manchester in 1799 had become commonplace in other parts of England. In 1811, it was reported that a General Ned Ludd, who was probably not even a real person, sent warning letters to factory owners in Nottingham. Shortly thereafter, the followers of Ludd, known as Luddites, began nightly attacks on factories there, breaking in and smashing the machinery, which they feared would result in lower wages and lost jobs for all workers.

As a Matter of Fact

In 1851, Britain held a World's Fair known as the Great Exhibition of the Works of Industry of All Nations. The Great Exhibition highlighted the wonders of industry born in the Industrial Revolution. The icon of the Great Exhibition was Joseph Paxton's daring architectural feat known as the Crystal Palace; Paxton designed the building in less than two weeks. The structure, made entirely of iron and nearly one million square feet of glass from England, housed some 13,000 exhibits and hosted over six million visitors during the Great Exhibition. The Great Exhibition, the brainchild of Prince Albert, was located in Hyde Park in London.

Word of the attacks caused new attacks. Hundreds of factories fell victim, and by February of 1812 the government passed legislation known as the Frame Breaking Act that made factory attacks a capital offense punishable by death. Additionally, the government deployed thousands of troops to protect against further attacks. The attacks turned deadly later in 1812 when a group of Luddites attacked a factory where guards were waiting. Some of the guards died in the attacks and several of the Luddites eventually were executed for the attacks. By 1817, the Luddite craze died down and Luddite attacks virtually disappeared.

Would You Believe?

Some of the convicted Luddites were spared from the gallows and were sent to Australia instead.

State-of-the-Art Technology

As machinery became larger and more complex, new processes were needed to create and manufacture the parts in large quantities. Entire factories eventually were employed to create parts for other factories. Manpower and horsepower were now obsolete, and even water power had its shortcomings. Once again, necessity led to the development of something new. In this case, the need for more raw power for large machines led to the development of new devices that allowed man to find and harness energy like never before.

New Sources of Energy

In Britain, the iron industry consumed the forests at a rapid pace and by the mid-eighteenth century had virtually depleted the isles of all meaningful forests. As a result, the iron industry slowed in Britain. Manpower and horsepower no longer got the job done. Britain needed new sources of energy to break the pattern of relying on wood, humans, and horses.

Britain already relied on coal for heating homes and for making things like glass, but not for machinery. As the forests disappeared, coal mining grew in importance. The mines got larger and deeper as the need for coal increased. The main problem with mining coal, though, was that the mines tended to fill with water. Men and horses lost countless man-hours emptying the mines of the water so mining could resume. A simple device was developed that would eventually be revolutionary.

Thomas Savery (1650–1715) invented a steam-powered pump to clear mines of water. The pump used coal to create steam from water. The problem with Savery's invention, which had no moving parts, was that the high pressure made it very volatile and dangerous. Therefore, miners used it at very low pressures. Thomas Newcomen (1663–1729) improved upon Savery's general idea and built a true steam-powered engine complete with a boiler, a piston, and a cylinder. Newcomen's engine was a marvel compared to Savery's, but it was still highly inefficient.

In 1763, a brilliant Scot named James Watt (1736–1819) was repairing one of Newcomen's engines when he figured out the problem. Watt noticed that the cylinder was heated and then cooled with every single stroke of the piston. Watt decided that the engine needed a separate condenser so the steam could cool somewhere else besides the cylinder. He also sealed the top of the cylinder so the steam couldn't escape. Both improvements resulted in massive increases in both efficiency and raw power. It was a Watt engine that Arkwright used to power his mill; by 1800, hundreds of Watt engines powered mills across England.

Would You Believe?

Critics of Watt argue that his carefully guarded patents restricted further development of steam technology, thus slowing the Industrial Revolution.

The successful harnessing of steam rejuvenated the coal and iron industries, and production soared during the late 1700s. The iron industry also benefited from a new development by Henry Cort (1740–1800). Henry Cort invented a puddling furnace that allowed pig iron, or raw iron, to be refined with coke, created by baking coal to remove water and other things, to create iron more suitable for use in heavy industry. In other words, Cort's furnace allowed impurities to be removed from the pig iron. The stronger iron played a major role in the development of an industry that changed not only Britain but the entire world.

The Railroads

Railroads existed in England as early as the seventeenth century. Not that there were trains and locomotives yet. Railroads were simply roads consisting of two rails along which carts could be pulled more easily than along the ground. The first sets of rails, which were made of wood, were used to haul coal. As time passed and the loads got heavier, wheels and rails alike were changed to iron. By 1800, rail companies actually transported passengers along the rails using steam-powered engines. The first passengers enjoyed speeds up to a hair-raising 10 miles per hour.

In 1813, a locomotive called the Puffing Billy made its debut. George Stephenson (1741–1848) improved upon that model and his new locomotive allowed the transportation of passengers and cargo at the same time. As the success of steam-powered locomotives became apparent, railways began appearing across England. The first real rail line was the Liverpool and Manchester Railway. At the famous Rainhill Trials, inventors competed to see whose locomotive would operate on the new railway. At a blazing 16 miles per hour, Stephenson's locomotive, the Rocket, won the right to run the rails between Liverpool and Manchester. The Liverpool and Manchester Railway served as a prototype that investors and engineers from around the world came to observe before building their own railways.

The railways were invaluable for carrying goods from one point to another. Likewise, passengers could travel throughout England more quickly than ever before. The railways made a fortune for the investors who financed their construction, mostly because there was no competition initially. However, the rails remained relatively lucrative even after rails crisscrossed all of Europe. The rails also produced a new group of workers. Large numbers of laborers were necessary for the construction of the rails and huge numbers of unskilled poor workers found work building the railways.

Labor and Reform

The Industrial Revolution created financial opportunities for people at all levels of the social order. The capitalists who invested grew financially secure and often wealthy. They joined the well-to-do merchants who made up the middle class of society. A new class of workers also found new financial opportunities in the factories.

The Industrial Revolution created not only new groups of people but also new sets of issues that society was forced to address. Granted, wages improved. However, concerns about work conditions, the length of the work day and work week, child labor, the sexual division of labor, and exploitation of workers grew as quickly as the industries themselves. When workers were unable to solve the problems themselves, they formed unions or turned to the government for intervention.

Better Wages but Worse Conditions

Both contemporary observers and modern historians have debated the extent to which wages rose for the factory workers during the Industrial Revolution. The most reliable figures indicate that wages and buying power didn't improve significantly for factory workers until after about 1820 in Europe; until that time, improvement in wages came slowly. Certainly, though, economic conditions improved markedly after 1850 for most workers across Europe.

Why did workers go to work in the factories if the wages weren't much better? Because of the population boom, there were simply more people in Britain and then in Europe. At the same time, new agricultural techniques allowed more food to be produced by fewer people. Simply put, there were more workers, and less agricultural work to do.

Conditions for factory workers ranged from good to horrible during the Industrial Revolution. For those who previously had made a living in the cottage industry, factories seemed like a major step backward. In the cottage industry, workers set their own schedules rather than working set hours (usually 12 per day), for a set number of days each week. Likewise, the former cottage workers despised the pace of work in the factories.

The machinery in factories also presented problems that cottage workers and those who came in from the fields had never faced before. The early machines were an open tangle of gears and levers and moving parts. Loose clothing, long hair, and fingers frequently got caught in the machinery, resulting in maimed workers. Factories often were dark, loud, and gloomy, sweltering in the summer and freezing in the winter.

Exploitation of Children

Owners often hired entire families to work in factories, including the children. The husbands often negotiated a wage for the family unit rather than separate wages for each member of the family. The entire family worked in the cottage industries, so it was only natural for workers to do the same in the factories. While the men did the heaviest and hardest labor, the women often operated the machines. Children, too, operated machines but they also swept, picked up scraps, and did other menial chores. Children worked the same hours under the same conditions as their parents.

Would You Believe?

Many factory owners who hired families only wanted children older than about ten years of age. However, many parents only took jobs where their children would be hired, too, so factory owners often employed children as young as six or seven.

There were occasions when families negotiated with factory owners to send their children to live in poorhouses and work in the factories. The children worked in the factories in exchange for room, board, and a tiny wage that was sent to the parents. In such cases, the children often were exploited terribly. The children's supervisors demanded strict discipline. The children worked in frightening conditions among dangerous equipment for pitiful food. Records show that children were sometimes forced to meet quotas before they could eat, take bathroom breaks, or even go to bed for the night. It should be no surprise that children who worked in factories rarely received an education.

Blame It on the Factory Owners

Early factory owners grew very wealthy and ascended to the heights of the middle class. As the Industrial Revolution moved into the middle of the nineteenth century, though, opportunities for first-time entrepreneurs grew increasingly rare because of the competitive nature of industry and because of the large number of factories that sprang up early on.

Usually the wealthy factory owners were "new money," meaning that they were not from a wealthy family but had made their fortunes only recently. Critics blamed these entrepreneurs for the poor working and living conditions of the workers. Critics like Marx and Engels (see Chapter 17) maintained that the owners of the capital exploited the workers.

Many factory owners did exploit their workers, children and adults alike. However, to be fair, financial success was not guaranteed for the capitalists, and they constantly dealt with the challenge of managing production costs while maintaining a reasonable margin of profit. More so than the landed aristocracy, who managed estates and plantations, the factory owners often recognized the plight of the workers and the widening gap between labor and management. After all, many factory owners were themselves from humble origins.

The Reform Movement

As early as the first two decades of the nineteenth century, socially conscious reformers worked to eliminate the terrible conditions of the factories and mills. Government committees visited factory after factory to see for themselves if conditions were as bad as critics claimed. Reformer after reformer spoke before Parliament and urged politicians to take action.

Their cries did not fall on deaf ears. The British government eventually responded, as it did to cries for liberal political and social reform, with the Factory Act of 1833. The legislation limited the workday for children between 9 and 13 to 8 hours and the workday for teenagers to 12 hours. It also prohibited the hiring of children less than 9 years of age and required those children to attend school. The Factory Act of 1844 further restricted the hours for young workers and addressed work-related injuries and unsanitary conditions in factories. In 1847, the Ten Hours Act limited the workday for both women and young workers to a maximum of 10 hours. (The bill actually created a workweek that averaged 10 hours of work per day rather than limiting work to only 10 hours each day.)

Early Labor Movements

Guilds and workers combinations, which were primitive forms of unions, offered some protection for workers dating back several centuries. However, the prominence of the idea of economic liberty caused many politicians to work toward eliminating the old way of doing things. Around the turn of the nineteenth century, the British adopted the Combination Acts. The Acts effectively made trade unions illegal and prohibited unions from striking or harassing management about better hours or more pay. The legislation did not have the desired effect; many workers either disregarded the acts altogether or simply took their union underground. Parliament repealed the Combination Acts in 1824 and unions became part of industrialization by 1825.

Workers had not been very successful with trade unions, so a reformer named Robert Owen (1771–1858) decided to create a national union for workers, stemming from his plan for creating a new society. In 1834, Owen created the Grand National Consolidated Trades Union. He tried again in 1835 with his Association of All Classes and All Nations. Both attempts failed. Owen's mills at New Lanark were a model of what he thought society could be: happy workers productively doing their jobs in a safe, healthy environment. He even experimented in New Harmony, Indiana, with a Utopian society founded on the idea that once crime and the evils of society had been removed, man could be at peace. Like his unions, New Harmony didn't last. His attempts at creating national unions, however, had a lasting effect even if the unions didn't survive. Thanks in large part to Owen, unions grew in popularity and their strength and effectiveness likewise increased over time.

The Sewer of City Life

Nineteenth-century Europeans weren't so different from people in the twenty-first century. Some people liked the laid-back feel of the countryside, while others preferred the hustle and bustle of city life. There were plenty who lived in the country who were excited by the possibilities that the city offered. Men wanted to leave the rural life behind to find work in the cities, and women wanted to find men who found work in the cities. The factories attracted people by the thousands and cities soon filled to capacity and beyond, not just in Britain but everywhere industrialization took hold. The influx of people into the cities, most built in the Middle Ages and never intended for the population pressure of the nineteenth century, caused more than a few problems.

The Growing Cities

Factory owners often built their factories in cities because medieval cities were often built on rivers or along the seas. Rivers and seaports offered manufacturers easy access to raw materials that had been shipped in and offered an easy way to transport their finished products to other markets.

Cities grew at such a rapid pace during the Industrial Revolution that huge population shifts occurred. In England, for example, several million people moved from the countryside into the cities in the first half of the nineteenth century, doubling the percentage of England's population that lived in cities to fully one third of the country by 1850. After another 50 years, practically half of England's population were city-dwellers. Just a century before, the overwhelming majority of Englishmen lived in the country.

The phenomenon occurred elsewhere in Europe, too, with the most notable examples being France and Germany. While Britain's boom occurred beginning in the eighteenth century, the rest of Europe experienced the boom in the nineteenth century. This pattern reflected the birth of the Industrial Revolution in Britain in the eighteenth century and the spread of the Revolution to the continent the following century. The number of large cities, or those with a population of 100,000 or more, nearly tripled between 1800 and 1900. Some cities in Germany, for example, experienced growth of a full one percent for many years, a rate of growth that would have caused the cities' populations to double within two generations' time. The existing buildings in the cities were maximizing their space by housing two and three families per unit and the buildings were side by side by side. There existed almost no recreational space in the cities. The huge and ever-increasing populations of European cities did nothing to help the conditions that already existed there.

Overpopulation

Of course the infrastructures of these medieval cities felt the strain of such overpopulation, but it also created problems on a more personal, human level. Workers from the countryside often packed up and moved to the city with no intention of returning. Once in the city, the worker and his family settled wherever they could. Eventually, the finite number of apartments, or rather rooms, and living quarters filled up. When that happened, families frequently doubled up and in some cases packed three or more families into one room. Some families even rented attics and basements. The buildings that held these families were long, straight, tall buildings with as many rooms as possible crammed into the available space. The problem of overpopulation in European cities was exacerbated by the lack of running water, sewer systems, and the absence of public transportation.

Sanitation? What's That?

The living conditions in the overcrowded cities of post-industrial Europe were nothing short of sickening. With so many people packed into tiny places, disease ran rampant. Because most of the larger cities were medieval cities, sewage ran down the sides of streets rather than in underground sewers. People commonly threw their waste out windows and into the streets as they always had. Outhouses overflowed. Sewage was everywhere, creating a permanent stench. People walking to and from work tracked the waste into their homes and workplaces. Passing carriages splashed the sewage on everyone around. Runoff from the streets frequently seeped into cellars and basements where families lived. Such incidents were widespread and not just isolated, extreme occurrences.

The unsanitary conditions were worsened by the lack of transportation, as most people walked everywhere they went. The fact that people rarely took baths also complicated matters. Even the medieval architecture aggravated the problem. The tall buildings that towered over the narrow, winding streets prevented sun and wind from drying the streets so they remained damp, if not wet and muddy, all the time.

One of the biggest reasons that the conditions were so bad, in addition to all the other reasons, was the ignorance of the population. Most people never thought twice about being dirty. Furthermore, no one had any concept of germs until about the mid-1850s, when Louis Pasteur (1822–1895) discovered living organisms called bacteria. Until then, people believed that they contracted diseases by smelling bad odors. Pasteur's discovery of bacteria proved that the waste material carried the bacteria and not the waste material's odor. As such, it should be no surprise that *cholera* ran wild in many cities and claimed countless lives.

Define Your Terms

Cholera is a potentially fatal gastrointestinal disease caused by bacteria; it is often contracted from unsanitary drinking water.

Cleaning Up Their Act

Socially conscious politicians and scientists knew that something had to be done to clean up the awful conditions in the cities. Pasteur's discovery of bacteria combined with Joseph Lister's (1827–1912) antiseptic strategy had profound effects. Lister knew that by using chemicals on wounds, bacteria would die and would, therefore, not cause sickness. Doctors used this knowledge in operating rooms and throughout hospitals. Eventually, as this knowledge trickled down to the general population, people became somewhat more conscious of dirt and filth. Politicians used the newfound knowledge to combat sickness in cities. If bacteria in water caused sickness, the water needed to be cleaned up.

Would You Believe?

The modern mouthwash Listerine is named for Joseph Lister, the father of antiseptics.

Napoleon III and engineer Georges Haussmann (1809–1884) took the lead in the effort to clean up European cities. They knocked down buildings in slums, built wider streets, and encouraged new construction in Paris. They also improved existing sewer systems and built aqueducts that carried fresh water into the city. Later in the nineteenth century, Paris added a rail system and public transportation. Other European cities weren't as quick to get into the act, but they did eventually follow the French lead.

How Romantic

About the time the Enlightenment peaked in France, an altogether different movement was emerging in Germany. The Enlightenment existed as a purely intellectual movement, and really only among the elite of Europe who had the means to support intellectual pursuits. The fledgling movement in Germany eventually would reach far beyond German borders and beyond Europe. Furthermore, the movement would reach far beyond salons and even beyond the political arena. The movement that would become known later as *Romanticism* eventually would affect literature, music, and art, and it found an audience not just with the European high-brows who for the most part looked down on the ordinary and the mundane.

Define Your Terms

The term **Romanticism** is derived from the "romances" written in the vernacular of the Romance languages during the Middle Ages. The Romance languages include French, Italian, and Spanish.

While Romanticism was to an extent an intellectual movement, it also was an artistic movement. It manifested itself in many ways and included individuals from many walks of life. As diverse and broad as the movement seems in retrospect, it had enormous influence on Europe in the seventeenth and eighteenth centuries. Arguably, the Romantic movement still lingers in places such as the United States, Germany, and England today.

Romantic Ideals

Romanticism began in Germany about the time of the Enlightenment in France. The movement most probably had its beginnings with the Grimm brothers' collection of popular folk tales and other Germans' interest in popular folksongs and ballads. This set the stage for the movement that would, at least to some extent, rise in reaction to the intellectualism and rationalism of the Enlightenment. The interest in folk literature and music showed that the "people," as Enlightenment thinkers would have referred to them, were just as capable as the intellectuals of developing ideas and creating art and literature. What followed not only in Germany but also in England was a fascination with things from the past; in particular, stories from the past. Medieval stories about heroic individuals and great deeds captured the imaginations of Romantics. Romantics embraced all things medieval and exotic.

A real departure from, and probably a reaction against, Enlightenment ideals, Romanticism generally dismissed cold, stoic rationalism in favor of creativity, imagination, and, above all, emotion. It also favored individuality and uniqueness instead of conforming to traditional standards. Romantics viewed religion from an artistic perspective rather than from the perspective of submissive devotees. It is perhaps ironic that Romanticism blossomed at exactly the same time industrialization swept the continent. Romanticism embraced nature. Whereas scientists and intellectuals examined the biological aspects of a flower or the geologic conditions of a mountain, Romantics saw the beauty and majesty. The Romantics lamented the destruction of nature and the pollution of the natural world by the factories of the Industrial Revolution.

One of the more interesting side effects of the Romantic movement was the promotion of nationalism. The interest in national languages, folklore, customs, and geography was obvious in Romantic works, especially in Romantic music. Clearly, the ideals of Romanticism are so broad that the movement cannot be fit neatly into a box or easily described and defined. However, the Romantic ideals can be easily seen where they manifest themselves in literature, art, and music.

Romantic Literature

Romantic literature has its roots in two places. In Germany, the *Sturm und Drang* literary movement rose as a reaction to the overly rational traditional forms of literature that existed in Europe before the 1760s. The "storm and stress" literature, inspired partly by the Enlightenment thinker Rousseau (see Chapter 12), featured a passionate or emotional individual struggling with an issue often related to the stress of society. Rousseau himself could have been the main character of such a story.

The best early example of such a work was Goethe's (1749–1832) *The Sorrows of Young Werther*, the story of a passionate young artist. In Britain, the earliest example of Romantic literature often is attributed to Samuel Taylor Coleridge (1772–1834) and William Wordsworth (1770–1850), whose *Lyrical Ballads* in 1798 broke all the traditional rules about poetry, ballads, and lyrics. They were followed by such literary giants as William Blake, Lord Byron, and John Keats.

Gothic literature, a form of Romantic literature, definitely stirred the emotions of readers. Beginning with Horace Walpole's (1717–1797) *The Castle of Otranto* in 1764 and culminating in the 1818 classic *Frankenstein* by Mary Shelley (1797–1851), gothic literature featured such things as ghosts, brooding characters, dark and gloomy settings, castles, and tales of horror and suspense. Sir Walter Scott (1771–1832) cashed in on the Romantic fascination with the Middle Ages in his novel *Ivanhoe* (1820) and popularized the historical novel. Victor Hugo (1802–1885) made his contribution with, among other titles, *The Hunchback of Notre Dame*. Interestingly, during the age of Romanticism, the work of William Shakespeare made a triumphant comeback and grew perhaps more popular than during his own lifetime.

Romantic Art and Music

Romantic art appeared as a reaction against the unemotional art of the neoclassical movement, of which Jacques-Louis David was one of the greatest. The strict and structured neoclassical movement reacted against the flowery and decorative art of the Baroque and sought to mimic the great classical styles of Greece and Rome. The Romantic artists did away with conventional standards and painted passionate, stirring works on a variety of subjects.

Two of the most prominent of all Romantic painters, both English, painted the same subject but in markedly different ways. J.M.W. Turner (1775–1851) and John Constable (1776–1837) were fascinated by nature. Turner painted tempestuous, stormy, and wild natural scenes. Constable, on the other hand, painted peaceful landscapes depicting farmers, cottages, and other serene scenes. In France, Eugene Delacroix (1798–1863) and Theodore Gericault (1791–1824) painted drastically different scenes from their British counterparts. Delacroix painted scenes of the exotic but his most famous painting remains a political one. His *Liberty Leading the People* (1830) celebrated the French Revolution of 1830 and depicted the passion and emotion of such an uprising. Gericault, who painted during the last years of Napoleon, found his greatest inspiration in human stress and suffering. His seminal work, *Raft of the Medusa* (1819), depicts the languishing survivors of a shipwreck floating on a raft with the majestic sea and sky as a background.

Would You Believe?

Delacroix is believed in some circles to have been the illegitimate son of French minister Charles Talleyrand.

The Romantic musical period followed the classical music period and reacted strongly against that period of music. The classical music period featured structure and traditional stylings. The Romantic musicians, though, worked hard to separate themselves from the classical style. Beginning with the great Ludwig von Beethoven (1770–1827), Romantic musicians sought to stir the emotions and take listeners on an emotional journey. Beethoven, and later Richard Wagner (1813–1833), used chords as no composers had before and placed new emphasis on musical themes. One of the most popular of the Romantic musicians was Franz Liszt (1811–1886), one of the greatest pianists of all time. Liszt enjoyed enormous popularity and produced volumes of musical pieces.

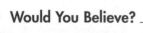

Would You Believe?

Liszt was a great humanitarian. He often taught lessons for free and he bestowed generous amounts of money on orphanages and disaster relief funds.

The Least You Need to Know

◆ Britain was the birthplace of the Industrial Revolution. The cottage industry grew in Britain and, later, Britain had plenty of natural resources, a surplus of labor, markets in the colonies, and freedom from interruptive war on British soil.

◆ As early manufacturing grew, looms and mills were moved to larger locations and became factories. The factories, in theory, threatened the jobs of many hand weavers and other artisans so the Luddites attacked hundreds of factories in protest.

◆ The railroads transformed all of Europe by making transportation of goods and people faster. Those who invested in the railroads made fortunes.

◆ As the Industrial Revolution attracted millions of workers to the cities of Europe, the cities overflowed with people. The result was filthy cities where cholera ran rampant.

◆ Europe's leaders eventually tackled the poor conditions in the cities with knowledge of the germ theory and with plans for new sewer systems, wider streets, and aqueducts.

◆ Romanticism contrasted greatly with the rationalistic Enlightenment. Romanticism emphasized individuality, emotions, passion, and beauty.

Chapter 17

Intriguing New Ideologies

In This Chapter

- Utopia—not quite what More had in mind
- Workers of the world, Marx is your man
- The foundations of socialism
- Not exactly your father's family unit
- Women and children from a new perspective

The years leading up to 1800 were years of intellectual and ideological change as well as radical political upheaval. The years following 1800 were also years of intellectual and ideological change; the political upheaval would come mostly in the mid-1800s. Political ideas like nationalism and liberalism challenged conservatism. Intellectual and artistic ideas of Romanticism challenged rationalism. As the revolutionary fever moved across the continent in the intellectual and political arenas, many Europeans began to dream of socioeconomic change. For these Europeans, socialism appeared to be the only logical choice.

Socialism

The early socialists believed that socioeconomic progress, improvement, and reform should go hand-in-hand with political reform. Unfortunately for these socialists, neither the French Revolution nor the Age of Napoleon produced the kinds of long-lasting changes they desired.

Socialism is a broad term and has come to mean a variety of things. Initially, socialism referred to a classless, competition-free society in which everyone worked together to create a better, if not ideal, society. Characteristics of such a society included cooperation among all members with the means of production controlled by the collective and not by profit-seeking individuals. Socialists believed that decisions affecting society should be made with concern for the greatest good for the greatest number of people. Though that exact idea and wording is attributed to the English-man John Stuart Mill (1806-1873), a nineteenth-century philosopher who advocated utilitarianism, the idea predated Mill by a few generations.

Socialism grew and developed and took on many forms. Some socialists were violent and some were not. Some branches of socialism advocated a classless society that would follow capitalist society. Some branches advocated a workers' revolution to overthrow those capitalists who had, for generations, been exploiting the workers. Later in the nineteenth century, many socialist groups became concerned primarily with the relationship between labor and management.

However fragmented socialism may have become, though, it proved to be a force to be reckoned with in the nineteenth century. Furthermore, its appeal to the working man has given it staying power that makes it significant even into the twenty-first century.

French Utopian Socialism

Some of the first socialists were Frenchmen who sought a utopia similar to that writ-ten about hundreds of years before by Sir Thomas More (see Chapter 2). These socialists were products of their environment who owed most of their ideas to what they experienced and witnessed. The earliest socialists experienced the turmoil of the French Revolution and the decline of conditions for workers during the Industrial Revolution.

The French utopian socialism began with Count Henri de Saint-Simon (1760–1825). Saint-Simon believed the secret to creating a socialist society lay in its planning and organization. Saint-Simon believed that men of science should help organize a society that would exist to better the world. He believed that those who were best suited to make decisions should receive the power to do so. He also believed that each member of society should contribute according to his ability and receive according to his need. Saint-Simon argued that the number-one priority of society ought to be the betterment of the poor. Therefore, society should be organized so that the goal of improving life for the poor, and ultimately eliminating poverty altogether, could be reached. To help reach these goals, Saint-Simon and his followers advocated the abolishment of rules of inheritance and the transfer of control of all wealth to social groups for redistribution. Though some of Saint-Simon's followers lingered for some time in France, they never successfully grew into a major force.

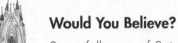

Would You Believe?

Some followers of Saint-Simon attempted to live communally, but disagreements, and perhaps jealousies, prevented the community's success.

Another French utopian socialist who proved more influential than Saint-Simon was Charles Fourier (1772–1837). Fourier outlined very specifically the details of his ideal society. The communities were to include about 1,600 residents on 5,000 acres of land. His view included apartment buildings where the rich lived at the top and the poor on the ground floor. In his society, which centered on caring and cooperation among all citizens, people earned income according to the job they did. The people working pleasant jobs received very little pay while those who did unpleasant jobs were paid more. To encourage everyone to work, he hoped to find a way to make work more like play.

In his society, there would be no marriage but rather freedom to form sexual unions whenever people wanted. He and many other socialists believed that marriage was a form of prostitution and exploitation of women; women in his society were to be emancipated.

From there, Fourier departed into his own world, one not based on the reality that most other Europeans experienced. Like many socialists, he viewed history in epochs, or stages. For Fourier, the Industrial Revolution marked only a passing phase that would be replaced in time by an epoch in which industrialization would be a thing of the past. Therefore, in his writings, he basically ignored the problems of industrialization that other socialists attacked. Fourier had some thoughts about the future, too. He predicted that eventually multiple moons would orbit the earth, that the extreme weather of the poles would become tropical and that the earth would one day be populated by millions of poets, scientists, and writers who would equal or surpass Homer, Newton, and Molière.

Other French utopians who struck a chord with the workers of France were Louis Blanc (1811–1865) and Pierre Joseph Proudhon (1809–1865). Blanc said the root of all evils in society was competition. The plight of the poor of the industrial world could be traced directly to the capitalists who owned the industries. He advocated equalization of wages and universal voting rights. He also called on the government to guarantee employment for all who desired work. In his mind, the right to work held as much as importance in the world as the right to life and liberty. He outlined his political beliefs in an 1839 essay called *The Organization of Work*.

> **Would You Believe?**
>
> Fourier's wildest idea might have been that the world's oceans would one day become lemonade.

Proudhon went even further than Blanc regarding the plight of the poor workers. He argued that the profit from manufacturing belonged to the workers and not to the capitalists. He opposed capitalism and advocated a system in which the workers and artisans controlled the means of production and then traded their manufactured goods. He also opposed communism, though, because he believed in individual property as long as that property was not stolen; he believed the profits made by capitalists were stolen.

Early Attempts at Utopia

A number of utopian socialists attempted to establish their ideal societies, but none of the attempts amounted to much. Robert Owen tried to create an ideal society in New Harmony, Indiana. Followers of a socialist named Etienne Cabet (1788–1856) also tried to build their ideal society in the United States. The Icarians, as they were known, tried in Iowa, Texas, and then Missouri. None of the settlements lasted. Fourier's followers established the community of La Reunion outside of Dallas, Texas. The population of 350 lasted only five years because of harsh weather and grasshoppers. Dozens more like La Reunion sprung up around the United States only to meet the same fate. France, too, witnessed the rise and fall of utopian societies. One of the most famous communes grew in Paris in the late 1800s.

Marx and the Manifesto

The French utopian socialists were influential in that later socialists read their works. However, the French utopians had such far-fetched ideas that utopian socialism never succeeded long-term. The socialists who followed the utopians read their ideas, weeded out the information that seemed impractical, and built upon the rest. Among the basic ideas that influenced later socialists were the idea that the capitalists were exploiting the workers, the idea of creating a classless society where the workers were no longer exploited, and the idea that the workers should control the means of production.

Two of the people influenced by these ideas were Karl Marx (1818–1883) and his important but often forgotten friend Friedrich Engels (1820–1895). These two would use the ideas of the utopians to create one of the most important economic works of the last 200 years, *The Communist Manifesto*. In the *Manifesto*, Marx and Engels combined French utopian socialism, German philosophy, and English labor economics to produce a statement of beliefs that would be hugely influential in Europe in the late nineteenth and early twentieth centuries.

Not One of the Marx Brothers

Karl Marx was born in Germany to a prominent Jewish family. Despite the family's Jewish ancestry, Marx's father converted to Christianity so he could remain a lawyer. The family became known as very liberal and progressive. Marx attended college, first in Bonn and then in Berlin, where he became fascinated with the philosophy of Georg Hegel.

Hegel's idea was that the state developed through a series of dialectics. Although he didn't use the terminology, his idea is best explained as thesis, antithesis, and synthesis. In other words, Hegel believed that history was developed through a reaction to something, the rise of something that contradicts the reaction, then the result of the tension between the two. This theory would have a profound influence on Marx and his view of the world.

As a Matter of Fact

Marx viewed the world as dynamic and not static. He viewed history that way, too. His dialectical approach to the study of history implies that capitalism, for example, grew out of the struggle between classes. One class won the struggle, ended up with the means of production, and proceeded to exploit the other class. According to the dialectical approach, though, capitalism will ultimately be replaced by something else as a result of struggle or conflict.

Engels, also a German by birth, was the son of a factory owner. His father sent him to England to manage the family textile industry, where he discovered the plight of the workers. Engels was appalled at what the Industrial Revolution and capitalism had done to the workers.

After spending some time in journalism, Marx moved to France, where he met Engels. They discovered they had similar ideas regarding capitalism, and Engels convinced Marx to become interested in economics. In 1845, Marx was expelled from France so he moved first to Belgium and then to England with Engels. Over the next several years, Marx moved to Germany, France, Belgium, and back to England again. During this time, Marx and Engels wrote extensively on a variety of topics. They wrote critiques of socialism, they wrote about poverty, and they wrote about politics. In England, in 1848, they wrote the *Manifesto*.

In 1864, Marx formed the International Workingmen's Association, a political activist group later known as the First International. His organization only lasted about five years, though. During his time with the organization, he researched and then wrote his other landmark piece, *Das Kapital*, or *Capital: A Critique of Political Economy*. In this work, written in German, Marx critically examined capitalism with the economic theories of Adam Smith and David Ricardo; the philosophy of Hegel; and the socialist thought of Charles Fourier, Henri de Saint-Simon, and Pierre Joseph Proudhon. His goal was to apply a scientific and philosophical examination to economic history to justify the rise of socialism. In *Das Kapital* he outlined many of his ideas about how the capitalists, who own the means of production, exploit the workers. Marx had plans for multiple editions of *Das Kapital*, but he died after the publication of the first one. His friend and partner, Engels, completed later editions by reconstructing Marx's notes and rough drafts.

As a Matter of Fact

Marx spent nearly his entire life with little or nothing to his name. He survived mostly by living off the generosity of Engels. Engels never married but lived with a woman, Mary Burns, until her death, when he moved in with his sister. He spent much of his later life working on feminist issues. He tied communist theory to marriage by implying that throughout history man has dominated woman within the institution of marriage much the way the capitalists have dominated the workers.

Workers of the World, Unite

In 1836, a group of German workers living in England formed the League of the Outlaws, later called the League of the Just, and finally the League of the Not Half-Bad. Engels attended one of their meetings in 1847 in London. Initially the group followed utopian socialist ideas. However, after Engels and Marx influenced the group, the League reorganized and changed its name to the Communist League. They even adopted Marx's slogan of "Workers of the world, unite." They declared their 1847 meeting to be the first congress of the new Communist League and agreed to hold a second congress later in the year. At the second congress, the Communist League requested that Marx and Engels write for them a *manifesto* for communists.

Define Your Terms

A **manifesto** is a statement of beliefs and principles.

In the *Manifesto*, Marx and Engels outlined the beliefs of communism, a system that advocates communal ownership of all property. Marx explained in the *Manifesto* that "The history of all hitherto existing society is the history of class struggle." In other words, all of history can be divided into stages or epochs. Each epoch is marked by class struggle, or conflict between the different social classes. The struggle in each epoch occurs because one socioeconomic class exploits or oppresses another.

When the *Manifesto* was written, the world was in the capitalist epoch, which had followed the feudal epoch. According to Marx and Engels, capitalism would fall after a revolution. The proletariat, or working class, would rise up against the bourgeoisie, or the capital-owning middle class. The authors believed that the rise of the proletariat eventually would lead, after a transitional period of socialism, to a classless society similar to the one dreamt about by so many utopians. Included in the communist system the authors advocated were things like the abolition of private property and land, the abolition of inheritance laws, the nationalization of the means of production, and even the abolition of the family unit and marriage.

Would You Believe?

Critics of the *Manifesto* have always asked the question, "How did Marx expect a revolutionary state to simply give way to a communal society?" Though many nations in the twentieth century adopted communism, the states never "withered away" into the communal society Marx anticipated.

The *Manifesto* was hardly popular or even widely known after its publication in 1848. However, its influence spread in the decades following 1848. The *Manifesto* was printed in new editions twice in the late 1800s. In addition to the *Manifesto*, Marx's ideas stayed alive through the Second International which Engels founded after Marx's death. The idea of Marxism grew later in Marx's life and after his death, although the popular Marxism didn't necessarily mirror the ideas of Marx and Engels. Many "Marxists" simply use the vocabulary of proletariat, bourgeoisie, class struggle, and more.

The Socialist Movement

By 1850, the Industrial Revolution had reached nearly every corner of Europe, and workers in other countries faced the same problems experienced by English workers during its early days. This led socialists to conclude that capitalism did indeed exploit workers wherever it manifested itself. No wonder, then, that workers throughout Europe fell in love with socialism. Though it grew and developed into a wide variety of forms, socialism maintained that society should be for the benefit of all, yet capitalist society existed solely for the benefit of the small, elite group of people who controlled the means of production. From the perspective of the workers who often felt exploited, socialism had a great deal of appeal.

Early Socialists

Try as they might, the utopian socialists never really made things happen. Those who followed had greater success seeing their socialist ideas amount to something tangible. However, many found themselves in direct competition with Marx and his followers. For example, Marx strongly opposed a Russian socialist named Mikhail Bakunin (1814–1876). Unlike Marx, Bakunin believed that the egalitarian, classless society sought by socialists could only be achieved through anarchy. In other words, the revolutionary government between capitalism and communism, as described by Marx, was neither

practical nor possible. In 1869, Bakunin
organized groups of workers into the Social
Democratic Alliance with the intent to join
Marx's First International. Marx, however,
refused his Alliance entry. The Alliance dissolved and the members joined the International on their own.

Would You Believe?

Bakunin was fiercely
anti-semitic and attacked Marx
for his Jewish heritage.

Ferdinand Lasalle (1825–1864) had quite an impact on the manifestation of socialist
ideas. A German Jew who studied both philology and philosophy and advocated
Hegel's ideas, Lasalle joined the Communist League. In the 1860s, Lasalle traveled
Germany and worked to call the working classes to action; he believed government
action would not be sufficient to ease the frustrations of the workers. Despite being
a member of the Communist League, Lasalle, like Bakunin, received nothing but
criticism from Marx and Engels. In 1863, Lasalle founded the Allgemeiner Deutscher
Arbeiterverein, or the General German Workers' Association. This party, later called
the Social Democratic Party of Germany, became the first labor party in Germany,
even before Germany unified (see Chapter 18). Marx's followers did not join the
party. Lasalle died in a duel the following year with the suitor of his love interest.

Socialism and Labor

Socialists more often than not were idealists who dreamed of creating ideal societies
where the working class enjoyed freedom from economic oppression, and they
worked diligently to spread their message to the working class of Europe. Ironically,
their progress was impeded somewhat by the workers themselves.

Many times labor's sole interest was the formation of trade unions to fight for better
conditions, wages, and benefits. Many workers lacked the foresight to imagine a new
society; they just wanted food on the table. Another explanation for the reluctance of
workers to join radical groups was the improving economic and political conditions
for workers after 1850. If conditions were
getting better, workers would be less inclined
to join radical groups bent on revolution.
Germany serves as a good example because
only a small percentage of the workforce even
belonged to a union.

Would You Believe?

At the turn of the twentieth century, economist Eduard
Bernstein asserted that Marx was
flat wrong when he predicted
that the working class would slip
further and further into poverty.

However, socialism and labor movements
became synonymous throughout the late nineteenth century. Despite the best efforts of many

European nations to squash socialist movements, as Bismarck did in Germany (see Chapter 18) because of the revolutionary potential inherent in socialism, it never died out. Socialists won the right to have legal labor unions in many nations between 1850 and 1900. Furthermore, by the end of the century, socialists had begun to win elected positions in governments across Europe.

New Ideas About Family

As much of Europe experienced industrialization and urbanization during the nineteenth century, ideas and values concerning the family unit changed. Things were bound to change. After all, at the turn of the nineteenth century, the family unit still often existed as an economic institution whose purpose was to work the family farm or work in the family's cottage industry. The lifestyle of the rural family unit hadn't changed much since the Middle Ages, and the urban family unit, particularly in an industrialized Europe, remained a relatively new development. Changes within the family were due in large part to the emergence of new classes, especially the solidified middle class that accompanied industrialization. The changes included ideas about sex and marriage, gender roles, children, education, money, and morality.

An Emerging Middle Class

The true middle class emerged during the nineteenth century in Europe. Unlike the middle class of modern America, characterized by comfortable but modest living conditions, the nineteenth-century European middle class included the most successful businessmen, bankers, and industrialists who were very wealthy, and the middle-of-the-road accountants, lawyers, merchants, engineers, managers, government employees, and industrialists who had yet to strike it rich. At the bottom were the small business owners, small-scale merchants, and other workers who used their brains rather than their backs for a living. Even schoolteachers and nurses worked their way up into the middle class. Perhaps the unifying characteristic of the new middle class was the use of their minds for their living and the general lifestyle they enjoyed.

The nineteenth-century middle class enjoyed a reasonable amount of disposable income that it spent on good food and domestic servants, both luxuries never before available to many of the middle class. The middle class also used the new surplus income for socializing. The middle class, the upper echelon more than the bottom, threw dinner parties and enjoyed "cultured" activities such as the opera and the theater. As the nineteenth century wore on, fashion became increasingly important to the middle class. The middle class also spent more and more money on their children's education.

The nineteenth-century middle class developed a sense of morality and family values. The commitment to family and moral living was shared by both the middle and working classes, but the working class had a necessary commitment to frugal living that was lost on the middle class. Despite the rise of social drinking by both men and women, drunkenness and heavy drinking were frowned upon. Temperance movements frequently moved through the predominantly Protestant areas of Europe. The champions of the temperance movements blamed alcohol for nearly all of society's woes and advocated abstinence. The middle class looked down on promiscuity, too.

Would You Believe?

The number of servants employed by middle-class families served as a sort of status symbol, much the way automobiles serve as a status symbol today.

As a Matter of Fact

The Victorian Age spanned from 1837 to 1901, the years of Queen Victoria's reign in Britain, and marked the pinnacle of British culture and industry. During this age, a set of moral standards emerged, often referred to as Victorian Morality, often viewed as a reflection of Victoria when in fact Victoria was probably a reflection of her times. The concept of Victorian Morality is something of a paradox. While the Age did see an increased emphasis on public improvement, morality, restraint, and frugal living, a strict class system existed throughout the United Kingdom, particularly overseas. Though Christianity was generally accepted by Europeans in the Victorian Age, not everyone attended church. Nevertheless, religion played a significant role in shaping Victorian Morality.

A change in the reasons people married in the nineteenth century allowed for a strict view of promiscuity. For centuries, Europeans at the upper end of the socioeconomic scale married for financial or political reasons and participated in arranged marriages. Poorer Europeans often waited relatively late to marry, until the man of the house had enough money to support a family.

With the financial opportunities available to both the middle and working classes in the nineteenth century, people married earlier than ever before. The fall of financial considerations and changes in the conditions of marriage also saw the rise of romantic

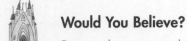

Would You Believe?

Despite the new emphasis on morality, sexual experimentation flourished, evidenced by the large number of illegitimate births early in the first half of the nineteenth century. Illegitimacy did seem to decline after 1850, though.

notions of marriage. When people had typically waited until their late twenties to marry, society often chose to ignore promiscuity. When people began to marry earlier, promiscuity became an evil condemned by many. Along the same lines, sexual conduct of children and teenagers became a real concern for families who valued their fine reputations. Men and women often repressed their children's sexuality in rather drastic ways. In extreme cases, boys seldom were left alone and girls were forbidden from riding bicycles or from riding horses in any way other than side-saddle.

Women's Changing Roles

The roles and status of women changed over the course of the nineteenth century, particularly after 1850 when industrialization had swept over the continent. These changes occurred both in and out of the family unit. Statistics show that most women of the nineteenth century married. For an unmarried woman, the place to find a husband was the city.

Droves of rural girls moved to the city to find employment and a husband, often taking jobs as maids. The rise of the middle class provided plenty of opportunity for those seeking jobs in the domestic services. An unfortunate side effect of the increase in young women working in other households was the surprising number of incidents of sexual harassment and abuse of these workers. Young, unmarried women often faced abuse and exploitation in the world's oldest profession, too. Prostitution, despite the sweeping morality, thrived in European cities and provided employment for women who couldn't find work elsewhere.

In the early part of the century, women often continued to work after they married. Before the nineteenth century, many wives helped provide for the family unit. As Europe's population became more and more urban and industrial, the husband more and more became the sole bread winner as economic conditions picked up after 1850. Especially among the middle class, the woman was expected to be at home with the children while the man worked to provide for the family.

This ideal contributed to a very rigid division of labor in European cities. When women, married or otherwise, sought employment, they often had no options other than domestic work, teaching schoolchildren, or working in the *sweated* industries. The sexual division of labor had created a situation in which the better jobs simply were not available to women. Furthermore, in any decent jobs available to both men and women, women received markedly lower wages. Chivalry may have been dead, but misogyny was alive and well. The lack of financial opportunities was mirrored by the lack of educational opportunities and the lack of legal rights for women in many places, too. Frequently, women were the legal property of their husbands or, at the very least, their incomes were.

Many women rebelled against the oppressive nature of the male-dominated nineteenth century. Socialism looked especially good to many women, who agreed that marriage equated to legalized prostitution. Several women's organizations, socialist and otherwise, formed to fight for equal rights, equal financial opportunities, and the right to vote. While many women did have almost complete control of the household, this wasn't enough for many. Women's groups demanded to be allowed the opportunity to be doctors, lawyers, and other professions limited almost entirely to men.

Define Your Terms

Sweated refers to labor that requires long hours of work in unsanitary conditions for low wages.

Would You Believe?

Toward the end of the nineteenth century, even liberal and forward-thinking men championed women's rights issues. The father of utilitarianism, John Stuart Mill, was outspoken in favor of granting women the right to vote.

New Attitudes Toward Children

During the Middle Ages and the few centuries that followed, families had attitudes about children that might seem shocking today. The infant mortality rate was high across Europe until the last few hundred years or so. Poor diet of the mother, a lack of hygiene, rudimentary medical knowledge, and generally unhealthy living conditions made childbirth tricky even for wealthy Europeans. The odds were only about 50/50 that a child would survive infancy, and just slightly better that an infant would survive past toddlerhood. Once a child reached age 10 or so, he or she was in good shape.

Because the survival rate for those children that survived childbirth remained relatively low, parents rarely developed deep emotional ties to their children. Evidence of emotional distance between parent and child can be found in a few examples of life prior to the nineteenth century. Wealthy women rarely breastfed their own children and instead hired wet nurses to do that for them. Also, the use of swaddling clothes, or tightly wrapped cloth that restricted all movement of an infant, to comfort children reduced the amount of time that women held their children. A child in swaddling clothes could be laid down to suckle a cloth dipped in milk while the mother worked or did chores.

By the end of the nineteenth century, evidence clearly showed that earlier trends in childrearing had fallen away. One of the biggest pieces of evidence relates to family size. Nineteenth-century families, especially within the middle class, had fewer children than families of centuries before. In previous centuries, more pregnancies resulted in better odds that several children would survive to adulthood. In the nineteenth century, families had fewer children so that they could devote the necessary attention to them. In centuries past, especially in rural areas, many families had several children to help in the fields and around the house. Especially in urban settings, extra children were no longer necessary for helping to provide income for the family.

The attention given to children also serves as evidence of deeper emotional ties. Families with extra income made the commitment to providing clothing, good diets, medical care, and education for their children. Mothers took better care of infants because they better understood infants' needs, and because they had better odds of surviving. Many women even breastfed their own children. This may be partially responsible for the deeper attachment to children. The fact that many women ran the household rather than working also helps explain the new attachment to the children. While the number of abandoned children and orphans remained high compared to modern standards, the numbers declined during the late nineteenth century.

The concern for children did reach interesting extremes. For example, many parents believed that the moment of conception and the moment of childbirth were pivotal moments in children's lives. Therefore, parents often tried to conceive while both parents were happy and healthy.

Would You Believe?

The concern for children's health often led to repression and overprotection of them. Many natural tendencies and curiosities, especially of a sexual nature, were carefully guarded against, even with medical procedures. Circumcisions, for example, often were recommended to discourage masturbation among boys.

The Least You Need to Know

♦ In the years following 1815, ideas of socialism spread across Europe. Socialists believed society should exist for the good of all and not just for the good of the elite, who owned virtually all the wealth in Europe.

♦ The rise of socialism must be considered in the context of the Industrial Revolution. The industrialization of Europe left workers feeling exploited because the industrialists grew rich after selling the goods produced by the workers.

♦ The most influential of all socialists were Karl Marx and Friedrich Engels who, in 1848, published *The Communist Manifesto*.

♦ Socialism and labor went hand in hand throughout the second half of the nineteenth century. Socialist intellectuals often were frustrated with workers who were reluctant to sign on to radical ideology.

♦ A new middle class emerged in Europe as an effect of industrialization and urbanization. The middle-class values emphasized hard work, discipline, and moral living. The role of women in the workplace and in the home changed, and children grew far more important to the family unit.

Nineteenth-Century Growing Pains

In This Chapter

- ◆ The Revolutions of 1848
- ◆ Napoleon rises again
- ◆ Italy gets it together
- ◆ Bismarck unites the Germans
- ◆ Making Russia not quite so backward

The years beginning with 1848 saw more turmoil and change across Europe than perhaps any 50-year stretch in centuries. Though the year 1848 would become synonymous with revolution, it was the events and conditions leading up to 1848 that caused those in control to lose nearly everything during that fateful year.

Before the Watershed

Industrialization was spreading from one European state to the next. Liberals, nationalists, and socialists all wanted change. The conservatives, led by Metternich, resisted it for as long as they could.

The British Parliament, controlled by the conservative aristocrats, had the power to deal with liberal challenges. The conservative government began with changes to the longstanding Corn Laws, which regulated the import of foreign grain. While at war with France, British grain and bread prices rose because they couldn't import grain. After the fall of Napoleon (see Chapter 15), imported grain brought down bread prices. In a selfish move, the aristocrats pushed through changes that allowed grain imports only after domestic prices reached a certain level, causing higher bread prices for the common Brit but more income for those who owned land. The law prompted protests, which Parliament controlled with the Six Acts restricting assemblies and the press.

The 1820s proved less oppressive but the real change came in 1832. The Reform Bill of 1832 did away with "rotten boroughs" or voting districts in which few or no voters actually lived. Some of the rotten boroughs were tracts of land where peasants once lived. After enclosure, many of the peasants left the land. It was not uncommon for rotten boroughs to be home mostly to sheep. Nevertheless, these boroughs still sent two representatives to Parliament. In the meantime, boroughs in heavily populated areas also sent two representatives. By redoing the boroughs, the Reform Bill increased the number of voters by about 50 percent. Middle-class citizens finally had a real vote in Parliament. The less conservative Parliament went on to repeal the Corn laws in 1846, but only after the Irish potato crops failed, and the Ten Hours act in 1847 (see Chapter 16). These liberal ideas were having a harder time taking hold on the continent, though.

> **Would You Believe?**
>
> The radicals in England at this time were the Chartists, who called for universal suffrage. Despite hundreds of thousands of signatures on petitions and a few protests, Parliament rejected the Chartists' pleas.

1848: Year of Revolts

The Parliamentary reforms in Britain probably saved the Brits from the kind of revolution that occurred almost everywhere else in Europe in 1848. Russia, too, managed to escape 1848 revolution-free, but only because it lacked a true middle class. The revolutions were ostensibly led by liberals against oppressive conservatism, but there was more going on in Europe prior to 1848 than just liberalism and nationalism versus conservatism.

After 1815, Europe was a wreck. Napoleon left a mess and the Congress of Vienna tried to clean it up. Economies were in shambles, crop failures left poor Europeans hungry, and hungry poor people always cause problems. The hunger peaked after 1845 when the Irish potato famine left Ireland desperate for food and the rest of

Europe dealing with Irish refugees. To make matters worse, Europe had embraced industrialization, but the workers had yet to really be rewarded for their labor. Socialists produced thought-provoking literature about ideal societies and hinted at revolution. Europe was ready to listen.

Revolution in France

After Napoleon's final defeat in 1815, Louis XVIII took the throne and maintained order basically by not doing anything stupid. His brother, Charles X, wasn't so interested in maintaining order.

From the moment of his ostentatious coronation in 1824, he sought to reestablish absolute monarchy in France, finally succeeding in 1830. He took voting rights away from many citizens and tightened controls on the press. Paris took to the streets, and for "three glorious days," as the event was remembered, revolutionaries created chaos. Charles fled for his life and, after some tricky maneuvering, the upper middle class declared the throne vacant and replaced Charles with Louis-Philippe (1773–1850).

Would You Believe?

One of the things that irritated the French most about Charles X was his insistence on getting rid of the *tricolore*, the blue, white, and red French national flag adopted during the French Revolution.

The Revolution of 1830 accomplished almost nothing in the long run. Louis-Philippe's government suffered from inactivity and corruption. He refused election reforms to allow people other than the rich to vote. Socially conscious citizens complained about the lack of social welfare under his rule. Economic conditions worsened throughout the 1840s, and the situation grew more volatile with each passing month.

In February of 1848, the people of Paris did what they always seemed to do when they got mad and hungry: the combined forces of the workers and the middle class barricaded the streets and revolted. The prime minister resigned and Louis-Philippe abdicated the throne in favor of his grandson, but Parisians were through with monarchies. They created the Second Republic, named after the First Republic that followed the 1789 Revolution.

Though all the revolutionaries agreed on a republic, the people were divided on what to do next. The moderate middle class didn't want to grant universal male suffrage, nor did they want too many social programs. As the situation worsened, the government set up National Workshops in Paris at the urging of socialist Louis Blanc and a worker named Albert, guaranteeing employment for tens of thousands of Parisians.

The disorganized government managed to stage elections in April and the people of France elected monarchists, moderate middle-class representatives, and socialists to the Constituent Assembly, the legislative body of France. The middle and upper classes, along with the rural peasants, feared the radical socialists. Furthermore, the rural poor and the middle class did not want to be taxed to guarantee jobs for the urban poor.

The government cut ties with Blanc and moved away from socialism, so reactionary urban poor and artisans from Paris stormed the Assembly in May and tried to form a new state. The National Guard crushed their attempts. In June, the government closed the workshops, touching off violent warfare between the classes. Unfortunately for the socialist urban workers, the National Guard brutally put down the revolution in three days, called the "June Days." Because deep divisions between all parties promised instability, the Assembly wrote the constitution so that the executive branch of the government had significant power. In December, a national election placed the authoritarian nephew of Napoleon Bonaparte in charge as president. The failure of the revolutionaries to work together resulted in the ultimate failure of France's 1848 revolution. It was successful only in that the king was gone.

Revolution in Austria

The situation in Austria's holdings greatly resembled that of France in 1848. Liberals from all walks of life demanded voting rights, constitutions, and other liberal concessions. As word of uprisings spread through Europe, liberals got their hopes up and revolution erupted in Vienna. In Hungary, which had long had nationalist ideas, nationalists demanded universal suffrage, liberty, and even independence from Austrian rule. Slow to act initially, Habsburg ruler Ferdinand I (1793-1875) agreed to some liberal concessions after rebellious students took to the streets. In addition to pressuring the conservative Metternich to step down, Ferdinand abolished serfdom in Hungary. This may have seemed like a victory for Hungarian revolutionaries, but it actually divided them. The serfs were rural poor who, after being freed, lost interest in radical action. The urban workers and the middle class then found themselves divided over socialist ideas.

Would You Believe?

After Metternich resigned, he disguised himself and fled to England.

The nationalist Hungarian government created a new constitution that would unite all of Hungary into a single nation and restrict participation in the process to Hungarian speakers only. Minorities like the Serbs and Croats had national aspirations of their own—and powerful allies in Austria and Russia. After a year of fighting over the creation of an independent state, Hungarian nationalists seemed close to their goal. However, Austria had put down uprisings everywhere else in its territory and turned its attention to Hungary. Led by Francis Joseph (1830–1916), the new emperor, the Austrians, with aid from the Russians coming in the form of additional troops, dashed Hungary's revolutionary hopes. The troops surrounded and recaptured the major cities that the Hungarians had captured. For years, Austria ruled Hungary with an iron fist and forbade such activities as public gatherings and the display of Hungarian nationalist colors. Again, the lack of solidarity among the revolutionaries prohibited the success of the revolution.

Prussians Make Demands

The 30-plus states of the German Confederation took notice when Louis-Philippe abdicated the throne in France. Liberals from all the German states had for some time longed for a unified German state under a constitution. Prussian liberals followed the French lead and called for reform by petitioning Prussian King Frederick William IV (1795-1861) in the Prussian capital of Berlin. The workers of Berlin took to the streets and joined the liberals in cries for reform. Frederick William buckled under the pressure and agreed to grant Prussians a constitution and to merge Prussia into a German state. Once again, though, the moderate middle class and the urban workers were divided over how democratic and socialist the new government should be, and conservatives of the middle class were able to convince Frederick William to change his position.

Plans for a unified German state led by Prussia were already being worked on by the National Assembly in Frankfurt. At the same time, an assembly of Prussians were hard at work on a Prussian constitution in Berlin. In the midst of the planning for a federal German constitution, Denmark attempted to annex Schleswig-Holstein, a region full of Germans. The National Assembly called on the Prussian army, which went to war with Denmark. The National Assembly finished its constitution in 1849 and offered Frederick William the chance to be emperor of the new German state. Having been persuaded by conservatives in Berlin, Frederick refused. He disbanded the assembly back in Berlin and returned Prussia to a state under rule as King of Prussia rather than under the government of bureaucracy. The uprisings around Prussia had been put down and the opportunity for unification had been squandered. Frederick William later wanted the German kings to make him emperor, but Austria wouldn't agree. He tried to exclude Austria from the union of German states but Austria resisted so he backed down. Yet again, division among the revolutionaries had resulted in a failed revolution.

Failed liberal uprisings occurred in Poland and in Italy in 1848, too. Again the revolutionaries had initial successes, then spent their time bickering over the direction of the new government. In each case, the old regime used the revolutionaries' period of indecisiveness to regroup and quell the revolutions. The revolutions of 1848 were failures in the short-term, but they would eventually give revolutionaries some of what they wanted. For example, Italy and Germany each would undergo major changes over the next 20 years. Also, in 1867, Hungary forced Austria to grant it dual monarchy status, resulting in the Austro-Hungarian Empire.

> **Would You Believe?**
>
> Frederick William later remarked that he wanted to be asked by his peers to be emperor and that he didn't want a crown "from the gutter," with "the stink of revolution."

Another Napoleon

When Charles Louis Napoleon Bonaparte won the national election in France in 1848, he became President Bonaparte. When he moved from president to emperor, he took the name Emperor Napoleon III of France. When was there a Napoleon II? Both times the original Napoleon abdicated, in 1814 and in 1815 (see Chapter 15), Napoleon's son by his second wife, Marie Louise, took over as emperor … sort of. Just three and four years old each time respectively, Napoleon II (1811–1832) never technically ruled France, but he did hold the title of emperor from June 22 to July 7, 1815.

> **Would You Believe?**
>
> Napoleon II died in Austria of tuberculosis at the age of 21. In 1940, Adolf Hitler sent his remains back to France so Napoleon II could be buried alongside his father at Les Invalides in France. King Louis-Philippe had Napoleon's remains brought to France from St. Helena in 1840.

How to Get Elected Using a Famous Name

Louis Napoleon, the nephew of the original Napoleon Bonaparte, tried twice to overthrow the government of Louis-Philippe, in 1836 and 1840. His second attempt landed him in jail, where he wrote a pamphlet promoting his political ideas titled *Napoleonic Ideas and the Elimination of Poverty*. He escaped in 1846 and went to Britain, returning to France after the revolution in 1848.

Though he had no political experience, Louis Napoleon decided to run for president. He established a platform that appealed to the masses and campaigned wisely. Louis Napoleon took advantage of the universal male suffrage and took his plan to the middle class and rural property owners, most of whom had never voted before. Napoleon knew that most rural voters had no interest in the radical socialist ideas spreading through the cities. Louis Napoleon vowed to provide a government tough on socialism. Louis Napoleon believed that the government should help the people improve their economic conditions, but not through socialism. France, he declared, needed a strong leader who answered to no one so that he could effectively serve the interests of all classes—a page he took directly out of his uncle's book.

One of the deciding factors in Louis Napoleon's election was simply the use of his uncle's name. Napoleon had left a bad taste in the mouths of most Europeans, but the Romantics idolized him, and by 1848 the French people remembered him as a hero. Napoleon symbolized a proud, strong France, a pillar of strength among other European nations. The French longed for such a time again. For the majority of the French voting public, Louis Napoleon appeared to be the strong leader they needed to restore order, even if it meant sacrificing some liberal ideas. Louis Napoleon won the election in a landslide.

First a Republic, Then an Empire

Louis Napoleon began his four-year term as president in 1849, facing a very conservative National Assembly. He was willing to work with the Assembly, though, because he would need concessions from it—namely a constitutional change allowing him to run for a second term in a few years. As a show of good faith, Louis Napoleon signed two laws, one that allowed the Catholic Church to control education and another that stripped some of the poorest voters of their rights.

To his chagrin, the Assembly didn't scratch his back as he had scratched theirs, so Louis Napoleon spent 1851 conspiring and planning against the Assembly. In December of 1851, Louis Napoleon dismissed the Assembly and staged a coup. Despite some minor uprisings, Louis Napoleon, with the help of the army, maintained control easily. He returned universal male suffrage to the French voters and held a plebiscite to give the voters a chance to legitimize his actions. They did just that by electing him to a 10-year term as president. Still not satisfied, the following year Louis Napoleon held another plebiscite and the French agreed to make him their emperor.

Napoleon's government, though authoritarian, proved successful for France. His public works projects and improvements boosted the French economy and his railroads helped France catch up with the rest of the industrialized world. He eventually gave back some power to the Assembly. He allowed members of the Assembly to be elected every six years by universal male suffrage. To keep control, Napoleon and his ministers often encouraged strategic members of French society to run for Assembly seats.

Toward the end of his rule, Napoleon allowed more and more liberal reforms. He granted labor the right to form unions and the right to strike, and he granted a new constitution. His foreign policy, though, proved less beneficial to France than his domestic policies.

Cleaning Up the Mess

Industrialization had hit Paris hard. The overcrowding put such pressure on the city that it was a disaster when Louis Napoleon took over. He made major improvements to the city (see Chapter 16), doing more than just improving the aesthetics. His reclamation project, headed by Georges Haussmann, and his public works projects served as a major shot in the arm for the unemployed. He also improved security by rebuilding the streets so that revolting Parisians couldn't barricade them; the streets were so wide that it was practically impossible for people to construct barricades from one side to the other. In a controversial move that paid off, Napoleon and Haussmann tore down much of the medieval part of Paris that lay behind walls, and in their place built offices, stores, theaters, and other buildings that greatly enhanced city life. City planners from elsewhere in Europe frequently visited Paris for inspiration.

As a Matter of Fact

While Georges Haussmann is remembered as the mastermind of the restructuring and rebuilding of Paris during the rule of Napoleon III, he hardly was celebrated during his day. The people of Paris greatly resented the destruction of the old, historic city even though much of Paris was dirty, run-down, and poverty-stricken. Many Parisians also objected to the extremely high cost of the project. Even Napoleon III eventually turned on the man he had hired; Napoleon fired Haussmann, largely as a result of outcries of negative public opinion. The very things Haussmann fell under fire for during his lifetime—wide streets filled with trees, shops and cultural centers—are the things modern Parisians and visitors love most about the city.

Nation Building: Italy and Germany

The liberal revolutions of 1848 failed in the short term, but their attempts to unite Germany and parts of Italy were not completely in vain. As industrial nations like

Britain and France developed strong economies, it became obvious to a few visionaries that small, independent states would soon fall behind in terms of financial and political importance in Europe. Based on the idea that a larger, stronger state would have more influence in Europe, revolutionaries helped unite regions into nations. In the cases of Germany and Italy, nationalism proved to be the glue that bound the smaller states together. Channeling the nationalism toward a common goal was the trick.

Unification of Italy

Italy had never been united. Over the centuries, the region had been controlled by the French, the Austrians, the Spanish, the papacy, and various Italians. The north was industrialized and the south highly agricultural, but many Italians wanted a unified Italy despite the traditional cultural and regional differences. Over the years, three legitimate plans arose for the unification of Italy into a single nation. Some people wanted a democratic state with universal suffrage. Some wanted a union of states under the authority of the papacy. Still others wanted an Italian kingdom headed by Piedmont-Sardinia, itself a kingdom.

Piedmont-Sardinia had a liberal constitution, so many Italians thought of it and its king, Victor Emmanuel II (1820–1878), as liberal. Sardinia's leading statesman, Count Camillo di Cavour (1810–1861), wanted a unified Italy under Sardinian leadership, but only made up of the northern states. To do so, the Austrians had to be expelled from Lombardy and Venetia, which he knew couldn't be done without help.

Cavour secretly formed an alliance with Louis Napoleon of France, convincing him to render aid in the event Sardinia fell under attack. Then, in 1859, Cavour picked a fight with Austria. Just like he planned, France came to his aid. After Austria was defeated, though, Napoleon III pulled out of the alliance. As a result, Sardinia received only Lombardy. Disgusted, Cavour resigned.

However, the Austrian troops' "invasion" of "Italy" enraged nationalists all over Italy, so Cavour returned to work. He worked a deal with Napoleon to smooth over any objections the French had about a new Italian state, and the central Italian states joined Sardinia. Half of Italy was united, but half remained independent.

Would You Believe?

Napoleon pulled out of the Sardinian alliance because French Catholics were upset that Napoleon supported an enemy of the pope.

Cavour next had to control a zealous, patriotic radical named Giuseppe Garibaldi (1807–1887), whose thousand-man army of "Red Shirts" threatened Cavour's plan for unification. Garibaldi led an interesting, mercenary-style life prior to his activity in the Italian unification process. He once traveled to South America where he met Anita, his lover who would become both his wife and comrade-in-arms, and fought in a rebellion there. Garibaldi even led the Uruguayan navy against Argentina. Several years later, in 1849, Garibaldi defended Rome against Napoleon III.

Continental Quotes

"I offer neither pay, nor quarters, nor food; I offer only hunger, thirst, forced marches, battles and death. Let him who loves his country with his heart, and not merely with his lips, follow me."

—Giuseppe Garibaldi

In 1860, Garibaldi invaded Sicily and easily defeated the much larger armies there, then set his sights on Naples and Rome. Cavour went in behind Garibaldi, used Sardinian troops to occupy the conquered or "liberated" states, then organized elections. (He also stopped Garibaldi from attacking the pope so as not to upset Catholic France any further.) As Garibaldi moved through Italy, the locals rallied behind him and people all over Italy fell in love with him and welcomed him as liberator. After he conquered Sicily, Garibaldi earned renown not only in Italy but across Europe.

Though Garibaldi disliked Cavour, he believed Victor Emmanuel was the right person to finish the unification process and to be King of Italy. After liberating Italy, Garibaldi simply resigned and refused to take any reward or recognition for his accomplishments. When the dust settled, the people of southern Italy voted to join Victor Emmanuel and Sardinia as a unified kingdom of Italy in 1860. Venice and Rome later joined Italy, too. The Italian states were now united, but the Italians still had issues. The Sardinian administrators ruled strictly and undid many of the reforms Garibaldi instituted, and, in the beginning at least, very few Italians enjoyed suffrage.

Would You Believe?

Cavour never got to see Venice and Rome united with Italy. He died just months after the 1860 unification.

Unification of Germany

Just as Cavour played the lead role in the unification of Italy, the master politician Otto von Bismarck (1815–1898) almost single-handedly created the unified German state. From his earliest days in politics, Bismarck's goal was the strengthening of Prussia at the expense of Austria. Tensions existed between Austria and Prussia long before Bismarck's time, however.

One source of tension was the Zollverein, a German customs union designed to help boost the economies of the states in the German confederation. The German states enjoyed free trade within the Zollverein and paid customs duties on imports. The catch was that Austria was not included in the Zollverein, so they missed out on the economic benefits. After 1848, Austria tried to seduce the southern German states to leave the Zollverein, but the states stayed put.

Two years after the beginning of the unification process in Italy, William I (1797–1888), eventually *Kaiser* Wilhelm I, replaced Frederick William IV in Prussia. His plan was to double the size of the Prussian army so as to be ready in case of war. The Prussian parliament rejected William's demands for higher taxes to fund his new army and insisted that the army be responsible to the people, not the king. The parliament also intended to prove that the supreme power lay with parliament and not with the king. Determined to have his way, William chose Otto von Bismarck to get the job done for him any way he could. He appointed Bismarck prime minister, a position responsible only to the king and not to the parliament.

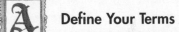

Define Your Terms

Kaiser is a German word for emperor derived from the Roman Caesar; it is the equivalent of czar in Slavic. William I was the first of three German rulers to use the title.

Bismarck set out to make Prussia one of Europe's great powers. He considered several strategies and decided to channel the German people's intense nationalism. The fiery Bismarck moved ahead with William's plans without the consent of parliament, declaring that only through "blood and iron" would things get accomplished, not through "speeches and resolutions." Bismarck ordered that taxes be collected regardless of parliament's disapproval. Bismarck also overhauled the military. As Bismarck focused German ire on foreign enemies, Germans eventually rallied to support his plans; initially Bismarck had the support only of the Prussians.

In 1864, Denmark tried to take Schleswig-Holstein again, as it had in 1848, and Prussia joined Austria in the relatively easy defeat of Denmark. Bismarck saw an opportunity to get Austria out of German affairs for good. He goaded Austria into the Austro-Prussian War and then defeated it. Rather than crushing Austria, he let them off easily; in return, Austria agreed to stay out of German politics forever.

After the war, the mostly Protestant northern German states formed the North German Confederation, led of course by Prussia, while the southern states formed an alliance with Prussia. Bismarck then drew up the constitution for the new Confederation. Each state kept its own government but recognized William as king and Bismarck as chancellor. The king and the chancellor handled virtually all affairs of the

Continental Quotes

Always a strategist, Otto von Bismarck once said, "One must always have two irons in the fire."

Confederation while the two houses of the legislature made the laws. The lower house consisted of members elected by universal male suffrage—a huge step for liberals in Germany, which helped bring liberals who often criticized Bismarck's authoritarian ways on board. Germany now found itself in a similar situation as the Italians only a few years before: half united and half to go.

Bismarck finally persuaded several of the southern German states to participate in the customs parliament that had been created from the old Zollverein. However, the southern states' interest in unification stopped there, at least partly because of the strong religious differences between north and south. Bismarck decided to stir up nationalist zeal again to bring the southern states on board, too.

Would You Believe?

Bismarck said the release of the Ems Dispatch was like waving a red cape in front of a bull. The infamous note was released to the public in the German city of Ems, hence the name of the dispatch.

He picked a fight with France in 1870 and began the Franco-Prussian War. To get France mad enough to fight, Bismarck used the notorious Ems Dispatch. William met with a French ambassador who requested that no Hohenzollern ever accept the Spanish throne, which would effectively push France into a corner. The conversation was polite, but William refused. Bismarck reworded the account of the meeting and gave it to the press. Bismarck's account made the French feel insulted by Germany and the Germans feel insulted by the French. Less than a week later, France declared war.

The southern German states quickly rallied behind fellow Germans and Bismarck's plan drew ever nearer to completion. Of course, he first had to win a war, but the German troops handled the French with little trouble and even captured Napoleon III at the Battle of Sedan. In Paris, a Third Republic was created, but it capitulated after several months of being starved by Germany. In victory, Germany hit France with tough sanctions including huge reparations and the loss of Alsace-Lorraine. To add insult to injury, William became German Emperor and was crowned in the Hall of Mirrors in Versailles.

Would You Believe?

Napoleon III, with no empire to go home to, fled to England, where he lived out his last few years in exile.

The victory over the French created a huge swell of nationalism in Germany that arguably carried over into the early twentieth century. In less than a generation, Bismarck had taken an obstinate and divided Germany from worst to first among the powers of Europe. His transformation of Germany made Germany a force to be reckoned with for the next 75 years.

Reforming Russia

The reforms of Peter the Great (see Chapter 10) helped Russia progress some. However, the resistance of the Russian nobles and subsequent czars to succumb to westernization went a long way toward preventing further progress. Furthermore, the geography of Russia, so far removed from the rest of Europe, kept Russia isolated and insulated from much of Western culture. Developments in western Europe, both political and technological, took a long time to appear in Russia, and Russian leaders, unlike Peter the Great, did not strive to bring new ideas into Russia. As a result, Russia once again lagged behind western European nations.

Nineteenth-century Russia resembled a Europe from centuries gone by far more than it resembled its contemporary neighbors. Even by 1850 industrialization had yet to truly make its way into Russia, which still depended on an inefficient if not obsolete agrarian economy. Russia employed a system of serfdom long after the rest of Europe had moved beyond feudalism. Lords bought and sold serfs as they had for hundreds of years. Most farmers still used their serfs in the open-field system, also left over from the Middle Ages.

Russia hadn't caught up with the rest of Europe politically, either. There were no revolutions of 1848 in Russia. Very few liberals called Russia home, and the wave of liberalism and nationalism dissipated before it made it that far east. Russia was still an empire that incorporated many nationalities and ethnicities. Therefore, Russia's main concern was not changing the government but holding together the many peoples under the Russian umbrella.

Russia got its wake-up call in the 1850s when it fought the Crimean War. Until then, France had the responsibility of protecting Catholic holy sites in the Ottoman Empire, and Russia was in charge of the Eastern Orthodox holy sites. In the early 1850s, a dispute arose between the Ottomans, the French, and the Russians. Russia, led by Czar Nicholas I (1796–1855), occupied a few small Ottoman principalities, which Nicholas didn't think anybody but the Ottomans would mind, since Russia had helped some nations squash their revolutions in 1848.

Nicholas was wrong. He found himself fighting the French *and* the British, who jumped at the chance to prevent this strong power from creeping in from the east, along with the Ottomans. When Austria threatened to join the fight, Russia withdrew from the area along the Danube River. Britain and France continued warring against Russia and finally forced a treaty in 1856 with Nicholas's successor, Alexander II (1818–1881).

The military defeat, which included the loss of the entire Russian fleet on the Black Sea, made Alexander and his ministers realize that Russia had to change or be totally left behind.

The So-Called Great Reforms

The single greatest challenge facing Russia at the beginning of Alexander's reign was to revamp the backward system of serfdom. What would they do with the serfs if they were freed? Alexander decided to emancipate the serfs and give them land—for a price, of course. In 1861, he signed the law that ended serfdom throughout Russia. The former serfs were given land, but they had to pay hefty prices and the land was often of poor quality.

Alexander recognized the dilemma, so he made each village collectively responsible for the sum of the payments of the village families. His hope was to prevent a growing class of peasants who could not afford land. He also hoped to create a sense of unity among the peasants. Actually, by making the peasants financially responsible to the villages, Alexander effectively restricted the peasants from movement.

Alexander also introduced a new system of local government to increase the Russian people's participation in government. The *zemstvo*, made up of representatives from towns, noble landowners, and peasant villagers, was an assembly meant to deal with local issues. However, they turned out to be more bureaucratic than anticipated and never led to more liberal reform as liberals and peasants had hoped. Other reforms instituted by Alexander include a revamping of the judicial system with a civil and penal code similar to the French Code Napoleon. Alexander also reformed the army, the navy, and the police force. These reforms were much more successful than the ones designed to help the peasants.

Would You Believe?

Alexander II survived several assassination attempts, including an assassin wielding a handgun, an explosion on the tracks near his train, and a bomb beneath his dining room.

Throughout his reign, Alexander remained relatively liberal. There had even been talk between Alexander and one of his chief ministers about the possibility of creating some form of parliamentary body. However, after several assassination attempts, Alexander's enemies finally caught up with the emperor. Russia had seriously suppressed various nationalist movements throughout the empire, and Polish nationalists in particular were mad. A group of Poles threw hand-made grenades or bombs at Alexander as he drove through St. Petersburg.

Upon Alexander's death, Alexander III (1845–1894) took over and brought the reforms to an end. Alexander III had three main goals for Russia. He wanted to increase Russian nationalism, which he attempted by outlawing languages other than Russian and establishing Russian schools in the non-Russian areas of the empire. He wanted to strengthen the Eastern Orthodox Church, so he eliminated as many remnants of Polish, German, and other cultures as he could. Finally, he wanted to secure and increase the autocratic power of his position, which he did through a number of repressive actions and the undoing of reforms that Alexander II, his father, had started.

Catching Up with the Rest of Europe

Both Alexander II and Alexander III realized that Russia needed to modernize. Modernization required industrialization. In the early 1860s, the gigantic Russia had less than 2,000 miles of railway. Over the next 20 years, the government subsidized the construction of railroads, increasing them tenfold. This allowed for faster transportation of goods within Russia and allowed Russia to export vast amounts of valuable grain. Factories and entire industrial towns popped up along the railways, and with them a new group of workers developed. Russia was on its way to becoming an industrialized nation. However, even late in the nineteenth century, the Russian economy still struggled. Alexander III appointed Sergei Witte (1849–1915) to do something about the sluggish economy.

During his tenure with the Russian government, Sergei Witte served as finance minister, transportation minister, and director of railways. With his background in railway transportation, Witte knew that the strides Russia had made in developing the railroads were important but still insufficient. Under his leadership, Russia doubled its mileage of track yet again. Witte knew Russia needed more industrialization, so he encouraged foreign investors to come to Russia to build factories and manufacturing centers. By doing this, Russia did not have to spend its own money to build factories. Foreign investors footed the bill and Russians went to work producing cheap goods for Russian consumers.

Would You Believe?

Witte's one failure was in the administration of the peasant economy. Under his administration, the condition of the rural peasants worsened and peasant unrest ensued.

The plan worked brilliantly. Witte encouraged protective tariffs to bolster the Russian economy and protect Russian goods. He also put Russia on the gold standard, an economic system in which the value of a nation's currency is based on a fixed amount of gold. When several nations use the gold standard, exchange rates are essentially fixed. This enabled Russia to more actively and efficiently participate in international trade. By the turn of the twentieth century, the once-backward nation of Russia had become one of the world's leading steel-producing nations and an industrial force in Europe. Sergei Witte cannot receive enough credit for this miraculous transformation.

The Least You Need to Know

♦ Liberal revolutions in Prussia, France, Italy, Poland, and Austrian holdings were short-lived because revolutionary factions couldn't agree on their next steps.

♦ Louis Napoleon was elected president in France after the 1848 revolution. His appeal to the masses eventually resulted in the French people's endorsement of him as Emperor Napoleon III.

♦ Cavour used nationalism, combined with clever politics, to unify Italy.

♦ Bismarck, like Cavour, used nationalism and a policy of "blood and iron" to unify German states under Prussian leadership.

♦ Alexander II, taking the defeat in the Crimean War as a hint, instituted liberal reforms in Russia including freeing the serfs and codifying the legal system. By building railroads and encouraging Western investment, Russia managed to become an industrial power by 1900.

Chapter 19

What a Tangled Web

In This Chapter

- ◆ A truly global economy
- ◆ Imperialism is back
- ◆ Civilizing the savages
- ◆ You can have too many friends
- ◆ The arms race
- ◆ Trouble brews in the Balkans

In 1750, Europe was a collection of agricultural states that differed very little from other places around the world. As industrialism, liberalism, and nationalism spread over the next hundred years, though, Europe began to distance itself from the rest of the world, with only the United States running a close second. As the economy became more diverse, fewer Europeans depended solely on agriculture, which meant fewer people suffered from poor harvests or crop failures. Additionally, the advent of railways allowed quick distribution of goods to areas hit by bad harvests. Europe's economy picked up steam in the second half of the nineteenth century as all of Europe embraced railroads and factories and the general living conditions improved. Europe began to look elsewhere for new markets for its manufactured goods and new sources of raw materials. As it did, it spread European values, ideas, and technology to the rest of the world.

A Global Market

During the nineteenth century, Europe turned the entire world into its marketplace. Europe profited from goods purchased or acquired in other parts of the world and from the European-made goods sold in other parts of the world. Such worldwide trade once seemed unimaginable to Europeans, but technology had conquered previously insurmountable distances. Faster was always better, and railroads certainly facilitated fast movement not only of goods but also people. The construction of railroads on other continents also allowed European goods to be transported to markets far away from port cities. In the period of colonial imperialism, railroads were often built before colonists even moved in.

The steam engine likewise allowed for faster and more efficient transportation of goods around the world. As engineers developed more streamlined ships and more fuel-efficient steam engines, the cost of shipping dropped tremendously. The drop in shipping prices made the transportation of inexpensive goods feasible for the first time. Passengers increased on the steamers, too. Toward the end of the nineteenth century, refrigerated railcars and ships revolutionized the global economy the way steam had done generations before. Refrigerated ships carried huge cargos of meat and other perishable goods to markets all over the world. Refrigerated ships also carried tons of meat from foreign markets back to Europe.

> **Would You Believe?**
>
> The completion of the Suez Canal in 1869 and then the Panama Canal in 1914 also contributed to the efficiency of global shipping.

There were challenges in the global marketplace, though. European nations constantly faced protective tariffs in competing markets. When a traditional market raised such a tariff, European businessmen were forced to look elsewhere to peddle their wares. At first glance, such tariffs seem detrimental to the economy of the European nations who faced them; in reality, new markets were often discovered that proved even more lucrative. For example, when the United States put tariffs on foreign textiles to protect its own textile industry, Europe found new markets in places like India.

The Growing Gap

The more industrialized Europe grew, the more profitable it became. Europe wasn't alone, though. For every part of the world that was industrializing, there existed a direct relationship between industrialization and the overall strength of the economy. The average income of people in the industrialized world skyrocketed between 1750 and 1900, whereas incomes in underdeveloped and nonindustrialized parts of the world barely changed. Despite initial sanitation problems and related issues, citizens of the industrialized world also enjoyed longer life expectancies and better overall health and well-being than the regions not yet industrialized.

The disparity between rich and poor nations has been examined and explained from the perspective of two main schools of thought. One school argues that the industrialized nations used innovation and ingenuity to tackle the problems of illiteracy, disease, and the like. The other school of thought maintains that the industrialized nations used their head-start to steal resources and wealth that the undeveloped nations could have used to industrialize, modernize, and improve the lives of their own citizens. There is perhaps some truth in both assertions.

Foreign Investment and Markets

The buying and selling of goods in foreign markets was just part of the secret to Europe's financial success. European governments and private investors made large sums of money in European and non-European investments alike. Investors put money into the development of railroads and factories in lands that were just being industrialized. As in most cases in Europe, new railroads abroad had virtually no competition and a monopoly was practically guaranteed for at least several years.

Along the same lines, European investors financed other things necessary for development and settlement of unindustrialized lands. The desire to invest in foreign markets greatly benefited banking centers in Europe, too, who gladly loaned huge sums of money to Europeans for capital investments. Britain invested more heavily than any other European nation of its day and a large percentage of British investments went to the Americas.

Would You Believe?

During the late nineteenth century, nearly a third of all capital for U.S. railroad construction came from European investors.

Opening the East

Europeans had managed to trade with the isolated Asians who lay beyond Russia even as far back as the Middle Ages. As European society seemed to advance, though, China, in particular, seemed to retreat into a deepening isolation. A superiority complex combined with a genuine desire to never be like the strangers from Europe influenced the Chinese to carefully guard their empire.

In the seventeenth and early eighteenth centuries, the few European traders allowed into China were restricted to the city of Canton. While in town, the foreigners were made to follow strict laws, trade only with certain merchants, and refrain from the worst of all possible activities: selling opium. Opium is a drug derived from certain poppy flowers that has intoxicating and painkilling side effects. Codeine and morphine are derived from opium.

The British grew opium in India, which it owned through imperialism, and then smuggled the opium into China. The opium trade with China grew so lucrative that opium smugglers begged British officials to find a way to gain access to other Chinese cities. When the Chinese government decided in 1839 to clamp down on opium smuggling in Canton, the Brits refused to sign a promise not to smuggle opium. One British ship defied the British refusal to sign; the captain signed and made his way into Canton. The Chinese attempted to protect another British ship that did the same, and shots were fired. Thus began the Opium Wars.

The British had their way with the Chinese; British gunboats attacked coastal cities and occupied wherever they pleased. They even seized the Chinese tax barges full of valuable goods. The British firearms drew little resistance. The British strangled the Chinese into submission in 1842 and forced the Treaty of Nanking. Britain won the island of Hong Kong along with a sizable payment of cash. The British also won the right to trade in more Chinese cities. Several years later, the two countries fought the Second Opium War with practically the same result. Britain had managed to bully its way into the Chinese market against China's wishes. Europe had opened up the East—by force.

Would You Believe?

The Japanese were even more isolationist than the Chinese until 1853, when American gunboats led by Commodore Perry threatened Japan with war if Japanese ports were not opened for trade.

Europeans Scatter Throughout the World

Because of the overall rise in Europe's standard of living and the new scientific and medical knowledge during the nineteenth century, Europe's population doubled between 1800 and 1900. The fact that over 400 million people lived in Europe at the beginning of the twentieth century is staggering when you consider that tens of millions of Europeans *emigrated* elsewhere during the nineteenth century. These migrants moved mostly to areas where other white *immigrants* lived, places like the United States, Australia, and parts of South America. Each European nation's experience with immigration was different. People did not leave all the nations in Europe at the same time or for the same reasons. Many British left after industrialization fully saturated the British Isles, while nations like Germany began to retain population after industrialization.

Define Your Terms

To **immigrate** means to enter a country to settle.

To **emigrate** means to leave a country for settlement elsewhere.

The overwhelming majority of those who migrated from European nations were rural farmers. They were neither the wealthy landowners nor the poorest of the poor; they were just farmers with poor land. Many farmers with little or no land went to the United States and Australia, where governments were giving away large tracts of land just for settling there. Another large group of immigrants were artisans who were squeezed out of business by the cheaper goods of industrialization. Although some migrated from Europe to escape legal or financial troubles and others left because industrialization had put them out of work, most simply wanted to make a better living. Some immigrants fled their countries to escape religious persecution, as was the case for so many Jews in the late 1800s. Most migrants were relatively young, often under the age of 35.

There were several benefits of the European migrations for the rest of the world. First, the immigrants took with them pieces of their native land: traditions, dress, language, cuisine, religion, and more. The influence of so many cultures undoubtedly contributed to the development of places like Australia, Canada, and the United States. Second, just as other parts of the world were industrializing and needing workers, here were plenty of Europeans ready and willing to work. Third, frontiers like the American west needed settlers and hardworking families to develop the virgin territory. Again, here were Europeans anxious to get land and opportunity. Fourth, the mass exodus from Europe relieved population pressures there. Had all the Europeans stayed home in the nineteenth century, the quality of life for many would have remained dismal their entire lives.

The White Man's Burden

While millions of Europeans landed on foreign shores with knapsacks on their backs, others were running ashore with gun in hand. The Europeans with guns weren't fighting wars, though. They were civilizing the "uncivilized." During the nineteenth century, the leading nations of Europe developed an insatiable appetite for colonizing and expanding empires, much the way the expansionist French, English, and Spanish had done in the 1500s. The European nations were of course looking for new markets and new raw materials for manufacturing. The European powers were locked in a fierce competition and they needed more land and more wealth. Places like Africa had just what the Europeans needed.

The only problem with colonizing Africa was that Africa was inhabited by millions of native Africans. To justify taking land and resources away from other peoples, not just in Africa but in India and other places, Europeans developed a sense of "responsibility." They believed that Europe was responsible for taking civilization to the barbarians in the primitive and uncivilized parts of the world. The "White Man's Burden," or the "burden of civilized Europeans to civilize the uncivilized," made it easier for nineteenth-century Europeans to practice an imperialism that was in some ways similar to and in some ways different from the old imperialism. In no place was this imperialism demonstrated more than in Africa. What resulted was a rush to snatch up as much land as possible before the other countries did. The late 1800s proved to be a bad time to live in the Third World.

Would You Believe? ___

It would be nearly impossible to calculate accurately the number of non-Europeans conquered during old imperialism. It is estimated under the system of new imperialism, though, that the Europeans managed to conquer or subjugate about half the world's non-European population.

New vs. Old Imperialism

Historians have adopted the terminology "old imperialism" and "new imperialism" to distinguish between the two distinct periods of imperialism and expansion in European history. The old imperialism of the fifteenth and sixteenth centuries featured primarily Portugal, Spain, England, and France exploring uncharted lands in search of gold and other treasures (see Chapter 6). These nations also hoped to find new lands full of souls that could be added to their kingdoms. There was indeed a sense of competition among the European powers that drove them to explore and colonize. Under the system of old imperialism, natives suffered from all sorts of things brought on by Europeans including slavery, war, and disease. In extreme cases, entire civilizations died off from war, disease, or both.

The new imperialism occurred in the late nineteenth century and shares some similarities with old imperialism. The new imperialists also wanted natural resources not available in their homelands, including gold, diamonds, tea, and more. Like the old imperialism, indigenous peoples suffered heavy population losses. With the invention of the rapid-fire guns toward the end of the 1800s, the indigenous peoples of Africa had no chance at all. There were several documented incidents of tens of thousands of natives being executed or killed in combat by European imperialists. Also like the old imperialism, new imperialism grew partly out of a sense of competition among major European powers including Britain, France, Germany, and Italy.

But new imperialism was unique, too. In the nineteenth century, imperialism was motivated at least partly by the enormous population pressure in Europe and the desire of smaller nations like Britain to have a place for the population to overflow. Also, new imperialism involved the search not only for new sources of raw materials but also for new markets for manufactured goods. In some ways, industrialization encouraged imperialism. There were plenty of intangible reasons for imperialism, too.

Justification for Imperialism

Rudyard Kipling (1865–1936), born in India and educated in England, earned a great deal of popularity for writing stories like the children's favorite *The Jungle Book*. However, Kipling also earned a measure of notoriety for his poem *White Man's Burden*. Written in 1899 to encourage the United States to invest in the development and the civilization of the Philippines, the poem reflects much of the sentiment of Europeans toward imperialism. The following lines epitomize the odd sense of duty Europeans claimed:

> *Take up the White Man's burden—*
> *The savage wars of peace—*
> *Fill full the mouth of Famine*
> *And bid the sickness cease;*

Europeans saw Africans, native Australians, Pacific Islanders, and others as primitive savages plagued by war, poverty, disease, and ignorance. The sense of duty to "civilize" the nonwhite peoples of the unindustrialized lands ranged from genuine religious and humanitarian concerns at one end of the spectrum to snobbery and arrogance at the other. Some Europeans wanted to spread Christianity while others

Continental Quotes

"Remember that you are an Englishman, and have consequently won first prize in the lottery of life."

—Cecil Rhodes, demonstrating the typical European sense of superiority during the nineteenth century.

Would You Believe?

Darwin's theories appalled the religious community because his theory of evolution appeared to contradict the Biblical account of creation.

wanted to prove that the nonwhite peoples were inferior beings. Many believed that administration of the nonwhite people by European governments would keep the savages safe from tribal warfare.

Many Europeans justified the expansion into Africa and other unindustrialized areas by calling the moves "social Darwinism." Charles Darwin (1809–1882) built upon an already-existing theory called evolution. In his shocking books *On the Origin of the Species* (1859) and *The Descent of Man* (1871), he outlined his take on evolution and natural selection. He maintained that species that are weaker tend to die out and species with superior traits tend to survive, hence the idea of "survival of the fittest." Contemporary Europeans applied this idea to imperialism. They pointed out that the stronger species, Europeans, would eventually overrun or stamp out the inferior species, the nonwhites, simply by laws of nature. These Europeans saw imperialism as part of the natural order of things.

India under British rule serves as a perfect example of such ideology. The British followed the Portuguese into India in the 1600s, but had more staying power. The powerful British East India Company succeeded in subjugating India in its entirety by the mid-1800s. Indians tried to get rid of the oppressive British for centuries, having one last go at it in 1857 and 1858. The British put down the Great Rebellion and continued to rule India. A tiny detachment of Brits administered the government there. They were elitists who considered the Indians inferior just as other Europeans thought of Africans. The British did bring some improvements to India, including some education and massive miles of railways. However, except for a few Indians who worked as government officials, the majority of the Indian population saw no change in their quality of life.

The Land Grab in Africa

Colonization of Africa occurred relatively late in the nineteenth century for the most part. The French had settlers in Algeria earlier in the century, as did the British and Dutch in South Africa. The Dutch were in South Africa first, but the British took it from them. After 1850, the descendants of the Dutch in South Africa, called Boers or

Afrikaners, declared their independence from Britain. Portugal had a few holdings along the African coast.

Aside from those European-dominated areas, Africa remained free from European rule until about 1880. After 1880, the European powers fell into a feeding frenzy and tried to gobble up as much African land as they could. Twenty years later, the whole continent "belonged" to Europe. The British grabbed South Africa, Rhodesia, Egypt, Sudan, Uganda, Nigeria, the Gold Coast, and some smaller states. Included in the British takeover was the violent Boer War against the Boers. The French ended up with Madagascar, French West Africa, the Ivory Coast, Morocco, Algeria, and French Equatorial Africa. The Italians managed to hang on to Libya and parts of Somalia, while the Germans clung to Cameroon, German East Africa, German Southwest Africa, and Togo. Belgium got the Belgian Congo, which they ruled ruthlessly. Ethiopia and Liberia managed to maintain relative independence, although Italy would attempt to colonize Ethiopia in the twentieth century. As the land grab unfolded, nations picked sides, worked together, plotted against others, and basically created a diplomatic nightmare that eventually would lead to heated rivalries and showdowns.

Would You Believe?

It was during the scramble for African land that the dark side of new imperialism really showed. For example, during the Battle of Omdurman in 1898, as the British dominated Sudan with the machine gun, the British suffered about 50 deaths and 500 wounded while the Sudanese lost 10,000 men, with 15,000 wounded and 5,000 taken prisoner.

Entangling Alliances

The colonization of Africa unfortunately coincided with a period in European history when each power was doing everything it could to enhance its European status. The English and French tried to hang on as Germany and even Russia tried to climb to the top of the heap. As the nations competed for land, power, and status, they often quietly arranged strategic alliances with other nations to get a leg up on more immediate rivals.

What resulted was a system of ridiculous treaties and alliances, jealousy and envy, and hurt feelings and egos, along with genuine military hostilities. German Chancellor Otto von Bismarck (see Chapter 18) often receives much of the credit as well as much of the blame for what developed. On the one hand, Bismarck helped defuse the ticking time bomb of Africa. On the other hand, Bismarck initiated a system of tricky networks and alliances that would not end well.

Ground Rules for the Land Grab

Perhaps the two most important early events in the scramble for Africa were the British occupation of Egypt and the Belgian affairs in the Congo. In the Congo, Leopold II of Belgium (1835–1909) established his own private state by pretending to send a scientific team to explore the region. He actually had a company establish a colony that he later used to control the region.

Bismarck knew something had to be done to keep these shenanigans from happening again and to keep the European powers at peace while they gobbled up Africa. He called representatives from Germany, France, Britain, the United States, Austria-Hungary, Belgium, Italy, the Netherlands, Portugal, Russia, Spain, and Sweden to a conference in Berlin. Known as the *Kongkonferenz* in German, or the Congo Conference, the meeting often is remembered as the Berlin Conference. The delegates assembled in Berlin in 1884 and 1885 to get some things straight about how they were going to carve up Africa.

The conference concluded in 1885, having resolved a number of issues. First, under the General Act of the Berlin Conference, the delegates agreed to allow Belgium to keep its state in the Congo. This was a huge success for the tiny Belgium. Second, the delegates agreed that free trade in Africa was in everyone's best interest. Therefore, Africa was to be a free trade region and the Nile and Congo Rivers were declared free for shipping. As for the actual grabbing of land, the delegates agreed that a nation could claim land only if it possessed land. In other words, a nation's representative could not land on the coast and claim the land from the coast to the African interior. A nation had to have settlements or colonies on the land to have a legitimate claim. Furthermore, once a nation claimed a piece of land, it had to officially notify all the other nations present at the conference. Finally, and perhaps most importantly, the delegates agreed to prohibit the international slave trade.

Would You Believe?

The exploration of the *terra incognita*, or the last unknown and unmapped territory, of Africa's Congo River Basin in the 1870s by Sir Henry Morton Stanley led to Leopold's interest in the Congo.

Too Many Treaties, Allies, and Enemies

If Bismarck had not been bent on maintaining peace in Europe, things would have fallen apart on the continent much sooner. Bismarck created a powerful German state and was satisfied. Despite some land-grabbing in Africa, Germany had no desire to do as Napoleon had tried to do (see Chapter 15). Bismarck decided that the best policy for Germany, as well as for the rest of Europe, was for Germany to use its leverage to maintain peace on the continent.

Bismarck planned to do this in a few ways. First, Bismarck wanted to prevent France from getting any crazy ideas about revenge for the Franco-Prussian War (see Chapter 18) and the loss of Alsace-Lorraine. He also wanted France to have as few allies as possible. Second, Bismarck wanted to keep eastern Europe as stable as possible. Austria-Hungary and Russia had separate interests in the Balkans, especially with the Ottoman Empire fizzling out. Bismarck created the League of the Three Emperors in 1873 to accomplish both goals.

Things changed by 1879, and Austria and Russia were again at odds over the Balkans. At a conference in Berlin, Bismarck worked with Austria-Hungary to make sure they got the upper hand in the Balkan region. This infuriated the Russians. Just to be safe, Bismarck forged a military alliance with Austria against Russia. A few years later, Italy joined that alliance because of tensions with France; this alliance became known as the Triple Alliance. In 1881, Bismarck brought both Austria and Russia to their senses and all three signed a treaty forming the Alliance of the Three Emperors, kept secret from Europe. In 1887, Russia dropped out of the Alliance over issues in the Balkans. To keep his alliance with Russia, Bismarck worked a deal between Russia and Germany only.

For 20 years, Bismarck worked round the clock to keep peace in Europe through treaty after treaty. However, things took a bad turn in 1890. Kaiser Wilhelm II, also known as William II (1859–1941), dismissed Bismarck as chancellor; he hated Bismarck's friendly relationship with the Russians and favored an expansionist foreign policy.

Bismarck left a fascinating legacy. Despite his *Kulturkampf* attacks on the Church and other political opposition and his "blood and iron" style of getting things done, he deserves credit for unifying Germany for the first time and for maintaining a tenuous European peace after German unification.

After Bismarck's forced resignation, Wilhelm II refused to renew the alliance with Russia in 1890. France saw the chance to finally get an ally, so the French courted Russia. The two nations signed a treaty to remain allied as long as the Triple Alliance of Germany, Austria, and Italy remained intact. At this point, Europe stood

Define Your Terms

Kulturkampf means literally "culture fight"; this was Bismarck's attempt to reduce Catholic influence on German politics in the early 1870s. He eventually joined Catholics in a fight against socialism.

divided into two sides. All eyes were on Britain, which remained uncommitted. No one really liked Britain at this point; the other nations resented the ever-expanding British Empire that sprawled across the globe. At the same time, nobody wanted Britain to be on the opposite side.

Too Much Tension

Just after 1900, Britain smoothed over relations with the United States and signed a formal treaty with the Japanese. In 1904, Britain sided with France and created the Anglo-French Entente. France joined with Britain on the condition of mutual support. France was to support Britain in Egypt and Britain was to support France in Morocco. The agreement between the two nations was known as the Entente Cordiale, which means "friendly agreement." The Entente Cordiale eventually led to the Triple Entente between Britain, France, and Russia.

Would You Believe?

When Britain and France teamed up, Germany demanded the dismissal of Théophile Delcassé, the brilliant French diplomat who negotiated several treaties between several European nations in efforts to keep peace, and who negotiated the Entente Cordiale. Germany really was testing French loyalties.

Germany tried to strain the alliance by making demands of France and holding an international conference to deal with the Morocco issue; Germany had no real plan, though, other than to weaken the Entente. The plan backfired and Germany was left mad, embarrassed, and with no real ally aside from Austria-Hungary because its former alliance, like so many of this era, dissolved. Britain, France, and Russia started to see the true colors of the new post-Bismarck Germany. They all feared what might happen if Germany grew too powerful. Germany at the same time began to feel paranoid and suspected that the other nations were ganging up on it. Things really got tense after Russia signed the Anglo-Russo Agreement in 1907. It seemed that Germany was isolated geographically in the center of a hostile Europe.

Keeping Up with the Joneses

Germany wasn't the only European nation feeling paranoid at the turn of the twentieth century. With the recent history of secret treaties and shifting alliances, no one really felt safe. Additionally, in the age of imperialism and far-flung imperial holdings, the glue that seemed to hold everything together for imperial powers was the navy.

A powerful navy allowed a nation to dominate the seas and thus maintain the security of its colonies.

At the time of rising tensions between Germany and the Anglo-French Alliance, the British had the dominant navy and a colonial empire that stretched around the world. A famous saying noted that the sun never set on the British Empire. Germany decided that it would need to expand its navy if it were to keep pace with Britain militarily. Under the leadership of Grand Admiral Alfred von Tirpitz (1849–1930), Germany set out to create a new and improved navy. Tirpitz expressed his desire to compete with the British navy when he said that Germany "must have a fleet equal in strength" to Britain's. His dream for the High Sea Fleet was an awesome 60-ship fleet which would be updated constantly. Tirpitz wanted to create such a navy that no one, not even the British, would run the risk of challenging the High Sea Fleet.

Britain threw a wrench in the German plans in 1905, though, with the launching of the Dreadnought class of battleships. Britain had always maintained a naval policy called the "two power standard." This policy meant that Britain kept its navy as large as any two other powers combined. This gave Germany a lofty goal. With the Dreadnought battleships in 1905, named for the ship the *HMS Dreadnought*, Britain separated itself even further from the rest of the world. The Dreadnought class of ships was the biggest, fastest, most heavily armed class of ships the world had ever seen. Germany found itself in double trouble by 1905 because the funding for the German navy had fallen into jeopardy. The army was jealous of naval expenditures, Germany lacked the funds to keep up with Britain, and some members of the German government didn't like the direction Tirpitz was taking the nation. By 1914, Tirpitz and his plan for the High Sea Fleet was way behind schedule. Ironically, the naval arms race among the European powers did not result in war. However, the rising tensions definitely contributed to the brewing storm in Europe.

The Balkan Powder Keg

For decades the region of the Balkans ticked like a time bomb just waiting for the right time to explode. Historians often refer to the region as a powder keg that waited for a spark, a place that "produces more history than it can consume locally." Either way, the highly volatile region would soon be the epicenter of a major disaster in European history.

The fading Ottoman Empire owned much of the Balkan region at the turn of the twentieth century. Austria-Hungary administered part of the region, and Russia envied the lands along the Black Sea and the Dardanelles. Bismarck had managed to keep Austria-Hungary and Russia separated, but Bismarck wasn't around anymore.

The tensions between the two rivals may well have been enough by themselves to cause an outbreak of fighting without any further help. However, there were more factors that made the situation even more complex and volatile.

The specter of nationalism that had haunted European conservatives for nearly a century appeared in the Balkans and caused great distress among nations like Austria-Hungary. In Serbia in 1903, a coup d'etat dethroned King Alexander and his wife, both of whom were murdered in their bedroom and then thrown out a window. King Peter I (1844–1921), an ally of Russia, replaced him and immediately introduced a number of reforms in Serbia. Serbia had a deep sense of nationalism and Peter wanted to annex Bosnia, home of hundreds of thousands of Serbs. In 1908, after the Young Turks overthrew the Ottoman government, Austria-Hungary took Bosnia. Serbia looked to Russia for help but Russia, fearing war with Austria-Hungary, its long-time rival, was not in a position to go to bat for Serbia.

Montenegro turned up the heat in 1912 when it declared war on Turkey and started the First Balkan War. Soon after the outbreak of war, Albania declared its independence from Turkey. Serbia, Montenegro, and Greece pounced on Albania quickly. At the peace conference in December, Albania was taken from the three nations and given its independence. In return, Serbia, Montenegro, and Greece were given the land that Bulgaria took amidst all the confusion. Bulgaria was understandably upset and tried using the military to resist the treaty's conditions. In July of 1813, the Second Balkan War erupted. Serbia, Greece, and Montenegro defeated Bulgaria and forced the Treaty of Bucharest. The victors got the spoils and Bulgaria got very little. The treaty redrew lines that violated informal national and ethnic boundaries, creating a volatile, chaotic situation that would not last long as nationalism burned stronger than ever in the Balkans.

> **Would You Believe?**
>
> Bulgaria had no choice but to accept the terms of the treaty since it was completely surrounded by the nations that forced the treaty on the Bulgarians.

Nationalism in the British Isles

Britain underwent huge political changes in the late nineteenth century. In the 1860s, Parliament extended the right to vote to more males than ever before. Then, in 1884, the franchise was granted to practically every male in Britain. Class tension developed in the early years of the new century between the conservative, aristocratic House of Lords and the House of Commons. When the House of Commons tried to pass the People's Budget in the first decade of the century, the Lords vetoed the legislation.

In addition to funding the naval expansion, the People's Budget would fund insurance, pensions, and social programs that did not interest the aristocratic House of Lords. When the king threatened to create new peers, or effectively replace the members of the House of Lords, the House changed its mind and approved the budget.

Part of the support for the People's Budget came from the Irish, who wanted home rule. The British slowly moved toward giving Ireland its own government a few times during the late 1800s, but never went through with it. Religion stood as the huge obstacle in the home rule issue. Ireland was split between hard-core Catholics and fiery Protestants; the majority was Catholic. The Catholic majority desperately wanted home rule, or independence, while the Protestants, most notably those in Ulster, detested the idea, wanting to maintain the balance of power by remaining British subjects. The Ulsterites raised an army and swore to resist Irish home rule. Parliament passed a home rule bill in 1914, but the actions resulting from the bill were suspended. Something more pressing was unfolding on the continent.

As a Matter of Fact

One of the leaders in Ireland's push for independence, seen either as a patriot or as a criminal depending on one's perspective, was Michael Collins. Collins joined the Irish Republican Brotherhood and participated in the Easter Uprising of 1916. After 1916, Collins organized and spearheaded violent resistance to all forms of British authority in Ireland. His Irish Republican Army and British forces volleyed violence back and forth until 1921 when Collins helped negotiate a treaty between the two sides. The treaty granted dominion status to Ireland and the right for Ireland to govern itself within the British Empire. The treaty met with mixed emotions in Ireland and Collins was assassinated in 1922.

A Sordid Affair

France had its own issues to deal with at the end of the nineteenth century. In 1894, a Jewish military officer in the French army was accused of treason and found guilty. The case eventually set off a violent reaction throughout the nation and virtually split the country into two camps.

Investigators accused Alfred Dreyfus (1859–1935) of giving secrets to the Germans. Their evidence was a handwritten document said to be of Dreyfus's doing. Dreyfus received a life sentence on Devil's Island off the South American coast. In 1896, the army discovered that the real spy was a man named Ferdinand Esterhazy (1847–1923). For less than $500 per month, Esterhazy provided the Germans with information

Would You Believe?

The Dreyfus camp even appealed to famous novelist Emile Zola (1840–1902) for help. The novelist published a letter concerning the case that landed him in court where he was accused of libel. After his conviction, Zola fled to England. The French Supreme Court later exonerated Zola and he returned to France.

about artillery and the like. The army refused to reopen the case, though, because it didn't want to admit its mistake. The press in France eventually caught wind of the scandal and went crazy. After it was clear the scandal would not go away, the army tried Esterhazy with a court martial; to no one's surprise, Esterhazy was acquitted.

The nation split over the Dreyfus Affair. Anti-Semites, the Catholic Church, and the military demanded that the decision against Dreyfus stand; admitting a mistake would cause the military and Catholic leaders to lose face. Civil libertarians and Jews demanded that Dreyfus be freed. The government finally agreed to a retrial but once again convicted Dreyfus. However, Dreyfus received a pardon and was allowed to return to the army. Tensions remained so high in France over the Dreyfus Affair that France basically disallowed anyone from talking about the incident for years.

The Least You Need to Know

- The development of rail and steam engine transportation made the world a smaller place. European nations took advantage of overseas markets for both suppliers of raw materials and consumers of finished goods.

- During the nineteenth century, millions and millions of Europeans migrated from Europe to other parts of the world. Many were farmers looking to take advantage of frontier land in developing nations.

- The European nations looked overseas and found enticing land that belonged to the various indigenous peoples there. Undaunted, Europe launched an era of violent new imperialism that led to European domination and colonization of much of the world.

- Bismarck and his contemporaries spent the final 30 years of the 1800s creating and undoing entangling alliances in an effort to keep peace. Ironically, the result was paranoia that would contribute to World War I.

- Nationalism created tension in Britain over the Irish home rule issue, and nationalism led to a series of wars in the Balkans that ultimately settled nothing.

Part 5

Big Wars and Big Bangs (Twentieth Century)

Europe spiraled into two world wars as a result of competition, arms races, nationalism, and greed. Russia pulled out of World War I to fight its own bloody civil war. World War I ended in 1919 but the hostilities remained, to be exploited by dictators to create powerful armies and states. The failings of the treaty that ended the First World War contributed to the outbreak of the Second World War, a global conflict that turned out to be worse than the first one. The atomic age ended the war, but left everyone nervous for generations as east faced off against west in the Cold War. Communism dominated eastern Europe and then collapsed at the end of the twentieth century, leaving Europe with a whole new set of challenges, especially in eastern Europe. Finally, a few current events of interest and importance point the way to the challenges on the horizon for Europe.

Chapter 20

Turning the World Upside Down

In This Chapter

- ◆ The First World War
- ◆ Revolution strikes in Russia
- ◆ What a worthless treaty
- ◆ Europe gets anxious
- ◆ Europe, along with everyone else, gets depressed

The nineteenth century had been one of growth, expansion, growing pains, scientific and technological advancement, and war. The roller-coaster ride that was the nineteenth century seemed tame in comparison with the first 30 or so years of the twentieth century.

The first years of the twentieth century were characterized by rising tensions among the European powers that seemed to escalate with each passing year. The competition for military supremacy and for economic resources abroad were complicated by entangling alliances, which were supposed to make Europe feel safer but ultimately left everyone paranoid and wondering who actually was trustworthy. The powers sat divided into two sides, or blocs, with each side just daring the other to make a hostile move.

Exacerbating the situation, particularly in eastern Europe, were nationalist desires for self-determination. When war finally did erupt, nobody expected the utter disaster that it brought down on Europe. When it was over, Europe was utterly exhausted, with deep emotional scars, faced with a long, tedious rebuilding process complicated by economic problems unlike anything Europeans had ever experienced. The first 30 years left Europeans scratching their heads and wondering where the world was headed.

The War That Was Supposed to End All Wars

The wars of the late nineteenth century sharply contrasted with the Napoleonic Wars and those of centuries before in one major way. Early wars seemed to drag on and on because no nation had the ability to deliver a knockout punch. That changed in the nineteenth century and the wars, for the most part, seemed shorter and less costly. The Austro-Prussian War, the Franco-Prussian War, the battles resulting from imperialism, and the Balkan Wars were nothing compared to the Hundred Years' War, the Thirty Years' War, or the Napoleonic Wars.

This played a large part in the decisions of European nations to go to war in 1914. The threat of war was not the deterrent that it should have been. World War I, of course, was not called that until after Europe had a second such war. It was simply known as the Great War, and later the War to End All Wars.

When fighting began in mid-1914, most governments believed the war would be over by Christmas. Little did they know that Europe would soon find itself in a familiar position. Though armies, ships, and guns were larger, more powerful, more destructive, and more deadly than ever, nobody could land the knockout punch. That, combined with the particular style of warfare used during the Great War, made the war seem like it would never end.

How Did This Happen?

The events that led to the outbreak of war were almost unbelievable. The chain of events that sparked the war began in Bosnia. The heir to the Habsburg throne, Archduke Franz Ferdinand (1863–1914), visited Sarajevo in Bosnia, which was controlled by Austria-Hungary. As Ferdinand drove through the streets of Sarajevo on June 28, 1914, a radical Serbian nationalist named Gavrilo Princip (1894–1918) attacked the motorcade and assassinated the archduke and his wife.

Austria was outraged and blamed Serbia, claiming that Serbia had supported the terrorist organization known as the Black Hand with which Princip was affiliated. Austria had already been leaning toward challenging Serbian nationalism, and this provided the perfect opportunity. After an investigation, the Austrian government issued an ultimatum: Serbia must cease all anti-Austrian activity and submit to an all-out investigation of such activity. Serbia refused to comply and the dominoes began to fall.

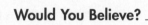

Would You Believe?

Princip actually threw a hand grenade at the Archduke's car but did not hit his target. A few moments later, when the Archduke's driver made a wrong turn, Princip finished the job with a handgun as the car drove by slowly.

Austria-Hungary declared war on Serbia. Germany had already thrown its support behind Austria by issuing the infamous "blank check," promising Austria that they would provide any financial or other support for Austria in the case of war. Germany and Austria both knew that Russia was an ally of Serbia and would likely enter the fray if Austria attacked Serbia, but that didn't matter.

Austria declared war on Serbia on July 28, 1914. In response, Russia mobilized its forces. Germany then issued an ultimatum to Russia to stand down. On August 1, Germany declared war on Russia. Since France was an ally of Russia, Germany declared war on France two days later. Britain warned Germany that if it invaded neutral Belgium to get at France, Britain would be forced to retaliate.

Ignoring the warnings, Germany invaded Belgium, and Britain declared war on Germany on August 4. Over the next 10 days, Austria declared war on Russia, and France and Britain declared war on Austria. Italy declared it would remain neutral. In less than a month, the belligerent Germany and Austria had dragged an entire continent into war.

Would You Believe?

During the war, the two sides were the Triple Entente or the Allies, Britain, France, Russia, and later Italy and the United States and the Central Powers, including Germany, Austria-Hungary, and later Turkey and Bulgaria.

War on the Western Front

Generally speaking, the war played out in two main theaters, the Western Front and the Eastern Front. On the Western Front, the Germans enacted the Schlieffen Plan as soon as war became imminent. The Schlieffen Plan was a German battle plan dictating that France must be knocked out first—military necessities outran political concerns. The plan called for rapidly mobilizing German troops and then plowing the troops through Belgium into France. The goal was not to take strategic French locations but rather to surround the French army.

Germany expected a two-front war, with France in the west and Russia in the east. Russia would take several weeks to fully mobilize its troops, so the plan called for immediate mobilization of almost all German troops to the west for an attack on France via Belgium and Holland. The remaining troops would establish a defensive position in the east and await the Russian attack.

As the plan unfolded on the Western Front, the Germans faced the British and Belgians in Belgium, then the French. By September the Germans were forcing an Allied retreat through France and the French government left Paris in case the Germans occupied the city. The Germans crossed the Marne River and engaged the French at the First Battle of the Marne. The battle involved more than two million troops. The French held their own and forced the Germans to abandon the Schlieffen Plan. With the battle fought to a draw, both sides dug in and began the terrible strategy known as trench warfare.

> **Would You Believe?**
>
> The outmanned French actually used taxis to transport reserves to the First Battle of the Marne.

Life in the Trenches

The two sides dug trenches meant to protect soldiers in defensive positions for a short amount of time. However, with the armies stalemated across from each other, they eventually grew longer, more complex, and more permanent; over time, the maze of trenches stretched along the entire French border. The complicated system of trenches often featured a front trench, a supply trench behind that, then a third trench in the rear where troops could gather for an attack.

The problem was that there was little attacking. Soldiers camped in the sucking mud of the trenches and exchanged volleys of rifle and artillery fire. The open land between the Allied and German trenches was known as "no man's land," because of the obvious danger of entering the unprotected area. Occasionally troops would attack over the ground, but the use of artillery, grenades, and gas made it easier to just dig in defensively. Neither side gained more than several hundred yards of territory over the course of years of trench warfare.

Conditions in the trenches were miserable. Aside from the immediate threat of enemy fire, the greatest threats to the soldiers were disease, rats, lice, and exposure. After the short initial burst of fighting, the duration of the war on the Western Front was epitomized by trench warfare, which cost both sides millions of soldiers. Not until the end of the war in 1918 did the British finally break through the German trench system and force the Germans to retreat toward Germany.

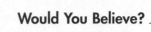

Would You Believe?

In 1929, German author Erich Remarque published the classic *All Quiet on the Western Front*, a novel about a young soldier in the deadly trenches of World War I. Nazi Germany eventually banned the book and accused Remarque of being Jewish.

War Spreads Across Europe

On the Eastern Front, the war had a much different character. The vast spaces and wide-open battlefields necessitated mobile troops and massive movements. At the beginning of the war, the huge Russian armies won victory after victory over the German and Austrian forces. However, as the Germans relocated troops from the Western to the Eastern Front and as Russia developed internal problems, the tide turned for Germany. Russia suffered enormous loss of life, ran short on weapons and supplies, and second-guessed what it was doing in the war. Russia would soon bow out entirely.

In the south, the Central Powers occupied the Balkans early in the war. Also in the south, the British faced off against the Ottomans in the Dardanelles in an attempt to resupply the Russians via the Black Sea. The British finally withdrew attacks on the Turks and concentrated on Ottoman forces in Palestine and the surrounding area. Britain called upon Australia, New Zealand, Egypt, and India for help there. Italy entered the war in 1915 by declaring war on Germany. Austrian troops then engaged the Italians along the Isonzo River in northern Italy; more than two million troops fought over a dozen major offensives there. The war turned global, too, as Allies of the Entente took Germany's colonies.

The turning point in the war came in 1917. First, the United States declared war on Germany because of Germany's unrestricted submarine warfare in the Atlantic. Two years earlier, a German sub had sunk the *Lusitania*, a passenger ship carrying a number of Americans. The United States issued a stern warning, but hoped to stay out of the war. When Germany resumed the use of subs to starve the British, the Americans jumped on board.

In addition, by 1917 Germany was really feeling the strain of war. The economy was shot and strikes broke out. In response, Germany established a dictatorship. With Russia out of the war because of the Russian Revolution, Germany turned toward France to deliver the knockout punch once and for all. They hoped to get to Paris before the American reinforcements arrived. Unfortunately for Germany, the American troops began arriving in Europe in small numbers in early 1918 and then in larger numbers by summertime. In July of 1918, British, French, and American forces engaged the Germans at the Second Battle of the Marne and turned the tide for good. For the first time, the Central Powers did not have the upper hand. The Allied forces then marched toward Germany. In the south, the British and Egyptian forces knocked out the Ottomans and the Italians forced a stalemate with the Austrians.

The Total War Effort

Because the powers involved in the First World War had no idea how long they would be involved in the war, early estimates of wartime costs fell far short of actual expenditures. It soon became obvious that the war was going to drain the nations' economies far more than anyone imagined.

That realization prompted the governments to temporarily abandon their traditional economic systems and establish command economies. Governments took over the means of production and mandated what was to be produced and in what quantities. In Germany, laws required men of working age to work only at jobs that benefited the war effort. Despite this strategy's effectiveness at streamlining the national economies, the governments of Europe alienated many workers.

The governments went a step further, too. In most countries, everyone got involved in the war. The men went to war, the women often worked in factories where the men used to work, and the children worked to collect scraps of metal to be used for military manufacturing purposes. The governments also instituted price controls and rationing, especially for food. Precious food often was denied to citizens so that the available supply could be used to feed soldiers. Through these extreme measures, with Germany's being the most extreme, the European governments were able to compensate for and manage shortages of all sorts of raw materials and necessary supplies.

Would You Believe?

To keep everyone on board with the war effort, governments used propaganda posters and pamphlets to promote the war. Government propaganda typically featured patriotic messages and often portrayed enemies as villains or monsters.

The efficiency demonstrated by some governments in the total war effort strengthened the arguments of socialists who advocated government control of means of production as well as the responsibility for the redistribution of wealth. The mobilization of entire societies proved invaluable to the war effort on both sides.

The Russian Revolution

Russia's involvement in the First World War was actually predated by the Russian Revolution of 1905. The hangover from the 1905 revolution would come back to haunt Russia in 1917 and force it to withdraw completely from the war.

The Revolution of 1905 resulted from a number of issues. First, the peasants never completely enjoyed the elimination of serfdom (see Chapter 18) because the conditions remained poor. Second, the urban workers developed many of the same complaints that factory workers had earlier in the century in Britain. The poor working and living conditions in the cities prompted the workers to form unions even though unions were illegal. These issues finally came to a head on a cold Sunday in January 1905.

Led by Father George Gapon (1870–1906), founder of the Assembly of Russian Factory and Plant Workers, thousands of peaceful demonstrators marched through St. Petersburg to the Winter Palace. With religious icons in hand and hymns ringing in the air, the crowds hoped to present Czar Nicolas with a petition. Little did they know that Nicholas had left the city two weeks earlier. Troops around the palace opened fire on the protestors and killed as many as 1,000 of them. The incident, known as Bloody Sunday, sparked strikes and revolts throughout the rest of 1905. The revolts never amounted to much, though, because they were neither organized nor goal-oriented; they were basically spontaneous violence.

Tired of the grumbling, Nicholas issued the October Manifesto in October and granted the Russian people some civil rights and a representative body known as the Duma. The Manifesto satisfied the liberals but the Social Democrats hated the move. In response, they unsuccessfully revolted in Moscow.

The End of the Czars

The Russian people found their Duma very disappointing. The czar maintained the right to veto anything the Duma did, so the people's voice wasn't actually heard. When the first Duma deadlocked with Nicholas's ministers, Nicholas dismissed the Duma. The next Duma, much to the czar's chagrin, turned out to be more liberal and obstinate than the first. Once again, Nicholas dismissed the Duma, and then rewrote the laws so that more of the propertied class would be elected and be loyal to the czar.

In the meantime, rumblings continued among the peasants and workers. They often acted out violently against the police and government officials. To get a grip on the unruly peasants, Nicholas appointed Pyotr Stolypin (1862–1911) prime minister in 1906. Stolypin introduced both industrial and agrarian reform to provide the unruly peasants and workers with ways to get themselves out of poverty, hoping to create a class of not-so-poor people who would be more loyal to the government. He was tough on radicals, though, and executed thousands during his administration. The gallows of Russia earned the nickname "Stolypin's necktie."

> **Would You Believe?**
>
> Stolypin's policies were what he considered a "wager on the strong" because he hoped that the strong Russians would make his legislation pay off for Russia.

In 1914, Russia found itself at war with the Central Powers in the eastern theater. Initially things went well for Russia, but by 1915, Russian soldiers were dying at a horrific rate. On the home front, the Russian people were getting fed up with the planned economy, with the war effort, and with Nicholas. They clamored louder than ever for rule by the Duma and not by the czar. The Russian people for generations had been dissatisfied with the czars. They disapproved of the czars' refusal to grant liberal reforms and they resented the czars' lack of commitment to the workers. After the debacle of the Russo-Japanese War and in light of the current state of affairs in Russia, the Russian people had little or no confidence that Nicholas could successfully guide Russia through the war. In the face of this popular unrest, Nicholas made a very bad decision. He dismissed the Duma yet again, then went to the front lines to rally his demoralized troops, leaving the country in the hands of his wife, Alexandra (1872–1918).

Alexandra had no talent for government at all; she shuffled the country's top ministers like cards. Alexandra carried the rare blood disease hemophilia and passed it on to her son. Since no doctors could help, Alexandra turned to Grigori Rasputin (c.1869–1916). Associated with a fringe sect and claiming to be a prophet and holy man, Rasputin developed a bizarre relationship with Alexandra; he reportedly could heal her son's bleeding when no one else could. With Nicholas gone to the front lines and Alexandra making political hirings and firings at Rasputin's request, three men murdered Rasputin. Alexandra fell into a state of shock because Rasputin prophesied bad things for Alexandra if he died. He was right.

As a Matter of Fact

The Mad Monk Rasputin actually was not a monk at all but rather a religious pilgrim of sorts. One of the more interesting beliefs of Rasputin was that God granted grace to those who corrected or repented of sins so sinning was important for finding God's grace. Considering the large number of women he reportedly slept with over the years, it should be no wonder that he preached this message to many of those ladies with whom he was acquainted.

The state of things in Russia declined quickly after Rasputin's murder. Within a few months bread shortages resulted in riots in St. Petersburg and the entire city fell into chaos. Nicholas, still foolishly at the battlefront, sent orders for the military to deal with the problem. The soldiers joined the riotous crowds instead. The Duma knew the end was at hand and declared a provisional government to rule in place of the doomed czar. The czar's family, and the czar when he returned, remained under house arrest until they were later moved to Siberia; they were executed after the subsequent revolution. Their remains weren't discovered and exhumed until the 1990s.

As a Matter of Fact

The Russian royal family died at the hands of executioners in 1918 but one of the bodies never surfaced—that of one of the daughters, Anastasia. Rumors of Anastasia's survival abounded for decades following the execution and prompted a sort of cult of fascination with the notion of her survival. The idea that Anastasia survived the execution led to several impersonation attempts, the most famous of which were by two women, an American named Eugenia Smith and Anna Anderson. In the 1960s, anthropologists and handwriting experts denounced Smith as a fraud; Smith also declined DNA tests. Despite Anderson's failed DNA tests, she acquired a rather large contingent in the 1970s of those who believed her to be the Grand Duchess.

The Provisional Government

From the very beginning the provisional government faced competition from the Petrograd Soviet, a council of a few thousand workers, soldiers, and intellectuals. The Petrograd Soviet formed when the czar abdicated, to act as the representative body for the workers of Petrograd (the Russian name for St. Petersburg). In May, the Petrograd Soviet issued Army Order Number One, which voided authority of military officers and put the authority in the hands of the regular soldiers. The *Soviet* intended this order to strengthen the military, but chaos ensued.

In the meantime, the new provisional government focused its attention on the war effort. The government, heavily influenced by Alexander Kerensky (1881–1970), wanted to launch one more major offensive against Germany before the peasant soldiers completely fell apart. Kerensky faced a huge challenge, though. Russians were demanding peace, the peasant soldiers were deserting left and right to return to their families, and a new threat to the provisional government emerged in Russia. During the summer of 1917, the peasants went crazy and stole land wherever they could. Russia stood on the verge of collapse at home and on the verge of defeat in the First World War.

Define Your Terms

Soviet is a Russian government council.

The Bolshevik Revolution

Waiting out the war in Switzerland until early 1917 was Vladimir Ilyich Lenin (1870–1924). Lenin had been exiled from Russia earlier in the century for his socialist ideas and he used his time away to study Marx and fraternize with other socialists. He believed in the revolutionary message of Marxist communism and believed there could and should be no peaceful transition to socialism. However, whereas Marx believed a violent revolution would occur naturally, Lenin believed it would be necessary to instigate a revolution with professional soldiers. Lenin and his followers were known as Bolsheviks and the less radical Russian socialists were known as Mensheviks. When war broke out in 1914, Lenin believed the time was drawing near for a socialist uprising in Russia.

In 1917, after Nicholas abdicated, Germany happily arranged for Lenin to make his way back into Russia, putting him in a sealed railway car and forbidding him to get off the train before he crossed the German border. From the moment he arrived in Petrograd, he denounced the provisional government. He encouraged the Bolsheviks in Petrograd to not cooperate with it. By July, after the rough days of June, the Bolsheviks attempted a takeover of the provisional government. The coup failed, though, and Lenin fled. In September the provisional government faced another takeover attempt, this time from General Lavr Kornilov (1870–1918). During the Kornilov Coup, Kerensky distributed

Would You Believe?

Lenin's brother, Aleksandr Ulyanov, died at the hands of an executioner in 1887 for conspiring to take the life of Czar Alexander III.

thousands and thousands of rifles to the Petrograd workers to defend the government. Kornilov's troops bailed on him and his coup failed. After the coup attempt, many of the armed Petrograd workers switched to the side of the Bolsheviks. Lenin, waiting for the right moment to return, saw his opportunity.

Central to the Bolshevik Revolution was the leadership of Lenin's right-hand man Leon Trotsky (1879–1940). Trotsky was a dynamic speaker who could electrify a room full of people. He used his oratory skills to convince the Petrograd Soviet, where the Bolsheviks gained a slim majority in October, to pass all military power to him. He then convinced the Soviet to stage a coup not for the Bolsheviks but for the other soviets throughout Russia, who happened to be holding a congress in Petrograd.

On November 6, Trotsky's men, along with the Bolsheviks, staged their coup. They took government buildings, then went to the congress of soviets to win its approval. The Bolshevik majority there declared Lenin the head of a new government where the power lay with the soviets. The power vacuum needed filling and the dynamic leaders Lenin and Trotsky filled the void. The desperate times facing Russia put the Russian workers in a position such that they simply needed a leader with a message. Lenin's message was simple: the political power would pass to the soviets, the land would go to the peasants, and Russia would get out of the war with Germany at all costs.

Lenin approached the issue of the war realistically. He knew that Russia was done even though some around him still wanted to fight, out of a sense of Romantic duty and obligation to the Allies. In December 1917, Russia signed an armistice with the Central Powers and began peace negotiations. The Germans drove a hard bargain during negotiations. The Treaty of Brest-Litovsk required that Russia give up claims to a ridiculous amount of territory. Included in the lands that Russia had to cede were Finland, Poland, Belarus, Ukraine, and the Baltic region, where the future states of Latvia, Estonia, and Lithuania would be. The Central Powers decided in 1918 to add high war reparations for Russia, too. Many of the Bolsheviks in the government initially refused to accept such harsh conditions for peace. However, the Germans began a march into Russia in early 1918 that, combined with Lenin's persuasiveness, changed their minds. Russia was officially out of the Great War in 1918, and not a moment too soon. Staying in the war would have resulted in a national disaster for Russia.

The Bolsheviks Win

When Lenin and Trotsky took control, they explained that theirs would be a provisional, temporary government until elections could be held and an assembly put together. The elections didn't go as planned, though. The Russians elected a majority of Socialist Revolutionary party members and a minority of Bolsheviks to the Constituent Assembly. Therefore, Lenin ordered the Bolshevik army to disband the Assembly. The Russian people were in disbelief that their elected representatives had been stripped of their power and the people were once again subjects of a dictatorship.

Would You Believe?

The Bolsheviks called their enemies *Whites* for two reasons. First, white stood in stark contrast to the red of the Bolsheviks. Second, the color white often was associated with the czar.

The Whites, or the Russian political and military forces who opposed the Bolsheviks, organized to fight for the soviets and launched a civil war to unseat the hated Bolsheviks from power. Additionally, regional governments popped up across Russia, further undermining the Bolshevik authority. Finally organized into a legitimate army by the end of 1918, the Whites marched on the Bolsheviks in Moscow, the new home of Lenin's government since March. Lenin's Red Army, though, withstood the attacks across Russia and had the Whites on the run. By 1921, the Reds had completely defeated the Whites and had won the civil war.

Lenin and Trotsky receive much of the credit for the victory over the Whites. Lenin's unwavering confidence inspired the Bolsheviks. The reinstated military draft and Trotsky's stern discipline helped shape up the Red Army. Any infractions resulted in harsh penalties, including execution. The Bolsheviks maintained control of central Russia while the Whites had to move in from the frontier regions of Russia. The Bolsheviks also used an intimidating secret police force known as the Cheka to hunt down those who opposed the Bolshevik cause. After an assassination attempt on Lenin, the Chekists turned up the heat and began the Red Terror. Perhaps hundreds of thousands were executed as enemies of the Bolsheviks during this period, which finally ended with the end of the civil war.

Would You Believe?

By the end of the civil war in Russia, the Cheka had become so ruthless and hated by the Russians that Lenin dissolved the organization and replaced it with a new secret police.

Let's Call the Whole Thing Off

By 1918, even with the withdrawal of Russia, things weren't exactly going as planned for the Central Powers. The reinforcement of the European troops with fresh, energetic American soldiers spelled doom for the Central Powers. Germany's Spring Offensive, the last attempt to salvage the war, got the Germans very close to Paris, but they stalled just short. In July and August, the Entente's troops made big surges and the Germans retreated each time. By October, German leadership faced a tough decision: fight until Germany was annihilated or sign a peace treaty. Rumors of German defeat spread through the German ranks and mutiny became a legitimate possibility everywhere; some of the German High Sea Fleet did mutiny. German public opinion ran in favor of an end to the fighting. On November 8, 1918, at Germany's most desperate hour, Kaiser Wilhelm II abdicated and gave way to the new Weimar Republic in Germany.

Bulgaria became the first Central Power to capitulate. They gave up in September 1918. The Ottomans then signed an armistice on October 30, followed by the Austrians on November 4. Germany finally signed an armistice agreement, on the eleventh day of the eleventh month, poetically at the eleventh hour, too.

The terrible war that saw the first use of chemical weapons and air combat, tragic trench warfare, and millions dead had finally drawn to a conclusion. With the final tallies done, fully 9 million men lost their lives in the war. Germany lost over two million, Russia lost 1.7 million, and France and Austria-Hungary also lost over a million lives. Surely this would be the war to end all wars.

As a Matter of Fact

One of the technological advances made during the war was the development of the modern tank. Introduced into combat in 1916 for the first time, the British D1 tank rolled into action at breakneck speeds of up to four or five miles per hour on level ground. Intended to break the stalemate created by trench warfare, the tanks proved very unreliable and high-maintenance on the uneven battlefields.

The Treaty of Versailles

In 1919, the representatives of "the Big Four" met at the Paris Peace Conference to work out the formal details of a treaty. Georges Clemenceau (1841–1929) represented France, David Lloyd George (1863–1945) represented Britain, Vittorio Orlando (1860–1952) represented Italy, and President Woodrow Wilson (1856–1924) represented the United States. Germany was represented but had no say in the proceedings. Russia, busy dealing with domestic problems, was not represented. Bulgaria and Turkey, home of the Ottomans, weren't involved at Versailles but signed the Treaty of

Neuilly and the Treaty of Sevres, respectively, which dealt harsh blows to the small nations and forced them to cede much land.

Would You Believe?

The Big Four met immediately with ideological problems. Wilson pushed the idea of national self-determination but France and Britain had no intention of letting go of their colonial empires.

Most of the delegates to the conference had their own agenda. Clemenceau hoped to exact revenge on Germany and deliver a crippling blow to it as a European power. Lloyd George also wanted Germany to pay for its crimes, but did not want blood like Clemenceau did. Wilson approached the meetings idealistically hoping to promote his idea for a League of Nations, an international peacekeeping organization. The League was part of Wilson's Fourteen Points, a plan that called for arms reductions, free trade, and more. In the end, Clemenceau and Lloyd George got their way.

The Treaty of Versailles required that Germany accept all responsibility for the war, fairly or not. Germany lost huge amounts of land to other nations, perhaps most notably the hotly contested region of Alsace-Lorraine to France. Germany found itself with a bill for 132 billion gold marks, a figure actually reduced from over 200 billion gold marks. The sum was still unrealistically high. The treaty placed serious limitations on the German military. The treaty limited Germany's army to 100,000 men and no draft, no tanks, and no heavy artillery. Likewise, the treaty limited the German navy to 15,000 men and no submarines. The treaty also created a DMZ, or demilitarized zone, along the Rhine to serve as a buffer between the two rival states. Though the Treaty of Versailles served as the major peace settlement after the war, other treaties dealt with the smaller nations involved in the war. The other treaties redrew political boundaries and resulted in the creation of new nations like Finland, Romania, Poland, Hungary, Lithuania, Estonia, and Latvia, to name a few.

Continental Quotes

"I don't know whether war is an interlude during peace, or peace is an interlude during war."

—Georges Clemenceau

Failings of the Treaty

The harsh treaty crushed Germany emotionally as well as fiscally. Britain and France were pleased with the outcome, but Wilson was disappointed. The Treaty of Versailles left Germany as the sole guilty party, a fact that would create deep resentment in Germany. Furthermore, the treaty did not address the very things that caused the war in the first place. In the end, the United States was the only one of the powers that did not sign the treaty.

The Treaty of Paris provided for the League of Nations to intervene in military aggression. Members in the League were to be obligated to defend other members who were attacked in the future. Because the American Congress had the sole constitutional power to declare war, the Congress refused to give that power away by signing such a treaty. Britain eventually backed out of its alliance with France, so Britain, France, and Germany were all left feeling relatively isolated. Germany felt wronged. Austria lost its empire. Some nationalists got their wish in Europe, but not all of them. Tensions were almost as high at the end of the war as they were at the beginning.

An Exhausted Europe

As if the loss of more than nine million lives wasn't enough for Europe, probably twice that number suffered some kind of physical injury as a result of the fighting. Buildings, factories, homes, farms, churches, and even entire villages and towns were completely destroyed. In France alone, 750,000 families lost homes as a result of the war. With that kind of destruction, the European economy also lay in rubble. Many nations ran up huge war debts through deficit spending and by taking loans to finance the war effort. After the war, though, they had no way to repay their debts.

The death and destruction of the war left a lasting impression on everyone involved. The threat of war hadn't been much of a deterrent when trouble brewed in the Balkans, but now war seemed like the worst thing imaginable. Man had created weapons of such destructive power that no one alive at the end of the war ever wanted to go to war again. Unfortunately, Europe's determination not to fight would actually lead to more fighting by mid-century.

One of the most profound and lasting effects of the war was one that no one really considered at the time. The collective psyche of Europe was almost irreparably damaged. The total destruction and chaos of the war led many to question and doubt all they had ever known or believed. These questions and doubts became apparent during the years after the war in areas including art, religion, psychology, and philosophy.

The Age of Anxiety

After 1919, Europe was dazed and confused like a boxer at the end of a terrible match. People were faced with the unsettling task of putting their lives back together. However, it became clear to everyone in Europe that things were never going to be the same as they were before the wars. The wars changed everything. The European economy had fallen to pieces, the politics of Europe had changed, and even the map of Europe had been redrawn. People were amazed at the destruction of the war and deeply disturbed that humans could inflict such destruction and suffering on humanity. These deeply troubling psychological issues manifested themselves in many areas of European life after the war and remained present in Europe arguably until after World War II.

Unsettling Philosophy

Intellectuals of the late nineteenth and early twentieth centuries had delivered ominous warnings even before the outbreak of the First World War and the Russian Revolution. One of the darkest nineteenth-century philosophers was Friedrich Nietzsche (1844–1900). The German philosopher emphasized in his works the fact that Western society has always repressed the individual and discouraged creativity. Nietzsche believed that religion, particularly Christianity, did the same thing. He argued that religion was for the meek, the weak, and the masses who were unable to think for themselves. Nietzsche argued that religion led humans to "slave morality" or the willingness to submit the individual will to the strong. The individual as manifested in the *übermench*, or superman, should be the goal of man. Man should not be satisfied with being part of the herd. Nietzschean thought, combined with aggressive German nationalism, contributed to the rise of a new Germany in the interwar years under Hitler (see Chapter 21).

> **Continental Quotes**
>
> Nietzche's most infamous quote is "God is dead." Often misinterpreted, Nietzsche meant that according to his observations of nineteenth-century Europe, God effectively had been killed or rendered obsolete by Christians because he no longer remained important to them.

Another philosopher who questioned rationality was the Austrian Ludwig Wittgenstein (1889–1951). Wittgenstein promoted logical empiricism. He maintained that anything that cannot be analyzed through philosophical study of the language that expresses it is a waste of time. In other words, statements about abstractions like happiness, liberty, or the existence of God are just as abstract because they cannot be expressed logically or mathematically. Basically, Wittgenstein's message to the world was, "If you can't express something logically, don't bother thinking about it." Europeans seeking answers or explanations for the recent tragic events of the wars found no reassurance in Wittgenstein.

In many ways, the existential thought of philosophers like Jean-Paul Sartre (1905–1980) proved just as disturbing. The French existentialist denied the existence of God and said that man just appeared. Once here, man is on his own. As a free being, a man has no choice but to act, to do something. What each man does provides meaning and definition for his life, thus each man defines his own existence; the idea that man's existence should be defined or guided by religion or morality is nonsense. However, existentialists did argue that man could overcome hardships by acting. The catch was that man acted on his own.

Would You Believe?

The desperate times during and following the wars also led to the revival of Christian thought, led by such thinkers as Søren Kierkegaard and Karl Barth.

New Physics

Just as the foundations of what humans believed about their world changed after the Scientific Revolution and the scientific advancements of the late nineteenth century, things changed again in the early twentieth century. The most unsettling scientific ideas that emerged in the early 1900s dealt with the atom, the basic building block of the world.

Until the 1900s, scientists believed that the atom was a stable piece of matter that was unbreakable and unshakable. However, the German scientist Max Plank (1858–1947) brought that into question when he invented modern quantum physics. Another German scientist, Albert Einstein (1879–1955), dealt a serious blow to science with his theory of special relativity. According to his theory, both space and time are relative, with the only constant through both space and time being the speed of light. Einstein went on to do further work related to what is now known as quantum physics. In the 1930s, after Adolf Hitler assumed power (see Chapter 21), Einstein wrote a letter to U.S. President Franklin D. Roosevelt urging him to explore atomic energy as a possible means of military technology. Einstein, greatly fearing the Nazis, believed Hitler would work toward that end with his Nazi physicists.

Further unsettling ideas about the basic building blocks of the world came out in 1919, when Ernest Rutherford (1871–1937) proved that

Would You Believe?

Hard sciences weren't the only sciences to experience upheaval. Sigmund Freud's psychology, based on psychoanalysis, maintained that human behavior was irrational and based on sexual and other desires that remained in constant conflict with rational thought.

atoms could be broken, or split. In the years that followed, scientists even discovered the existence of subatomic particles. Once again, all that man knew about science turned out to be incomplete data. Interestingly, the knowledge of atom-splitting coincided with the rise of the dictators against whom the threat of atomic weapons eventually would be used.

Art and Literature Break All the Rules

The camera single-handedly changed the world of art in the late nineteenth century. For centuries, artists strived to make their paintings as lifelike as possible. With the photograph, though, artists no longer had a need to paint a picture exactly as it might appear in real life. Beginning with the impressionists like Claude Monet (1840–1926) and Auguste Renoir (1841–1919), paintings took on a different form. Rather than faithfully recreating scenes, these artists painted works that left the impression or feeling of a scene. The expressionists like Paul Gauguin (1848–1903) and Vincent van Gogh (1853–1890), and the postimpressionists like Paul Cezanne (1839–1906) and Pablo Picasso (1881–1973), continued to push the edge of the artistic envelope. They placed emphasis on ideals like form, color, shapes, and lines, and painted those things rather than what the eye perceives an object to look like.

The artists of the late nineteenth and early twentieth centuries helped blaze a trail that made a real departure from tradition. The artists who spearheaded the artistic movements known as Dadaism and surrealism were anything but traditional. These movements sought specifically to challenge all rules and authority in the art world. They painted dreamlike scenes, and scenes that seemingly had no basis in reality. They fashioned nonsensical structures and presented as art many things that contemporaries considered obscene. The music of the early twentieth century, in many ways, challenged authority, too. Atonal music and risqué themes shocked audiences who had grown accustomed to classical music. Two of the most significant atonal composers were Alban Berg and Arnold Schoenberg, both of Vienna.

The literature of the early years of the century embraced unconventional thought as much as the art did. Virginia Woolf (1882–1941) and James Joyce (1882–1941) used stream-of-consciousness novels to explore the inner workings of the human psyche. In such works, random thoughts come and go and the reader is left to put all the pieces together collectively rather than in a linear fashion. Many writers, like their contemporary philosophers, rejected notions of progress in the wake of the wars. Writers such as Franz Kafka (1883–1924) and George Orwell (1903–1950) predicted futures that were dark and disturbing. Little did they know that their writings would be so prophetic.

The Great Depression

The first years after the end of the First World War were characterized by obvious economic hardships as well as agricultural difficulties often directly caused by the destruction of the war. As the economic situation picked up for some, the desire to live life to the fullest in the wake of the war led to unwise borrowing and spending habits. Millions of people in Europe and the United States extended their credit beyond safe limits. To make matters worse, millions of people around the world borrowed money to speculate on stocks. In other words, they invested borrowed money, money that would have to be paid back one day. As investors poured more and more money into stocks and other investments, stock prices soared to unrealistically high levels. As a result, the stock market in America crashed in 1929 and left speculators and investors with nothing except debt.

As the American economy started down the slippery slope toward disaster, banks called in loans from everyone. American banks also called in loans from foreign countries that had borrowed for the war or for the rebuilding process after the war. The foreign nations, though, could scarcely afford the interest on those loans. With the supply of money seemingly disappearing, consumers everywhere held on to their cash and made runs on banks. Spending dropped, so producers dumped as many goods as they could, thus causing prices to fall dramatically. As demand slowed, so did production. As production slowed, so did employment. Unemployment skyrocketed. Then, in 1931, the leading bank in Europe, the Credit-Anstalt, collapsed. Britain and other leading countries took themselves off the gold standard and suddenly it was every man for himself.

The brilliant economist John Maynard Keynes (1883–1946) recommended that countries spend their way out of the debt. He encouraged governments to create jobs to infuse money into the economies. Instead, governments reduced spending and held on to their cash, too. By the 1930s, some governments, such as America under President Franklin Roosevelt, began recovery programs like the New Deal. For most nations around the world, though, only World War II provided the economic stimulation necessary to climb out of the doldrums. It was against this economic backdrop that the strong leaders of the interwar years emerged.

The Least You Need to Know

◆ When a Serb assassinated the Austrian heir, Archduke Franz Ferdinand, Austria, prompted by Germany, issued an ultimatum to Serbia, despite knowing that Russia would enter any war on Serbia's side. Russia did, as did France, Britain, and Turkey. The Great War had begun.

◆ The war on the Western Front consisted mostly of trench warfare. Thousands of miles of mazelike trenches covered France and led to four years of virtual stalemate. War in the east featured more land and massive troop movements. Russia met with initial success but domestic problems drove it out of the war.

◆ Russia experienced revolution and civil war in 1917. Lenin and the Bolsheviks won the fight to be leaders of Russia. At a high price, Russia pulled out of World War I.

◆ America's entry tipped the scales against the Central Powers. In 1919, the allies forced the Treaty of Versailles on Germany, which was made to make serious restrictions on its military and pay huge reparations in cash and land.

◆ The war left Europe in a state of shock, bewilderment, and anxiety that manifested itself in the art, music, and literature of the time. The turn-of-the-century science and philosophy also left Europeans unsure about the world and the future.

World War: Second Verse, Worse Than the First

In This Chapter

◆ Stalin, Hitler, and Mussolini take the stage

◆ Appeasement—worst idea ever?

◆ World war all over again

◆ The horrible, horrible Holocaust

As Europe tried to move forward from the disastrous First World War, uncertainty faced everyone on the continent. No one knew exactly how long the rebuilding process would take or how much it would cost. No one knew if the tenuous peace of the Treaty of Paris would hold up, or for how long.

Continental Drift

This sense of uncertainty heightened as Britain and France drifted apart after the war. The two nations already differed greatly over how to treat post-war Germany. Britain definitely wanted Germany punished, but not to the extent that France did. France's animosity toward Germany led to icy relations with Britain and with the United States. Feeling alone, France turned to the fledgling states of Poland, Czechoslovakia, Romania, and Yugoslavia as allies.

The relationship between France and Germany looked as though it might improve after Germany made its first installment reparations payment in 1921, but things changed when Germany couldn't pay in 1922. Britain wanted to cut Germany a little slack, but France wouldn't dream of it. In 1923, France marched into Germany and occupied the Rhineland. Rather than fight back with guns, the Germans of the Rhineland simply quit working. The factories closed and France grew more frustrated than ever. In late 1923, Germany got new, moderate leaders in the government who called off the strikes. In return, they asked France to reevaluate Germany's ability to pay. Remarkably, France agreed and things looked up again.

The United States, Britain, and France sent financial experts to Germany to reevaluate the situation and settled on what became known as the Dawes Plan, which set Germany's payments based on realistic German productivity. It also created a strange system of loans. The United States loaned money to Germany so that Germany could make reparations payments to Britain and France so that Britain and France could repay loans to America. Things got a little more cordial in 1926 when Germany joined the League of Nations, and things looked up again, at least for idealists, in 1928 when a number of nations signed the Kellogg-Briand Pact, an official declaration that war should not be used as foreign policy. Realistically, the Pact did nothing; neither did the League of Nations.

What little optimism existed amidst the widespread anxiety in 1928 vanished with the Stock Market crash the next year. Little did Europe know that the tough times ahead would give rise to a few of the worst regimes to ever rule in Europe.

Dictators Seize Power

In the years known later as the interwar years, the people looked for strong leaders to take command and lead them to a better life. Three men in particular rose above all others and took command. In Russia, Germany, and Italy, dictators rose and took control of the national governments. The circumstances of each dictator's ascension differed from nation to nation, as did the politics of each dictator, but each ruled with an iron fist, trampling human rights—and human life. In the end, their citizens were not sad to see them go.

The Rise of Stalin

In the new Soviet Union, Lenin and Trotsky pulled off the unimaginable. The trick was not taking power but keeping it. On their way to the top, though, they and the Bolsheviks ruined the economy. To rebuild, Lenin instituted the NEP or New Economic Policy to replace the War Communism or command economy during the Civil War. The NEP allowed some economic freedom, something the Bolsheviks did not allow in their rise to power. As a result, the Soviet economy grew, repression eased slightly, and things seemed to be turning around for the Soviets.

> **Would You Believe?**
>
> Joseph Stalin's original surname was "Dzughashvili." In 1913 he adopted "Stalin" which in Russian means "man of steel."

In 1924, however, Lenin died, with no plans for a successor. At the time Joseph Stalin (1879–1953) was the general secretary of the Communist Party, a position that didn't actually hold much power. Stalin and two others, Leon Trotsky and Nikolai Bukharin (1888–1938), vied for leadership of the Soviet Union. Stalin positioned himself politically between Trotsky on the left and Bukharin on the right. By 1928, Stalin emerged from the group with the most power. He did this by first aligning against Trotsky. Once Trotsky had been eliminated as a political threat, Stalin aligned with Bukharin's enemies, the moderates.

> **As a Matter of Fact**
>
> Amidst the power struggle with the Stalin-led Communists, Trotsky and his followers were expelled from the Communist Party in 1927. In 1929 he was expelled from the Soviet Union and forced to live in exile. Trotsky spent time in Turkey, France, and Norway before retiring permanently to Mexico. While in exile, he wrote extensively against Stalin's communism and expounded on his own version of communism, which featured a state of permanent revolution. In 1940, Stalin sent an assassination squad to kill Trotsky but he survived. Later that year, though, an assassin drove the pick of an ice axe into Trotsky's skull, mortally wounding him. Within days, Trotsky was dead.

In 1928, Stalin instituted the first of the Five Year Plans, the economic replacement for Lenin's NEP. Stalin's goal was a new, industrialized Soviet Union. He would achieve this goal with Five Year Plans that specifically defined what the goals were for the nation's heavy industry, agriculture, and so on. The first Five Year Plan, to run from 1929 to 1933, set very high goals. Industrial production was to increase over twofold and agricultural production one and a half times. To accomplish the agricultural goals, Stalin arranged for about one out of every five peasants to give up their own land and work on collective farms. Stalin hoped to boost the economy and simultaneously get rid of any lasting economic freedoms left over from the NEP.

Stalin also wanted to deal with the problem of the peasants. The hard-core socialists believed that landed peasants would one day drift toward capitalism and pose a threat to the communist state. In a process known as collectivization, Stalin moved the poorest peasants to collective farms. The better-off peasants, though, often met a different fate. Known as *kulaks*, the better-off peasants became targets for Stalin's brutality. Stalin wanted the kulaks gone—all of them. Many were deported to Siberia or to forced labor camps. Those who offered the least bit of protest or resistance were shot immediately. Most were never heard from again.

This plan did not pay off. The first Five Year Plans saw virtually no increase in agricultural efficiency. Nevertheless, within 10 years, 9 out of every 10 peasant families had been removed from their land. The loss of life in the process of collectivization boggles the mind. Stalin actually told Winston Churchill that he estimated 10 million of his own people died during the process. The process of industrialization, however, greatly improved under the plan. Steel production alone increased five-fold during the first two plans. Society suffered, though, and dealt constantly with food shortages, harsh conditions, and repressive measures from Stalin.

The peasantry weren't the only ones who suffered in the Stalin regime. Those closest to Stalin were never safe, especially once the Great Purges began in the 1930s. In order to become an absolute, autocratic ruler, Stalin had to eliminate people around him, and anyone else he could find who opposed his regime. He launched an offensive against enemies of the state beginning with his closest advisor. Stalin had his secret police make literally millions of arrests. Those arrested included government officials, workers, peasants, intellectuals, and members of the military. In all, Stalin purged several million Soviets. Some estimates place the number of dead near 7 million; other estimates soar as high as 10 million. These deaths were the result of executions as well as deaths in labor camps. Those targeted in the purges either died, suffered torture, or found themselves in Siberian labor camps. While there certainly were those who opposed Stalin, especially once he reached the pinnacle of Soviet power, Stalin's paranoia got the best of him, costing countless Soviets their lives.

The Soviet Union under Stalin's iron-fisted regime certainly wasn't what millions of Communist followers envisioned when Lenin took control years before. The people had wanted a government unlike the one under the long line of czars, which would be sympathetic to the workers, a government that would create a people's state. Though Lenin and Stalin steered the Soviet Union away from the old czarist Russia and got the economy moving again, they abandoned the Marxist philosophy that would have eventually caused the government to disappear and be replaced by a classless society. Stalin was power-hungry and would never consider relinquishing control. The result, Stalin's purges, was one of the worst tragedies in all of human history.

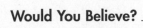

Would You Believe?

The head of the secret police was finally relieved of his duty, tried for treason, and shot. Some historians believe Stalin had this done to shift the blame for the purges away from himself.

The Rise of Mussolini

Benito Mussolini (1883–1945) was the original practitioner of the form of government known as *fascism*. Hitler, like Mussolini, would turn to fascism as his political system of choice. Fascists, unlike Communists, had no interest in elevating or equalizing the classes. Fascists had as their primary motive the promotion and glorification of the state. Industry and war were two of the primary ways fascists glorified the state.

War held great Romantic value for the fascists. To incite the people to support the state in its endeavors, fascists used intense nationalism, in particular the theme of the common enemy. The use of government propaganda and government control of the media were highly effective tools for fascists. The elimination of second and third parties also helped unite the people to the common cause of the state. Also unlike Communists, fascists had no interest in state-controlled means of production. When the state needed industrial production it simply commanded the private sector to do what was necessary. Individuals were subordinate to the state in every aspect of their lives.

Define Your Terms

The word **fascism** derives from the Latin *fasces*, or an ax with a bundle of sticks tied around it, the symbol of civic unity in ancient Rome.

Benito Mussolini created the *Fasci de Combattimento*, or the League of Combat in 1919. Mussolini and many others were glad that Italy finally entered the First World War but they felt betrayed and let down by the Treaty of Versailles. The *Facsi* gave like-minded Italians a voice for their frustrations. Most of the members feared the spread of communism and socialism into Italy from Europe, too; for fascists, there was always an enemy somewhere.

Despite being frustrated with the parliamentary system under King Victor Emmanuel III (1869–1947), Mussolini joined parliament in 1921. Parliament proved inefficient and, in Mussolini's opinion, inept. Mussolini organized a squadron of thugs known as *squadristi*, who terrorized and threatened socialists and Communists not to run for election. In 1922, Mussolini and his fascists organized a massive march on Rome to demand a new government. Though not really threatened by the march, King Victor Emmanuel III knew that he had to give power either to the fascists or the socialists in order to prevent a civil war between the two groups. In October 1922, Victor Emmanuel named Mussolini prime minister, the youngest ever in Italian history. Victor Emmanuel remained king of Italy, although the power lay with Mussolini.

Mussolini's first order of business was to establish complete control. With the help of the Parliament, Mussolini assumed dictatorial powers for one year to fix Italy's problems. He changed voting methods, rigged elections, instituted strict censorship, and bullied opponents with his brigands, the Blackshirts. In 1925, he assumed complete control of the government. He used propaganda to spread the message of fascism and to hype himself as "the great leader," or *Il Duce*. He used the schools, taught by teachers who had taken an oath of allegiance to fascism, to indoctrinate the schoolchildren of Italy and he encouraged fascist youth organizations. He used dramatic speeches to instill fascist values, especially intense nationalism, in crowds who cheered him wildly.

Would You Believe?

In 1929, to secure the support of Italian Catholics, Mussolini recognized the sovereignty of the Vatican in return for papal recognition of the fascist Italian state.

Mussolini never created the totalitarian regime of Hitler and Stalin, though, and he never committed the atrocities of the other two. He hoped to help the peasants and workers, although he often gave special concessions to big business and industry. He never even destroyed the monarchy, and he went to the pope for support.

The Rise of Hitler

Perhaps the most infamous man in all of history, Adolf Hitler (1889–1945) actually may rank second behind Joseph Stalin in terms of lives taken. Nevertheless, Hitler definitely made his mark on the world through brutality and iron-fisted rule. Ironically, Hitler's rise to power was not what might be expected of a ruthless dictator. Born in Austria, Hitler spent much time in Vienna, where he fell under the influence of the mayor of Vienna, Karl Lueger (1844–1910), an anti-Semite, and Hitler was set upon his path toward fierce nationalism and anti-Semitism.

Hitler joined the German army in 1913 and served in World War I. After the war, Hitler developed the idea that a Jewish and Communist conspiracy had cost Germany the war. Hitler became politically active and joined the German Workers' Party. Within just a few years, Hitler had taken control of the party and had attracted many new party members. He took his party and marched on a beer hall in Munich in an attempt to overthrow the local government and then the failing government of the Weimar Republic; the attempt was known as the Beer Hall Putsch. When the storming of the beer hall failed to produce the desired effect, World War I General Ludendorff convinced Hitler and his men to march on the Defense Ministry building, where things deteriorated. The takeover didn't go so well and Hitler ended up being tried and jailed. In jail, having plenty of time to think, Hitler planned a legal rather than a forceful takeover of the government.

Would You Believe?

In 1918, Hitler suffered temporary blindness as a result of an attack with poisonous gas.

Hitler worked hard to find members for his National Socialist German Workers' Party, or Nazi Party, and managed to get membership to about 100,000. That membership won twelve seats in the German legislature, or *Reichstag*, in 1928. Only four years later, as the Great Depression took hold in Germany, Hitler's pro-socialism and anti-capitalism message reaped big rewards to the tune of having the largest party in the *Reichstag*. His message appealed especially to the lower and middle classes of workers and to the disillusioned German youth.

Hitler ran for president in 1932 but lost. Then in 1933, unable to cooperate with the Nazi-dominated *Reichstag*, President Paul von Hindenburg (1847–1934) appointed Hitler chancellor and appointed two other Nazis to key positions. In February, the *Reichstag* fell victim to arson and Hitler persuaded Hindenburg to suspend civil liberties "until further notice." The March 1933 elections once again put Nazis in control of the *Reichstag*, which in late March passed the Enabling Act, giving Hitler dictatorial powers. Shortly thereafter the government banned all other political parties. When President Hindenburg died in 1934, the government combined the offices of president and chancellor, and Hitler had total control of the government as *Fuhrer* for four years.

With supreme power, Hitler declared "A Thousand Year Reich," or empire, and proceeded to win the favor of the German people. To rein in all threats to his power, Hitler arrested and executed some 1,000 SA or storm trooper leaders. The storm troopers were the Nazi paramilitary organization often known as brownshirts; the brown uniforms distinguished them from the blackshirts, the Nazis' protective squadron known as the SS. The execution of the SA leadership took place on what has become known as the Night of the Long Knives in 1934. The SS eventually became the premier Nazi fighting force and, under the direction of Heinrich Himmler (1900–1945), assumed the responsibilities of the Gestapo, or the German secret police. Hitler required that the military swear an oath of loyalty to him personally. Hitler stood as the supreme commander of the government and the military.

Under the Third Reich, the first two empires being the Holy Roman Empire and the Prussian Empire, Hitler instituted a system of fascism much like Mussolini in Italy. Hitler greatly expanded the German economy, mostly through the expansion of the military and industry. He also constructed numerous roads, highways, dams, and other public works projects. Whether the average German actually enjoyed a better standard of living as Hitler promised has been debated, however. Hitler controlled the culture of Germany in the same way he did the economy and the politics. Like a good fascist, he encouraged men to work and women to stay home where they could have and raise children. By sending women home from the workplace, German propagandists claimed that unemployment reached an all-time low; that fact remained true only because the workforce had been reduced drastically.

Appeasement—Seemed Like a Good Idea at the Time

After the First World War, Europeans didn't want to fight anymore. They wanted to try to pick up the pieces of their lives. Governments wanted to get economies back on track. Both citizens and governments found their desires hard to satisfy, though. Doom and gloom prevailed for a while before prosperity returned. The prosperity was short-lived, though, because so much of the money going back into the economies of Europe was borrowed. As hard times hit in 1930, radical political groups emerged all over Europe because the established governments didn't seem to be getting the job done. Tensions remained among a few nations; however, none wanted to go back to fighting. The League of Nations convinced itself that it would actually be able to prevent war in the future.

Would You Believe?

As the governments changed under Stalin, Hitler, and Mussolini, European nations took notice but did little else. Though nations like France and England weren't particularly fond of dictatorships, no one wanted trouble, so they didn't dare rock the boat by interfering in other nations' affairs.

Not surprisingly, with all that was preoccupying the rest of Europe, nobody noticed as Germany picked itself up and dusted itself off. Germany's government seemed to be turning things around. Maybe the people didn't benefit much, but production was way up. Hitler worried a number of leaders, but the moderate national leaders didn't want to instigate anything;

there was already enough post-war tension. Therefore, other than the equivalent of a few stern glances in his direction, Hitler didn't have to deal with much interference as he carried out his master plan. In short, the nations that watched Hitler rise to power and annex territories chose appeasement, or nonaction in order to maintain harmony, over confrontation.

The Rough Interwar Years

The interwar years were toughest on Germany, Russia, and France. The Soviet people suffered under Stalin, but his Five Year Plans got production and the economy going. Germany finally managed to expand its economy and its production when the reparations no longer choked the life out of the German budget. France, though, struggled mightily as did Britain. France in particular had counted on the German reparation payments to help rebuild, but what payments did come in did little to stabilize France's economic crisis.

Economically, France struggled with stabilizing its currency and controlling prices. Politically, France experienced unbelievable turnover during the interwar years; the average French government between the two world wars lasted about a year. Diplomatically, France found itself at odds with almost everyone over its harsh demands of Germany.

Britain's economic and political landscape, though not as stormy as France's, faced uncertainty. The British had a difficult time readjusting to peacetime life. Labor lashed out at management. Control of the government went back and forth from one party to the other. When the Depression hit, Britain's leaders quarreled and dragged their feet. The government experienced more turnover just as things heated up with Germany again. David Lloyd George resigned and Neville Chamberlain (1869–1940) succeeded him, but foreign policy did not change.

In eastern Europe, the fledgling states experienced quite a few growing pains. Poland and Hungary found themselves under dictatorial control and the other eastern states, save Czechoslovakia, barely got by; Czechoslovakia actually did fairly well, but nationalism sent many running for Nazi Germany once the Depression hit.

In Spain, leftists and monarchists battled over the government in an all-out civil war. In 1931, the Spanish monarchy was unseated and a

Would You Believe?

Pablo Picasso's famous painting *Guernica* represented the horrors of the Nationalist bombing of the town of Guernica during the Spanish Civil War. As the bombs fell, Nationalists massacred people while they tried to escape.

provisional government installed in its place. For several years the nation stood divided between monarchists and socialists. Fed up with the chaos, General Francisco Franco (1892–1975) led a group of generals in an overthrow of the government. Hitler and Mussolini both offered support to Franco while the Soviet Union, as well as liberal idealists from everywhere, supported the Republicans, or those fighting Franco. Franco and his Nationalists finally won the war in 1939, and Spain remained a dictatorship until 1975.

Hitler Breaks Some Rules

With so much going on in Europe, Hitler believed, arrogantly but correctly, that no one would notice if he bent the rules just a little. Hitler and all of Germany resented the Treaty of Versailles and he had no intention of following it. In 1935, after establishing control of the government and the military, Hitler instituted a military draft, a direct violation of the Treaty of Versailles. In the same year, he began work on a bigger, stronger navy and a new air force known as the *Luftwaffe*. France and Britain protested but Hitler was undeterred. A year later, Hitler secretly moved his troops into the Rhineland, the area that was set aside as a demilitarized zone. Hitler instructed his troops to retreat if France showed even the slightest resistance. France did nothing.

As a Matter of Fact

When Adolf Hitler marched his troops into the Rhineland in 1936, he rolled the dice and held his breath. Hitler gambled that France would do nothing about the presence of some 32,000 Nazi troops. His troops had orders to retreat at the slightest hint of resistance, but the French did nothing and the gamble paid off. Hitler later said, "If France had then marched into the Rhineland, we would have had to withdraw with our tails between our legs." Hitler also commented that the 48 hours following the initial occupation were the most nerve-racking of his career.

Since nobody seemed to mind too much, Hitler pushed for unification with Austria. After successfully adding Austria, Hitler targeted the Sudetenland, part of Czechoslovakia inhabited by many Germans. This finally prompted the Munich Conference in 1938; Europe had started to worry about Hitler's rearmament and aggression. Hitler exaggerated his strength through inflated military figures, and no one wanted to call his bluff—even though he appeared to have exceeded the parameters laid out in the Treaty of Versailles.

Europe expected war but the conference accomplished its goal; war had been averted. The Munich Agreement gave Hitler the Sudetenland as long as he agreed to stop there. Of course Hitler agreed. Britain's Chamberlain returned to England and told cheering crowds that he believed they had secured "peace in our time." *Time* magazine made Hitler their 1938 Man of the Year. Given Hitler's track record, why was anyone surprised when Hitler took the rest of Czechoslovakia in 1939?

The Price of Appeasement

After Hitler took Czechoslovakia, Britain and France finally mobilized their troops. Hoping to avoid another war at all costs, the European powers had repeatedly ignored Hitler, his rearmament, his aggression toward weaker states, and his blatant disregard for the Treaty of Versailles. The powers generally did not fear Hitler the way they feared Stalin, so perhaps they didn't take him seriously. They also thought the League of Nations would handle problems like Hitler. Pretty much every member of the League agreed to use force if a member nation were attacked, but the League wasn't unanimous on using force against belligerent nations. No nation in Europe had the budget to rearm after the First World War, and challenging Hitler probably would have required building armed forces again.

Regardless of the reasons, the appeasement of Hitler cost Europe dearly in the long run. Hitler, of course, didn't stop after Czechoslovakia. In August, he signed a secret treaty with Stalin known as the Molotov-Ribbentrop Pact or the Non-Aggression Pact. The pact earned its name because of the two agents who negotiated for their leaders: Vyacheslav Molotov (1890–1986) for Stalin and Joachim von Ribbentrop (1893–1946) for Hitler. With the treaty, the two nations agreed not to fight in case of war. The treaty also included a secret provision for the mutual division of states like Poland and Finland after the fighting ceased.

Total War

At first, the Second World War remained isolated on the continent of Europe, but it soon grew to involve nations from six continents. The invasion of Poland generally marks the beginning of the war, but Japan had invaded China two years earlier. As the war unfolded, the Allied Powers of Britain, France, Poland, and eventually the United States fought against the Axis Powers of Germany, Italy, and Japan. Australia, South Africa, and Canada also declared war on Germany a few days after the Polish invasion. Yugoslavia, China, and the Soviet Union eventually joined forces with the Allies, while Bulgaria, Romania, Hungary, and Finland joined the Axis Powers. By the time the war ended, it would be the deadliest and costliest in human history.

Britain and France Finally React

Britain suspected Hitler was up to no good but could do little more than issue an ultimatum to Germany. Hoping that France would follow its lead, Britain advised Germany that Poland would receive British assistance if Hitler invaded. Nevertheless, Hitler invaded Poland on September 1, 1939, and took it in just four weeks using a style of warfare known as the *blitzkrieg*, or lightning war. Totally different than any style of warfare used in World War I, the *blitzkrieg* was a quick attack using planes and tanks. Hitler could have taken Poland even more quickly, but German troops committed atrocities on their way through in an attempt to annihilate as many Poles and Jews as possible.

The British and the French officially gave Hitler two days to withdraw from Poland, but Hitler ignored them. Britain and France declared war when the two days had expired. Though the Allies declared war on September 3, the only war initially was a "confetti war" of anti-Nazi propaganda dropped over Germany. This period of cold war was called the "sitzkrieg." The real fighting began in 1940 with the Nazi takeover of Denmark and Norway, followed by the much-anticipated invasion of Belgium and France. The British and French were ready for the Germans in Belgium, where they had dug in with obsolete World War I-style trenches. Little did they know how effective the *blitzkrieg* would be against the old, ineffective style of warfare.

The British found themselves squeezed between two German armies, only managing to save the army by executing the miraculous evacuation of 300,000 of their troops using every available ship and fishing boat on the Channel. Within a week, German *Luftwaffe* air raids flew over Paris, and 10 days later the Germans broke the French defenses and marched toward Paris. On May 22, 1940, France gave up and Hitler installed the so-called Vichy government of French collaborators. For the duration of the war, resistance forces and underground agents led by Charles de Gaulle (1890–1970) fought against the Vichy regime.

Britain knew that Hitler planned to use France and Belgium as a launch pad for an invasion of the British Isles, so it took drastic measures. In Operation Catapult, Britain gave the French fleet several options to avoid falling into German hands, but the French wouldn't cooperate. In a terribly difficult and tragic decision, the British sunk its ally's fleet and killed over a thousand sailors.

Just a week after Operation Catapult, the first German bombers began their air war on Britain. The air attack culminated on Eagle Day in August when Germany attempted the knockout punch with 1,400 aircraft attacking England. Winston Churchill (1874–1965) inspired his people and the Royal Air Force withstood the attacks. In fact, the RAF lost one third as many planes as the *Luftwaffe*.

After the failure of Eagle Day, Hitler committed a major error. He ordered the *Luftwaffe* to move away from military and industrial targets and commence attacks on civilians in the cities, hoping to brutally crush the spirit of the British. This tactical error allowed British production to continue enough to keep it in the war; furthermore, the fearful but inspired British remained undaunted despite heavy civilian casualties, especially in London. After months of the Battle of Britain, Hitler gave up on the idea of invading Britain.

Britain found itself engaged in the Mediterranean, too, as Italy joined the war against France and Britain. After an initial success in Africa against the British, the Italians performed miserably. In Egypt and Greece, for example, Mussolini got in over his head against superior forces. In North Africa, Hitler had to step in by sending his premier tank commander, Field Marshal Erwin Rommel (1891–1944). Hitler also deployed troops to Greece. The Germans took Greece pretty easily but they got bogged down in the deserts of North Africa. Italy's poor showing ultimately cost Hitler much-needed forces, busy cleaning up Mussolini's mess.

Continental Quotes

Let us therefore brace ourselves to our duty, and so bear ourselves that, if the British Commonwealth and the Empire last for a thousand years, men will still say, 'This was their finest hour'."

—Winston Churchill in 1940 in preparing his nation for the Battle of Britain

Would You Believe?

As Germany bombed Britain, British bombers were returning the favor by firebombing Berlin. The air war of World War II was the first of its kind in human history.

Russia and the United States Get Involved

Had Hitler read *The Complete Idiot's Guide to European History*, he would have known from Napoleon's example that an invasion of Russia is an ill-advised undertaking (see Chapter 15). Nevertheless, as he had planned all along, Hitler turned on his pseudo-ally Stalin and invaded Russia in June 1941, estimating that his superior army could take Russia in six weeks. Shortly after the invasion, Stalin ordered the execution of the scorched-earth policy. As the Germans advanced, the retreating Soviet armies and civilians burned everything as they went. For an army that counted on living off the land it invaded, this was a devastating blow. The Germans pushed onward, though, and approached Moscow by October. The Russian citizens dug barbed-wire-covered trenches around the entire city, however, and stopped the German advance.

The winter of 1941 marked a turning point for the Russians as major as the Battle of Britain had for the Brits. With winter setting in, Hitler ordered the German troops to continue their advance even though they had only summer uniforms. The winter took its toll on the Germans just as it did on Napoleon's men. The winter of early 1942 really did them in as the Soviet air defense and the outrageous weather conditions prevented the Germans from resupplying. As German soldiers froze and starved, the German general in command defied Hitler and surrendered. The battle for Stalingrad, a major city to the south, proved costly for Germany but the Russians sustained astronomical losses, too. The siege of the city cost the two sides some two million lives. By holding out as long as they did, the Russians outlasted the Germans and scored a major victory.

Would You Believe?

Millions and millions of Russian soldiers, civilians, and Jews died at the hands of the Germans as they marched through Russia. The Germans were working toward one of Hitler's goals for western Russia: depopulate the land as much as possible so that Germans could pour in and settle the land when the war was over.

No Quiet on the Eastern Front

Japan was already in a bad mood by 1941. It had hoped to conquer all of eastern Asia, including the eastern part of the Soviet Union, ideally with Germany's help. But Germany signed the Non-Aggression Pact with Stalin and ruined that plan; nevertheless, Japan signed the Tripartite Act with Germany and Italy in 1940. Thus began the Axis Powers. Then in 1940, the United States, in reaction to Japan's hostile actions toward Indochina, enacted embargoes on iron, steel, and petroleum to Japan that drastically hurt the Japanese economy. The United States turned up the heat in mid–1941 when it placed an embargo on oil to Japan, too. In November 1941, the Japanese fleet set sail eastward toward the tiny Hawaiian Islands and launched a sneak attack on the U.S. naval base at Pearl Harbor.

Until the December 7 attack, the United States remained officially neutral but not actually neutral. Like Europe, the United States didn't want to fight another war. As a result of the isolationism but out of a desire to help the "good guys," the United States sent aid to the Allies via the Lend-Lease Act; technically, the United States was loaning and leasing equipment to the Allies, who would settle up later, but everyone knew the United States would never get the supplies back. After the Pearl Harbor attack, the United States declared war on Japan, and Germany declared war on the United States. The war was now truly global.

The entry of the United States into the war made an impact rather quickly, at least in the Pacific Theatre. Early in 1942, the United States launched its war in the Pacific aimed at defeating Japan through naval and air battles and occupation of Pacific islands, a strategy known as island hopping. The Battle of Midway in June 1942 helped turn the tide against the Japanese in favor of the United States, and it put the Japanese on the defensive.

In late 1942, American troops made their initial contribution in North Africa with Operation Torch. In 1943, President Franklin Roosevelt and Prime Minister Winston Churchill met in Casablanca in modern-day Morocco and discussed strategy. They planned an Allied invasion of Europe via the English Channel in 1944 and they sent word to Stalin that they would help defeat Germany. The two decided most importantly that they would accept nothing but "unconditional surrender" from Germany. Later that year in Tehran, Iran, the two leaders met with Stalin and decided to take out Germany first, then Japan; Stalin agreed to help against Japan once Germany had been defeated.

Unconditional Surrender

The newly strengthened Allied forces made serious headway against the Axis Powers in late 1942. After the British defeated the Germans at El-Alamein in North Africa, Allied troops invaded North Africa in Operation Torch. With Rommel, the "Desert Fox," temporarily away from the front lines, the Allies took 1,000 miles of African coastline. The allies invaded Sicily in mid–1943 and then invaded mainland Italy and knocked Mussolini out of the war altogether. After a pivotal battle at Kursk between Soviet and German armored divisions, the Soviet armies forced Germany into a westward retreat. As the Soviets pushed westward back through Russia, Ukraine, and Poland, they discovered evidence of the atrocities that had been committed by the Germans.

> **Would You Believe?**
>
> It was during the German westward retreat and the Soviet pursuit of the Germans through Poland that Soviet troops discovered the first proof of German concentration camps.

After German double-agents helped convince the Germans that the Allied invasion of Europe would take place at the English Channel's narrowest point, the Allies launched Operation Overlord under the direction of U.S. General Dwight Eisenhower (1890–1969). On June 6, 1944, the Allies invaded the beaches at Normandy—not the narrowest point at all—almost immediately after the Allies liberated Rome. Over the following weeks, two million Allied troops would enter France in the largest invasion by sea in history. After weeks of bitter and bloody fighting, the Allies finally pushed inland and reached Paris on August 25.

By late 1944, the Allies had Germany surrounded. Germans who saw the writing on the wall made several attempts on Hitler's life, but none succeeded. German troops made one last surge toward Antwerp in the Battle of the Bulge, an attempt to salvage victory with a surprise attack in the Ardennes forests. Initially the Germans were successful, but Allied troops finally drove the Germans back in January 1945. Stalin, Churchill, and Roosevelt met in the Crimean resort of Yalta and decided, first, to have Allied troops meet in Berlin and, second, to divide Germany into zones of occupation after the war.

As the end drew near, things fell apart quickly for the Axis Powers. The Soviets liberated eastern Europe by March and Vienna by April. In late April, U.S. and Soviet troops met in Germany and surrounded Berlin. Hitler committed suicide in his Berlin bunker, though he had ordered his troops and the newly conscripted army in Berlin to fight to the death. Only days earlier, Italians had executed Mussolini in Italy. Germany surrendered a week later, and May 8 became known as V-E Day, or Victory in Europe Day.

In the Pacific theater, now-President Harry S. Truman (1884–1972), who assumed presidential responsibilities upon the death of President Franklin D. Roosevelt (1882–1945) due to a cerebral hemorrhage in April 1945, considered the possibility of using atomic weapons to avoid an American invasion of the Japanese mainland. After intelligence reported that perhaps a million American lives would be lost taking Japan, the United States dropped an atomic bomb on Hiroshima, Japan, on August 6, and another on Nagasaki, Japan, on August 9. Less than a week later, Japan surrendered. August 15 became V-J Day. The war finally had drawn to a close. Historians estimate that as many as 50 million people died in World War II.

Would You Believe?

As horrific as the effects of the atomic bombs were, the incendiary bombing attacks conducted earlier on Japan killed more people than did the atomic bombs.

The Holocaust

Perhaps the saddest and most disturbing chapter in all of human history was written during World War II. While the Allies worked to put down the Axis Powers' political aggressions, the Germans quietly worked to eliminate as many Jews, eastern Europeans, and "impure breeds" of humans as they could. The word *Holocaust* derives from a Latin word the Romans used to describe a sacrifice completely consumed by fire in ancient Judaism. The word has come to be associated with the atrocities and mass executions of the Jews and others between about 1938 and 1945.

The Holocaust resulted from the deep anti-Semitism Hitler developed as a youth and the intense German nationalism he felt. German nationalism prior to World War II promoted a sense of German superiority that suggested other ethnicities were somehow less human. Hitler used this anti-Semitism and nationalism as part of his master plan to depopulate as much of eastern Europe as possible to create "living space" for his superior race. He targeted not only Jews but also Poles, Ukrainians, Gypsies or Roma, and homosexuals. Sadly, few heeded his warnings—and there were warnings.

Would You Believe?

Jews have suffered persecution time and time again throughout European history. The Crusaders attacked Jews en route to the Holy Land, people blamed the Black Death on a Jewish conspiracy, and Jews were not allowed in England for centuries prior to Cromwell's protectorate. The Holocaust was, by far, the worst persecution of Jews not just in European history but in human history.

He Said It in *Mein Kampf*

Adolf Hitler began dictating *Mein Kampf*, which translates to "My Struggle," while in jail in the early 1920s. In his book, which is somewhat autobiographical, Hitler tells of early experiences that contributed to his anti-Semitism. He even presented himself as the "superman" or "superhuman" of which Nietzsche wrote. Hitler rambled on about "the Jewish peril" and the conspiracy among Jews to take over Europe and the world. He spoke of Jews as "parasites" and questioned the value of Jewish life. He used convoluted logic to divide up all of humanity into different races with the blonde-haired, blue-eyed Aryans at the top of the order. The Jews and Gypsies or Roma were at the bottom of the order.

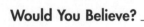

Would You Believe?

The Gypsies, or Roma, who also suffered terribly at the hands of the Nazis, use their language to describe the atrocities as "The Devouring."

According to Hitler, the Jews were hurting the Aryans by holding them back in lives of mediocre equality rather than their natural superiority. He even mentioned the use of gas on the Jews, but not in the context of concentration camps. He hated the Communists, too, and hoped to one day eliminate them. The best estimates show that some 10 million copies of the book circulated through Germany by the end of the war, even though many people purchased the book just to show support of the Nazi party.

The Jewish Problem

In 1942, a group of Nazi officials met at the Wannsee Conference to discuss the so-called "Jewish question" or "Jewish problem." The leaders of the conference wanted to realize Hitler's dream of living space for Germany. To do so, however, meant removing the inferior races like Gypsies and Jews from Germany, Poland, and other eastern European lands. The talk focused on physically moving the Jews and sterilizing those who could not be moved. The conference then dealt with who exactly the Jews were and how to determine which people would and could be classified as Jews. The transcripts of the conference revealed that the delegates discussed a "final solution," a target of 11 million; they did not specifically address how, other than deportation, this number was to be reached. The transcripts made it clear, though, that the deportation of the Jews had become more tedious and expensive than the Nazis had hoped. That, perhaps, served as motivation for the use of the death camps and concentration camps in Poland.

Concentration Camps

Persecution of the Jews by the Nazi party began in 1938 with the *Kristallnacht*, or Night of the Broken Glass, when Nazis ruthlessly destroyed Jewish synagogues, businesses, and homes. Thereafter, Nazis moved the Jews to ghettos. In the invasions of Poland and the Soviet Union, the Nazis shot Jews on sight and then moved on to mass executions, which gradually became more and more organized and planned.

As the numbers of Jews who had to be "dealt with" increased, the Nazis in 1940 began constructing camps where mass executions could be carried out on a regular basis. Almost all such camps were in Poland and were supervised by Heinrich Himmler's SS troops. Although some prisoners of these camps did hard labor, most prisoners arrived and faced execution almost right away. The camps used large gas chambers and incinerators to kill those who arrived daily. German scientists and "doctors" also performed gruesome and torturous experiments on countless prisoners. All told, some six million Jews and perhaps that many Slavs, Gypsies, and homosexuals died in the concentration camps. The worst of the concentration camps was located at Auschwitz, where a million or more died.

The Nuremburg Trials

After World War II, a series of trials were held at the Nuremburg Palace of Justice in Nuremburg, Germany. As Allied troops made their way through Poland and discovered the horrors of the extermination camps, word spread quickly. After the war, the Allies rounded up as many "war criminals" as could be located, including those responsible for the concentration camps.

The most famous of the trials at Nuremburg was the International Military Tribunal from 1945 to 1946. The Tribunal tried the Nazis for crimes against peace, war crimes, and crimes against humanity. Among those on trial were Hermann Göring, commander of the Luftwaffe; Rudolph Hess; Joachim von Ribbentrop; and Alfred Rosenberg, mastermind behind many racial and ethnic Nazi policies. Though Hess was sentenced to life in prison, the others mentioned here received the death penalty. The trials resulted in the Nuremburg Principles and the Nuremburg Code, which strictly prohibit crimes against humanity, such as those performed by the Nazis.

Would You Believe?

The Nuremburg Trials were bound by no rules of evidence. The tribunal was allowed to hear and consider any evidence it deemed useful.

The Least You Need to Know

◆ During the interwar years, European nations faced economic and political uncertainty. As a result, many Europeans looked for strong, confident leaders.

◆ The nations of Europe wanted so badly to remain at peace after World War I that they allowed Hitler to ignore the Treaty of Versailles, build his armies, and conquer territories.

◆ Finally, after the invasion of Poland in 1939, Britain and France declared war on Germany. The Soviet Union joined the Allies against the Germans after Hitler invaded Russia and the United States joined after Japan's attack on Pearl Harbor.

◆ Germany finally succumbed to the Allies after the Allies invaded France via Operation Overlord and pushed through France toward Germany. The Allied and Soviet forces met in Berlin.

◆ Japan surrendered only after the United States dropped two atomic bombs on Japan, one at Hiroshima and one at Nagasaki.

◆ The war cost humanity some 50 million or more lives, including 10 million or more victims of Nazi genocide.

Chapter 22

The Cold War Era

In This Chapter

- ◆ The rivalry between east and west
- ◆ Rebuilding after the war
- ◆ Coming out of the Cold War
- ◆ European powers say goodbye to their colonies
- ◆ The economy takes hit after hit

People around the world celebrated the end of the war. Perhaps their celebrations were premature, though. Germany and Japan, both guilty of aggression and crimes against humanity, had been defeated. Subjugated nations had been liberated. Prisoners who were sure to die had been freed from captivity. The hated Hitler and Mussolini were dead. All that remained to do was to put the pieces back together.

But the victors of World War II never saw eye to eye about much of anything after the war, or even before the war for that matter. The idealistic United States and the iron-fisted and aggressively Communist Stalin had different visions for the European landscape. During the war the two sides were merely military allies against a dictator bent on the domination of Europe—strange bedfellows who would never have cooperated in anything else. Immediately after the war, the two sides went in opposite directions.

What resulted was a long and bitter relationship of fierce rivalry and competition between two nations and the allies of those nations. Over the next 45 years, the world seemed to divide into two camps and two spheres of influence—the east and the west. The tense relationship between the two parts of the world deteriorated into a war of wills and words known as the Cold War. The Cold War featured diplomatic and economic warfare but not military warfare, at least not between the United States and the Soviet Union. Against the backdrop of this Cold War, Europe made a remarkable recovery after World War II.

Nations United or United Nations?

The United States and Britain teamed with the Soviet Union only to knock out Germany. They signed no treaties, long-term agreements, or any other documents obligating them to future cooperation. When the Big Three, as they were known, met in Tehran, Iran, to finalize strategies for the remainder of the conflict, Roosevelt and Stalin agreed to surround Germany and meet in Berlin. They did just that in 1945. By doing so, the powers gave Europe a sign of things to come. The American and British forces were the saviors of western Europe while the Soviet Union, alone, was the savior of eastern Europe. The two sides were not partners, though.

Even before the fighting ceased in 1945, a new organization was in the works in San Francisco. Representatives from 50 nations met to draft a charter for an organization known as the United Nations, a name suggested by Franklin Roosevelt; the representatives left a blank for Poland, which signed later. Open to "peace-loving states," the United Nations Organization was designed to be an international peace-keeping organization much as the League of Nations had once hoped to be. The premise of the organization was collective security. The organization hoped to prevent future wars, protect human rights, offer assistance in times of crisis, aid in peace-keeping after conflicts, and deal with issues like arms races and atomic weapons.

The organization officially began operations in October 1945 after the Security Council ratified the charter. The permanent members of the Security Council were China, France, the Soviet Union, the United States, and Britain. The Security Council members may not have been political bedfellows but they all, at least theoretically, valued peace. The organization finally dropped the "O" from its name in the 1950s and became the UN. Fittingly, the UNO General Assembly's first item on its first agenda in 1946 was the issue of atomic weapons.

Would You Believe?

The UN created the state of Israel in 1948 as a homeland for Jews.

Pre–Cold War Tensions

Stalin's occupation of eastern Europe bothered the Allies, but there was nothing they could do about it. This created tension that complicated the task of deciding Germany's fate after Germany's unconditional surrender, as well as the fate of eastern European states. The powers agreed at Yalta that after Germany was defeated, it and Berlin would be divided up into zones of occupation. The zones were to be administered by the victors. The powers had a much more difficult time deciding the fate of eastern Europe, though, since Stalin had basically occupied the states as his troops moved through.

Roosevelt had no real grounds on which to tell Stalin to leave countries like Bulgaria, Romania, and Czechoslovakia. Because the United States traditionally pushed self-determination, Roosevelt and Churchill could only hope that Stalin eventually would pull out of eastern Europe; they knew that Soviet influence in the eastern states would not soon go away. Reluctantly, the Big Three agreed that the eastern states were to have freely elected governments. As part of the deal, Stalin got his wish that the eastern states would favor Russia. The tensions of the Yalta Conference carried over to the postwar conference at Potsdam in July of 1945.

The long-ill Roosevelt died and the presidency passed to Harry Truman, a staunch defender of free elections and democracy. At the conference, Truman lacked Roosevelt's conciliatory nature. He demanded free elections for the eastern European states. Stalin wasn't going to budge. Stalin knew that free elections in eastern Europe would probably mean the end of Soviet influence there, and he wasn't about to let those states slip away.

The two sides literally and figuratively were from different worlds. America, with its tradition of free elections, could not imagine states without self-determination. The Soviet Union, on the other hand, had suffered at the hands of Germany not once but twice. In Stalin's opinion, the only way to guarantee there never would be a third time was to control the states of eastern Europe so they remained loyal to the USSR and not to some other power. Stalin probably would have fought to maintain control of eastern Europe, and war was out of the question for the Allies. The Allies in Europe were exhausted from two wars in the last 30 years and had no fight left in them. The United States had the bomb but didn't feel that control of eastern Europe was worth fighting over. In eastern Europe, Stalin had won.

Would You Believe?

Winston Churchill announced in 1946 that an "iron curtain" had fallen across Europe. He meant that Germany, and the rest of Europe, had been divided into east and west.

East vs. West

Like two fighters, the east and the west went to their corners immediately following the war. Truman threw the first punch when he cut off financial aid to the Soviets in 1945. He went a step further and announced that the United States would not recognize any state established by force. In other words, the United States would not enter into any form of diplomatic or trade relations with such a state. As the western European nations outwardly showed their anti-Communist and anti-Soviet sentiments, the Communists came out of the woodwork.

Communist parties formed in western nations like Italy and France and worked to undermine capitalist ideologies. Communists throughout Europe tried desperately to convert others and to wage a verbal and philosophical war on behalf of the Soviet Union. The United States developed a plan to limit the spread of communism and to isolate Eastern Europe. The plan, known as the Truman Doctrine, was to offer support to any European state resisting communism and the Soviet Union. For starters, the United States offered military assistance to Greece and Iran, nations Stalin had already been pressuring in the short time since the end of the war. The United States knew that European nations would struggle to rebuild on their own and that democracy could ill afford for the Soviets to rush to the rescue. In 1946, U.S. Secretary of State George Marshall (1880–1959), hoping to exert democratic influence, offered financial aid to European nations. On behalf of the eastern European nations, Stalin declined the offer.

Things heated up yet again in 1948, when Stalin blockaded the western-controlled zone of Berlin, which was deep within the Soviet-controlled zone of Germany. Stalin was reacting to economic measures taken by Truman refusing to allow West German industries to pay reparations to the Soviet Union. The western zone of Berlin could be reached only by autobahn. Stalin, after closing Berlin, argued that no treaty ever guaranteed the western powers the right to travel through his zone of occupation. Technically, Stalin was right. Rather than escalate the situation with a ground attack as his advisors suggested, the Allies chose a different approach. Truman opted for an airlift to the citizens of Berlin. Beginning in late June, aircraft flew in and out of Berlin day after day for 324 days. The planes, called "raisin bombers" by the people of Berlin, carried everything from food to coal. The Soviets finally lifted the blockade on May 11, 1949, but the planes kept flying until September, just in case Stalin changed his mind. In total, the Berlin Airlift carried over two million tons of food and supplies to the citizens of Berlin, held hostage by Stalin.

As a Matter of Fact

The U.S. military nicknamed the Berlin airlift Operation Vittles. At the height of the operation, which infuriated the Soviet Union, an aircraft landed in West Berlin about once per minute. By the end of the operation, the Allies flew more than a quarter of a million flights into Berlin and gave the West Berliners more than two million tons of aid. The Soviets lifted the blockade in 1949 only after the Allies signed the North Atlantic Treaty which declared an attack on one Ally would be an attack on all of them.

NATO and the Warsaw Pact

The two sides after the war were pretty clearly delineated. However, at the time of the Berlin Airlift there existed no formal agreements between members of either side. The League of Nations didn't serve its purpose before World War II, so why would the United Nations Organization be any different? The western allies felt like they needed something tangible to prove their solidarity not to each other but to the Soviet Union. In 1949, the western allies—United States, the United Kingdom, France, Italy, Canada, Portugal, Norway, Belgium, Denmark, the Netherlands, Luxembourg, and Iceland—signed the North Atlantic Charter. Article V of the charter of the North Atlantic Treaty Organization, or NATO, stated "that an armed attack against one or more of [the member states] in Europe or North America shall be considered an attack on them all." As it turned out, the Soviets never invaded western Europe as everyone expected. The Soviets did respond to the creation of NATO, though.

Would You Believe?

The provision quoted from Article V of the NATO Charter was never invoked until after the September 11 attacks in New York City in 2001.

The Soviet Union created an organization of its own which basically mirrored the North Atlantic Treaty Organization. Ironically, the Soviets used a warmer, friendlier name for their organization. In 1955, in direct response to the threat of NATO, the Eastern Bloc nations of the Soviet Union, Poland, Hungary, Czechoslovakia, Romania, Bulgaria, and Albania signed the Warsaw Pact and formed the Treaty of Friendship, Cooperation, and Mutual Assistance. Interestingly, all the eastern European Communist states joined except for Yugoslavia. As with NATO, the members of the Warsaw Pact promised to retaliate if one of the member states were attacked. The single event that spawned the Warsaw Pact occurred in 1955 when West Germany joined NATO. East Germany, naturally, joined the Warsaw Pact in 1956. Because Stalin had died in 1953, the Soviet leader responsible for the Warsaw Pact was Nikita Khrushchev (1894–1971).

Although the Warsaw Treaty specifically stated that member states were to practice a policy of noninterference in the affairs of other member states, the body disregarded that fact twice. First, in 1956, Warsaw Pact troops interfered with the Hungarian Revolution. Though the Warsaw Pact troops initially withdrew after the government broke down, the troops reentered Hungary at the request of the leader of one of the factions. The troops quickly put down the opposing faction. Then, in 1968, Czechoslovakia criticized and condemned the Warsaw Pact and practically dared the Warsaw Pact to challenge the Czech military by vowing to defend its sovereignty by force if necessary. A large contingent of Warsaw Pact troops quickly brought Czechoslovakia back in line. Basically, the Soviet Union felt it had the right, if not the duty, to intervene any time a Communist state strayed off the path. This idea later became known as the Brezhnev Doctrine.

Would You Believe?

Albania withdrew from the Warsaw Pact after the incident in Czechoslovakia. The Warsaw Pact never again intervened in the affairs of its member states … but not because of Albanian protests.

Rising from the Ashes

Humanity really outdid itself with the Second World War. After the Great War, remembered as the War to End All Wars, nobody in Europe could have imagined anything worse, and practically everyone in Europe, aside from Germany, did everything to avoid another such war.

Europe's worst nightmares were realized, though, as the costliest and deadliest war in history played out largely in Europe. Almost miraculously, then, western Europe rebounded from the war and within a generation had become a bastion of world political, cultural, and economic leaders once again. And for the most part, the western nations accomplished this turnaround peacefully and without oppression. Eastern Europe did not experience the same recovery, mostly because of the tight Communist control over the Eastern Bloc nations that stifled the economies there.

The Devastation of the War

The cost of World War II can be counted in any number of ways. In terms of life, 50 million or more died, 10 million of them soldiers, the remaining 40 million, civilians. In many places, entire families, towns, and villages simply ceased to exist, eradicated.

National populations felt the blows of population loss, with the Soviet Union and Germany losing the greatest amount of people; the USSR lost perhaps 20 million citizens.

In terms of dollars, the devastation of the war can't be accurately measured. However, national governments ran up debts because of wartime deficit spending. Businesses and industries were wiped out. Countless individuals lost everything—homes, farms, savings, heirlooms, and more. Farmland suffered from looting, bombing, fire, and battle. Burned out trucks, tanks, and planes lay where they crashed. Bombing raids destroyed historic landmarks and architecture. Looters, particularly the Nazis, stole or lost many priceless works of art that have never been recovered. The economic outlook in Europe could hardly have been worse.

Western Europe Prospers

Just as the phoenix rose from its own ashes to live again, so did western Europe after the war. The triumph over devastation took cooperation, energy, and creative new ideas. The leaders of the most prominent western nations after the war were committed to change, cooperation, and recovery.

Part of the cooperation included the removal of old trade barriers and tariff walls. In Britain, as in other places in Europe, the socialists led the way to recovery. Despite his steadfast moral support of the British during the war, Winston Churchill was replaced by the Labour Party's Clement Atlee (1883–1967). The voters wanted to move toward a welfare state but Churchill opposed public health care and even some aspects of public education.

In France, the war hero Charles de Gaulle helped establish the Fourth Republic. He hoped for a strong central executive, but the people were wary of another Vichy regime. Despite frequent turnover in the government, the French economy did well.

In Italy, the brilliant Alcide de Gasperi (1881–1954), founder of the Christian Democrats or DC, won eight consecutive terms as Prime Minister of Italy. He and his Catholic constituents moved as far away from fascism as possible, and his reform-minded party dominated Italian politics until the 1990s.

To get their economies going again, each of these governments employed a new brand of economic policy developed by West Germans, an economic policy called a mixed economy. In the newly created Federal Republic of Germany, Konrad Adenauer (1876–1967) led the Christian Democrats much the way Gasperi did. A staunch opponent of Nazism who spent time in prison for his anti-Nazi views, Adenauer also centered his political career on Catholic values. Of the western nations,

France and Germany felt the greatest economic despair. Germany probably had the steepest hill to climb, though, because of huge population losses, severed ties with the eastern part of Germany, and the loss of those resources as well.

Would You Believe?

The Catholic Social Thought embraced by Christian Democrats included tenets such as care for the poor, protection of human rights, promotion of disarmament, and the rejection of both communism and laissez-faire economic systems.

Adenauer and his economics minister, Ludwig Erhard (1897–1977), introduced a new economic policy for West Germany known as a social market economy, featuring a state-controlled economy that emphasized low unemployment, welfare, low inflation, and social programs or public services. Theoretically, the social market economy combined some capitalism, some Catholic social thought, and some socialism. Adenauer and Erhard succeeded in reaching their financial and economic goals and engineered what Germans referred to as "the economic miracle" of prosperity in Germany.

The EEC

In 1951, the nations of France, West Germany, Italy, Belgium, Luxembourg, and the Netherlands signed a treaty that created the European Coal and Steel Community. Under the economic leadership of Frenchmen Jean Monnet (1889–1979) and Robert Schuman (1886–1963), the member nations created an economic union based on free trade. The smaller nations could not effectively compete in the European and global markets. As an economic union, though, the member states could compete in the coal and steel markets because the entire membership operated as a collective. On another level, the spirit of cooperation developed among and within the member states hopefully would help deter war in the future.

The plan worked so well that the six members created a new union in 1957 known as the European Economic Community. The new union greatly resembled the former but expanded the cooperation. By dropping tariffs and allowing free trade, the union created a huge market capable of fostering more success in each member state than they could possibly have achieved on their own. The EEC had as some of its goals complete economic unity, common prices for agricultural goods, common welfare and social programs, and similar foreign policies. The EEC would have to wait several decades before complete economic unity would be achieved. The economic

Would You Believe?

The European Coal and Steel Community dissolved in 2002 because its charter provided for a 50-year existence.

success of the EEC, later called the European Community, greatly benefited the member states. The EC's success also encouraged other nations to create economic communities and led to the eventual creation of the European Union (see Chapter 23).

A Nicer USSR?

Joseph Stalin didn't mellow in his old age. He got meaner. As the years passed, the United States slowly pulled away from western Europe as America became convinced that the western nations were going to be fine. Stalin, on the other hand, did no such thing in eastern Europe. In fact, as the Cold War wound down, Stalin tightened his grip on the satellite states and at home.

Rather than rewarding his war-torn nation for their valiant efforts against the German invaders, Stalin purged the Soviet Union again. This time the enemy was capitalism. For Stalin, war always loomed as long as capitalism lived. Therefore, he started the labor camps again and purged the Soviets of those who showed an inclination toward the evils of capitalism, western ideas, and Judaism. In the states under his influence, national leaders mirrored Stalin through collectivization of farms, reduction of civil liberties, and attacking unwanted ideologies. The only eastern state that escaped the influence of the Soviet Union was Yugoslavia under Josip Tito (1892–1980). Finally, in 1953, the "man of steel" died, leaving a mess for his successors to sort out.

No More Stalin

Stalin died after suffering an apparent stroke. After dinner with several prominent Communists, Stalin retired to his room and didn't get up in the morning. Finally, the following evening, guards found him in bad shape in his bed. Rather than rushing medical help to Stalin, the ministers took their time. Stalin finally died days later.

Some years later, theories surfaced that in fact Stalin had been murdered by one of the ministers. Although there is no way to be sure, it is reasonable to think that the ministers feared falling victim to Stalin's purges. While Stalin was alive, he created what has become known as a *cult of personality*. Stalin promoted himself as

Define Your Terms

Cult of personality is a phrase coined by Khrushchev to describe the unnatural praise and worship of an individual who purports to be a liberator or savior; examples include Stalin, Hitler, Tito, Castro, and Saddam Hussein.

much or more than he did the Fatherland and communism. Despite his oppression, people worshipped Stalin because of indoctrination and propaganda.

With Stalin out of the way, people finally started to say out loud what many had been thinking for years: things had to change. After his death, there was no clear-cut successor. Rather, a power struggle ensued between the conservative, old-school Communists who wanted to keep things the way they had always been and the reform-minded Communists who recognized that Stalin had done more harm than good for the Soviets. Among those who cried for reform the loudest was Nikita Khrushchev.

De-Stalinization

After Stalin's death, the power struggle turned ugly. The reform-minded Communists led by Khrushchev had as their main rival Lavrenty Beria (1899–1953), a rather unsavory fellow with myriad allegations against him. Khrushchev charged him with being on the British intelligence payroll and Beria eventually was tried and executed.

Khrushchev emerged in 1955 as the new leader of the Soviet Union. He went to work right away denouncing Stalin and the cruel form of communism he practiced. Khrushchev's most famous tirade against Stalin occurred in 1956 at the Twentieth Party Congress. In his speech, Khrushchev shocked the delegates with his indictment of Stalin's genocide, his torture and execution of loyal Communists, and his failures in both foreign and domestic policy. Khrushchev genuinely wanted to repair the damage that had been done in the Soviet Union. Furthermore, he wanted to undermine the power, authority, and public image of the hard-line Stalinists who opposed him politically. He recruited new party members and placed new members in leadership positions. Khrushchev made economic moves that improved life for the workers and resulted in an improved standard of living.

Khrushchev didn't stop with domestic policy. He initially wanted to reform the belligerent foreign policy that had left the Soviets isolated from the west. He shocked many within his party when he mentioned the possibility of a peaceful relationship with the west and the hated capitalists. What he meant, though, was that he perceived of the west as rivals rather than enemies. He seemed to change his tune, though, when he told the Western Diplomats in 1956, "We will bury you." However, his approach to the west remained basically the same. His tirade probably did not mean that the Soviet Union would kill the west but rather that the Soviets would still be around when the west, figuratively speaking, died. Then, in 1961, he gave East Germany his blessings for the construction of the Berlin Wall, a huge concrete wall that separated East and West Berlin.

East Germany began construction on the Berlin Wall, or *Die Berliner Mauer*, technically without the help of the Soviets. Workers constructed a barbed wire barrier around the three western sectors of Berlin. The barrier actually lay some distance inside East Berlin's territory so that in 1962 a second barrier could and would be constructed (also still on East Berlin's territory), creating a "No Man's Land" or "Death Strip" between the two barriers. Though the Berlin Wall kept East Berliners from entering West Berlin, East Germany claimed the Wall was to protect East Berlin from western aggression; its name was the Anti-Fascist Protection Wall.

By the time the Wall was completed in 1975, it stood approximately 10 feet high, more than three feet wide, and about 100 miles long. Bunkers, watchtowers, and armed guards reinforced the concrete wall. The three points through which people could pass from one side to another were Alpha, Bravo, and Charlie. During its existence, only about 5,000 people managed to escape to West Berlin. Nearly 200 died trying.

Would You Believe?

The U.S.-Soviet relationship took a major hit in 1960 when the Soviets shot down a U.S. U2 spy plane over Soviet air space. The United States claimed that the plane was a NASA research plane, but Khrushchev had the plane, the pilot, the camera, and the film. The United States had been caught red-handed by the Reds.

In 1962, Khrushchev played a dangerous game of chicken when he instigated the Cuban Missile Crisis by installing nuclear missiles in Fidel Castro's Cuba, the Soviet satellite state just 90 miles from the United States. Khrushchev removed the missiles only after President John F. Kennedy stood his ground and blockaded Cuba. For a few weeks in 1962, the world was eerily close to nuclear disaster. Khrushchev's foreign policy greatly concerned the party.

Khrushchev's kinder, gentler communism, or so his colleagues perceived it, caused quite a stir in the Soviet satellite states as the people there clamored for the relaxation of hard-line communism. This call for more liberal governments resulted in revolution in Hungary in 1956. The conservative Soviets used the Warsaw Pact troops to quickly put an end to liberal ideas in Hungary. Over the next several years, though, Khrushchev continued his policy of De-Stalinization. Conservative Communists couldn't stomach the thought of liberal ideas creeping into eastern Europe, where the USSR had worked so hard to destroy liberalism.

Would You Believe?

Khrushchev, famous for his boorish temper and rude interruptions, once banged his shoe on a table during a meeting of the UN General Assembly.

The Brezhnev Doctrine

The Communist Party had had enough of Khrushchev by the early 1960s, especially after the Cuban Missile Crisis. Party leaders deposed Khrushchev in 1964 and Leonid Brezhnev (1906–1982) replaced him. The hard-line Communists saw De-Stalinization as a threat to the authoritarian control Communists had always enjoyed.

To make sure they didn't lose what they had gained, the Communist Party leaders tightened their grip. They quickly ended any talk of domestic reform and instead accentuated the positive of Stalin's regime. The Soviets, under Brezhnev's leadership, also began an arms race with the United States to ensure that the Soviet Union never had to back down from the United States again. Foreign policy became aggressively old-school Stalinist. In 1968, Soviet-led Warsaw Pact troops occupied Czechoslovakia to end the growth of liberal ideas there and put down the bold Czech leader Alexander Dubček (1921–1992), whose "socialism with a human face" didn't strike a pleasant chord with the Eastern Bloc.

It was after the invasion of Czechoslovakia that Brezhnev declared the Brezhnev Doctrine. Brezhnev said, the "Communist Party is responsible not only to its own people, but also to all the socialist countries, to the entire Communist movement" and "the implementation of … 'self-determination' … [thus] Czechoslovakia's detachment from the socialist community, would have come into conflict with its own vital interests and would have been detrimental to the other socialist states." In other words, the Soviet Union reserved the right to intervene in the affairs of any Eastern Bloc nation that seemed to be straying from communism. This wasn't new; the same thing had happened when Stalin intervened on behalf of the Warsaw Pact, but what made the Brezhnev Doctrine special was the unilateral way in which it was intended to be implemented.

As a Matter of Fact

Part of Leonid Brezhnev's cult of personality, not to mention his fascination with himself, manifested itself with a medal fetish. Throughout Brezhnev's career he "received" medals for all sorts of feats, especially for his roles, no matter how minor, in combat. The Soviet Union also bestowed many medals on him for being a Hero of the Soviet Union. The USSR wasn't the only nation to shower Brezhnev with medals. Soviet satellite states like Afghanistan, Laos, Bulgaria, and Romania also presented the aging Brezhnev with medals. At the end of his life, Brezhnev's medal collection numbered well over 100. He wore many of them proudly on his chest for public appearances in order to enhance his public image.

Détente?

Throughout Brezhnev's administration, Soviet relations with China worsened, especially after a series of Soviet-Chinese clashes in the 1960s. Despite the conflict in Vietnam, the Chinese relationship with the United States began to improve by 1971. Brezhnev feared a Chinese-American alliance and decided not to be left out in the cold. Brezhnev began a series of negotiations with the United States, and at the beginning of the 1970s, the Cold War truly entered into the period known as *détente*.

The real sign that détente had arrived was the summit between Brezhnev and President Richard Nixon that resulted in SALT I, or the Strategic Arms Limitation Treaty of 1972, which froze current levels of strategic missiles. The détente continued when the Vietnam War ended in 1973. Though the era of détente culminated in progress in the 1970s, the seeds for such progress had been planted in the 1960s. The Soviet economy wasn't up to the challenge of the arms race and the space race with the United States. Also, European politicians like West Germany's Willy Brandt (1913–1992) worked relentlessly for peace. Brandt moved away from Adenauer's policy of trading only with the west and looked eastward instead in a policy known as *Ostpolitik*. Brandt especially wanted to ease political tensions between the east and west, particularly between East and West Germany. Brandt also helped ease tensions when he visited Poland and offered an official apology on behalf of Germany for the atrocities of Nazi Germany.

Define Your Terms

Détente is the term used for the reduction of Cold War tensions.

Détente continued into the mid–1970s with the SALT II treaty and other diplomatic negotiations between the United States and the USSR. For all the progress made during the 1960s and 1970s, though, détente ended in the late 1970s with the Iran hostage situation and the Soviet invasion of Afghanistan. Then, in 1980, the United States elected Ronald Reagan (1911–2004), a popular president bent on ending communism, escalating the arms race, and tearing down the Berlin Wall.

Letting Go Is Hard to Do

One of modern history's recurring themes—that of the desire for self-determination—appeared in Asia and Africa during the postwar years. The great empires of France and Britain were the last of their kind in the modern world and barely had been holding on to the last of their colonies.

Imperialism had always been predicated on the fact that Europeans simply were superior to the subjugated peoples of Africa and Asia. After the Second World War, opponents of imperialism often pointed out that Europe's failures offered irrefutable evidence that Europe was no better than the rest of the world. Furthermore, most Europeans were more interested in rebuilding their homes than worrying about foreign colonies. Asian and African peoples, for their part, became fascinated with western ideals and demanded independence.

The imperial powers were faced with difficult decisions concerning their colonial empires. Aside from the major empires of the British and French, other imperial nations released their colonies. Included were the Japanese recognition of Korea, the recognition of Indonesian independence from the Netherlands, the recognition of Libyan independence from Italy, and the recognition of the independence of the Belgian Congo and Rwanda from Belgium.

From British Empire to British Commonwealth

When war broke out between Britain and Germany, the British government worked a deal with India whereby Indian independence could be achieved after the war in exchange for Indian assistance against Germany during the war. Socialists in Britain had long opposed imperialism and its costs in light of the costs of staging a war and rebuilding a war-torn Britain. The election of the Labour Party in 1945 helped reaffirm Britain's commitment to Indian independence as well as the independence of other colonies.

In 1947, the British divided India into two states—India and the Muslim-dominated Pakistan. The independence excited India but the partition didn't please everyone. The Kashmir region, for example, became a hot spot for violence because the region, left in India, had a high concentration of Muslims. As a result, the Indo-Paksitani War broke out shortly after India received its independence.

Would You Believe?

In 1960, the UN passed Resolution 1514, denouncing colonization and promoting the transfer of the power of self-determination to subjugated peoples.

The United Kingdom went on to recognize the independence of Burma in 1947, Palestine (which became Israel) in 1948, Sudan in 1956, Malaya and Ghana in 1957, and a host of other states in the 1960s including Jamaica, Kenya, Zambia, Cameroon, Rhodesia, Barbados, and Fiji. The empire that once sprawled across the entire world had released its colonies and accepted its status as a commonwealth rather than as an empire.

French Decolonization

In the late nineteenth century, France conquered Vietnam and eventually combined it with Cambodia and Laos to form French Indochina. After World War II, France tried to reestablish itself as a power in the region of Indochina. After the war, imperialism held much value for France, and in fact many French saw France's profile in the postwar world as inextricably bound to its empire. However, the Communist Ho Chi Minh (1890–1969) led the Viet Minh against the French. After a long and frustrating battle, the Viet Minh, supported by China and the Soviet Union, won the war in 1954. The result was the partition of Vietnam into Communist North Vietnam and free South Vietnam backed by the United States and Britain.

France jumped right into trouble with Algeria in 1954. Algeria desperately wanted independence, but France was determined not to lose another of its colonies. After a long, violent war with Algiers, France finally gave in and recognized Algerian independence in 1962. The Algerian crisis emphasized the problems of the French Fourth Republic. Its frequent turnover of leadership and constitutional problems repeatedly left France in the lurch. Dismayed, France turned to de Gaulle to save the day again. Charles de Gaulle returned and helped create France's Fifth Republic. France hoped de Gaulle would put an end to the crisis in Algiers, but he didn't. He did, however, help France grant independence to other states much more easily, states including the sub-Saharan African states of Guinea, Cameroon, Chad, Niger, Madagascar, and the Ivory Coast.

> **Continental Quotes**
>
> "How can you govern a country with 246 varieties of cheese?"
>
> —Charles de Gaulle on governing France

The Economy Worsens

The Vietnam War, an example of a proxy war, helped mark the end of stability and prosperity for postwar Europe. A proxy war was one fought not between the major powers but between smaller, satellite states almost on their behalf. Student unrest and the cultural upheaval among the youth of America and Europe also indicated that Europe had entered a period of instability and uncertainty. The economies of European nations and of the United States had blossomed and contributed to a truly global economy. As a result, economic upturns and downturns were felt around the world. By the early 1970s, the economic policies of the United States that helped rebuild a devastated France came back to bite the United States in the wallet. The spiraling economy took a number of turns that affected the consumers badly.

The Fall of the Dollar

Over the 25 years following the Second World War, the United States funneled billions of dollars worth of U.S. aid into Europe. By 1970, though, the U.S. had nearly depleted its supply of gold bullion, the financial backing for U.S. currency. Europe, on the other hand, had managed to stockpile U.S. bullion. The postwar economy of Europe had developed in such a way that the international economy centered on the dollar. With a depleted supply of gold, the U.S. dollar suddenly wasn't worth what it once was. Investors in foreign markets caught on and dumped the dollar as quickly as they could to avoid taking losses on the currency.

President Richard Nixon (1913–1994) halted the sale of U.S. gold and started a chain reaction of economic events. First, the value of the dollar fell sharply. Since the postwar international economy was based on the dollar, inflation resulted as prices rose. With the plummeting value of the dollar, nations abandoned a fixed rate of exchange so their own currencies wouldn't suffer the fate of the dollar. Without a fixed rate of exchange, though, European economics became tricky business. Unfortunately for consumers around the world, the fallout from the dollar coincided with an energy crisis.

The OPEC Embargo

Part of the success of postwar Europe was wed to the availability of cheap oil from Arab oil-producing nations. As manufacturing costs rose during the 1960s, oil prices remained relatively constant. The Arab nations, members of OPEC or the Organization of Petroleum Exporting Countries, jacked up the price of oil and stood firm. The United States stood behind Israel in 1973 when Egypt and Syria attacked Israel. In order to get the United States out of the Arab-Israeli War, OPEC placed an *embargo* on the United States. Economists and governments around the world knew the embargo would have serious repercussions but no one intervened. As a result, the price of oil skyrocketed and energy became scarce. The world, and in particular the United States, had become so dependent on Arab oil that industries slowed to a crawl without it. As industry slowed, unemployment rose. High unemployment and high prices combined led to the worst economic depression around the world since the Great Depression of the 1930s (see Chapter 20).

Trouble hit again when Iran suffered revolution in 1979 and oil prices rose again. Remarkably, the Common Market, as the EC was known, stood firm and weathered the storm. The Common Market helped prevent European nations from engaging in renegade economics motivated by national interests. The energy crisis created in the United States and Europe an era of reevaluation. Governments and individuals took a long, hard look at where money was spent and how. Frugal living and conservative values reigned. In Britain, for example, the voters chose the more conservative Margaret Thatcher (b.1925) as their prime minister in 1979. France was the exception, though. Its president, François Mitterand (1916–1996), engaged in Keynsian spending to stimulate the economy.

Keeping an Eye on the USSR

A generation of Cold War babies grew up in the 1970s and 1980s with a sense of distrust for the Soviet Union. Since World War II, the east versus west mentality prevailed around the world. Therefore, the détente was viewed with much skepticism in the western world. The Soviet Union had demonstrated repeatedly that its word was shaky at best. Though Stalinesque brutality seemingly had disappeared from the Soviet Union, the Soviets still supported dictatorial regimes around the world and still remained belligerent toward the west. The Soviet invasion of Afghanistan didn't do anything to help its image. A renewed sense of Russian nationalism and hard-line communism led to intellectual repression in the Soviet Union and to the renewed oppression of the Jews.

With the Soviet Union still up to its old tricks, many in the western world felt a duty to keep an eye on the Soviets. President Ronald Reagan led the way against the Soviets as he ratcheted up American spending on defense. Reagan's conservative values helped earn him allies of Britain, under Thatcher, and West Germany under Helmut Kohl (b. 1930). Thatcher argued in the mid–1970s that the USSR was bent on world domination. Thatcher tackled the economic problems within her country by slowing the economy and raising taxes in the midst of the recession. Initially painful, the measures eventually reduced unemployment and slowed inflation. Kohl, with his conservative Christian Democratic values, aligned his economic, political, and even military policies with Britain and the United States, often against the Soviet Union.

The Least You Need to Know

- ◆ Even before the end of the war, the western nations and the Soviet Union were at odds over Soviet plans for eastern Europe following the war.

- ◆ After Germany was divided into zones of occupation, the two factions in Europe divided into two camps: NATO, consisting of the western nations and the United States, and the Warsaw Pact, consisting of the Soviet Union and its satellite states in the Eastern Bloc.

- ◆ The Cold War featured many showdowns between east and west, including the Berlin Airlift, the U2 incident, tensions resulting from the Brezhnev Doctrine, and the Cuban Missile Crisis.

- ◆ Decolonization proved relatively easy for the United Kingdom after the war, while France nearly found itself in civil war over the Algiers crisis. De Gaulle, who helped create France's Fourth Republic, guided France through de-colonization and then helped form the Fifth Republic in France in 1958.

- ◆ An economic crisis set in during the 1970s as a result of the falling dollar and the OPEC oil embargo.

- ◆ The tough times encouraged conservative values as the United States, Britain, and West Germany aligned themselves. The Common Market helped maintain a sense of European unity during the economic crisis.

Chapter 23

Changing Millennia

In This Chapter

◆ Communism in Europe is down for the count

◆ The USSR loses control

◆ Germany—back together again

◆ There's trouble in the Balkans again

◆ One currency—the Euro

◆ Europe takes on terror

Sitting just 10 years away from the new millennium, Europe still wasn't out of the woods. East-west relations had chilled again. Cries for self-determination were growing louder in traditionally Communist states. Religious and ethnic tensions heated up in the volatile Balkan region yet again. Dreams of European economic unity had not yet been fully realized. There were challenges ahead that Europeans could not possibly have imagined. A strange mix of nationalism and international unity would sweep across Europe over the next 15 years. A strange assortment of related and unrelated tragedies would strike Europe over the next 15 years, too. At the new millennium, Europe had prevailed over many challenges, while facing new challenges for the twenty-first century.

The Decline and Fall of Communism

Westerners had always hoped, both secretly and out loud, that communism would one day disappear altogether. Capitalists had long believed that the Communist system simply could not and would not last. Nevertheless, the Soviet Union, China, Cuba, and some Eastern Bloc nations clung to traditional Communist systems. At least in Europe, though, communism would meet its match in the voice it had traditionally tried to quiet—the voice of self-determination. Once the Communists opened the Pandora's Box of democratization, communism was doomed. The fall of communism spread like a disease from nation to nation. The rise of democratic and limited market-economy ideals occurred in smaller states, then shocked the world as even the mighty Soviet Union succumbed. The world stood in disbelief as the Cold War, the Berlin Wall, and the Soviet Union vanished within a few years of each other.

One Last Soviet Stand

The Soviet Union's Leonid Brezhnev continued the Cold War practice of proxy wars in the 1970s as his government indirectly affected conflicts in Angola, Ethiopia, and Somalia. Brezhnev also built the most powerful Soviet navy ever. Then Brezhnev extended his Brezhnev Doctrine one final time, invading Afghanistan in 1979 to help a struggling Communist government hang on to power. He couldn't allow the fate of another Communist state to have an adverse effect on the Soviet Union. In his final years, Brezhnev became increasingly preoccupied by foreign policy, two examples being the signing of the SALT II treaty in 1979 and the invasion of Afghanistan, and creating a cult of personality for himself.

Brezhnev and the other aging Communists jockeyed for more domestic political power; Brezhnev even took the title of Marshal of the Soviet Union, a title not used since Stalin's days. His attempts to appear bold and powerful were thinly veiled attempts to disguise that Brezhnev's brand of communism had stagnated. The Soviet Union was keeping up with the United States as a superpower, but the efforts weren't sustainable. In the eyes of the world, the Soviets had been defined by military and technological might, but the stagnant economy would not allow the huge expenditures on the military and the space program much longer. Brezhnev had lost sight of the domestic issues that faced the Soviet Union: poor working and living conditions, rampant alcoholism, corruption, and apathy gripped the Soviet Union.

Poland Makes Waves

The Communists were stumbling everywhere in the Eastern Bloc, but they truly struggled with Poland. Attempts to suppress the Catholic Church and the peasants in the 1950s were met with obstinate resistance. By failing to control those two important facets of Polish society, the Communists effectively failed to control Poland. As such, the poorly administered Polish economy struggled through the 1960s, then plummeted in the 1970s. In 1978, as the Polish people will testify, a wondrous thing happened to Poland when the Polish Cardinal Karol Wojtyla (1920–2005) became Pope John Paul II. The Polish pope would quietly become one of the dominant personalities of the next quarter-century.

The other dominant Polish personality emerged about the same time. In 1980, strikes broke out at shipyards in Gdansk, Poland, where Poles protested rising prices. An unlikely hero emerged from the strikes as the leader of the "Solidarity" movement. The staunchly Catholic Lech Walesa (b. 1943), an electrician by trade, was chosen to be the chairman of the Solidarity Free Trade Union. Walesa earned fame in 1980 when a strike broke out at the Gdansk Shipyard. Walesa illegally climbed the wall at the shipyard, rallied the workers, and effectively became the leader of the strike. In 1981, things got messy when the Polish government declared martial law and threw Walesa in prison where he remained until late 1982. The following year, under the watchful eye of the government, Walesa returned to work at the shipyards. He also won the Nobel Peace Prize in 1983, which he accepted by proxy, and donated the prize money to the Solidarity cause, headquartered safely out of the country. As the strikes spread, the Polish government finally caved to the demands of the workers. The strikers, showing unusual solidarity, won the right to organize unions, the right to strike, freedom of speech, and the promise of economic reforms.

In 1988, Walesa organized another strike demanding only that Solidarity be made legal again. The government finally agreed and Solidarity returned to Poland. The government had no idea the union would become a political force, and in the 1989 elections, the Solidarity "party" won parliamentary elections. The following year, Solidarity elected Walesa president of Poland. Though criticized for his abilities in government, Walesa won resounding praise for taking Poland from a Communist-controlled backward state to a democratic state with a free market economy. Walesa lost the next election in 1995, but continued to work behind the scenes in politics.

Would You Believe?

Lech Walesa was chosen in 1982 as *Time* magazine Man of the Year.

Reagan and the Pope Take on Communism

With the recent passing of both Ronald Reagan and Pope John Paul II, it has become trendy to pair the two as the men who defeated communism in Europe. As with most clichés, there is a large element of truth to the assertion. Though each attacked communism in different ways, each played a role in the disintegration of modern communism.

Ronald Reagan, not being bound by the same rules of religion as the pope, attacked communism from a variety of angles. First, Reagan and most capitalists had no faith in the economic stability of Communist states. Therefore, Reagan turned away from the détente of his predecessors and escalated the arms race, which established military superiority over the rest of the world for the United States and forced the Soviets to break the bank to keep up. Reagan also imposed economic sanctions on Communist nations such as Poland and the USSR. Finally, he used proxy wars to undermine communist regimes and to generally create more problems for the Communists.

Would You Believe?

In an interesting coincidence, both Reagan and Pope John Paul II were actors before they rose to prominence on the world stage.

Pope John Paul II, on the other hand, could not and would not condone violence or even sanctions that resulted in harm or deprivation for civilians. Along the same lines, the pope never judged governments, though he frequently criticized their actions and policies. Pope John Paul II preached freedom, peace, and openness. The pope never called for regime change but rather change within the regime. He placed human rights above all and spoke openly, even in the company of Communists, about the value of human life and the importance of human rights.

As a Pole who grew up under Communist oppression, Pope John Paul II understood the role of the Church in providing a safe haven for people. He continued the tradition in Poland of not allowing the Communist government to break the Church. As a result, the Church provided freedom for intellectual, religious, and even political expression within its sphere of influence. By preaching openness, religion slowly got its foot in the door of Communist nations. Lech Walesa and Mikhail Gorbachev both said that communism would not have fallen had it not been for Pope John Paul II. Of the pope, Walesa said, "The pope started this chain of events that led to the end of communism. Before his pontificate, the world was divided into blocs. Nobody knew how to get rid of communism. He simply said: 'Don't be afraid, change the image of this land.'" Walesa and the pope did just that.

1989

In one of the most remarkable years of the twentieth century, 1989, human rights scored victory after victory over oppression. The first revolution occurred in Lech Walesa's Poland, where he was elected as the first non-Communist leader in all of eastern Europe in more than a generation.

The democratic fever spread from Poland to Hungary. The Communists of Hungary replaced an old-school Communist with a reform-minded Communist government in 1988, with the hopes of increasing popularity for the party. The "reforms" didn't go over, so the government decided in 1989 to revoke one-party rule, thinking that the Communists would still be able to win any election they pleased. They were wrong.

The fever spread quickly to East Germany. Reform-minded Hungary opened its borders to East German "refugees," who traveled through Hungary, Austria, and into West Germany. So many people suddenly packed up and left East Germany that the East German government had no choice but to "tear down that wall," as Reagan demanded, in an effort to prevent chaos and depopulation. The old, hard-line Communists of East Germany found themselves suddenly dispensable as a reform-minded government took power and scheduled elections for 1990.

In Czechoslovakia, the Velvet Revolution unseated the Communists in December 1989. Peaceful student protests in Bratislava in November were dispersed by riot police and a week later 500,000 protestors had gathered in Prague. The Communist government rolled over and gave up. By the end of the calendar year, Czechoslovakia elected Vaclav Havel (b. 1936) as president in the first free election in Czechoslovakia in 43 years.

As a Matter of Fact

The last president of Czechoslovakia and the first president of the Czech Republic, Vaclav Havel once lived a life outside the political arena. As a young man, Havel worked as a stagehand and studied theater. He went on to write several plays including *The Garden Party* and *The Beggar's Opera*, as well as several books including *Letters to Olga* (written to his wife from prison) and *The Art of the Impossible*. Havel became increasingly political after 1968 and even spent five years in prison. Throughout his career, Havel has remained a proponent of nonviolent resistance to oppression.

While most of the Eastern Bloc regimes fell quietly in 1989, Romania was not as lucky. After violent clashes between peaceful protestors and state police, the aging and ruthless ruler Nicolae Ceausescu (1918–1989) and his wife reacted badly. They confronted crowds in a public square and lost control when shots were fired. They fled and their forces fell to an uprising of the Romanian people. After their capture, they faced trial in a kangaroo court and were executed immediately with machine guns. Footage of the corpses flooded media outlets worldwide. A new government emerged but Romania remained mired in economic and political turmoil for years. By the end of 1989 the Eastern Bloc didn't look so menacing to westerners anymore.

> **Would You Believe?**
>
> As Ceausescu and his wife faced the firing squad, they reportedly recited from the *Internationale*, the world's most famous socialist anthem which originally was meant to be sung to the tune of the French national anthem.

Germany Reunites

After Hungary opened its Austrian borders in 1989, East Germans escaped to the west in droves. Faced with a crisis, the East German government held an election and a new reform-minded government took over. The new prime minister, Lothar de Maizière (b. 1940), negotiated with West Germany's Helmut Kohl and with France, the United States, and the Soviet Union about the possibility of merging with West Germany. Helmut Kohl helped convince East Germans to agree to the reunification by offering an even trade on their East German marks. In other words, the sad East German currency could be traded for the strong West German marks. That was an offer the East Germans couldn't refuse. The biggest challenge facing Kohl was convincing the Soviets, before the USSR collapsed, that a unified Germany would not threaten peace in Europe. Cautiously, Gorbachev signed off on the plan when Kohl promised West German loans to the Soviets to help their struggling economy.

Finally, on October 3, 1990, the state of East Germany joined West Germany and the West German constitution. The reunification of Germany resulted partly from the anti-Communist movements of 1989, and in turn partly contributed to the disintegration of the Soviet Union.

The reunification came at a price for West Germany. By picking up the dead weight of the formerly Soviet-subsidized East German economy, the West German economy slowed. The pitiful industries in East Germany had to be transferred to private ownership and the currency had to be stabilized. Fifteen years later, the German economy still has yet to recover completely.

One of the driving forces behind the unification process was the desire for the two German states to successfully reunite their common history and common culture. After reunification, the German government spent billions of dollars to salvage that culture. East Germany remained poorer than West Germany after the war, and as a result, entire cities needed repair and refurbishment. In many cases, museums and galleries needed huge investments if the German culture in the east was to be salvaged. On a smaller level, many artists ventured into the east from the west and vice versa to catch up on the two generations of culture they had missed. Cultural centers like Leipzig and Dresden have flourished since reunification. Even today, Germany is working hard to preserve the old German culture and to create a single new German culture.

The Collapse of the USSR

The collapse of the Soviet Union could be considered a happy accident. As Brezhnev died and passed leadership on, most people within the government agreed that some amount of change was necessary. However, Yuri Andropov (1914–1984), who followed Brezhnev, didn't get the job done. In fact, the economy sunk even lower under Andropov. Andropov, often remembered for his ties to the KGB and his internal investigations for corruption, died of kidney failure in 1984. Konstantin Chernenko (1911-1985), also in poor health, lasted only a short while as Andropov's successor. During his brief stint, which ended in 1985 after a long illness, though, he escalated the Cold War and increased the harsh treatment of dissidents in the Soviet Union.

Would You Believe?

In early 1985 while Chernenko lay deathly ill in bed, a Politburo member physically hauled Chernenko out of bed and forced him to go the polls to vote.

Things were about to change drastically. Mikhail Gorbachev (b. 1931) worked his way up to prominence within the Communist Party and became the leader of the Soviet Union in 1985. A brilliant man with a genuine concern for the Soviet people, Gorbachev realized that the only way to save the stale and listless Communist Party was to introduce reforms. Gorbachev's plan began with the budget and the economy. He knew that the Soviet Union could not keep up with the United States in the arms race, and further attempts to would bankrupt the struggling economy. He planned to restructure the economy so that the military didn't eat up the budget, and he addressed the issue of corruption in government.

Gorbachev's restructuring plan was known as *perestroika*, or, simply, restructuring. Included in the restructuring were reduced price controls and reduced restrictions on private enterprises. At first the economy appeared to be looking up, but then it stalled. Gorbachev clung to power by introducing perhaps the most important ideological reform since the Russian Revolution: *glasnost*, or openness.

Glasnost contradicted everything the conservative, traditional Communists had done over the last 50 years. Gorbachev wanted the reformed government to be open and honest. He promoted free expression, free speech, and the relatively free flow of ideas. Gorbachev also introduced limited democratic principles, including free elections.

In that magical year of 1989, the Soviet people elected a few non-Communists. For the first time, political ideas were openly debated by politicians who weren't in the Communist Party. But once the door was cracked, the public wanted it wide open. As Soviets enjoyed some political expression, they of course wanted more say in the government. With the recent emphasis on Russian nationalism, many non-Russians now began to dream their own nationalist dreams—seemingly a very real possibility, having seen the Soviets stand by as the Eastern Bloc countries threw off the shackles of communism.

Would You Believe?

Because of his non-threatening demeanor, journalists enjoyed referring to Gorbachev as "Gorby." Gorby is probably the most famous person ever to have the birthmark known as the "port-wine stain," or *naevus flammus*, prominently displayed on his forehead.

Gorbachev completely shelved the Brezhnev Doctrine, and that gave Russian and non-Russian nationalists alike a sense of hope. Gorbachev drew fire from both conservative Communists and radical liberals who wanted nothing less than complete independence for the Soviet states. The Communists suffered a major defeat in the 1990 elections. Then, in a remarkable move, Lithuania declared independence. All eyes watched Gorbachev as he imposed an embargo on the state—but refused to send the military. Russia followed suit under the leadership of Russian Parliament leader Boris Yeltsin (b. 1931). Despite Gorbachev's efforts to save the union, nine more states declared their independence.

In a last-ditch effort, the old-school, hard-line Communists attempted a coup of the Gorbachev government, but to no avail. Though Gorbachev returned quickly to power after a kidnapping attempt during the coup, Gorbachev's Soviet Union slipped away. As of Christmas Day, 1991, the Soviet Union no longer existed; in its place stood fourteen independent states. Eleven of the states formed a confederation known as the Commonwealth of Independent Sates. Its members at the end of 1991 were Armenia, Azerbaijan, Belarus, Kazakhstan, Kyrgyzstan, Moldova, Russia, Tajikistan, Turkmenistan, Ukraine, and Uzbekistan. In 1993, Georgia joined the CIS after Russian troops intervened in Georgian affairs.

Would You Believe?

When Germany reunited, it technically was a member of both NATO and the Warsaw Pact at the same time. Interest in the Warsaw Pact waned and the member nations officially dissolved the organization in 1991.

Bad Days in the Balkans

If history were any indication, the Balkans seemed destined to have problems as anti-Communist sentiment moved through the Eastern Bloc. Nationalism had been a force to be reckoned with in the Balkans since even before World War I. For the last few generations, nationalist ideas in the Balkans had been dominated and suppressed by communism.

The hotbed of political tension in the 1990s would be Yugoslavia. The Socialist Federal Republic of Yugoslavia had been ruled by Josip Tito since 1953. The Republic included the Socialist Republics of Slovenia, Croatia, Bosnia-Herzegovina, Serbia, Montenegro, and Macedonia. Kosovo and Vojvodina were provinces of Serbia. With Tito's death in 1980, the ties that bound Yugoslavia together were undone. Suddenly the multi-ethnic states held more power and autonomy than ever before.

As was so typical of postwar European diplomacy, the boundary lines had been drawn without much regard for the ethnicities living in the area. The entire region was a hodge-podge of ethnicities, many of them harboring ancient grudges. For example, within Bosnia-Herezegovina's borders lived Serbs, Bosnians, and Croats or Croatians; none of the ethnicities had a majority. Within Serbia's borders lived Croatians, Serbs, and even Hungarians. Quite a few Serbs lived in Croatia, too. Complicating matters even more was the presence of both Christianity and Islam. The standard of living declined across the board in the years between Tito's death and 1989. The revolutions that broke out elsewhere in 1989 fueled the fire in the Balkans.

Would You Believe?

Tito actually was born Josip Broz. He adopted the codename "Tito" while working for an underground Communist organization in the 1930s.

The Breakup of Yugoslavia

When Tito died, political leaders around the world watched Yugoslavia to see if it could withstand the ethnic rivalries that were sure to develop. The effective leader of Yugoslavia after Tito was Slobodan Milosevic (b. 1941), a Communist from Serbia. Milosevic's immediate goal was to create a state dominated by Serbs, so he stirred up Serbian nationalism, alienating many other ethnic groups within Yugoslavia. He also reduced the autonomy enjoyed by Kosovo and Vojvodina.

After 10 years in power, Milosevic gave the Serb majority power over all of Yugoslavia by giving each person a vote rather than each republic a vote in the Yugoslav government. The Slovenians and Croatians were infuriated and left the proceedings of the 14th Congress of the League of Communists of Yugoslavia in disgust. Anti-Communist reform finally made its way to Yugoslavia and the republics created new governments within the Yugoslav system. At one extreme, Serbia and Montenegro created governments that favored a unified, Serb-dominated, Yugoslavia. Slovenia and Croatia created governments that leaned toward declaring independence. The Yugoslav People's Army wanted to declare martial law to restore order to the SFRY. Serbia, Montenegro, Kosovo, and Vojvodina voted for martial law; the others voted against the action. In 1991, Croatia, Macedonia, and Slovenia declared independence. Also in 1991, Bosnia-Herzegovina held the same referendum and decided to declare independence, but only because Bosnian Serbs there boycotted the vote. Thus the Yugoslav wars began, first in Slovenia and Croatia and then in Bosnia. The Yugoslav People's Army, with the breakup of Yugoslavia, disintegrated.

The Yugoslav Wars

War broke out in 1991 in Slovenia and in Croatia as an attempt by the Serb majority under Milosevic to keep Yugoslavia united, but the war ultimately deteriorated into bloody nationalist fights between Serbs, led by the ruthless Milosevic, and Croats, led by Franjo Tudman.

The war in Bosnia, which began in 1992, grew especially complicated because of the large Muslim population there. Instead of two sides fighting in Bosnia, three sides fought one against another against another. After fierce and bloody fighting for three years, and after UN troops had been deployed to the region, the three sides met in Dayton, Ohio, with President Bill Clinton's (b. 1946) administration to hammer out a peace agreement.

The Dayton Accords divided Bosnia-Herzegovina into two distinct entities to operate jointly as a single state. The Dayton accords also required the presence of NATO peace-keeping forces to maintain order in the region. Milosevic's oppression of the Albanian population within the province of Kosovo eventually led to the War in Kosovo in 1996, led by the KLA or Kosovo Liberation Army against the oppressive Serbs. When the government of Albania briefly collapsed in 1997 after election fraud sent the country into anarchy, much of the Albanian army's weapons ended up in Kosovo, thus heightening the conflict. The world's leaders really didn't want to get involved again and basically watched the events unfold. Finally, a U.S.-led coalition of NATO forces launched a bombing campaign to drive the Serbs from Kosovo so the refugees could return home. Conflict in the region continued in Macedonia and Serbia in 2001. To this day, the peace there is tenuous at best as nationalist interests still run high.

Ethnic Cleansing

The factor that finally led to the intervention of outside forces in the former Yugo-slavia was the practice known as ethnic cleansing. The term means the removal of an ethnicity or people from a region. Ethnic cleansing can be done by forcing people to flee, by deporting them, or by genocide. The Yugoslav wars featured all three. Horribly violent episodes of fighting, terrorist activity, and guerilla attacks left hundreds of thousands dead and millions displaced from their homes.

As international authorities made their way through the region in the years both during and after the wars, they documented the existence of numerous mass graves. According to testimony and eyewitness accounts, the practice of ethnic cleansing generally followed the pattern of warning an area that it was about to be cleansed, executing the potential political leaders, dividing the population into those who could fight and those who couldn't, executing the "fighting age" men, and then removing the rest of the undesired population from the area. Slobodan Milosevic was arrested and handed over to the United Nations in 2001 and charged with war crimes and genocide. The prosecution took two years to prepare the case and the trial has intermittently dragged on ever since.

> **Would You Believe?**
>
> Milosevic originally presented a list of over 1,600 witnesses for his defense but the court whittled that number down to about 200. As of late 2005, only about 40 had testified.

The trial hit a snag in October 2005, when the court announced that Milosevic, who finally won the right to defend himself, had already used 75 percent of the time allotted him and would receive no extensions of time. Facing the prospect of being accused of staging an unfair trial, which was originally scheduled to end in early 2006, the court has wrangled with the decision to extend Milosevic's time.

> ### As a Matter of Fact
>
> In 1984, the capital city of Sarajevo served as the host city for the Fourteenth Winter Olympics. The beautiful, multiethnic city captured the hearts and minds of the world with its beauty and hospitality. Then, less than 10 years later, ethnic fighting ripped the region and left the once-glorious city in ruins. Many of the Olympic venues were destroyed in the fighting. After the fighting ended, the city of Sarajevo, hardly multiethnic after the war, began the rebuilding process. In 2000, leaders in Sarajevo mounted a campaign to host the 2010 Winter Olympics. Though the International Olympic Committee gave funds for the rebuilding of the city, the IOC declined to officially recognize the city's bid for the games.

The European Union

In the decades following the Second World War, six nations of western Europe (Belgium, France, Italy, Luxembourg, the Netherlands, and West Germany) joined together to form the EEC, or the Common Market. Though it served as an economic organization designed to allow the region to function as a single economic unit, many people dreamed that one day all of Europe would belong to such an organization. Theoretically, by creating a single European economic community, the European economy would be more stable. Also, by creating a single currency the issue of exchange rates could be eliminated. A single currency could be used in Britain, France, Germany, and so on.

In the 1980s, that dream looked more and more like a reality as European leaders worked vigorously to hammer out details and convince the European people that such an organization wouldn't require the sacrifice of any sovereignty or national identity.

The Single European Act and the Maastricht Treaty

In 1986, the Single European Act established a general blueprint for a single European economic organization, much like the EC of old, which would allow free trade and the free movement of labor and goods within its borders. The act went into effect in 1993 and the organization took the name the European Union, or EU. France and Germany, under the leadership of François Mitterand and Helmut Kohl, respectively, pushed for a single European currency, too. The British held out the longest, but the advocates finally won the argument.

In 1991, the Maastricht Treaty set 1999 as the date the single European currency would become active. Inevitably, the move marked not only a step toward economic unity but also toward political unity. Because of that implication, many Europeans in nearly every nation were reluctant to jump on board. The fear of losing sovereignty and the idea of allowing bureaucrats in another country to control the international economy seemed pretty unsettling. Other concerns were over potential membership. Western nations were concerned about eastern nations joining and adding "dead weight" to the collective economy. To help calm nerves, the Treaty of Amsterdam in 1997 helped make the EU more democratic and more appealing to Europeans. In addition to handling economic issues, the EU also has departments for agriculture, justice, security, human rights, and more. It is increasingly becoming a political entity.

As a Matter of Fact

The idea of an integrated and unified Europe began in 1950 with a speech by Frenchman Robert Schuman. As French Foreign Minister, Schuman wanted to put to bed the postwar tensions between France and Germany so he invited Germany to help jointly manage the French and German coal and steel industries. This joint effort led to the European Coal and Steel union which, in turn, led to the development of the European Union.

The original members of the European Union include Austria, Belgium, Denmark, Finland, France, Germany, Greece, Ireland, Italy, Luxembourg, the Netherlands, Portugal, Spain, Sweden, and the United Kingdom. In 2004, the European Union added Cyprus, the Czech Republic, Estonia, Hungary, Latvia, Lithuania, Malta, Poland, Slovakia, and Slovenia.

Currently there are 25 member states in the European Union. The nations of Bulgaria and Romania have completed negotiations with the EU and are slated for membership in 2007. As of late 2005, the European Union announced that there were no further obstacles preventing Turkey from opening negotiations over membership in the EU. Those obstacles were laws in Turkey that the EU deemed in violation of human rights and civil rights. Croatia currently is a candidate nation, too.

Macedonia is hoping to join the EU in the near future as well. Switzerland has applied for membership but its citizens are split down the middle regarding membership. Norway, too, has applied for membership but its citizens have rejected its attempts to join in referendums.

Although there would seem to be strength in numbers, the European Union is not begging nations to join. In fact, interested nations have to meet certain criteria, known as the Copenhagen Criteria. The most important of these criteria include a sound market economy and the ability to maintain a democratic government and to protect human rights. Furthermore, member nations are expected to protect the rights of minorities. Based on these criteria, there are quite a few nations that will not be members anytime soon.

Here Comes the Euro

Although most of the members of the EU signed on to replace their currencies with the euro, a few did not. In 2002, the euro went into circulation in Austria, Belgium, Finland, France, Germany, Greece, Ireland, Italy, Luxembourg, the Netherlands, Portugal, and Spain. The euro currency features seven different denominations of banknotes or paper money and eight different coins. The EU printed about 14.5 billion banknotes and 50 billion coins totaling a whopping 664 billion euro, or ε664 billion. The coins have one side in common and one side unique to a member country so that there are twelve distinct euro coins for each denomination. Within the "euro area" as it is known, consumers can use any euro minted or printed in any euro member state. In other words, someone from France vacationing in Germany and Austria never has to change currencies or calculate confusing conversion rates that change daily. The euro is traded one-for-one within all member states that use the euro.

Would You Believe?

When the euro hit the market in 2002, collectors, history buffs, and people who were curious bought countless sets of the new currency through auctions on eBay, often for far above face value.

The More Things Change

After 600 or so years of modern European history, several things have become apparent to casual observers and historians alike.

First, the desire for self-determination is one of the most powerful forces known to humanity, proven time and time again to be something worthy of great, even ultimate, sacrifice.

Second, ideological differences and religious differences simply are part of life. While diversity is difficult sometimes, oppression in the name of order and assimilation always leads to violence.

Third, regardless of how tough things seem to be, humans persevere. Whether the challenges were related to disease, war, economic depression, uncertainty about science and religion, or simply the ability to coexist peacefully, European civilization has always managed to find a way not only to survive but to thrive.

Fourth, in spite of all the turmoil history has thrown at Europe, Europe still managed to produce some of history's most brilliant and creative minds. People often say that history repeats itself. It doesn't. However, people are and have always been the same. Therefore, just as there have always been conflicts in the past, there will be conflicts in the future; hopefully just not as many and not as destructive as in the past. Likewise, future Europeans undoubtedly will surpass the Europeans of the past intellectually and creatively, just as past Europeans surpassed those who came before them.

Finally, just as the past has presented a never-ending supply of fascinating characters and stories, so will the future. As the nineteenth-century author Alphonse Karr said, "The more things change, the more they remain the same."

Responding to Terror

Throughout European history, those not inclined to diplomatic means have resorted to violence, threats of violence, fear, and oppression to deal with problems. Most often these problems arose over religion and politics, although economic conditions occasionally sparked such attacks. In the twenty-first century, although much has changed since the Middle Ages, people are still the same. There are still people in the world who cannot deal with diversity and differences of opinion. For these few extremists, the way of handling diversity and change is through cowardly attacks and the threat of fear. Acts of terror can be committed by individuals, by groups, and even by states. The most frequent acts of terror include car bombing, suicide bombing, assassination, and hijacking. On a greater level, terrorism includes bio-terrorism and nuclear terrorism.

Numerous terror attacks occurred in Europe throughout the late twentieth century, including the 1972 Munich Olympics attacks; numerous Irish Republican Army bombings in the 1970s, 1980s, and 1990s; the 1986 bombing of a discotheque in

Berlin; and the 1988 bombing of Pan Am Flight 103 over Lockerbie, Scotland. However, after the September 11, 2001, terror attacks in the United States, Europe faced a new kind of enemy. Though Europe had been relatively safe from non-European attacks, as had the United States, that era was over. On March 11, 2004, a bomb exploded in a commuter train in Madrid and killed 191 people. That same year, a bombed Russian airplane killed 90. Also in 2004, terrorists took schoolchildren hostage in Russia and 344 died. In July 2005, terrorists detonated three bombs in London's public transportation system on the eve of the G8 summit, killing more than 50.

British Prime Minister Tony Blair (b. 1953), despite taking heat at home, took the lead in the European response to terrorism. Blair immediately sided with the United States in the days and months following the September 11 attacks, and he committed British troops to the "war on terror."

Since 2001, intelligence and counter-terrorist measures are reported to have greatly increased security throughout Europe, but security officials will attest that there is still room for improvement. In Spain, for example, Spanish authorities have increased surveillance in strategic locations and have increased the frequency of anti-terror raids on suspected terror cells. In the wake of bombings of the London bus and underground systems in July 2005, English Prime Minister Blair proposed new measures to help in the war on terror. Among the proposals were the refusal of asylum to former terrorists, making glorification of terror a crime, increasing the power to close a place "fomenting extremism" even if the place is a house of worship, and deportation on the grounds of fostering hatred. These proposals go beyond the traditional responses of increasing security at target areas and increasing intelligence activities. In eastern Europe, Russian President Vladimir Putin has been relentless in using troops to respond to acts of terror such as the frequent activities of Chechen rebels. Furthermore, Putin has encouraged European powers not to stand by but to become actively involved in the war on terror.

> ### Continental Quotes
>
> "In the global context true security cannot be achieved by a mounting build up of weapons-defence in the narrow sense—but only by providing basic conditions for peaceful relations between nations, and solving not only the military but also the non-military problems which threaten them."
>
> —Willy Brandt

Challenges for the Future

Considering what the last century has been like for Europe, the continent is in remarkably good shape. The overall economy is fair, no European powers currently threaten to upset the peace or balance of power for the rest of the continent, and the economy is becoming more globalized and, at least theoretically, less volatile.

However, there remain several challenges that will have to be dealt with in the coming years. Perhaps most fresh on everyone's mind is the challenge of dealing with terror. Creating a political entity in the European Union without challenging the sovereignty of nations will certainly be a challenge. Both the UN and NATO face the constant challenge of policing the continent. Furthermore, just in the last few years, the two organizations have had to reevaluate their mission and role in the political affairs of sovereign states. States will continue to face challenges regarding alliances and the way those alliances affect relationships with other European states, particularly alliances with the United States and China.

The Least You Need to Know

- Communist states, once they became smitten with democratic ideals, fell one after another, especially in 1989. Eventually, Communist East Germany joined with a democratic West Germany.

- The mighty Soviet Union fell in 1991 after Mikhail Gorbachev introduced changes to save communism there. Ironically, the liberal changes intended to save communism actually spelled doom for it.

- After Tito died, Yugoslavia experienced terrible nationalist wars between Serbs and minorities. The wars featured genocide and ethnic cleansing, both of which are charges facing former Serb leader Slobodan Milosevic.

- The former EC developed into a 25-member economic and political entity known as the European Union. Many of the member states traded in their national currencies for the common currency of the EU, the euro.

- The British royal family has experienced triumph and tragedy, romance and heartache. It remains the most popular and widely followed royal family in the world.

- The most pressing challenges facing Europe include the development of the EU, the response to terrorism, and the effective administration of NATO and the UN.

Major Events in European History

1337–1453—Hundred Years' War between England and France.

1347—The bubonic plague, or the Black Death, invades Europe.

c.1350—Publication of Boccaccio's *Decameron*.

1377–1418—The Great Schism.

1378—The Ciompi revolt in Florence.

c.1390—Publication of Geoffrey Chaucer's *Canterbury Tales*.

c.1450—Johann Gutenberg invents the movable type printing press.

1455–1485—The English Houses of York and Lancaster fight in the War of the Roses.

1469—Ferdinand and Isabella marry and unite Castile and Aragon, or modern-day Spain.

1485—The Tudor Era begins in England after the War of the Roses.

1492—Christopher Columbus sets sail westward for Asia and then lands in the Bahamas.

1492—Ferdinand and Isabella kick Jews out of Spain.

1503–1506—Leonardo da Vinci works on *Mona Lisa*.

1508–1512—Michelangelo paints the Sistine Chapel ceiling.

1513—Niccolo Machiavelli writes *The Prince*.

1516–1519—Desiderius Erasmus produces his Greek and Latin translations of the New Testament. Both, according to Erasmus, are more accurate than the Vulgate.

1517—Johann Tetzel begins sale of indulgences.

1517—Martin Luther writes and perhaps posts his *95 Theses*.

1519–1522—Ferdinand Magellan's expedition circumnavigates the globe.

1521—Charles V and the Diet of Worms outlaw Martin Luther.

1521—Cortés destroys Aztec Empire.

1525—German peasants revolt in Luther's name.

1527—King Henry VIII asks for a divorce from Catherine of Aragon.

1529—Diet of Speyer uses "Protestant" for the first time.

1530—Henry VIII receives annulment of marriage to Catherine of Aragon.

1530—Pizarro destroys Inca Empire.

1534—Act of Supremacy makes Henry VIII head of Church of England.

1536—Publication of John Calvin's *Institutes of the Christian Religion*.

1543—Publication of Copernicus's *On the Revolution of the Heavenly Bodies*.

1549—Thomas Cranmer issues the *Book of Common Prayer* for the Church of England.

1555—The Peace of Augsburg allows German princes to choose the religion of their principalities.

1558—Elizabeth I becomes Queen of England.

1568—The Netherlands revolt against Spain.

1588—Defeat of the Spanish Armada.

c. 1590—William Shakespeare begins writing.

1598—Henry IV issues Edict of Nantes.

1603—James VI of Scotland becomes first Stuart king of England.

1611—Publication of the King James Bible in England.

1618—Defenestration of Prague begins the Thirty Years' War.

1628—William Harvey develops theory on the circulation of blood.

1632—Publication of Galileo's *Dialogues on the Two Chief Systems of the World*.

1633—Trial of Galileo.

1642–1649—The English Civil War.

1643–1715—Louis XIV rules France.

1648—The Peace of Westphalia ends the Thirty Years' War.

1653–1658—Cromwell rules the Protectorate in England.

1685—Louis XIV revokes Edict of Nantes.

1687—Publication of Sir Isaac Newton's *Principia*.

1688—The Glorious Revolution in England.

1689—Peter the Great becomes czar of Russia.

1698—Thomas Savery creates first steam engine.

1701–1713—War of the Spanish Succession.

1721—Johann Sebastian Bach completes the *Brandenburg Concertos*.

1733—John Kay creates the flying shuttle.

1740—Pinnacle of Prussian military state under Frederick William I "the Soldiers' King."

1751—Publication of Diderot's *Encyclopedie*.

1755—The Lisbon earthquake.

1756–1763—Seven Years' War.

1759—Publication of Voltaire's *Candide*.

1762—Catherine the Great begins her rule in Russia.

1764—Wolfgang Amadeus Mozart writes first symphony at age eight.

1765—James Hargreaves invents the cotton spinning jenny.

1776—British colonies in America declare their independence.

1776—Publication of Adam Smith's *Wealth of Nations*.

1787—Louis XVI calls for Assembly of Notables.

1789–1794—French Revolution.

1793—King Louis XVI of France is executed for treason.

1796—Edward Jenner develops smallpox vaccine.

1798—Publication of Thomas Malthus's *Essays on the Principle of Population*.

1798—Publication of *Lyrical Ballads* by Wordsworth and Coleridge.

1799–1815—Napoleon takes control of French government; begins Napoleonic Era.

1799—Combination Acts in England ban labor unions.

1808—Ludwig von Beethoven completes *Fifth Symphony*.

1812—Napoleon suffers defeat in Russia.

1815—Napoleon loses to Wellington at the Battle of Waterloo.

1815—The Congress of Vienna ends Napoleonic Era.

1815–1848—The Age of Metternich.

1818—Creation of Prussian *Zollverein*.

1825—George Stephenson invents the locomotive.

1829—Frederic Chopin's first piano concerts in Vienna.

1830—Revolution erupts in France, again.

1832–1846—Reform legislation passes in England including Reform Bill of 1832, Poor Law, and the repeal of the Corn Laws.

1845–1846—Great Potato Famine in Ireland.

1848—Publication of *Communist Manifesto* by Marx and Engels.

1848—Revolutions break out in Paris, Hungary, and Vienna; the rise of nationalism.

1851—Louis Napoleon becomes Emperor Napoleon III of France.

1859—Publication of Charles Darwin's *Origin of the Species*.

1860—Giuseppe Garibaldi and his 1,000 Red Shirts invade Sicily.

1861—Unification of Italy.

1862—Prince Otto von Bismarck becomes minister-president of Prussia.

1866—First transatlantic cable from Europe to the United States.

1866—Austro-Prussian War.

1870–1871—Franco-Prussian War.

1871—Unification of Germany.

1880–1900—The scramble for Africa; imperialism.

1894—The Dreyfus Affair in France.

1898—The Boxer Rebellion in China.

1898—The Spanish-American War.

1898—Marie Curie discovers radium.

1899—Publication of Rudyard Kipling's *White Man's Burden*.

1899–1902—The British fight Afrikaners in the Boer War.

1905—The First Russian Revolution.

1905–1910—Albert Einstein works on theory of relativity.

1914—World War I begins with assassination of Archduke Franz Ferdinand.

1914–1918—World War I, also known as the Great War and the War to End All Wars.

1917–1918—Russian Revolution or Bolshevik Revolution.

1919—The Treaty of Versailles.

1922—Benito Mussolini rises to power in Italy.

1928—Stalin begins Five-Year Plans.

1929–1939—The Great Depression.

1929—Publication of Erich Remarque's *All Quiet on the Western Front*.

1930—Talkies become part of entertainment culture.

1933—Adolf Hitler rises to power in Germany.

1936—Hitler and Mussolini back Franco in the Spanish Civil War.

1936—Publication of John Maynard Keynes's *The General Theory of Employment, Interest and Money*.

1939—Hitler and Stalin sign non-aggression pact.

1939—Hitler invades Poland.

1939–1945—World War II and the Holocaust.

1946—First meeting of the General Assembly of the United Nations.

1947—The Marshall Plan.

1948—The Berlin Airlift.

1948—Israel becomes a nation.

1950–1970s—Cold War.

1955–1962—De-Stalinization in Soviet Union.

1957—Russians launch Sputnik satellite into orbit.

1957—Treaty of Rome creates European Common Market.

1960—U-2 spy plane incident.

1961—Construction of Berlin Wall.

1962—The Cuban Missile Crisis.

1970s—Détente in Cold War.

1979—Margaret Thatcher becomes British prime minister.

1979—Soviet Union invades Afghanistan.

1986—Nuclear accident in Chernobyl.

1989—Fall of Berlin Wall; reunification of East and West Germany.

1989—Fall of communism in Europe.

1991—The Soviet Union collapses.

1991–1995—War in former Yugoslavia.

1992—The Treaty of Maastricht creates the European Union.

1997—Mother Theresa dies.

2002—Trial of Slobodan Milosevic begins.

2005—Pope John Paul II dies.

Online Resources for Further Research

Part 1: Climbing Out of the Middle Ages (c.1300–1600)

1. The End of the World as We Know It

The Bubonic Plague:
www.emedicine.com/emerg/topic428.htm

The Bubonic Plague:
www.themiddleages.net/plague.html

The Hundred Years' War:
www.theotherside.co.uk/tmheritage/background/100yearswar.htm

The Hundred Years' War:
www.100yearswar.co.uk

The Crusades:
www.medievalcrusades.com

2. The Renaissance: Civilization Reborn

Italian Renaissance:
www.wsu.edu:8080/~dee/REN/BACK.HTM

Humanism:
www.loc.gov/exhibits/vatican/humanism.html

Humanism:
www.learner.org/exhibits/renaissance/printing_sub.html

Renaissance Art:
www.artchive.com/artchive/renaissance.html

3. Time for a Change in the Church

John Wycliffe:
www.wycliffe.org/history/JWycliff.htm

Jan Hus:
justus.anglican.org/resources/bio/7.html

Luther's *95 Theses:*
www.iclnet.org/pub/resources/text/wittenberg/luther/web/ninetyfive.html

4. Time for an Alternative to the Church

John Calvin:
www.ccel.org/c/calvin

John Knox:
www.newgenevacenter.org/biography/knox2.htm

The Anabaptists:
www.anabaptists.org

English Reformation:
www.bbc.co.uk/history/state/church_reformation/english_reformation_01.shtml

Henry VIII:
www.tudorhistory.org

5. The Catholic and Counter Reformations

The Catholic Reformation:
mars.acnet.wnec.edu/~grempel/courses/wc2/lectures/catholicreform.html

The Counter-Reformation:
www.historylearningsite.co.uk/counter-reform.htm

The Council of Trent:
www.newadvent.org/cathen/15030c.htm

Texts from the Council of Trent:
history.hanover.edu/texts/trent.html

The Index of Prohibited Books:
www.fordham.edu/halsall/mod/indexlibrorum.html

Part 2: Might Makes Right, Right? (c.1450–1750)

6. God, Gold, and Glory

The Age of Exploration:
www.mariner.org/educationalad/ageofex

Christopher Columbus:
www.ucalgary.ca/applied_history/tutor/eurvoya/columbus.html

Christopher Columbus:
www.fordham.edu/halsall/source/columbus1.html

Conquistadores:
college.hmco.com/history/readerscomp/mil/html/mh_012000_conquistador.htm

The Spanish Armada:
www.nmm.ac.uk/server/show/conWebDoc.171

7. Our Religion Is Better Than Your Religion

French Wars of Religion:
www.lepg.org/wars.htm

Letters of Philip II:
www.lib.byu.edu/~rdh/phil2

Mary I and Elizabeth I of England:
www.tudorhistory.org

The Witch Hunts:
www.gendercide.org/case_witchhunts.html

The *Malleus Maleficarum:*
www.malleusmaleficarum.org

8. The Rise and Fall of the Holy Roman Empire

The Holy Roman Empire:
www.ucalgary.ca/applied_history/tutor/endmiddle/holy.html

The Thirty Years' War:
www.pipeline.com/~cwa/TYWHome.htm

The Thirty Years' War:
www.shsu.edu/~his_ncp/Thirty.html

9. Am I in Charge? Absolutely!

Cardinal Richelieu:
www.newadvent.org/cathen/13047a.htm

Louis XIV:
www.louis-xiv.de/louisold/louisxiv.html

Versailles:
www.chateauversailles.fr/en

James I of England:
www.luminarium.org/sevenlit/james

The English Civil War:
history.boisestate.edu/westciv/english

The Glorious Revolution:
www.bbc.co.uk/history/timelines/britain/stu_glorious_rev.shtml

10. The Eastern Absolutists

The Habsburgs:
www.h-net.org/~habsweb

The History of Prussia:
web.ics.purdue.edu/~mbishop/frames/prusshist.html

Ivan the Terrible:
mars.acnet.wnec.edu/~grempel/courses/russia/lectures/09ivanIV.html

Peter the Great:
www.fordham.edu/halsall/mod/petergreat.html

Baroque Music:
www.baroquemusic.org

Baroque Art:
www.ibiblio.org/wm/paint/glo/baroque

Part 3: Revolutions Galore (c.1500–1800)

11. Revolt of the Scientists

The Scientific Revolution:
web.clas.ufl.edu/users/rhatch/pages/03-Sci-Rev/SCI-REV-Home

Galileo:
galileo.rice.edu

Sir Isaac Newton:
www-groups.dcs.st and.ac.uk/~history/Mathematicians/Newton.html

Bacon and Descartes:
www.thingsrevealed.net/dscrtbacn.htm

12. Enlightening the Public, Not the People

The Enlightenment:
www.wsu.edu/~dee/ENLIGHT/ENLIGHT.HTM

John Locke:
plato.stanford.edu/entries/locke

Voltaire:
www.online-literature.com/voltaire

Jean-Jacques Rousseau:
www.wabash.edu/Rousseau

Texts by Enlightened Absolutists:
www.fordham.edu/halsall/mod/modsbook11.html

13. The Agricultural Revolution and an Expanding Europe

Agricultural Revolution:
www.bbc.co.uk/history/society_culture/industrialisation/
agricultural_revolution_01.shtml

Agricultural Revolution:
www.saburchill.com/history/chapters/IR/006.html

Mercantilism:
en.wikipedia.org/wiki/Mercantilism

Adam Smith:
www.blupete.com/Literature/Biographies/Philosophy/Smith.htm#TOC

14. The French Revolution

French Revolution:
chnm.gmu.edu/revolution

French Revolution:
www.historychannel.com/frenchrevolution

French Revolution:
www.historyguide.org/intellect/lecture11a.html

Documents of the French Revolution:
www.fordham.edu/halsall/mod/modsbook13.html

Part 4. You Say You Want More Revolution? (c.1800–1900)

15. A "Little" Guy Named Napoleon, a Big Wig Named Metternich

Napoleon:
www.napoleonguide.com

Napoleon:
www.pbs.org/empires/napoleon

Napoleon:
www.napoleon.org/en/home.asp

The Napoleonic Code:
www.history-magazine.com/codenap.html

Memoirs of Metternich:
www.h-net.org/~habsweb/sourcetexts/mettsrc.htm

16. The Industrial Revolution

Documents of the Industrial Revolution:
www.fordham.edu/halsall/mod/modsbook14.html

Industrialization:
www.bbc.co.uk/history/society_culture/industrialisation

Luddites:
www.spartacus.schoolnet.co.uk/PRluddites.htm

Romanticism:
www.wsu.edu:8080/~brians/hum_303/romanticism.html

Romantic Literature:
www.fordham.edu/halsall/mod/modsbook15.html

Romantic Art:
www.artcyclopedia.com/history/romanticism.html

17. Intriguing New Ideologies

Socialism:
www.the-wood.org/socialism

Utopian Socialists:
cepa.newschool.edu/het/schools/utopia.htm

Marx:
www.historyguide.org/intellect/marx.html

Marx:
www.marxists.org

Communist Manifesto:
www.anu.edu.au/polsci/marx/classics/manifesto.html

18. Growing Pains

Revolutions of 1848:
www.cats.ohiou.edu/~Chastain/contents.htm

Revolutions of 1848:
www.age-of-the-sage.org/history/1848/revolution_of_1848.html

Napoleon III:
www.newgenevacenter.org/biography/louis-napoleon2.htm

Unification of Italy:
www.arcaini.com/ITALY/ItalyHistory/ItalianUnification.htm

Bismarck and Unification of Germany:
www.zum.de/whkmla/region/germany/bismarck.html

19. What a Tangled Web

Bismarckian Alliances:
www.aldridgeshs.eq.edu.au/sose/modrespg/imperial/britanicares/britanica4.htm

White Man's Burden:
historymatters.gmu.edu/d/5478

The Balkans:
www.lib.msu.edu/sowards/balkan

Part 5. Big Wars and Big Bangs (Twentieth Century)

20. Turning the World Upside Down

World War I:
www.firstworldwar.com

World War I:
www.worldwar1.com

Russian Revolution:
www.spartacus.schoolnet.co.uk/Russian-Revolution.htm

Russian Revolution:
www.historyguide.org/europe/lecture5.html

Great Depression:
Documents of the Great Depression:
www.fordham.edu/halsall/mod/modsbook41.html

21. World War: Second Verse, Worse Than the First

World War II:
www.bbc.co.uk/history/war/wwtwo

World War II:
www.spartacus.schoolnet.co.uk/2WW.htm

Holocaust:
www.holocaust-history.org

Holocaust:
www.historyplace.com/worldwar2/holocaust/timeline.html

22. The Cold War Era

United Nations:
www.un.org

NATO:
www.nato.int

Warsaw Pact:
www.shsu.edu/~his_ncp/WarPact.html

Cold War:
www.cnn.com/SPECIALS/cold.war

Cold War:
www.coldwar.org

23. Changing Millennia

Revolutions of 1989:
www.lib.msu.edu/sowards/balkan/lect24.htm

Berlin Wall:
www.wall-berlin.org/gb/berlin.htm

Collapse of the Soviet Union:
http://newarkwww.rutgers.edu/guides/glo-sov.html

Milosevic Trial:
hague.bard.edu

Ethnic Cleansing:
balkansnet.org/ethnicl.html

EU:
europa.eu.int

Index

Numbers

1989, decline and fall of communism, 387-388
95 Theses Against the Sale of Indulgences, The, 48-49

A

absenteeism, 45
absolutism, 139
  Eastern absolutists
    Austria, 158-161
    Baroque style, 169-170
    plight of the peasants, 157-158
    Prussia, 161-163
    Russia, 164-168
  England, 148-149
    Charles I, 150-151
    Cromwell, Oliver, 151-153
    Glorious Revolution, 154-155
    Hobbes, Thomas, 153-154
    King James I of England, 149
    Restoration of 1660, 153
  Enlightenment, 201
    Catherine the Great, 202-203
    Frederick the Great, 201-202
    Joseph II, 203-204
    Theresa, Maria, 203
  Louis XIV, 144-145
    Age of Louis XIV, 148
    defense of faith, 146
    interest in the military, 147
    mercantilism, 146-147
    Versailles, 145-146
  origins of, 140
    Bethune, Maximilien, 141
    Henry IV, 140-141
    Mazarin, Jules, 143-144
    Richelieu, Cardinal, 142-143
Adenauer, Konrad, 371
administrative monarchy. *See* absolutism
Adolphus, Gustavus, 132
Africa, colonization and development of alliances, 314-318
aftermath
  Thirty Years' War, 133-136
  World War I, 339
    age of anxiety, 339
    art and literature, 342-343
    Continental Drift, 345-346
    Great Depression, 343
    scientific ideas, 341
    unsettling philosophies, 340-341
  World War II, 370-372
Against the Murdering, Thieving Hordes, 54
Age of Louis XIV, 148

Agincourt (Hundred Years' War), 9
Agricultural Revolution, 205
  Atlantic Economy, 214-218
  open-field system, 206-208
  origins of, 205-206
  population explosion, 211-212
  rural industry, 212-214
  technology, 208-211
agriculture
  British industrialization, 259
  Thirty Years' War, losses, 135-136
Alexander I, 248
Alexander II, 304
Alexander III, 305
Alexandra, 332
Algeria, independence from France, 379
All Quiet on the Western Front, 329
Allgemeiner Deutscher Arbeiterverein (General German Workers' Association), 283
Alliance of the Three Emperors, 316-318
alliances (expansionism), 315
  Africa, 314-318
  Alliance of the Three Emperors, 316-318
  Balkan powder keg, 319-320
  Congo Conference, 316
  nationalism in British Isles, 320-321

rising tension between Germany and Anglo-French Alliance, 318-319
Triple Entente, 318
American colonies, rebellion against Britain, 220-222
Amish, 66
Anabaptists, 65-66
Anderson, Anna, 333
Andropov, Yuri, 389
Angelice, 82
Anglican Parliament, 153
Anglo-French Alliance, 318-319
Anglo-French Entente, 318
Anglo-Russo Agreement, 318
anti-Communist sentiment, 384
1989, 387-388
Balkans, 391
breakup of Yugoslavia, 392
ethnic cleansing, 393-394
Yugoslav wars, 392-393
collapse of Soviet Union, 389-391
John Paul II, Pope, 386
Poland, 385
Reagan, President Ronald, 386
reunification of Germany, 388-389
Soviet Union, 384
Anti-Fascist Protection Wall, 375
anti-Semitism, Hitler, Adolf, 350-352
Antoinette, Marie, 228
apostolic succession, 71
appeasement, 352, 355
architecture, Baroque style, 170
Aristotle, 177
Arkwright, Richard, 259

Armada, Spanish, 117-118
armies of the Mongols (Golden Horde), 164
armistice, World War I, 336-337
Army Order Number One (Petrograd Soviet), 333
Arouet, François Marie (Voltaire), 197-198
art
Baroque style, 169
Northern Renaissance, 36
post–World War I, 342-343
Renaissance, 30-33
Romanticism, 272
Art of the Impossible, The, 387
Assembly of Russian Factory and Plant Workers, 331
assignats, 229
Association of All Classes and All Nations, 267
astrolabe, 94
Atlantic Economy, 214-215
slavery, 217
Smith, Adam, 216-217
Triangle Trade, 217-218
Atlee, Clement, 371
atom, scientific ideas post–World War I, 341
Austria
absolutism, 158
Habsburg Empire, 108, 159-160
Pragmatic Sanction, 161
War of the Spanish Succession, 160
declaration of war on Serbia, 326-327
revolutions of 1848, 294-295
Austro-Hungarian Empire, 296
Avila, Theresa of, 84

B

Babylonian Captivity, 14-15
Bacon, Sir Francis, 184-185
Bakewell, Robert, 210
Bakunin, Mikhail, 282
balance of power politics, 245
Bourbon dynasty restoration, 246
Congress of Vienna, 247-249
Italian states, 245-246
Balkans
anti-Communist sentiment, 391
breakup of Yugoslavia, 392
ethnic cleansing, 393-394
Yugoslav wars, 392-393
Balkan powder keg, 319-320
Ball, John, 43
banking families, Renaissance, 24-26
Barnabites, 82
Baroque style, 169-170
Barth, Karl, 341
Bastille, storming of, 226-227
Battle of Borodino, 243
Battle of Castillon, 11
Battle of Hastings, 4
Battle of Nations, 244
Battle of Omdurman, 315
Battle of Waterloo, 244-245
Bayle, Pierre, 192
Beer Hall Putsch, 351
Beethoven, Ludwig von, 272
Beggar's Opera, The, 387
Belgium
German invasion of, 327
independence of Belgian Congo and Rwanda from, 378
Berg, Alban, 342

Beria, Lavrenty, 374
Berlin Airlift, 368
Berlin Conference, 316
Berlin Wall construction, 374-375
Bethune, Maximilien (Duke of Sully), 141
Big Three, Cold War era, 366
bio-terrorism, 397
Bismarck, Otto von, 315
    Berlin Conference, 316
    League of the Three Emperors, 316
    unification of Germany, 300-302
Black Death, 6
Blair, Prime Minister Tony, 398
Blake, William, 271
Blanc, Louis, 278
blank slate theory (*tabula rasa*), Enlightenment, 193
Bohemian Phase (Thirty Years' War), 130-131
Boleyn, Anne, 69
Bolshevik Revolution, 334-336
Bonaparte, Charles Louis Napoleon, 238, 296
    appointment to First Consul, 240
    balance of political power after defeat at Waterloo, 245
        Bourbon dynasty restoration, 246
        Congress of Vienna, 247-249
        Italian states, 245-246
    Battle of Borodino, 243
    Battle of Nations, 244
    Battle of Waterloo, 244-245
    Concordat of 1801, 240-241
    early life and background, 238-239
    election of, 296-297

foreign policy goals, 242-243
Hundred Days, 244
military career, 239
Napoleonic Code, 241
participation in plot to overthrow the Directory, 238
reclamation and public works projects, 298
restructuring of French government, 241
rule of France, 297-298
Bonaparte, Lucien, 238
Book of Common Order, The, 63
Book of Common Prayer, 72
Book of Martyrs, The, 71
Bosnian war, 392
Bourbon dynasty restoration, 246
boyars, 165
Brahe, Tycho, 178
Brandt, Willy, 377
Brezhnev, Leonid, 376
    invasion of Afghanistan, 384
    summit with Nixon, 377
Brezhnev Doctrine, 376
Britain
    American colonies rebellion against, 220-222
    declaration of war on Germany, 356-357
    Dreadnought class of battleships, 319
    interwar years, 353
    textile industry, 258-261
British East India Company, 314
British Empire, decolonization, 378
British Isles, nationalism, 320-321
British Parliament, 292
brownshirts, 351

Broz, Josip, 391
Brunelleschi, Filippo (Renaissance artist), 32
bubonic plague, 5-7
Bukharin, Nikolai, 347
Burckhardt, Jacob, 22
Byron, Lord, 271

C

Cabal, 153
Cabet, Etienne, 278
Cabot, John, 103
Calas, Jean, 198
calls for human rights (philosophes), 219
Calvin, John, 59-60
    reaction to Scientific Revolution, 182
    theology, 60-62
Candide, 198
canonization of Joan of Arc, 10
Cape of Good Hope, 97
Capital: A Critique of Political Economy, 280
Carafa, Cardinal, 85
caravel, 94
Carlsbad Decrees, 254
Cartier, Jacques, 102
cartography, 92
Cartwright, Edmund, 260
Castillon, Battle of, 11
Castle of Otranto, The, 271
Catalan World Atlas, 93
Catherine of Siena, 15
Catherine the Great, 202-203
Catholic Church
    influence during the Middle Ages, 12
        Babylonian Captivity, 14-15
        change in Church's power, 16-17

Conciliar Movement, 16
Crusades, 13-14
Great Schism, 15-16
reaction to Scientific
Revolution, 182-183
Reformation, 40
hierarchy and governance
of the Church, 40-41
Hus, Jan, 43-44
Luther, Martin, 46-55
problems with the
Church, 44-45
Wycliffe, John, 41-43
Catholic Emancipation in the
United Kingdom, 245
Catholic Reformation, 76
Congregation of the
Inquisition, 85-87
Council of Trent, 79-81
humanists, 77-78
monasticism, 82-84
Oratory of the Divine Love,
78
Catholic Social Thought, 372
Catholics versus Protestants,
115
defeat of the Spanish
Armada, 117-118
Elizabeth I, 116
Tudor, Mary, 115-116
Cavaliers, 151
Cavour, Count Camillo di, 299
Ceausescu, Nicolae, 388
Cezanne, Paul, 342
Chamber of Deputies, 246
Chamber of Peers, 246
Chamberlain, Neville, 353
Champlain, Samuel, 102
Charlemagne (Charles the
Great), 4, 124
Charles I
death of English absolutism,
153-155
English Civil War, 150-151

Charles II, 153
Charles the Fair, 7
Charles the Great
(Charlemagne), 4, 124
Charles V, 109, 127
Charles VI, Pragmatic
Sanction, 160-161
Charles X, 246, 293
Chartists, 292
Châtelet, Madame du, 197
Cheka, 336
Chernenko, Konstantin, 389
chiaroscuro technique
(Renaissance art), 31
chivalry, 8
cholera, 269
Christian Democrats, 371
Christian humanism, 35-36
Christian IV, 131
Christianity, influence during
the Middle Ages, 12
Babylonian Captivity, 14-15
change in Church's power,
16-17
Conciliar Movement, 16
Crusades, 13-14
Great Schism, 15-16
Church, The, 43
Church of England, 71
Churchill, Winston, 367, 371
Ciompi Revolt, 26-27
city life, Industrial Revolution,
267-269
city-states, 23, 26-27
civil code of 1804, 241
*Civilization of the Renaissance in
Italy in 1860, The*, 22
classes of citizens (France),
National Assembly, 224-227
*Declaration of the Rights of
Man, The*, 228
status of women, 228
written laws, 229

Clemenceau, Georges, 337
clergy (French class of citizen),
224
Coalitions, 242
Code of Chivalry, 8
Coercive Acts, 221
Colbert, Jean-Baptiste, 146-147
Cold War era, 365
Big Three, 366
decolonization, 377-379
east versus west, 368
Berlin Airlift, 368-369
formation of Communist
parties, 368
NATO (North Atlantic
Treaty Organization),
369
Warsaw Pact, 369-370
economy, 379-381
distrust of the Soviet
Union, 381
fall of the dollar, 380
OPEC embargo, 380-381
pre–Cold War tensions, 367
Soviet Union, 373
Brezhnev Doctrine, 376
De-Stalinization,
374-375
death of Stalin, 373
détente, 377
United Nations
Organization, 366
WWII aftermath, 370-372
Coleridge, Samuel Taylor, 271
Coligny, Admiral Gaspard, 111
collapse of Soviet Union,
389-391
Collins, Michael, 321
colonies, 103
Africa, 314-318
American colonies' rebellion
against Britain, 220-222
function of mercantilism,
215-218

Columbian Exchange, 104-105
Columbus, Christopher, 98-100
Combination Acts, 266
command economies, 330
commercial revival (Renaissance), 24
Committee of Public Safety (National Convention), 231-233
Common Market, 381
commoners (French class of citizen), National Assembly, 225-227
    Declaration of the Rights of Man, The, 228
    status of women, 228
    written laws, 229
Commonwealth of Independent States, 391
communes, 26
communism
    Cold War era, 368
    Communist Party, Brezhnev Doctrine, 376
    decline and fall of, 384
        1989, 387-388
        Balkans, 391-394
        collapse of Soviet Union, 389-391
        Poland, 385
        Pope John Paul II, 386
        Reagan, President Ronald, 386
        reunification of Germany, 388-389
        Soviet Union, 384
    Marx, Karl, 281-282
    Stalin, Joseph, 347-349
Communist League, 281-283
Communist Manifesto, The, 279-282

concentration camps, 362
Concert of Europe, 247
Conciliar Movement, 16
Conclusions (Lollards), 42
Concordat of 1801, 240-241
Concordat of Bologna, 109
Confession of Faith, 63
Congo Conference, 316
Congregation of the Inquisition, 85-87
Congress of Troppau, 253
Congress of Vienna, 247-249
    conservatism, 251-252
    liberalism, 250-251
    nationalism, 249-250
conquistador expeditions, 100-101
conservatism, 251-254
consistory, 61
Constable, John, 272
Constituent Assembly, 294
Constitution of Year X, 240
Constitution of Year XVIII, 240
construction of Berlin Wall, 374-375
consubstantiation, 53
consul, 238
Contarini, Gasparo, 78
Continental Drift, 345-346
Continental System, 243
convents, 82
Conversations on the Plurality of Worlds, 191
conversos, 84
Copenhagen Criteria, 396
Copernicus, Nicholas, 177-178
Corday, Charlotte, 233
Corn Laws, 292
Coronado, Francisco, 102
Cort, Henry, 263

Cortés, Hernán, 100-101
cottage industry, 212-214
cotton "spinning jenny," 258
Council of Ancients, 234, 238
Council of Constance, 16, 43
Council of Five Hundred, 234, 238
Council of Trent, 79-81
Council of Two Hundred, 60
Counter-Reformation. *See* Catholic Reformation
Courtier, The, 32
Coverdale, Miles, 68
Cranmer, Thomas, 68
Crécy, Battle at, 8-9
Credit-Anstalt collapse, 343
Cresques, Abraham, *Catalan World Atlas*, 93
Crimean War, 303
Crompton, Samuel, 260
Cromwell, Oliver, 151-153
Cromwell, Richard, 152
Cromwell, Thomas, 70
crop rotation, 207
Crusades, 13-14
Crystal Palace, 261
Cuban Missile Crisis, 375
cult of personality, 373
Cult of Reason, 232
Cult of the Supreme Being, 232
czar, Russian, 165
Czech Brethren, 44
Czechoslovakia, 387

D

d'Ailly, Pierre, *Image of the World*, 95
d'Alembert, Jean le Rond, 196
d'Holbach, Baron Paul, 199

D1 tanks, 337
da Gama, Vasco, 97-98
da Vinci, Leonardo, 32
Dadaism, 342
Danish Phase (Thirty Years' War), 131
Dark Ages, 4
Darwin, Charles, 314
Das Kapital, 280
David, Jacques-Louis, 226, 233, 272
Dawes Plan, 346
Dayton Accords, 393
de Balboa, Vasco, 102
de Gaulle, Charles, 371, 379
de Soto, Hernando, 102
de' Medici, Catherine, 110
De-Stalinization of Soviet Union, 374-375
Death of Marat, 233
Death Strip (Berlin Wall), 375
Declaration of Independence, 221
Declaration of Pillnitz, 229-230
Declaration of the Rights of Man, The, 228
Declaration of the Rights of Woman, 228
decline of the Holy Roman Empire, 134-135
decolonization of United Kingdom, 377-379
deductive reasoning, 185-186
Defenestration of Prague, 129-130
deism, 194
Delacroix, Eugene, 272
Delcassé, Théophile, 318
demilitarized zone (DMZ), 338
Descartes, René, 185-186
Descent of Man, The, 314

détente, 377
Dialogue on the Two Chief Systems of the World, 180
Dias, Bartholomew, 97
dictatorships, post–World War I, 346
   Hitler, Adolf, 350-352
   Mussolini, Benito, 349-350
   Stalin, Joseph, 347-349
Diderot, Denis, 196
Diet of Speyer, 55
Diet of Worms, 51-52
Directorium inquisitorium, 86
Discourse on Methods, 185
disease, bubonic plague, 5-7
division of labor in European cities, 286
DMZ (demilitarized zone), 338
doctrines, 41
domestic policy, Khrushchev, Nikita, 374
Donatello (Renaissance artist), 32
Drake, Sir Francis, 103-105
Dreadnought class of battle-ships, 319
Dreyfus Affair, 321-322
Dreyfus, Alfred, 321
Dubček, Alexander, 376
Ducos, Roger, 238
Duke of Sully (Maximilien de Bethune), 141
Dutch trade, 103

E

east versus west (Cold War era), 368
   Berlin Airlift, 368-369
   formation of Communist parties, 368

NATO (North Atlantic Treaty Organization), 369
Warsaw Pact, 369-370
Eastern absolutists
   Austria, 158
      Habsburg Empire, 159-160
      Pragmatic Sanction, 161
      War of the Spanish Succession, 160
   Baroque style, 169-170
   plight of the peasants, 157-158
   Prussia, 161-163
   Russia, 164
      czar, 165
      Ivan IV, 165-166
      Mongol Yoke, 164
      Peter the Great, 166-168
      Time of Troubles, 166
Eastern Front
   World War I, 329-330
   World War II, 358-359
eastern trade, global economy, 310
EC (European Community), 373
economy, 307
   Cold War era, 379-381
   eastern trade, 310
   European migrations, 310-311
   foreign investments and markets, 309
   relationship between indus-trialization and economy, 309
   Thirty Years' War, 135-136
   worldwide trade, 308
Edict of Nantes, 112-113
Edict of Restitution, 131
EEC (European Economic Community), 372

Einstein, Albert, 341
Elizabeth I
 defeat of the Spanish
  Armada, 117-118
 restoration of Anglican
  Church, 73
 return of England to
  Protestantism, 116
Elizabethan Settlement, 117
embargo, OPEC (Organization
 of Petroleum Exporting
 Countries), 380-381
emigration, 311
Emile, 200
Emiliani, Jerome, 82
Emmanuel, Victor, III, 299
Emperor Charles V, 113
Emperor Sigismund, 16
enclosure movement
 (Agricultural Revolution), 208
encomenderos, 104
Encyclopedie, 196
Engels, Friedrich, 279-280
England
 absolutism, 148-149
  Charles I, 150-151
  Cromwell, Oliver,
   151-153
  Glorious Revolution,
   154-155
  Hobbes, Thomas,
   153-154
  King James I of England,
   149
  Restoration of 1660, 153
 Hundred Years' War, 7-8
  battle at Crécy, 8-9
  Battle of Castillon, 11
  Joan of Arc, 10-11
  rise of nationalism, 11-12
  Treaty of Troyes, 9

Protestants versus Catholics,
 115
 defeat of the Spanish
  Armada, 117-118
 Elizabeth I, 116
 Tudor, Mary, 115-116
English Civil War, 150-151
English Reformation, 67
 Church of England, 71
 Henry VIII, 68-69
 Reformation Parliament,
  70-71
 restoration of Anglican
  Church by Elizabeth I, 73
 return of England to
  Catholicism by Mary
  Tudor, 72-73
 Tyndale, William, 68
Enlightenment
 absolutists, 201
  Catherine the Great,
   202-203
  Frederick the Great,
   201-202
  Joseph II, 203-204
  Theresa, Maria, 203
 contrast to Romanticism,
  270-271
 Encyclopedie, 196
 late Enlightenment, 198
  d'Holbach, Baron Paul,
   199
  Hume, David, 199
  Rousseau, Jean-Jacques,
   199-200
 link to Scientific Revolution,
  190-193
 philosophes, 193-194
  France, 194-195
  push for tolerance,
   196-197
  Voltaire, 197-198

Entente Cordiale, 318
epicycles, 177
Erasmus, Desiderius, 36, 77
Erhard, Ludwig, 372
*Essay Concerning Human
 Understanding*, 193
*Essay on the Principle of
 Population*, 212
Essays, 192
estates (French legal classes),
 224-225
Estates-General, 223-226
Esterhazy, Ferdinand, 321
et Minh, 379
ethnic cleansing, 393-394
EU (European Union), 395
euro currency, 396
European Coal and Steel
 Community, 372
European Coal and Steel
 union, 395
European Community (EC),
 373
European Economic
 Community (EEC), 372
European exploration, 91-92
 motivations, 95-97
 overseas exploration, 92-93
  advanced technologies,
   93-94
  Cartier, Jacques, 102
  Columbus, Christopher,
   98-100
  conquistadors, 100-101
  d'Ailly, Pierre, 95
  Dutch trade, 103
  Magellan, Ferdinand, 102
  Ponce de Leon, Juan, 102
  Portuguese expeditions,
   97-98
  Spanish expeditions,
   104-105

European Union (EU), 373, 394-396
expansionism
    alliances, 315
        Alliance of the Three Emperors, 316-318
        Balkan powder keg, 319-320
        Congo Conference, 316
        nationalism in British Isles, 320-321
        rising tension between Germany and Anglo-French Alliance, 318-319
        Triple Entente, 318
    imperialism, 312-315
    White Man's Burden, 312
experiment (scientific method), 187
exploitation of children, Industrial Revolution, 265
explorations of Europeans, 91-92
    motivations, 95-97
    overseas exploration, 92-93
        advanced technologies, 93-94
        Cartier, Jacques, 102
        Columbus, Christopher, 98-100
        conquistadors, 100-101
        d'Ailly, Pierre, 95
        Dutch trade, 103
        Magellan, Ferdinand, 102
        Ponce de Leon, Juan, 102
        Portuguese expeditions, 97-98
        Spanish expeditions, 104-105

F

factories, rise of (Britain), 259-261
Factory Act of 1833, 266
Factory Act of 1844, 266
fall of communism, 384
    1989, 387-388
    Balkans, 391
        breakup of Yugoslavia, 392
        ethnic cleansing, 393-394
        Yugoslav wars, 392-393
    collapse of Soviet Union, 389-391
    John Paul II, Pope, 386
    Poland, 385
    Reagan, President Ronald, 386
    reunification of Germany, 388-389
    Soviet Union, 384
fall of Holy Roman Empire, 134-135
family unit ideas (nineteenth century), 284
    attitudes about children, 287-288
    emerging middle class, 284-286
    status of women, 286-287
Farel, Guillaume, 59-60
Farnese, Alexander, 114
Fasci de Combattimento (League of Combat), 349
fascism, Mussolini, Benito, 349-350
Federal Republic of Germany, 371
Fens land, 209
Ferdinand I, 128, 294

Ferdinand II, 128
Ferdinand III, 128, 159
Ferdinand, Archduke Franz, 130, 326
Festival of Reason, 232
fiefs, 4
financial consequences of World War II, 371
First Balkan War, 320
First Battle of the Marne (WWI), 328-329
First Book of Discipline, The, 63
First Coalition, 229
First Consul appointment, Bonaparte, Napoleon, 240
First International, 280
Five Year Plans (Stalin), 347
fleet convoy system (Spain), 105
Florence, Ciompi Revolt, 26-27
flota, 105
flying shuttle, 258
Fontenelle, Bernard de, 191
foreign investments/markets (global economy), 309
foreign policy
    Bonaparte, Napoleon, 242-243
    Khrushchev, Nikita, 374-375
foundations for modern scientific method, 186-187
Fountain of Youth, 102
Fourier, Charles, 277
Fourteen Points (Woodrow Wilson), 338
Fourteenth Winter Olympics, 394
Fourth Coalition, 242
Fourth Republic, 371
Fox, George, 67

France
  Algerian crisis, 379
  alliance with American
    colonies against Britain,
    222
  Bonaparte's rule of, 297-298
  declaration of war on
    Germany, 356-357
  decolonization, 379
  Dreyfus Affair, 321-322
  Enlightenment, 194-195
  First Battle of the Marne,
    328-329
  Hundred Years' War, 7
    battle at Crécy, 8-9
    Battle of Castillon, 11
    Joan of Arc, 10-11
    rise of nationalism, 11-12
    Treaty of Troyes, 9
  interwar years, 353
  invasion of England under
    Bonaparte, 242
  legal classes of citizens,
    224-225
    National Assembly,
      225-229
  restructuring of govern-
    ment, 241
  revolutions of 1848,
    293-294
  Wars of Religion, 110-113
Francis I, 109
Franco, General Francisco, 354
Frankenstein, 271
Frederick III, 162
Frederick V of the Palatinate,
  130
Frederick the Great, 201-202
French absolutism
  Bethune, Maximilien, 141
  Henry IV, 140-141

Louis XIV, 144-145
  Age of Louis XIV, 148
  Colbert and mercantil-
    ism, 146-147
  defense of faith, 146
  interest in the military,
    147
  Versailles, 145-146
Mazarin, Jules, 143-144
Richelieu, Cardinal,
  142-143
French and Indian War, 215
French Indochina, 379
French laws, Napoleonic Code,
  241
French Phase (Thirty Years'
  War), 132-133
French Resistance, 11
French Revolution, 219
  American colonies rebellion
    against Britain, 220-222
  Declaration of Pillnitz,
    229-230
  establishment of the
    Directory, 234
  Louis XVI, 223
    call for a meeting of the
      Estates-General,
      223-226
    restoration of power to
      parlements, 223
    storming of Bastille,
      226-227
  National Assembly takeover,
    227-229
  National Convention, 230
    Committee of Public
      Safety, 231-233
    split into Girondists and
      the Mountain, 230-231
    Thermidorian Reaction,
      233

French utopian socialism,
  276-278
fundamental laws of planetary
  motion (Kepler), 179
future of Europe, 399

G

Galen, 187
Galilei, Galileo, 179-180
galleons, 105
Gapon, Father George, 331
Garden Party, The, 387
Garibaldi, Giuseppe, 300
Gasperi, Alcide de, 371
Gauguin, Paul, 342
Gdansk Shipyard, 385
General Act of the Berlin
  Conference, 316
General German Workers'
  Association, 283
Geoffrin, Madame Marie-
  Thérèse, 195
George, David Lloyd, 337
Gericault, Theodore, 272
German Confederation, 248
German Confederation of the
  Rhine, 242
German Workers' Party, 351
Germany
  aftermath of Thirty Years'
    War, 135-136
  declaration of war by Britain
    and France, 356-357
  declaration of war on
    Russia, 327
  First Battle of the Marne,
    328-329
  Hitler, Adolf, 350-352
    appeasement of, 355
    military draft, 354-355
    Munich Conference, 354
    storm on Rhineland, 354

invasion of Belgium, 327
reunification, 388-389
Schlieffen Plan, 327
tension with Anglo-French
 Alliance, 318-319
unification of, 300-302
Gestapo, 352
Girondists (National
 Convention), 230-231
glasnost, 390-391
global economy, 307
 eastern trade, 310
 European migrations,
  310-311
 foreign investments and
  markets, 309
 relationship between indus-
  trialization and economy,
  309
 worldwide trade, 308
Glorious Revolution, 154-155
Goethe, *The Sorrows of Young
 Werther*, 271
Golden Horde (armies of the
 Mongols), 164
Gorbachev, Mikhail
 glasnost, 390-391
 perestroika, 389
Gouges, Olympe de, 228
government propaganda,
 World War I, 330
Grand Empire, 243
Grand National Consolidated
 Trades Union, 267
Grand Retreat, 244
Great Depression, 343
Great Exhibition of the Works
 of Industry of All Nations,
 261
Great Purges (Stalin), 348
Great Schism, 15-16
Great War. *See* World War I
Great Witch Hunt, 120-122

Grenadiers, 163
Grey, Lady Jane, 72
Guernica, bombing of, 353
Gutenberg Bible, 34
Gutenberg, Johann, 33-34

H

Habsburg Empire, 127-129
 eastern absolutism in
  Austria, 159-160
 Habsburg-Valois Wars,
  108-109
 Thirty Years' War, 129
  agricultural, economic
   and population losses,
   135-136
  Bohemian Phase,
   130-131
  Danish Phase, 131
  decline of the Holy
   Roman Empire,
   134-135
  Defenestration of Prague,
   129-130
  French Phase, 132-133
  Peace of Westphalia,
   133-134
  Swedish Phase, 132
Hammer of Witches, The, 120
Hardenburg, Karl von,
 Congress of Vienna, 247
Hargreaves, James, 258
Harvey, William, 188
Hastings, Battle of, 4
Haussmann, Georges, 269, 298
Havel, Vaclav, 387
Hegel, George, 279
heliocentric theory
 (Copernicus), 178
Henry II, 110
Henry IV, 112-113, 140-141

Henry of Navarre, 111
Henry the Navigator, 93
Henry VIII, 68-69
High Middle Ages, 4
High Sea Fleet, 319
Himmler, Heinrich, 352
Hindenburg, President Paul
 von, 351
Historical and Critical Dictionary,
 192
Hitler, Adolf, 350-352
 appeasement of, 355
 Holocaust, 360
  concentration camps, 362
  Mein Kampf, 361-362
  Nuremburg Trials, 363
  Wannsee Conference,
   362
 military draft, 354-355
 Munich Conference, 354
 storm on Rhineland, 354
Hobbes, Thomas, 153-154
Hohenzollern family, 161-162
Holocaust, 360-361
 concentration camps, 362
 Mein Kampf, 361-362
 Nuremburg Trials, 363
 Wannsee Conference, 362
Holy Alliance, 253-254
Holy Office, 85-87
Holy Roman Emperor, 109
Holy Roman Empire, 124-125
 Habsburg Empire, 127-129
  eastern absolutism in
   Austria, 159-160
  Habsburg-Valois Wars,
   108-109
  Thirty Years' War,
   129-136
 right to rule as emperor,
  125-126
 union of church and state,
  126-127

House of Bourbon, 110-111
House of Commons, 320
House of Guise, 110-111
Hudson, Henry, 103
Hugo, Victor, 271
Huguenots, Wars of Religion,
110-111
    Edict of Nantes, 112-113
    War of the Three Henrys,
    111-112
humanism, 77
    Christian humanism, 35-36
    Renaissance, 27-29
Hume, David, 199
Hunchback of Notre Dame, The,
271
Hundred Days, Napoleon's
rule of France, 244
Hundred Years' War, 7
    battle at Crécy, 8-9
    Battle of Castillon, 11
    Joan of Arc, 10-11
    rise of nationalism, 11-12
    tensions between France
    and England, 7-8
    Treaty of Troyes, 9
Hungarian Revolution, Warsaw
Pact, 370
Hus, Jan, 43-44
hypothesis (scientific method),
186

I

Icarians, 278
iconoclastic fury, 114
iconoclasts, 58
icons, 58
Ignatius of Loyola, Jesuits
(Society of Jesus), 83
Image of the World, 95

immigration, 311
Immortal Seven, 154
imperialism
    colonization of Africa,
    314-315
    justification, 313-314
    new versus old imperialism,
    312-313
Index librorum prohibitorum
(Index of Prohibited Books),
86
India, division into two states,
378
individualism, Renaissance, 30
Indo-Paksitani War, 378
Indonesia, independence from
the Netherlands, 378
inductive reasoning, 184-185
Industrial Revolution, 257
    British textile industry, 258
    conditions in Britain
      resulting in industrial-
      ization, 258-259
      Luddite attacks on facto-
      ries, 260-261
      rise of factories, 259-261
    influx of people into the
    cities, 267-269
    labor and reform, 264
      development of unions,
      266-267
      exploitation of children,
      265
      influence of factories,
      265-266
      reform movement, 266
      wages and work condi-
      tions, 264
    need for energy sources,
    261-263
    railroads, 263

industrialization
    relationship with economy,
    309
    Russian modernization,
    305-306
*Inquiry into the Nature and
Causes of the Wealth of Nations*,
216
inquisition, Congregation of
the Inquisition, 85-87
*Institutes of the Christian
Religion*, 61
Instrument of Government,
151
intellectual movement, 249
    conservatism, 251-254
    liberalism, 250-251
    nationalism, 249-250
intendants, 142
International Workers' Day,
282
International Workingmen's
Association, 280
Internationale, 388
Interregnum, 153
interwar years, 346
    appeasement of European
    nations, 352
    Britain, 353
    eastern Europe, 353
    France, 353
    Germany, 354-355
    Hitler, Adolf, 350-352
    Mussolini, Benito, 349-350
    Soviet Union, 353
    Spain, 353
    Stalin, Joseph, 347-349
Irish Republican Army bomb-
ings, 397
iron industry, 263

Italy
  Libyan independence from, 378
  Mussolini, Benito, 349-350
  Renaissance, 23-24
  unification of, 299-300
Ivan I, 164-165
Ivan III, 164
Ivan IV (Ivan the Terrible), 165-166
Ivanhoe, 271

J

Jacobins, 230
Jacquerie, 17-18
James I of England, 149
James II, 154
Jansenists, 146
Jesuits, 83
Jewish people, Holocaust, 360-361
  concentration camps, 362
  Mein Kampf, 361-362
  Nuremburg Trials, 363
  Wannsee Conference, 362
Joan of Arc, 10-11
John Paul II, Pope, 386
Joliet, Louis, 102
Joseph, Francis, 295
Joseph II, 203-204
Joyce, James, 342
June Days, 294
junkers, 162
justification for imperialism, 313-314

K

Kafka, Franz, 342
Kashmir region, 378
Kay, John, 258

Keats, John, 271
Kellogg-Briand Pact, 346
Kepler, Johannes, 178-179
Kerensky, Alexander, 334
Keynes, John Maynard, 343
Khrushchev, Nikita, De-Stalinization of Soviet Union, 370-375
Kierkegaard, Søren, 341
King Charles IX, 111
King Charles VII, 10
King Charles VIII, 108
King James I of England, 149
King Philip the Fair, 14
Kipling, Rudyard, 313
KLA (Kosovo Liberation Army), 393
Knox, John, 62-64
Kohl, Helmut, 381, 388
Kongkonferenz (Berlin conference), 316
Kornilov, General Lavr (Kornilov Coup), 334
Kosovo, 393
Kosovo Liberation Army (KLA), 393
Kramer, Heinrich, *The Hammer of Witches*, 120
kulaks, 348
Kulturkampf attacks (Bismarck), 317

L

labor issues
  Industrial Revolution, 264
    development of unions, 266-267
    exploitation of children, 265
    influence of factories, 265-266

    reform movement, 266
    wages and work conditions, 264
  socialism, 283
Labour Party, 371
Lafayette, Marquis de, 222
laissez faire economic policy (Smith), 216
Lasalle, Ferdinand, 283
Last Supper, The, 33
laws of planetary motion (Kepler), 179
lay investiture, 45
League of Combat (*Fasci de Combattimento*), 349
League of Nations, 338
League of the Just, 281
League of the Not Half-Bad, 281
League of the Outlaws, 281
League of the Three Emperors, 317
Lenin, Vladimir Ilyich, 334
Leopold II, 316
Letters to Olga, 387
liberal revolutions (revolutions of 1848), 291-300
  Austria, 294-295
  Bonaparte, Charles Louis Napoleon, 296-298
  France, 293-294
  Prussia, 295-296
  unification of Germany, 300-302
  unification of Italy, 299-300
liberalism, 250-251
Libertines, 60
Liberty Leading the People, 272
liberty or freedom (philosophes), 219
Libya, independence from Italy, 378
Lister, Joseph, 269

Liszt, Franz, 272
literature
   post–World War I, 342-343
   Romanticism, 271
Lithuania, 390
Liverpool and Manchester
   Railway, 263
Locke, John, 155, 193
Lollardy, 42-43
London, public transportation
   system, 398
Louis XIV (absolutist), 144
   Age of Louis XIV, 148
   defense of faith, 146
   interest in the military, 147
   mercantilism, 146-147
   Versailles, 145-146
Louis XVI, role in the French
   Revolution, 223
   call for a meeting of the
      Estates-General, 223-226
   restoration of power to par-
      lements, 223
   storming of Bastille,
      226-227
Louis XVIII, 246
Low Countries, 113
Lower Middle Age, 4
Loyalists, 221
Ludd, General Ned, 261
Luddites, 260-261
Luftwaffe, 354
Lusitania, 329
Luther, Martin
   reaction to Scientific
      Revolution, 182
   Reformation, 46-47
      Diet of Speyer, 55
      Diet of Worms, 51-52
      effects of ideas, 53-54
      exception to Tetzel's sale
         of indulgences, 48-49

Protestant thought versus
   Catholic dogma, 52-53
*Resolutions Concerning the
   Virtue of Indulgences*, 50
status of women, 55
struggle with salvation,
   47-48
Twelve Articles of the
   peasants, 54
Lyrical Ballads, 271

M

Maastricht Treaty, 395
Machiavelli, Niccolo, 25
Madrid bombing, 398
Magellan, Ferdinand, 102
Maizière, Lothar de, 388
Malleus maleficarum (*The
   Hammer of Witches*), 120
Malthus, Thomas, 212
Manifesto (*The Communist
   Manifesto*), 279-282
maps, age of exploration, 93
Marat, Jean-Paul, 233
Marquette, Jacques, 102
Marx, Karl, 278-281
Mary of Burgundy, 113
Masaccio (Renaissance artist),
   32
mass production of textiles,
   259-261
Maximilian II, 128
Maximilian III, 128
May Day, 282
Mazarin, Jules, 143-144
Medici family, 25-26
medieval art, 31
medicine, Scientific
   Revolution, 187-188
Mein Kampf, 361-362
Menshevik, 334

mercantilism, 146-147
   colonies as a function of,
      215
   slavery, 217
   Smith, Adam, 216-217
   Triangle Trade, 217-218
mercantilist economic system
   (Britain), 258
Merici, Angela, 84
Metternich, Prince Klemens
   von, 252-253
   Carlsbad Decrees, 254
   Congress of Vienna, 247
   Holy Alliance, 253-254
Michelangelo, 33
Middle Ages, 4-5
   bubonic plague, 5-7
   Hundred Years' War, 7
      battle at Crécy, 8-9
      Battle of Castillon, 11
      Joan of Arc, 10-11
      rise of nationalism, 11-12
      tensions between France
         and England, 7-8
      Treaty of Troyes, 9
   influence of the Catholic
      Church, 12
      Babylonian Captivity,
         14-15
      change in Church's
         power, 16-17
      Conciliar Movement, 16
      Crusades, 13-14
      Great Schism, 15-16
   peasant revolts, 17-18
   Reformation, 40-87
      Amish, 66
      Anabaptists, 65-66
      Calvin, John, 59-62
      Catholic Reformation,
         76-87
      English Reformation,
         67-73

Farel, Guillaume, 59-60
hierarchy and governance
  of the Church, 40-41
Hus, Jan, 43-44
Luther, Martin, 46-55
problems with the
  Church, 44-45
Quakers, 67
Reformation of the
  Common Man, 58-59
spread to Scotland, 62-64
Wycliffe, John, 41-43
Renaissance, 21-36
  art, 30-33
  city-states, 26-27
  commercial revival, 24
  communes, 26
  humanism, 27-29
  individualism, 30
  Italy, 23-24
  Northern Renaissance,
    34-36
  power of banking fami-
    lies, 24-26
  printing press, 33-34
  republics, 26
  secularism, 29-30
middle-class emergence,
  284-286
Middle Passage, 218
migration (European migrations), 310-311
military draft (Hitler), 354-355
Mill, John Stuart, 276, 287
millennium, 383
  decline and fall of commu-
    nism, 384
    1989, 387-388
    Balkans, 391-394
    collapse of Soviet Union,
      389-391

John Paul II, Pope, 386
Poland, 385
Reagan, President
  Ronald, 386
reunification of
  Germany, 388-389
Soviet Union, 384
European Union, 394-396
Milosevic, Slobodan, 392
Minh, Ho Chi, 379
Mirandola, Pico della, 29
misogyny, 119-120
Mitterand, François, 381
mixed economy, 371
modern quantum physics, 341
modernization, 305-306
Molotov, Vyacheslav, 355
Molotov-Ribbentrop Pact, 355
monarchs
  English, 148-149
    Charles I, 150-151
    Cromwell, Oliver,
      151-153
    King James I of England,
      149
  New Monarchs, 140
monasticism, 82-84
Monet, Claude, 342
Mongol Yoke, 164
Mongols, 164
Monnet, Jean, 372
Montaigne, Michel de, 192
Moravians, 44
More, Sir Thomas, 35, 77
Mountain (National
  Convention), 230-231
Munich Conference, 354
Munich Olympics attacks, 397
music, Romanticism, 272
Mussolini, Benito, 349-350
mysticism, 85

N

Napoleon III, 269
Napoleonic Code, 241
*Napoleonic Ideas and the
  Elimination of Poverty*, 296
National Assembly, 225-227
  status of women, 228
  *Declaration of the Rights of
    Man, The*, 228
  written laws, 229
National Convention, 230
  Committee of Public Safety,
    231-233
  split into Girondists and the
    Mountain, 230-231
  Thermidorian Reaction, 233
National Workshops in Paris,
  293
nationalism, 249-250
  British Isles, 320-321
  Hitler, Adolf, 350-352
  influence of Romanticism,
    271
  rise of, Hundred Years' War,
    11-12
nationalization of the Church
  by National Assembly, 229
NATO (North Atlantic Treaty
  Organization), 369
Natural History of Religion, The,
  199
Navigation Acts, 215-216
Nazi Party (Hitler), 351
NEP (New Economic Policy),
  347
Nesselrode, Count Karl
  Robert, 247
Netherlands, 113
  Indonesian independence
    from, 378
  resistance, 114-115
  rule of Philip II, 113-114

New Deal (Roosevelt), 343
New Economic Policy (NEP),
347
New Heloise, The, 200
new imperialism, 312-313
new millennium, 383
   decline and fall of commu-
    nism, 384
     1989, 387-388
     Balkans, 391-394
     collapse of Soviet Union,
      389-391
     John Paul II, Pope, 386
     Poland, 385
     Reagan, President
      Ronald, 386
     reunification of
      Germany, 388-389
     Soviet Union, 384
    European Union, 394-396
New Model Army, 151
New Monarchs, 140
New Testament (Tyndale), 68
new worldview, Scientific
   Revolution, 176
Newcomen, Thomas, 262
Newton, Sir Isaac, 180-181
Nicholas I, 303
Nietzsche, Friedrich, 340
Night of the Long Knives, 352
Niña, 99
nitrogen replenishing crops
   (Agricultural Revolution),
   209-210
Nixon, President Richard
   halt of gold sales, 380
   summit with Brezhnev, 377
No Man's Land (Berlin Wall),
   375
nobles (French class of citizen),
   224
Non-Aggression Pact, 355
North Atlantic Treaty
   Organization (NATO), 369

North Vietnam, 379
Northern Renaissance, 34-36
Nostradamus, 110
nuclear terrorism, 397
Nuremburg Trials, 363

O

observation (scientific method),
   186
old imperialism, 312-313
old worldview, Scientific
   Revolution, 176-177
oligarchic government, 26
On the Origin of the Species, 314
*On the Revolutions of Heavenly
   Bodies*, 177
OPEC (Organization of
   Petroleum Exporting
   Countries) embargo, 380-381
open-field system (Agricultural
   Revolution), 206-208
Operation Vittles, 369
Oration on the Dignity of Man,
   29
Oratory of the Divine Love, 78
order of citizens (France),
   National Assembly, 224-229
    *Declaration of the Rights of
     Man, The*, 228
    status of women, 228
    written laws, 229
Order of the Barnabites, 82
orders (groups of clergy), 82-84
Organization of Petroleum
   Exporting Countries (OPEC)
   embargo, 380
Organization of Work, The, 278
origins
   absolutism, 140
    Bethune, Maximilien,
     141

    Henry IV, 140-141
    Mazarin, Jules, 143-144
    Richelieu, Cardinal,
     142-143
   Agricultural Revolution,
    205-206
Orlando, Vittorio, 337
Orwell, George, 342
ostentation, 44
Ostpolitik, 377
Otto I, 125
Ottoman Turks, 159
overseas explorations of
   Europeans, 92-93
   advanced technologies,
    93-94
   Cartier, Jacques, 102
   Columbus, Christopher,
    98-100
   conquistadors, 100-101
   d'Ailly, Pierre, 95
   Dutch trade, 103
   Magellan, Ferdinand, 102
   Ponce de Leon, Juan, 102
   Portuguese expeditions,
    97-98
   Spanish expeditions,
    104-105
Owen, Robert, 267

P

Pakistan, 378
Palatinate Phase (Thirty Years'
   War), 130
Pan Am Flight 103 bombing,
   398
papal bulls, 51
Paracelsus, 188
parlements, 223
Pasteur, Louis, 269

Paxton, Joseph, 261
Peace of Augsburg, 131
Peace of Utrecht, 160
Peace of Westphalia (Thirty
  Years' War), 133-134
peasants
  eastern Europe, 157-158
  Revolt of 1381, 18
  Twelve Articles, 54
Penn, William, 67
People's Budget (House of
  Commons), 320
perestroika, 389
Persian Letters, 195
Peter I, Serbian reform, 320
Peter the Great, 166-168
Petrarch, Francisco, 15, 28
Petrograd Soviet, 333
Philip II
  rule of the Netherlands,
    113-114
  Spanish Armada, 117-118
Philip IV of Spain, 128
philosophes, 193-194
  France, 194-195
  ideas as cry for French revo-
    lution, 219-220
  push for tolerance, 196-197
  Voltaire, 197-198
physiocrats, 216
Picasso, Pablo, 342
Piedmont-Sardinia, 299
Pinta, 99
Pizarro, Francisco, 100-102
Plank, Max, 341
plebiscite, 240
Plessis, Armand Jean du
  (Cardinal Richelieu), 142-143
pluralism, 45
Poitiers (Hundred Years'
  War), 9

Poland
  decline and fall of commu-
    nism, 385
  invasion of, 355
Pole, Cardinal Reginald, 72
political consequences
  actions of Martin Luther,
    53-55
  Hundred Years' War, 11
Polo, Maffeo, 91
Polo, Marco, 91
Polo, Niccolo, 91
Ponce de Leon, Juan, 102
Pope Boniface VIII, 14
Pope Calixtus III, 10
Pope Clement V, 14
Pope Gregory XI, 15
Pope John XII, 125
Pope John XXIII, 16
Pope John Paul II, 386
Pope Leo III, 124
Pope Martin V, 16
Pope Paul III, 78
Pope Paul IV, 86
Pope Tetzel, 48-49
Pope Urban II, 13
popolo, 26
population
  explosion, Agricultural
    Revolution, 211-212
  losses, Thirty Years' War,
    135-136
Portugal, expeditions, 93,
  97-98
posthumous execution of
  Cromwell, Oliver, 152
power loom invention, 260
Pragmatic Sanction, 113, 161
Pragmatic Sanction of 1438, 16
Praise of Folly, 77
pre–Cold War tensions, 367
prediction (scientific method),
  187

price controls, World War I,
  330
Prince William of Orange, 154
Prince, The, 25
Princip, Gavrilo, 326
Principia, 181
printing press, 33-34
progress (Enlightenment), 190
propaganda, World War I, 330
Protectorate, 151-153
Protestants, 52
  Colloquy of Marburg public
    forum, 58
  reaction to Scientific
    Revolution, 182
  versus Catholics, 115
    defeat of the Spanish
      Armada, 117-118
    Elizabeth I, 116
    Reformation, 52-53
    Tudor, Mary, 115-116
proto-industrialization, textiles,
  213-214
Proudhon, Pierre Joseph, 278,
  280
Prussia
  absolutism, 161-163
  revolutions of 1848,
    295-296
Ptolemaic universe concept,
  177
Ptolemy, 177
public works projects (France),
  298
puddling furnace invention,
  263
Puffing Billy, 263
Putin, President Vladimir, 398
putting-out system (cottage
  industry), 213

Q

Quadruple Alliance, 245
Bourbon dynasty restoration, 246
Congress of Vienna, 247-249
Italian states, 245-246
Quakers (Religious Society of Friends), 67
quantum physics, 341

R

Raft of the Medusa, 272
railroads, 263
Rainhill Trials, 263
raisin bombers, 368
Raphael, 33
Rasputin, Grigori, 332
rationing, World War I, 330
Razin, Stenka, 166
Reagan, President Ronald, 377, 386
reclamation projects (France), 298
Red Shirts (Garibaldi), 300
Red Terror, 336
reform
Industrial Revolution, 264
development of unions, 266-267
exploitation of children, 265
influence of factories, 265-266
reform movement, 266
wages and work conditions, 264
philosophes, 194

Russia in the nineteenth century, 303-304
Alexander II, 304
modernization, 305-306
Serbia, 320
Reform Bill of 1832, 292
Reformation, 40
Amish, 66
Anabaptists, 65-66
Calvin, John, 59-62
Catholic Reformation, 76
Congregation of the Inquisition, 85-87
Council of Trent, 79-81
humanists, 77-78
monasticism, 82-84
Oratory of the Divine Love, 78
English Reformation, 67
Church of England, 71
Henry VIII, 68-69
Reformation Parliament, 70-71
restoration of Anglican Church by Elizabeth I, 73
return of England to Catholicism by Mary Tudor, 72-73
Tyndale, William, 68
Farel, Guillaume, 59-60
hierarchy and governance of the Church, 40-41
Hus, Jan, 43-44
Luther, Martin, 46-47
Diet of Speyer, 55
Diet of Worms, 51-52
effects of ideas, 53-54
exception to Tetzel's sale of indulgences, 48-49
Protestant thought versus Catholic dogma, 52-53

Resolutions Concerning the Virtue of Indulgences, 50
status of women, 55
struggle with salvation, 47-48
Twelve Articles of the peasants, 54
problems with the Church, 44-45
Quakers, 67
Reformation of the Common Man, 58-59
spread to Scotland, 62-64
Wycliffe, John, 41-43
Reformation of the Common Man, 58-59
Reformation Parliament (English Parliament), 70-71
Reichstag (German legislature), 351
Religious Society of Friends (Quakers), 67
religious wars, France, 110-111
Edict of Nantes, 112-113
War of the Three Henrys, 111-112
Remarque, Erich, 329
Renaissance, 21-22
art, 30
Brunelleschi, Filippo, 32
changes in technique, 30-31
da Vinci, Leonardo, 32
Donatello, 32
Masaccio, 32
Michelangelo, 33
Raphael, 33
status of artists, 31-32
city-states, 26-27
commercial revival, 24
communes, 26
humanism, 27-29

individualism, 30
Italy, 23-24
Northern Renaissance,
    34-36
power of banking families,
    24-26
printing press, 33-34
republics, 26
secularism, 29-30
Renoir, Auguste, 342
Republic (Socialist Federal
Republic of Yugoslavia), 391
republics, 26, 230
Resolution 1514 (UN), 378
*Resolutions Concerning the Virtue
of Indulgences*, 50
Restoration of 1660, 153
restructuring of French gov-
    ernment, Napoleon
    Bonaparte, 241
resurrection of classical ideas.
    See Renaissance
reunification of Germany,
    388-389
Revolution of 1830, 293
revolutions of 1848, 292
    Austria, 294-295
    Bonaparte, Charles Louis
        Napoleon, 296-298
    building of nations (Italy
        and Germany), 298-302
    France, 293-294
    Prussia, 295-296
Rhineland, Hitler's storm on,
    354
Ribbentrop, Joachim von, 355
Richelieu, Cardinal (Armand
    Jean du Plessis), 142-143
rise of factories (Britain),
    259-261

rise of nationalism, Hundred
    Years' War, 11-12
Robespierre, Maximilien,
    231-233
Rocket (locomotive), 263
Roman Inquisition, 85
Romania, 388
Romanov, Michael, 166
Romanticism, 270-272
Roosevelt, President Franklin,
    New Deal, 343
rotten boroughs (voting dis-
    tricts), 292
Roundheads, 151
Rousseau, Jean-Jacques,
    199-200
Royal Academy of Sciences,
    197
Rump Parliament, 151
rural industry (cottage indus-
    try), 212-214
Russia
    Eastern absolutists, 164
        czar, 165
        Ivan IV, 165-166
        Mongol Yoke, 164
        Peter the Great, 166-168
        Time of Troubles, 166
    entry into World War II,
        357-358
    Germany's declaration of
        war on, 327
    nineteenth-century reform,
        303-306
    Revolution of 1905, 331-334
    terrorist hostage situation,
        398
Rutherford, Ernest, 341
Rwanda, independence from
    Belgium, 378

S

sacraments, debate at Council
    of Trent, 80
Saint-Simon, Count Henri de,
    276
sale of indulgences
    Luther's exception to
        95 Theses, 48-49
        Diet of Worms, 51-52
        Protestant thought versus
            Catholic dogma, 52-53
        *Resolutions Concerning the
            Virtue of Indulgences*, 50
    Wycliffe's exception to, 41
SALT I (Strategic Arms
    Limitation Treaty), 377
SALT II treaty, 377
sanitation, city life (Industrial
    Revolution), 268-269
sans-culottes, 231
Santa Maria, 99
Sarajevo, Fourteenth Winter
    Olympics, 394
Sartre, Jean-Paul, 341
Savery, Thomas, 262
Schlieffen Plan, 327
Schoenberg, Arnold, 342
Schuman, Robert, 372, 395
science
    post–World War I, 341
    scientific method, 186-187,
        190-191
Scientific Revolution
    Bacon, Sir Francis, 184-185
    Brahe, Tycho, 178
    consequences of, 186-188
    Copernicus, Nicholas,
        177-178
    Descartes, René, 185-186
    Galilei, Galileo, 179-180

Kepler, Johannes, 178-179
link to the Enlightenment, 190-193
new worldview, 176
Newton, Sir Isaac, 180-181
old worldview, 176-177
reaction of religion, 181-183
Scotland, Reformation, 62-64
Scott, Sir Walter, 271
Scottish National Church, 63-64
Sea Beggars, 114
Second Balkan War, 320
Second Battle of the Marne, 330
Second Coalition, 237
Second Continental Congress, Declaration of Independence, 221
Second International, 282
Second Republic, 293
second revolution, National Convention, 230
    Committee of Public Safety, 231-233
    split into Girondists and the Mountain, 230-231
    Thermidorian Reaction, 233
Secondat, Charles-Louis, 195
secularism, 29-30, 77
Security Council, 366
self-determination, 367, 397
September Massacres, 230
Serbia
    Austria's declaration of war on, 326-327
    reform, 320
Servetus, Michael, 61
service nobility, 164
Seven Years' War, 215
Seventeen Provinces (Netherlands), 113

Seymour, Edward, 72
Seymour, Jane, 72
Shakespeare, William, 271
Shelley, Mary, 271
ships, age of exploration, 94
Sicily, bubonic plague, 5
Sieyès, Abbé Emmanuel, 226
Sieyès, Emanuel Joseph, 238
signori, 26
Simons, Menno, 66
simony, 45
Single European Act, 394
Sistine Chapel, 33
Six Articles, 71
Sixth Coalition, 244
Sixty-Seven Conclusions, 58
slavery, 217
Slavs, 164
Smith, Adam, 216-217
Smith, Eugenia, 333
social consequences
    actions of Martin Luther, 53-55
    Hundred Years' War, 11
Social Contract, The, 200
social Darwinism, 314
Social Democratic Alliance, 283
Social Democratic Party of Germany, 283
social market economy, 372
socialism, 276
    Engels, Friedrich, 279-280
    French utopian socialism, 276-278
    labor issues, 283
    Marx, Karl, 278-281
    socialist movement, 282-283
    utopian socialists, 278
Socialist Federal Republic of Yugoslavia, 391
Society of Jesus, 83

Solidarity Free Trade Union, 385
Solidarity movement, 385
Somaschi Order of Regular Clerics, 82
Sorrows of Young Werther, The, 271
South Vietnam, 379
Soviet Union
    Cold War era, 373
        Brezhnev Doctrine, 376
        De-Stalinization, 374-375
        death of Stalin, 373
        détente, 377
    collapse of, 389-391
    decline and fall of communism, 384
    interwar years, 353
    Stalin, Joseph, 347-349
Spain, interwar years, 353
Spanish Armada, 117-118
Spanish Civil War, 353
Spanish expeditions, 100
    Columbian Exchange, 104-105
    conquistadors, 100-101
    fleet convoy system, 105
Spanish Habsburgs, 108
Spanish Inquisition, 85
Spanish Netherlands, 115
"spinning jenny," 258
spinning mule invention, 260
spinsters, 214
Spirit of the Laws, The, 195
Sprenger, James, 120
Spring Offensive (Germany), 337
squadristi, 350
St. Bartholomew's Day massacre, 111
St. Francis of Assisi, 82

St. Petersburg, 168

Stalin, Joseph, 347-349
  blockade of western-
    controlled zone of Britain,
    368
  death of, 373

Stamp Act, 221

Stanley, Sir Henry Morton,
  316

status of women
  influence of Martin Luther,
    55
  National Assembly, 228
  nineteenth century, 286-287

Statute in Restraint of Appeals
  (Reformation Parliament), 70

status of women, misogyny,
  119-120

steam-powered inventions,
  262-263

Stephenson, George, 263

Stolypin, Pyotr, 332

"storm and stress" literature,
  271

Strategic Arms Limitation
  Treaty (SALT I), 377

surrealism, 342

survival of the fittest, 314

sweat labor, 287

Swedish Phase (Thirty Years'
  War), 132

synod, 64

system of balance of power pol-
  itics, 245
  Bourbon dynasty restora-
    tion, 246
  Congress of Vienna,
    247-249
  Italian states, 245-246

system of congresses (Concert
  of Europe), 247

System of Nature, 199

T

tabula rasa theory (blank slate),
  193

Talleyrand, Charles, 238, 247

technology
  Agricultural Revolution,
    208-211
  contribution to expeditions,
    93-94
  Industrial Revolution,
    261-263

Ten Hours Act, 266

Tennis Court Oath, 226

terrorism, 397-398

Test Act of 1763, 153

textile industry, 213-214,
  258-261

Thatcher, Margaret, 381

Theatines Clerks Regular, 78

theology of John Calvin, 60-62

Theresa of Avila, 84

Theresa, Maria, 203

Thermidorian Reaction, 233

Third Coalition, 242

Third Reich, 352

Thirty Years' War, 129
  agricultural losses, 135-136
  Bohemian Phase, 130-131
  Danish Phase, 131
  decline of the Holy Roman
    Empire, 134-135
  Defenestration of Prague,
    129-130
  economic losses, 135-136
  French Phase, 132-133
  Peace of Westphalia,
    133-134
  population losses, 135-136
  Swedish Phase, 132

Thirty-Nine Articles (Anglican
  Church), 73

Thousand Year Reich (Hitler),
  351

three-field system (crop rotation), 207

Time of Troubles (Russia), 166

Tirpitz, Admiral Alfred von,
  319

Tito, Josip, 391

Toledo, Fernando Alvarez, 114

total war effort, World War I,
  330

Townsend, Charles, 210

trade routes (exploration of
  Europe), 92

translation of the scriptures,
  Council of Trent, 80

transmission of the bubonic
  plague, 5

Travels, 92

*Travels of Sir John Mandeville,
  The*, 92

A Treatise on Tolerance, 198

Treaty of Amsterdam, 395

Treaty of Brest-Litovsk, 335

Treaty of Cateau-Cambrésis,
  109-110, 114

Treaty of Friendship,
  Cooperation, and Mutual
  Assistance, 369

Treaty of Neuilly, 338

Treaty of Sevres, 338

Treaty of the Pyrenees, 133

Treaty of Troyes (Hundred
  Years' War), 9

Treaty of Versailles, 337-339

trench warfare, 328-329

Triangle Trade, 217-218

Triennial Act, 150

Triple Alliance, 317

Triple Entente, 318

Troppau Protocol, 253

Trotsky, Leon, 335, 347

Tudman, Franjo, 392
Tudor, Mary
    persecution of Protestants in
        England, 115-116
    return of England to
        Catholicism, 72-73
Tull, Jethro, 210
Turner, J.M.W., 272
Twelve Articles, 54
Twentieth Party Congress, 374
two power standard (Britain
    navy policy), 319
Tyndale, William, 68

U

Ulyanov, Aleksandr, 334
unification
    Germany, 300-302
    Italy, 299-300
union of church and state,
    Holy Roman Empire,
    126-127
Union of Utrecht, 115
unions, development of,
    266-267
United Kingdom, decoloniza-
    tion, 377-379
United Nations Organization,
    366
United Provinces, 115
United States' entry into
    World War I, 329, 357-358
universal suffrage, 251
Ursuline Order, 84
USSR. *See* Soviet Union
Utopia, 35, 77
utopian socialists, 278

V

Valla, Lorenzo, 30
Valois family, Habsburg-Valois
    Wars, 108-109
van Gogh, Vincent, 342
vassals, 4
Velazquez, Diego Rodriguez,
    128
Velvet Revolution, 387
Vermuyden, Cornelius, 209
Versailles
    Louis XIV, 145-146
    Treaty of Versailles, 337-339
Vesalius, Andreas, 188
Vespucci, Amerigo, 100
Vichy Regime, 11
Victorian Age, 285
Victorian Morality, 285
Vietnam, split into North and
    South, 379
*Vindication of the Rights of
    Man, A*, 228
*Vindication of the Rights of
    Woman, A*, 228
Virgin Queen (Elizabeth I),
    116
Voltaire (François Marie
    Arouet), 197-198
von Hohenheim, Theophrastus
    Bombastus, 188
voting districts (rotten bor-
    oughs), 292
Vulgate, 68

W

wages and work conditions,
    Industrial Revolution, 264
Wagner, Richard, 272
Walesa, Lech, 385

Wallenstein, Albrecht von, 130
Walpole, Horace, 271
Wannsee Conference, 362
wars
    Cold War era
        Big Three, 366
        decolonization, 377-379
        east versus west, 368-370
        economy, 379-381
        pre–Cold War tensions,
            367
        Soviet Union, 373-377
        United Nations
            Organization, 366
        WWII aftermath,
            370-372
    Hundred Years' War, 7
        battle at Crécy, 8-9
        Battle of Castillon, 11
        Joan of Arc, 10-11
        rise of nationalism, 11-12
        tensions between France
            and England, 7-8
        Treaty of Troyes, 9
    War in Kosovo, 393
    War of the Spanish
        Succession, 160, 215
    War of the Three Henrys,
        111-112
    War on Terror, 397-398
    War to End All Wars. *See*
        World War I
    Wars of Religion, 110
        Edict of Nantes, 112-113
        War of the Three
            Henrys, 111-112
    World War I. *See* World
        War I
    World War II. *See* World
        War II
Warsaw Pact, 369-370
water frame invention, 259

Waterloo, Battle of, 244-245
Watt, James, 262
Wealth of Nations, 216
Wellesley, Arthur, 245
west versus east (Cold War era), 368
  Berlin Airlift, 368-369
  formation of Communist parties, 368
  NATO (North Atlantic Treaty Organization), 369
  Warsaw Pact, 369-370
Western Front (World War I), 328-329
White Man's Burden, 313
White Terror, 246
Whites, 336
William I (Kaiser), 301
William of Orange, 114
William the Conqueror, 4
William, Frederick, 162
William, Frederick I, 163
William, Frederick IV, 295
Wilson, President Woodrow, 337
Winchilsea, Lord, 245
Wishart, George, 62
witch hunts, 118
  Great Witch Hunt, 120-122
  misogyny, 119-120
Witte, Sergei, 305
Wittgenstein, Ludwig, 340
Wojtyla, Cardinal Karol, 385
Wollstonecraft, Mary, 228
women
  misogyny, 119-120
  status of
    influence of Martin Luther, 55
    National Assembly, 228
    nineteenth century, 286-287
  Ursuline Order, 84

Woolf, Virginia, 342
Wordsworth, William, 271
work conditions and wages, Industrial Revolution, 264
world maps, 93
World War I, 326
  aftermath, 339
    age of anxiety, 339
    art and literature, 342-343
    Continental Drift, 345-346
    Great Depression, 343
    scientific ideas, 341
    unsettling philosophies, 340-341
  armistice, 336-337
  Bolshevik Revolution, 334-336
  chain of events leading to war, 326-327
  Eastern Front, 329-330
  Russian Revolution of 1905, 331-334
  total war effort, 330
  Treaty of Versailles, 337-339
  Western Front, 328-329
World War II
  aftermath, 370
    devastation of the war, 370-371
    EEC (European Economic Community), 372
    prosperity of western Europe, 371-372
  British and French declaration of war on Germany, 356-357
  Eastern Front, 358-359
  Holocaust, 360
    concentration camps, 362
    Mein Kampf, 361-362

  Nuremburg Trials, 363
  Wannsee Conference, 362
  invasion of Poland, 355
  Russian involvement, 357-358
  United States' involvement, 357-358
World's Fair (Britain), 261
worldwide trade, 308
Wycliffe, John, 41-43

X–Y–Z

Yalta Conference, 367
Yeltsin, Boris, 390
Yugoslav wars, 392-393
Yugoslavia
  ethnic cleansing, 393-394
  Milosevic, Slobodan, 392
  Yugoslav wars, 392-393

Zaccaria, Anthony, 82
Zola, Emile, 322
Zollverein, 301
zones of occupation (Germany and Berlin), 367
Zwingli, Ulrich, 58

Check Out These
Best-Sellers

Grammar and Style
SECOND EDITION

Laurie E. Rozakis, Ph.D.

1-59257-115-8 • $16.95

Buying and Selling a Home
FOURTH EDITION

Shelley O'Hara and Nancy D. Lewis

1-59257-120-4 • $18.95

Being a Groom
SECOND EDITION

Jennifer Lata Rung and Mark Rung

0-02-864456-5 • $9.95

Learning Spanish
THIRD EDITION

Gail Stein

0-02-864451-4 • $18.95

Personal Finance in Your 20s & 30s
SECOND EDITION

Sarah Young Fisher and Susan Shelly

0-02-864374-7 • $19.95

Organizing Your Life
FOURTH EDITION

Georgene Lockwood

1-59257-413-0 • $16.95

Total Nutrition
FOURTH EDITION

Joy Bauer, M.S., R.D., C.D.N.

1-59257-439-4 • $18.95

Positive Dog Training

Pamela Dennison

0-02-864463-8 • $14.95

The Bible
THIRD EDITION

James Stuart Bell and Stan Campbell

1-59257-389-4 • $18.95

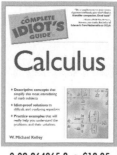

Calculus

W. Michael Kelley

0-02-864365-8 • $18.95

Music Theory
SECOND EDITION

Michael Miller

1-59257-437-8 • $19.95

The Perfect Resume
THIRD EDITION

Susan Ireland

0-02-864440-9 • $14.95

Playing the Guitar
SECOND EDITION

Frederick Noad

0-02-864244-9 • $21.95

Drawing Manga ILLUSTRATED

John Layman and David Hutchison

1-59257-335-5 • $19.95

Knitting and Crocheting
SECOND EDITION
Illustrated

Barbara Breiter and Gail Diven

1-59257-089-5 • $16.95

More than *450 titles* available at booksellers and online retailers everywhere